Sir Anthony Eden and the Suez Crisis

Sir Anthony Eden and the Suez Crisis

Reluctant Gamble

Jonathan Pearson

© Jonathan Pearson 2003

All rights reserved. No reproduction, copy or transmission of this publication may be made without written permission.

No paragraph of this publication may be reproduced, copied or transmitted save with written permission or in accordance with the provisions of the Copyright, Designs and Patents Act 1988, or under the terms of any licence permitting limited copying issued by the Copyright Licensing Agency, 90 Tottenham Court Road, London W1T 4LP.

Any person who does any unauthorised act in relation to this publication may be liable to criminal prosecution and civil claims for damages.

The author has asserted his right to be identified as the author of this work in accordance with the Copyright, Designs and Patents Act 1988.

First published 2003 by
PALGRAVE MACMILLAN
Houndmills, Basingstoke, Hampshire RG21 6XS and
175 Fifth Avenue, New York, N.Y. 10010
Companies and representatives throughout the world.

PALGRAVE MACMILLAN is the global academic imprint of the Palgrave Macmillan division of St Martin's Press, LLC and of Palgrave Macmillan Ltd. Macmillan® is a registered trademark in the United States, United Kingdom and other countries. Palgrave is a registered trademark in the European Union and other countries.

ISBN 0–333–98451–X

This book is printed on paper suitable for recycling and made from fully managed and sustained forest sources.

A catalogue record for this book is available from the British Library.

Library of Congress Cataloging-in-Publication Data
Pearson, Jonathan, 1971–
   Sir Anthony Eden and the Suez crisis : reluctant gamble / Jonathan Pearson.
     p. cm.
   Includes bibliographical references and index.
   ISBN 0–333–98451–X
   1. Egypt—History—Intervention, 1956. 2. Great Britain—Foreign relations—1945–1964. 3. Eden, Anthony, Earl of Avon, 1897–
   I. Title.
DT107.83 .P38 2002
962.05′3—dc21   2002072620

10 9 8 7 6 5 4 3 2 1
12 11 10 09 08 07 06 05 04 03

Printed and bound in Great Britain by
Antony Rowe Ltd, Chippenham and Eastbourne

To Doug and Joan Pearson

Contents

List of Abbreviations   viii

Acknowledgements   xi

Introduction   1

1   Nationalisation of the Canal: 26 July–3 August   20

2   Negotiation: 4 August–9 September   42

3   SCUA: 10 September–21 September   67

4   Mounting Pressure: 22 September–3 October   92

5   Transition to Force: 4 October–14 October   120

6   Collusion: 15 October–25 October   145

7   Finale: 26 October 1956–9 January 1957   158

Conclusion   169

Notes   181

Bibliography   233

Index   248

List of Abbreviations

Archival

ADM	UK Admiralty Files
AIR	UK Air Ministry Files
ALBP	Alan Lennox-Boyd Papers, Bodleian Library, Oxford
AP	Avon Papers, Heslop Room, University of Birmingham
BeP	Beaverbrook Papers, House of Lords Record Office, London
BLP	Bruce Lockhart Papers, Lilly Library, Indiana University, Bloomington, Indiana
BP	Butler Papers, Trinity College, Cambridge
BrP	Brendan Bracken Papers, Churchill College, Cambridge
CAB 128	UK Cabinet Meetings
CAB 129	UK Cabinet Memoranda
CAB 131	UK Defence Committee
CAB 134/1216	Egypt Committee Meetings
CAB 134/1217	Egypt Committee Memoranda
CCUKC	Cartoon Centre, University of Kent
CiP	Cilcennin Papers, Camarthenshire County Council Archives, Camarthen, Wales
CP	Churchill Papers, Churchill College, Cambridge
DDE	The Papers of Dwight David Eisenhower, Eisenhower Library, Abilene, Kansas
DEFE 4	UK Chiefs of Staff Committee Meetings
DEFE 5	UK Chiefs of Staff Memoranda
DEFE 32	UK Chiefs of Staff, Secretary's Standard File
DP	Sir William Dickson Papers, Churchill College, Cambridge
DSP	Duncan-Sandys Papers, Churchill College, Cambridge
FO 371	UK General Foreign Office Files
FO 800	UK Foreign Secretary's Private Files
GBP	Gore-Booth Papers, Bodleian Library, Oxford
GMP	Gilbert Murray Papers, Bodleian Library, Oxford
HP	Hayter Papers, in the private possession of Lady Hayter
JFDOH	John Foster Dulles Oral History, Seeley G. Mudd Manuscript Library, Princeton
KP	Kilmuir Papers, Churchill College, Cambridge
LHA	Liddel Hart Archive, Liddel Hart Centre for Military Archives, King's College, University of London
MP	Macmillan Papers, Bodleian Library, Oxford
NACP	US National Archives, College Park

NAW	US National Archives, Washington, DC
NBP	Norman Brook Papers, Bodleian Library, Oxford
PREM 11	UK Prime Minister's Files
PRO	Public Records Office, Kew, London
RG 218	Records of the US Joint Chiefs of Staff
RG 263	Records of the Central Intelligence Agency
SCP	Spencer Churchill Papers, Churchill College, Cambridge
SELO	Selwyn Lloyd Papers, Churchill College, Cambridge
SLA	Squerryes Lodge Archive, Churchill College, Cambridge
SOHP	Suez Oral History Project, Liddel Hart Archive, Liddel Hart Centre for Military Archives, King's College, University of London
T	UK Treasury Files
TNLA	*The Times* News Library Archive, News International, London
WCP	William Clark Papers, Bodleian Library, Oxford
WHP	William Hayley Papers, Churchill College, Cambridge
WMP	Walter Monckton Papers, Bodleian Library, Oxford
WO32	UK War Office Files on Suez Crisis
WP	Wright Papers, in the private possession of Sir Denis Wright

Other

ALPHA	The plan to give land to Egypt and financially compensate Israel (for more details, see PRO CAB 129/75. Memorandum by Macmillan, 11 June, 1955)
CASU	Co-operative Association of Suez Canal Users, an acronym superseded by SCUA (see below)
COS	Chiefs of Staff
DAFR	*Documents of American Foreign Relations* (New York, 1956–57)
DDF	*Documents Diplomatique Français*
EC	Egypt Committee
E(O)C	Egypt Official Committee
FO	Foreign Office
FRUS	*Foreign Relations of the United States* (Washington, DC, 1979–90)
HMG	Her Majesty's Government
IMF	International Monetary Fund
JIC	Joint Intelligence Committee
ME(O)	Middle East Official Committee
ME(O)(SC)	Suez Canal Sub-Committee of the Official Middle East Committee
OMEGA	The Anglo-American plan to destabilise Nasser's Regime by economic sanctions and covert activity
RIIA	Royal Institute of International Affairs

RIIR	Royal Institute of International Relations
SCUA	Suez Canal Users Association
SEATO	South East Asian Treaty Organisation
SIS	Secret Intelligence Service; MI6
SOE	Special Operations Executive
UNEF	United Nations Emergency Force
USDDRS	*United States Declassified Document Reference System* (Washington, DC, 1976–90)

Acknowledgements

I owe great debts of gratitude to the many people who have enabled me to complete this book. Firstly, I would like to thank everyone at Palgrave Macmillan and Keith Povey for their help in the preparation of the manuscript. Sincere thanks also to the archival staff in every institution cited in the course of my work. In the United Kingdom: the Public Record Office, Kew; Churchill College and Trinity College, Cambridge; the Barnes Library and the Central Library, Birmingham; the Liddell Hart Centre for Military Archives, King's College, London; the Carmarthenshire County Archives; the Cartoon Centre, University of Kent; and the British Newspaper Archive, Collindale, London. In the United States: The Lilly Library, Indiana University, Bloomington, Indiana; the National Archives, College Park; and the Seeley Mudd Library, Princeton. I would also like to give specific thanks to Miss Chris Penney at the University of Birmingham; Mr Brian MacArthur, for access, and Mr Eamon Dyas, for his help, at News International, *The Times* News Library Archive, London; Sara Campbell at the Wellcome Institute, Oxford; Colin Harris, Nia Mai Williams and Martin Maw at Modern Political Papers, Department of Special Collections and Western Manuscripts, Bodleian Library, Oxford; Laurie Millner at the Imperial War Museum; and Dwight Strandberg at the Eisenhower Library, Abilene, Kansas.

I would also like to thank Lady Avon and the Avon Trustees for granting me access to the Avon Papers, Mrs Virginia Makins for access and permission to use her father's, Lord Sherfield's, unpublished memoirs, the Macmillan Trustees for permission to use the Macmillan diaries, and Mr Donald Hayley for access to Sir William Hayley's papers. Others have been kind enough to grant me interviews. To them I express great thanks for their time, their experience and their patience: Lord Robert Carr; Sir Guy Millard; Sir Frank Cooper; Mr A. Nicholls; Mr Aleco Joannides; Mr Iverach MacDonald; and Sir Douglas Dodds-Parker, who suffered my questions on two occasions. Lady Hayter graciously agreed to an interview and kindly allowed me access to both her diaries for the period, as well as Sir William Hayter's papers. Sir Denis Wright also agreed to an interview and allowed me to view his unpublished memoirs. I also thank Sir Patrick Reilly, Sir Edward Playfair and Mr Julian Shuckburgh for their correspondence.

Various academics have advised me during my study. They are too numerous to include all, but I would like to convey my particular gratitude, with deference to those not mentioned, to Peter Hennessy, Colin Seymour-Ure, David Welch, John Young, Scott Lucas, Brian Atkinson and Anthony Sampson.

Above all, I owe a special debt of gratitude to George Conyne, for his continued faith, interest and patience.

My greatest strength has been derived from my family; my wife, Jo Fox, and above all, my parents, to whom I would like to dedicate this book.

JONATHAN PEARSON

Introduction

Recent studies of the Suez Crisis, and of Sir Anthony Eden's role, have tried to clarify his decision-making; however, none have traced this process, breaking through the discontinuity that has been hidden by the historiography, and not least by Eden himself. By focusing on Eden's personality and influences, this study contextualises his conduct of foreign relations, as distinct from a precise foreign policy, and reappraises his role in resolving the crisis. Historians, from the first to write publicly about the crisis, Paul Johnson and Hugh Thomas, to the more recent, Keith Kyle and W. Scott Lucas, have argued that Eden decided to use force in late July and finally saw the opportunity to act on that decision on 14 October 1956.[1] Specifically, Kyle and Lucas argue that Eden chose to use force in early July but then briefly sought a peaceful solution through the UN in October, before employing force on 14 October 1956. In their opinion, the decision to use force had been made and the 14th was merely the date of implementation. Thomas believed that the Prime Minister had been looking for a *casus belli* to remove Nasser since the Egyptian leader's apparent involvement in the dismissal of Sir John Glubb as head of the Arab Legion, on 1 March 1956.[2] These views fail to take account of the substantial evidence of confusion during the period.[3] The eventual use of force was not the fulfilment of a policy initiated in July, despite the dual-track policy decision made by Cabinet on 27 July. Eden and the Government backed a negotiated settlement of the crisis. However, if this failed, they believed that the use of force would be justified because of the severe political and economic implications of the nationalisation of the Canal Company for Western Europe and, specifically, Britain. Therefore, military contingency plans would be made to protect British interests, as Cabinet agreed on 27 July, in the 'last resort'.[4] Eden believed throughout August, September and early October 1956 that international pressure brought to bear upon Nasser would preclude the need for more drastic action. Military plans would also increase this pressure and force Nasser to relinquish control of the Canal. They were also a deterrent to any further action. Despite the dual-track policy, negotiation from a position of strength dominated Eden's search for a solution to the crisis to the extent that there is little evidence to suggest that he wanted to use force before October 1956. The decision to use the military was the eventual reaction to a need to fill a vacuum at a time when Eden's health had severely declined and he judged that both his country's interests and his own future were in danger. The use of force did not fulfil the military preparations of the 'dual track', but involved a hastily constructed plan in 'collusion' with the French and the Israelis, again suggesting that it was not a decision made at the beginning of the crisis but later, when Eden decided that the situation had become intractable by diplomatic means. Pressure had mounted on the Prime Minister to provide an active solution and diplomatic attempts to resolve the crisis had failed. Historians have failed to trace, in the same detail, the full extent of the pressures building upon Eden. David Dutton has drawn a much clearer picture of the French attempts to embroil the British in a war against Egypt, but convinced of Eden's early decision to use force, has placed little importance on the effect of these outside pressures on the Prime Minister.[5] Thus Dutton, as with the rest of the historiography, has seen Britain and France as partners in a military venture.

The majority of the misunderstandings of Eden and his situation reflected an overly critical historiography that misrepresented Eden's political dealings during the crisis. Many wrote defending themselves and were looking to lay blame because Suez was a failure, publicly revealing Britain's subjugation. As Harold Wilson recalled, Eden became the 'scapegoat'.[6] Eden did not help himself by the adamant defence of his action and the denial of any collusion. Few people in government circles knew of the secret talks at Sèvres before the end of 1956, while most people were unaware of the meetings before 1967. Even fewer knew of the tripartite agreement that settled the covert joint invasion plans of the French, Israelis and British. Eden justified Britain's military intervention as an extension of his military precautions. Keen to conceal the results of the meetings at Sèvres, and collusion, he explained that the invasion fulfilled 'the approved plan', which had been 'prepared by the Anglo-French military staff that had been studying the problem since the end of July'.[7] While Eden argued that his objectives were different in July and October, he tried to demonstrate that the plans were the same.[8] Having told only half-truths to the full Cabinet and having lied to the House of Commons, in October and November 1956 respectively, he needed to justify his actions. Accusations of irresolution coupled with the insecurity that his illness and prescribed medication exaggerated also gave him the opportunity to answer his critics. Thus, the majority of the Civil Service and Government did not have a full enough picture to judge Eden or his actions accurately, and, significantly, their timing. The public, opposition and world opinion were in an even weaker position, particularly as, while Eden sought to deal with the crisis, some of those around him, notably Harold Macmillan, had already set their own agenda and were working to their ends. Eden avoided any mention of collusion in his memoirs, which has meant that the rest of the work has tended to be ignored as being heavily biased or of dubious veracity. This ignores much useful, accurate information in the memoirs that reflect much of the Prime Minister's hopes and attempts to secure a negotiated settlement. Eden wrote to Selwyn Lloyd to help with the book, and Lloyd helped Eden to remember the facts.[9] The memoirs prompted Erskine Childers to write in 1962 'how Eden revealed far more of the truth than a surface reading of the *Memoirs* would suggest', but he was unable to get through to the real story of collusion.[10] Childers had begun his research into Suez in a 1959 article in *The Spectator*, which angered Eden. In a remark typical of Eden's thoughtless outbursts, he raged that, '[i]t seems to start on a false premise, that we did not want a United Nations' solution, ignores the consequences of the Soviet veto upon the twenty-two power proposals and thinks that there was a conspiracy because of the very appropriate observations you [Lloyd] and Pineau made on that topic. After this it has a characteristically Irish rebel mentality.'[11] He was annoyed that his attempt at redress to the UN had been belittled, but more importantly, he had been accused of plotting in a conspiratorial fashion. This moral slur offended Eden's sensibilities more than any accusation of warmongering, and hence he steadfastly avoided mentioning collusion. He developed an elaborate web of deception centred on showing the events of October 1956 as part of a continuous policy, adopted in late July 1956. This was not the case but perpetuated the myth that had been promoted by the misunderstanding of some of his colleagues and writers on the subject. Lucas's interpretation of Eden's explanation of Dulles's intentions remains a good example of how historians have refused to take the Prime Minister's memoirs at face value. Eden believed that Dulles's announcement that Nasser must be made to disgorge his control of the Canal signalled American commitment to promoting a solution to the crisis. For Lucas, it represented Eden's belief in Dulles's ultimate agreement to the use of force.[12] Further evidence, particularly personal meetings with his close friend Iverach McDonald, substantiate Eden's own version rather than that of the historiography.[13]

Restricted to a very limited distribution within Government circles, the first history of the Suez Crisis was written by Guy Millard, a private secretary of Eden's, after being suggested to Eden by Sir Norman Brook, the Cabinet Secretary.[14] The work, entitled 'Memorandum on Relations Between the United Kingdom, the United States and France in the Months Following Egyptian Nationalisation of the Suez Canal Company in 1956', was written in August 1957 and printed on 21 October 1957. However, while Millard reported the events, including collusion, the memorandum was altered in a number of small ways, which affected its tone.[15] Whether Eden knew of these alterations is unclear, but Brook destroyed Suez records, under instruction from Eden.[16] After the fall of the Eden Government, Brook ordered 'two middle-rank Foreign Office officials...to collect all sensitive files on Suez and put them in a file marked "SUEZ"'. This file disappeared when Brook left the Cabinet.[17] Eden, himself, removed many of the Foreign Office papers, particularly related to collusion.[18] These actions increased suspicion of Eden's warmongering during the crisis, but in fact they merely reflected his desire to hide the evidence of collusion rather than increased militarism.

The first published literature on Suez came in 1957, when Merry and Serge Bromberger first revealed details concerning the collusion between Britain, France and Israel, in *The Secrets of Suez*. This increased the criticism of Eden and the misunderstanding of his handling of the crisis.[19] However, it would be another nine years before a participant would actually reveal the co-operation between the three countries. In 1966, Moshe Dayan's *Diary of the Sinai Campaign* admitted to collusion. However, while an Israeli representative at the Sèvres meetings had written it, it did not directly refer to Sèvres. The first to refer to the meetings of 22 and 24 October was Hugh Thomas in his 1967 *The Suez Affair*. Thomas, the son-in-law of Gladwyn Jebb, resigned from the Foreign Office in 1957, apparently because of 'a general distaste for official life'.[20] He had written a novel, *The World's Game*, in 1957, which depicted, in fiction, what he believed to be the deliberate bellicose British involvement in the Suez Crisis. After Dayan's disclosure, he wrote an historical account which was serialised in *The Sunday Times* in 1966. Lloyd made a major contribution to producing the work.[21] However, he berated Thomas over his treatment of Eden and his Suez policy. Initially, criticising Thomas's failure to represent the extent to which Eden consulted 'his senior colleagues', he went on to say:

> I don't think that you bring out sufficiently clearly that our primary objective throughout was a peaceful settlement...I get the impression from your article that from the 26th of July we were all longing to have a physical smack at Nasser. That really is not true. Eden, [Antony], Head [Secretary of State for War and then Minister of Defence] and I had had too much over the Suez base to want to go back to a physical presence in Egypt other than that agreed under the 1954 agreement. This applied to the August Conference, the acceptance of SCUA, and to the final reference to the Security Council.[22]

Nonetheless, despite the remarks, the book remained the leading work on Suez and was reprinted in 1987. It was not until the works of Lucas and Kyle emerged in 1991 that *The Suez Affair* began to lose prominence.

In 1967, Anthony Nutting published *No End of a Lesson*. Both Eden and Lloyd were unimpressed by Nutting's account. Eden considered taking legal action but Lloyd advised him to ignore it.[23] This led the way for another civil servant, Geoffrey McDermott, to write his account. In 1969, he produced *The Eden Legacy and the Decline of British Diplomacy*. He did refer to Sèvres but his information was inaccurate which suggested that it was second-hand.[24] McDermott had believed that he 'was one of only three Foreign Office officials who were in on the political and strategic planning of the Suez campaign'.[25] However, as he later wrote, he believed that Eden only confided in one person, Lloyd, which compromised his own evidence.[26] Here was another official who assumed that Eden's deception and collusion were extensions of his military preparations. The two major studies by Kyle and Lucas finally broke through the confusion of the crisis, revealing the intricacies of the collusion. However, in attempting to clarify the situation they explained a series of events as a concerted policy by Eden, rather than the confused reaction to events that actually took place. They believed that Eden decided at the beginning of the crisis, in July, to use force. Therefore, any of Eden's subsequent actions were viewed as an attempt to achieve this goal or hide his intentions from a divided country and reluctant world.

However, while Eden intended to maintain British interests, he knew before the summer of 1956 that he could not act independently. In addition, his moral and diplomatic beliefs drove him toward negotiation, even if this might mean hard bargaining from behind the pressure of the US. The Prime Minister had long fostered a belief in exerting power through the US. This led to the following of an American line but the Americans vacillated under the misinterpretation of Eden's intentions. Thus, the character of the Prime Minister's process of making decisions was lost to certain contemporaries, consequently confusing the historiography.[27]

Adopted in October, the decision to use force offered a high-risk solution to an increasingly high-risk situation. In the two and a half months prior to the decision, Eden, in line with his moral and political beliefs, as well as his experience, attempted to bring the crisis to a peaceful conclusion within the limited parameters that British 'power' offered. This remained consistent with British conduct of foreign affairs. Britain had never been more than a status quo power in the twentieth century. She reacted to events in the hope of maintaining her world power status. However, even this power had waned, particularly since the two world wars. In the post-1945 world, Britain conducted foreign relations as opposed to foreign policy. The Second World War resulted in her replacement by the United States as the world's leading power impeding any possible pretensions of *weltpolitik* or even *machtpolitik*.[28] The post-war British governments had to accustom themselves to the new parameters of their role. Foreign policy became relegated to a day-by-day reaction to events rather than the fulfilment of measured policies. Studies of government perpetuated the myth of the traditional procedure of defining policies, as did the misunderstanding that while the precise nature of the role might have changed, its broader definition had not.[29] The majority of the British public still believed that its country was a leading world power with the ability to create her own policy and act independently. The Suez Crisis changed this perspective. Britain still had a role to play in world affairs, but Eden recognised that this role depended on the will of the US, despite historiographical criticism that his earlier experience, particularly of the Dictators, had made him more determined to exact a dynamic role for his country.[30] On a more personal level, Eden had spent his entire life under this modern reality. Born in 1897 he grew up in the declining years of British imperialism, and entered politics in 1923, when Britain's role and method for conducting foreign affairs was changing.[31] He remained under no illusion as to Britain's position with regard to foreign relations, although he maintained her world profile through his mediation and peaceful settlement of issues such as the Second World War, Civil War in Greece (1944), the Trieste problem (1954), and the French in Indochina (1954).[32]

Even in the Middle East, a traditional area of British power, he understood his country's limitations, believing that '[i]t is a case of new times, new methods... What we are trying to do in Egypt is not to run away from a regime which often says crude and hostile things, but rather to lay the foundations of security in the Middle East in the new and changed circumstances that now prevail there. By this I mean of course not so much the new regime in Egypt, as the changes in our position in the world.'[33] He then reiterated and emphasised this point: 'In the second half of the twentieth century we cannot hope to maintain our position in the Middle East by the methods of the last century. However little we like it, we must face that fact... If we are to maintain our influence in this area, future policy must be designed to harness these [nationalist] movements rather than struggle against them.'[34] Maintaining influence meant protecting British assets, in particular oil, but Eden understood the rising strength of nationalism within the Middle East.[35] He knew that if he wanted to maintain British 'interests' then he must do as little to antagonise the nationalist movements as possible. This meant that he could not afford to develop a distinct policy other than to accept these groups openly, maintaining passivity, and react to individual incidents if and when they occurred, but only when they threatened British interests directly.

The need for minimalist foreign relations was accentuated by the opinion of a public that had elected the Conservatives, in 1955, under the banner of 'Working for Peace'.[36] In his correspondence with Eisenhower, Eden stressed the need to ease world tension. However, this was not just a party question but a reflection of the deep desire of the whole British people.[37] Having led the 'scuttle' from the Canal base in 1954, Eden had shown his intention to minimise Britain's involvement in certain areas, principally with a view to cutting costs.[38] Shortly after the general election of 1955, he demonstrated the need 'to make economies in the defence programmes'. After talks with Minister of Defence Selwyn Lloyd, he cut spending to £1,535 million, despite calls for increased spending from the right-wing Conservatives. The economy of the country was not capable of taking the strain of increased defence spending and the need for economies had become engraved on Eden's mind.[39] On 28 September 1955, he had raised the issue of Britain's current disarmament programme with Macmillan. The Prime Minister knew that defence cuts worried the Americans, because of the obvious defensive/strategic implications, but believed that 'we must push on vigorously'.[40] He assumed that the US would involve themselves in Middle Eastern politics if it believed the area to be destabilised. Macmillan was then sent to New York to head the UK delegation at a disarmament conference. Eden continued to favour withdrawal from Egypt and a limitation to defence spending.

Criticism arose from the Suez Group, which consisted of a core of 28 right-wing, hardline imperialist MPs who had voted against the decision to 'scuttle'.[41] The group misunderstood Eden's conduct of foreign affairs by reaction to events, believing that 'he mistook diplomacy for foreign policy'.[42] As Julian Amery, one of the group's leading members, remembered, its size 'waxed and waned', but '[d]ouble that number were fairly regular attenders of group meetings'.[43] At this stage the group did little more than stoke up trouble, particularly in the media, but their influence would increase when Eden's health and will deteriorated in October 1956, culminating in their role at the Conservative Party conference at Llandudno. Churchill also opposed the withdrawal. Again, this had no direct effect on affairs until October 1956 when Eden began to rely more heavily on his advice and support. Despite his later use of the 'scuttle' to motivate Churchill to goad Eden into using force, Macmillan recorded, in 1954, that the withdrawal was 'the great event of the week' as '[t]here can be no doubt at all that we have acted wisely'.[44] In the early weeks of the crisis, both Churchill and Macmillan remained silent or, at least, private critics of Eden's actions. At this stage, they did not influence the Prime Minister.

Reflecting the form of foreign relations that Eden employed, the Prime Minister soon came under criticism. The majority of 1955 had seen little direct political action on Middle Eastern issues, fuelling Tory discontent and media anger. Despite his past association as an anti-appeaser, Eden was now seen as an appeaser of both the Arabs and the Russians.[45] Eden did not envisage a direct threat from either at this point. The Soviet issue lay dormant, and he still appeared optimistic of an Arab-Israeli peace that included Nasser. However, the media developed a campaign against him, led by Pamela Berry's *Daily Telegraph* and immortalised in Donald Maclachlan's article of 3 January 1956.[46] The 'Eden Must Go' campaign lasted for several months and focused on the Prime Minister and Government's indecisiveness, delay and 'confusing of policy decisions'.[47] It also showed that Eden was isolated at the time when he needed to convey his sentiments to politicians and the public.[48] At the point of extreme frustration and pressure in October 1956, this isolation from media assistance would have profound effects. Tony Shaw also held this view, but saw the point of isolation as occurring much earlier, concurring with the established historiography that Eden had decided in July to use force.[49] Having narrowed down his lines of advice Eden had already isolated himself from the public through the medium of the press.

Despite the significant difference between Eden and Churchill over imperialism, the country had long seen Eden as Churchill's anointed successor and his immediate succession after Churchill suggested continuity in thinking between the two men. However, even Churchill, the leading imperialist, had been forced to subjugate much of his pretensions because of the change in Britain's position.[50] He agreed to Cabinet's decision to begin the withdrawal from the Canal Zone but he could never reconcile himself to this anti-imperial sentiment, the frustration boiling over as he promoted a forceful solution to the crisis. However, Churchill remained unique amongst post-war leaders as the only one to defend the Empire openly. In 1952, he had referred to the Egyptians, directly to Eden, as 'lower than the most degraded savages now known' and had wished that he had 'taught the pashas and the very small class of educated Egyptians a lesson which they would not have forgotten for a decade'.[51] In 1953, Evelyn Shuckburgh, a private secretary of Eden's, had noted that Churchill '[a]lways...wanted a war with Egypt'.[52] Attlee had understood the need for change in the transitional period after the War. Eden, of the old school and so long heir apparent to Churchill, was also presumed to be a defender of the Empire. However, to Eden, the importance of control in Suez was not so much because of its effect on British imperial control in the Middle East, as its potential for the specific strangling of her oil supplies. Summarising his position to Cabinet, he referred to a 'general policy...founded on the need to protect our oil interests in Iraq and in the Persian Gulf'.[53] He knew that Britain was declining and had set out not to rock the boat, hoping to gain support to promote a deterrent against the compromising of the 'oil interests'.[54]

Succeeding Churchill also had another clouding effect on the understanding of Eden's political aspirations, which paralleled the accusations of imperialism. When he took over as Prime Minister, the Conservative Party still prided itself on its 'Bulldog reputation'. Some historians have used this to explain his frustration, and therefore imply an alleged impetuosity during the Suez Crisis.[55] Even Macmillan had thought that 'it must be difficult for Eden', waiting in the wings.[56] Yet, despite waiting for Churchill to 'move over' Eden did not enter his new role with the naivety of a man merely intent on leaving his mark, as his understanding of British foreign relations in the Middle East showed.[57] On taking over as Prime Minister, Eden deliberately distanced himself from Churchill. He called a general election for May 1955, just a month after assuming office, and chose not to ask Churchill to join the campaign. While he had respected and revered his predecessor, he did not always see eye to eye with him, especially over foreign issues and notably Egypt.[58] Eden had threatened to resign in 1953 because of disagreements over foreign affairs.[59] It was not until late September, 1956, that increasingly ill, he began to seek reassurance and often advice from Churchill, who adamantly believed that Nasser must be removed by force, and endeavoured to influence the Prime Minister. No historians have seen Churchill as such a strong influence upon Eden. Thomas, Lucas and Kyle all believed that Churchill favoured a forceful resolution of the crisis. Nevertheless, Lucas did not refer to Churchill's influence.[60] Similarly, Thomas has written that Churchill considered that this was a situation that could be met by force but despite his disappointment at the lack of action did not directly influence Eden.[61] Kyle believed that Churchill's support for force was in line with Eden's thinking. He has documented Churchill's attempts to influence Eden but believed that this was in order to change the military plan rather than incite military action.[62]

One area in which Eden did agree with Churchill was on maintaining Anglo-American relations to affect US assistance in areas where Britain could not afford to maintain an effective deterrent. Eden believed in the importance of Anglo-American co-operation: that had been the major reason for his resignation in 1938. His disillusion with Neville Chamberlain's appeasement of the dictators and failure to speed rearmament as a deterrent to the dictators turned to despair when Chamberlain rejected President Roosevelt's peace initiative of January 1938.[63] Eden was 'outraged and uneasy' because he had been working on increasing Anglo-American co-operation through discussion throughout 1937, and because of the abruptness with which Chamberlain dismissed the offer, knowing that Eden, away in the south of France, would be back in London in only twenty-four hours.[64] Eden wanted a formal alliance between the USA, Great Britain and France against the dictators.[65] Fundamentally, as he hinted to the House of Commons:

> I should not be frank with the House if I were to pretend that it is an isolated issue between my Right Hon. friend the Prime Minister and myself. It is not. Within the last few weeks upon one most important decision of foreign policy which did not concern Italy at all, the difference was fundamental.[66]

The failure to secure Anglo-American co-operation and not the appeasement of Italy had forced his resignation. He believed in the importance of Anglo-American relations but the decision also reflected the extent to which Eden remained a gentleman, in the traditional sense, and true to his principles.

In 1955/56, now Prime Minister, Eden acted on his deep-seated belief in developing an Anglo-American relationship. He was keen to maintain British interests with the US, backed by Commonwealth support.[67] Fearful of Nasser's brand of Pan-Arab nationalism, he hoped to gain US support to deter any direct action in the Middle East that might affect British resources, notably oil. Kyle and Lucas believed that Eden wanted US support for force.

At this stage, the Cabinet did not share Eden's views. However, Eden believed that the Americans shared his distrust of Nasser. While he had been Foreign Secretary, he and US Secretary of State John Foster Dulles had started discussions on a possible settlement of the Arab-Israeli dispute which would maintain the balance of power in the Middle East and prevent a destabilisation of an area that might be seized upon by Nasser, another Arab power or Israel. Talks proved especially difficult and long, but by June 1955 the details had been agreed, and even in the face of a poor balance of payments, Cabinet approved ALPHA, the plan to give land to Egypt and compensate Israel financially, 'in principle'.[68] In addition, Eden hoped the Americans, with their greater interests in Saudi Arabia and consequent influence, might have curbed the Saudis, whose bribery and corruption had started to create political problems within the Middle East and the Levant.[69]

Eden also tried to draw the US into the Baghdad Pact, which aimed at mutual co-operation against militants of the left, and to maintain 'friendly' countries with arms.[70] The only way of harnessing the growing nationalist movements in the Middle East appeared to be by buying favour.[71] By 26 September 1955, Shuckburgh saw the possibility when he set out the various alternatives before the Government, concluding that it must try to frighten Nasser and then 'bribe' him.[72] Eden also saw the potential. However, Nasser could not be frightened without US support, because it would also have meant appearing to resort to old tactics, of 'gunboat diplomacy', which the Americans would not have condoned because they smacked of colonialist values. Eisenhower had remarked that 'to Americans liberty was more precious than good government'.[73] Dulles had argued that 'the West had to demonstrate that "Colonialism" was a fake charge'.[74] More significantly for Eden, he did not have the money available to maintain a military deterrent in the Middle East and hoped that the US would be able to provide, if not a direct military deterrent, a more plausible indirect threat to Arab or Israeli moves. This reflected Eden's own belief in NATO and the principle of 'peace through strength'. The Prime Minister had always favoured the principle of collective security. He had been a staunch advocate of the League of Nations while serving as Parliamentary Private Secretary to Foreign Secretary Austen Chamberlain and as Minister for League of Nations Affairs.[75] In contrast, the historiography has seen Eden's past as a motive for an aggressive policy over Suez.[76]

However, there was an immediate divergence of opinion between the British and American leaders, based on President Eisenhower's apparent inability to distinguish between emerging Egyptian nationalism and Nasser's Pan-Arabism.[77] Eisenhower understood the situation but had his hands tied by a variety of bonds including public and Congressional opinion. This was the reason behind the essentially passive American role in foreign affairs and the subsequent crisis. In addition, there had been a number of problems between the British and Americans over ALPHA, in particular between

Dulles and Eden, which reflected the deliberate inaction of the Eisenhower Administration. Ironically, while Britain hoped to limit her own involvement in world affairs, whilst looking to the US to fill the vacuum, the Americans tried to scale down their own open foreign commitments. Eden never fully reconciled this apparent indifference, the cause of which he did not understand. Once again, this had little bearing on events until deep into the crisis when the Prime Minister, ill, tired and frustrated, decided to use force to settle the crisis regardless of US support.

The simplest way around this, for Eden, appeared to be enlisting American financial support to counter 'communist' infiltration. The Arab-Israeli dispute created instability within the Middle East and opened the area to Soviet penetration. However, Eden saw that the Soviets were not the threat that had been assumed by contemporaries at home and abroad. As early as 29 July 1955, he had suggested that 'they [the Soviets] were looking out for someone to hold their hands' and if they required British support in Europe, they would only endanger it by interfering in the old bastion and supposed remnant of British power, the Middle East.[78] Eden and Macmillan disagreed on the nature of the Soviet threat to Britain but the Prime Minister watched as his Foreign Secretary and Dulles inflamed each other's fear of the Communist threat.[79] By September 1955, Macmillan had developed a hatred of Nasser that inflamed his anti-communist feelings as the Egyptian leader received military aid from the Soviets through Czechoslovakia.[80] Eisenhower also saw Nasser's actions as communist inspired. Here was a good opportunity for Eden to influence American opinion. Historians have also seen Macmillan as rabidly anti-communist but they have assumed, as with his conviction to use force, that Eden had the same view.[81] Both Kyle and Lucas suggest little difference of opinion between Eden, Macmillan and Lloyd. Thomas believed that Macmillan overpowered Eden, quickly bringing him into line with his own designs for a solution.[82]

Despite the Prime Minister's attempt to influence the US, the Americans were not as anti-communist as the British assumed. At the time of the Eisenhower Administration's inauguration in 1953, the new president's advisers believed that the government had been 'languishing in a state of decay and disorder' which had abetted 'the world menace of communism'. However, they reacted by suggesting 'some show of resolution – spiced with some specific, but not too costly, show of force'.[83] The President was more concerned about publicly reacting against possible Soviet expansion than actually developing a specific global policy. On taking office, Eisenhower had immediately directed his Secretary of State to conduct a purge and had Dulles send a letter to 16,500 members of the State Department demanding 'positive loyalty' to the US Government.[84] This action demonstrated Dulles's anti-communism to the British, despite that, in hindsight, it was only a show of faith to the American people by a new President and his Secretary of State.[85] The British belief in the extent of Dulles's fear of communism increased. Early in 1953, he had conducted a tour of the Middle East that had led to an emphatic desire to strengthen the area against Soviet aggression. On 26 February 1953, addressing the *Philadelphia Bulletin* Forum, Dulles appraised Soviet policies. Despite acknowledging that there was a change in leadership and 'already a notable shift in Soviet foreign policy', he went on to warn that '[t]hroughout its 38 years of existence...[w]henever the opportunity has arisen, the Soviet Union has swallowed up its neighbors, or made satellites of them, or subordinated them in other ways'.[86] Dulles also supported the Baghdad Pact, praising the '"northern tier" concept' which had, 'without challenging the concept of Arab unity...drawn together for collective defense'.[87] In a meeting with Macmillan and French Foreign Minister Antoine Pinay, he suggested 'getting tough around here' if efforts to dissuade Nasser failed.[88] With this sense of strong anti-communism and the British believing that Dulles ran US foreign relations, there appeared to be leverage to influence the Americans into providing a deterrent in the Middle East. Dulles appeared to mistake the nationalism within the Middle East for communist insurrection but the British misunderstood and therefore exaggerated the extent of his anti-communism.[89] Publicly Dulles's fears were more strongly expressed because of the need to placate the Republican right wing. In private, and more indicative of his true view, the Secretary of State was not nearly so anti-communist; little more so than most of the Western post-war leaders. Hence, the British misjudged their ability to influence both Dulles and the President.

Despite ALPHA's failure, largely due to its withering on the vine as the Americans refused to support it, Eden sought to strengthen his policy of supporting friendly countries with arms or financial aid, a policy more acceptable to the US's 'informal empire' or 'influence'. The US also managed to threaten this scheme, reducing its agreed commitment of tanks to Iraq.[90] In reaction, Eden wrote to Eisenhower, playing on the Communist threat and pointing out that 'there is no question of money in this but only of security'.[91] Yet, it *was* a question of money, which Britain did not have. Throughout early 1956, Eden continued to suggest that the US join the Baghdad Pact. He knew that this was a political impossibility but wanted to benefit from the compromises that the US offered in lieu of membership. Eden understood that he must subordinate his own policy and maintain mediation if he wanted to obtain American assistance.[92]

Eden believed that Nasser feared Western power, whereas the Egyptian leader had developed such a strong sense of hatred for Eden that any such fear was only secondary to standing up to the British. Neither man understood the other's perspective. Eden had met with Nasser only once, on 20 February 1955, en route to Bangkok, for the South East Asian Treaty Organisation (SEATO) Conference. Anthony Nutting, Minister of State in the Foreign Office during the Suez Crisis, remembered how he 'greeted the President with the utmost coldness'.[93] The Prime Minister recorded little of the meeting in his memoirs, but was struck by the Egyptian leader's 'frustrated desire to lead the Arab world'.[94] He then put a new light on the famous photograph of the two men, taken before the meeting. Eden recalled, '[a]s the flashlights went off, he seized my hand and held it'.[95] This symbolised, to Eden, Nasser's desire to maintain Anglo-Egyptian relations publicly despite disagreement, particularly over the Turco-Iraqi Pact. Yet, while his Pan-Arabism was emerging, Eden remained calm. As Nutting recalled, although the Prime Minister did not like Nasser personally, 'he regarded him as a great improvement on King Farouk'.[96] However, the calm belied his fears, as Eden, writing to Dulles, predicted 'Nasser would denounce [the Turco-Iraqi] treaty at time of signature and...there would be Egyptian efforts in Iraq to bring about the downfall of Nuri [Sa'id].'[97] Nasser believed that Eden had talked down to him, and that the meeting had been conducted to deride the Egyptians. As one of the President's advisers remembered, Nasser became 'obsessed with this theme'.[98] A gulf of misunderstanding soon opened between them, but Eden's attitude reflected that he could still do business with the Egyptians, particularly if backed by American support. This was shown by his commitment to ALPHA, and OMEGA, the Anglo-American plan to destabilise Nasser's regime by economic sanctions and covert activity.[99] Again, it would only be later that, concerted with other pressures, this frustration would lead Eden to embark on a military solution in October 1956.

The role of MI6 has also clouded the interpretation of Eden's intentions in the Middle East. In particular, its aggressive stance, involving assassination attempts on Nasser, has suggested that Eden was using them to derive a forceful solution to his problems, particularly in Egypt. MI6 sought to disinform the Prime Minister in the hope that he would support a policy more in line with its role in the Cold War of protecting Britain and British interests from Communist incursion. Several sources show that Eden was receiving a stream of information from an agent within Nasser's personal entourage, which suggested that Nasser had tied himself extremely closely to the Soviets, to a greater extent than anyone had realised.[100] However, Evelyn Shuckburgh was not convinced of Nasser's subjugation, believing that he was 'playing East off against West to the last moment'.[101] In fact, information from 'Lucky Break', the codename of an informant within Nasser's Government, was presented to Eden as evidence of a move by Nasser towards the communists.[102] However MI6 was intent on influencing Eden, although the Prime Minister remained unaware of its intentions. The full extent of MI6/CIA subversion of policy remains unclear but their influence and policy engendered a belief of the British Government's bellicosity, which has confused contemporaries and historians alike. Lucas and Kyle have both seen the use or attempted use of MI6 to assassinate Nasser as indicative of Eden's warmongering and, by implication, his commitment to a solution at any cost.[103]

However, misunderstanding permeated the personalities and relationships of the key Anglo-American diplomats. This made it much more difficult to promote consensus and trust when the crisis developed. President Eisenhower had stolen Eden's thunder at the Geneva Conference, revealing the reality of both the post-1945 world order and the subordination of Eden as the world's leading diplomat. However, the situation was clouded by the inability of much of the Cabinet to take the President seriously.[104] Churchill exclaimed 'I am bewildered. It seems that everything is left to Dulles... This fellow preaches like a Methodist Minister, and his bloody text is always the same.' He believed 'that the President is no more than a ventriloquist's doll'.[105] Eden inherited and developed much of this misunderstanding, which increased during his dealings with the Americans both as Foreign Secretary and later as Prime Minister. Sir Philip de Zulueta, his private secretary, believed that his 'master' could 'never quite come to terms with Eisenhower's elevation from army officer to head of state'. Here Churchill too had thought of 'Ike' as a 'brigadier'.[106] Frederick Bishop, one of Eden's private secretaries, did not think that Eden's regard for the President was by 'any means wholehearted'. He believed that as the crisis developed, so Eden's regard for Eisenhower diminished. Eden did not think that the American was a 'particularly wise man', but possibly 'stupid' and, regarding international affairs, 'inept'. In short, he underrated the President.[107] The continuation of American passivity, inflamed by this disregard for Eisenhower's ability, would eventually infuriate Eden. However, until October, he continued to follow the American lead, particularly after the genesis of Dulles's idea for returning the Canal to international control, which mirrored Eden's own solution for the crisis.

While the British underestimated the Americans and Eden in particular disliked working with Dulles, the Americans did not enjoy a comfortable relationship with the British. They did not trust the word of Eden or Selwyn Lloyd.[108] Shuckburgh recalled that Dean Acheson, then US Secretary of State, said to Eden, after Lloyd had been negotiating over Korea in the UN, 'Don't bring a crooked Welsh lawyer with you next time.'[109] The Dulles/Eden relationship proved to contain even more misunderstanding and misjudgement. Shuckburgh recalled that 'Dulles didn't trust Eden' and the pair 'simply couldn't "gel"'. Even the different pace at which each man spoke elicited annoyance and mistrust from the other. This became such a problem that along with his American colleagues, Shuckburgh found himself in the position of trying to prevent 'misunderstandings... arising partly from that incompatibility of tempo in their speech'.[110] While 'Dulles mistrusted Eden', the Secretary of State's private secretaries disliked the Prime Minister.

Shuckburgh remembered that many of them thought that the Prime Minister was homosexual because he called them 'dear'.[111] Chester Cooper, the CIA representative in London, also believed that Eden's manner and demeanour affected his relationship with the Americans, describing him as an 'essence of a British Prime Minister', 'almost Gilbert and Sullivan'.[112] These cultural differences made direct communication and trust very difficult.

While the Americans misunderstood the Prime Minister, so too did contemporaries and, consequently, historians. For example, Eden has often been seen as possessing an impulsive nature and there is little doubt that he was motivated by a great deal of pride in his achievements, in the position he attained and in Britain's prestige. This has been voiced by Kyle, Lucas and Thomas who have also considered him extremely vain, leading to a misinterpretation of aspects of Eden's character and exaggerations of its worst excesses, notably, in their opinion, the decision to use force.[113] Eden's pride manifested itself in his immediate reaction to events, which could result in aggressive outbursts that did not reflect his opinion, more his frustration as he laboured to protect British interests without a foreign policy. After a short period of contemplation he retracted his remarks and employed a more moderate and considered reaction. This was representative of his reaction to the dismissal of Sir John Glubb from the leadership of the Arab Legion on 1 March 1956, by King Hussein of Jordan.[114] The telegrams that Eden sent in response to the Glubb incident conveyed a different tone and intent from the historiographical accusations of his anger and threats against Nasser. This was despite the fact that he immediately assumed Nasser had influenced Hussein and the potentially misleading Bellicose[115] and the scaremongering tone emanating from the British Embassy in Amman. King Hussein had been uncommunicative with the Ambassador and so Sir Alexander Kirkbride, former Ambassador to Jordan, was told by Eden to continue on his prospective trip to Jordan to draw out the King. Kirkbride reported his conversations such that the Prime Minister 'now realised that Hussein had acted on his own initiative'.[116] Eden had also met with Glubb at Chequers. The Prime Minister continued to employ his own passive crisis management. Publicly, and in his dealings with other governments/countries, Eden's reactions had been exemplary, in terms of both emotion and policy. Privately, again, he had let his temper get the better of him but his subsequent directives did not reflect this. Nevertheless, many contemporaries remained misinformed.

Yet, with Eden it was not just pride. He possessed a violent temper, inherited from his father, which, while under control for the majority of the time, came out when he was overtired.[117] This has become an additional reason why historians have assumed that Eden reacted aggressively against Nasser's nationalisation of the Canal.[118] Shuckburgh recorded that one of the biggest effects of Eden's medical complaint was sleep deprivation and a good night's sleep would be as little as five uninterrupted hours.[119] However, Shuckburgh knew these outbursts lacked importance. After one outburst he remarked, 'I am beginning to learn how to be a lightning conductor on these occasions, to innocent bystanders from scenes which appear far more serious to them than I know them to be'.[120] Sir William Hayter, British Ambassador in Moscow, recalled how Eden's anger should not be misinterpreted and demonstrated what it was that Eden actually wanted. During the visit of Khrushchev and Bulganin to Britain in April 1956, the Prime Minister would ring up Hayter, practically every morning. This was usually to complain about the press coverage and, as on one occasion, could be as trivial as bemoaning the larger number of column inches devoted to Bulganin than to himself. However, as Hayter concluded: 'He didn't want anything done. He just wanted to sound off about it.' Such was the ambassador's concern that his reply was 'Oh dear, how dreadful.'[121] When asked how he dealt with Eden's temper, Shuckburgh remembered: 'It wasn't too difficult because Anthony never kept up his anger. He would apologise afterwards. I don't think anybody ever regarded his tantrums as particularly wounding or dreadful.'[122] Those working closest with him continued to hold him in the highest regard in spite of his temper. They could see that it did not really represent his true character or feelings. Bishop explained: 'One thought of him very much as someone who was an arduous but agreeable taskmaster. His demands were considerable and indeed one could see at times his temper was not as equable as at other times, but on the whole the general atmosphere was very good.'[123] 'Under pressure [Eden] tended to get very nervy', undoubtedly increasing the frequency and volume of these outbursts.[124] This was represented during the growth of Nasser's nationalism, with its threat to Britain and, in particular, to Eden. However, as Millard concluded, 'to say [Eden] was not in command of himself is an exaggeration'.[125] In private, he vented his immediate dissatisfaction before he considered and enacted his decision. This showed the difficulty in understanding his private and public faces, both for contemporaries and for historians, who have ignored these differences. Those closest to him, such as Bishop, Millard, Iverach McDonald, Foreign Editor of *The Times*, and Shuckburgh, as well as those who had known him for some time, such as Hayter, recognised this distinction. Others, outside of this 'inner circle', took these outbursts to be more serious than they were, which compounded the problem of misunderstanding the Prime Minister.

He had very few close friends who understood him. Eden did not prove particularly easy to know or understand. He did not share Macmillan's ease of social mingling. Whereas the Chancellor would always retire to the Commons smoking-room or equivalent, Eden remained much more aloof. He preferred the company of a few close friends. Iain Macleod, the Minister of Labour and National Service, commented facetiously, although only with mild exaggeration, that the Prime Minister had 'absolutely no friends'.[126] This isolation deepened with his marriage to Clarissa Churchill, in 1952, who, as a most loyal wife, tried to protect him from criticism and provided a country retreat in Wiltshire where he tried to escape the rigours of government and, to a lesser extent, the scrutiny of the media. This trend increased with the development of the crisis, as attacks on Eden grew and as his medical condition worsened. So, normally aloof, by the critical period of the crisis in October, he had very few friends or advisers. McDonald, a friend for over twenty years, held a privileged position in maintaining Eden's confidence. Those outside of the small group of friends and closest colleagues, as with his contemporaries in government, found it much more difficult to know the full picture.

One area of Eden's life that has been the subject of much speculation but little understood was his illness. Historians have recognised that Eden was ill and that his health deteriorated after taking office in 1955. However, because of their own belief that he had already decided to use force in July, they see no relationship between the significant worsening of the Prime Minister's health in October and his subsequent use of force. In addition, they do not recognise the seriousness of Eden's decline, which left him requiring surgery on 6 October. However, a correlation exists between the deterioration of the Prime Minister's health in October 1956 and the consequent decision to use force to settle the crisis. Eden was ill by the time Nasser expropriated the Suez Canal. Even before he took on the premiership, he had been in poor health. He had suffered from suspected jaundice and a duodenal ulcer prior to taking over from Churchill, but his brief tenure as Prime Minister coincided with a worsening of his health, troubled as he was by gallstones, diverticulitis, and ultimately cholangitis. After a failed bile duct operation in April 1953 and two further failed attempts at corrective surgery, Eden's symptoms worsened. Because of the attentions of his doctors, in particular Sir Horace Evans, and the use of a variety of drugs, he managed to continue in senior ministerial office. However, by November 1956, Evans told R. A. Butler, by then Lord Privy Seal, that 'Anthony could not live on stimulants any more.'[127] Under increasing pressure, he was unable to steal more than a day or two away from London at his home in Wiltshire during the period 1953–7. Even here, accompanied by at least one private secretary, he would keep in touch with affairs by telephone.[128] As the crisis developed, so the strains of its management hastened the deterioration of Eden's health, a situation made worse by the time differences between London, New York, Washington and Cairo:[129] the Prime Minister, already an arduous worker, made himself available at all times of the day or night so that he could react to any changes in the situation. By October, this led to Eden's hospitalisation for corrective surgery.

The majority of the pressures that would finally push Eden to the use of force were already in place, as were the reasons for history's misunderstanding of his intentions. The Prime Minister remained flexible; he had always favoured the peaceful resolution of disputes and this was of even more importance at a time when Britain's power and, more importantly, the world perception of that power, was in decline and her financial equilibrium threatened. Nasser became, for Eden, the embodiment of all the threats to

British power, and so the Prime Minister steadily developed a personal hatred that often expressed itself in occasional fits of rage. Not only was Nasser threatening the balance of power in the Middle East, but he threatened Britain's oil supplies, her export trade and thus her livelihood, a situation of which Eisenhower was fully aware.[130]

Eisenhower, reflecting on the Arab-Israeli conflict, wrote: 'we must be friends with both contestants in that region in order that we can bring them closer together. To take sides could do nothing but to destroy our influence in leading toward a peaceful settlement of one of the most explosive situations in the world today.'[131] Given the notorious powder-keg relations of Middle Eastern politics, this quote summarised the viewpoint that quickly became lost in the British analyses of the crisis. It also underscored what was essentially, for the Americans, a passive role. Nevertheless, it reflected the belief that the US had in this policy as the best way to achieve what was always Washington and London's principal goal, maintaining free-flowing oil supplies. This was another source of misunderstanding between London and Washington. The British Government lost sight of the American view that the world situation dictated that diplomacy was the *only* route to achieving this goal. The British mistook American 'passivity' for indifference. Therefore, Eden tried to benefit from the compromises that the US offered in lieu of membership. It was in this way that the Prime Minister conducted his foreign relations in the period 1955–6. As Shuckburgh recalled, '[Eden] did believe that we had responsibilities, experiences and qualities of thought of a worldwide nature which we ought not to jeopardise', but he also understood that he must subordinate his country's pretensions. For his part, Eisenhower countered that 'under normal circumstances we were quite content for the experienced British to take the...initiative...in the Middle East, but when the Soviet Union threatened to become actively involved, the United States could no longer remain a silent partner'.[132] This bode well for the British who were keen to limit their involvement in world affairs and had been upset at the US for trying to do the same. However, while Eden's correspondence contributed to this stirring, the Americans remained silent. Therefore, the Prime Minister had to negotiate with Nasser under the auspices of the US if he wanted to derive a peaceful solution to the crisis.[133] He did not know that Dulles, being protective, believed that closer Anglo-American relations would 'throw an intolerable burden upon the President'.[134] The Americans continued to believe that Britain expected closer relations, which would involve US material, moral and physical assistance. However, Eden was not searching for such a relationship, just a US commitment to offering a deterrent in the Middle East. After Dean Acheson's denial of the Anglo-American special relationship in 1949, Eden had become aware of the US's reluctance to be openly involved in any such implication. That he was forced into trying to lure the US into offering help to fight the Soviet threat also indicated that he did not believe a 'special relationship', in this way, was likely.

Fundamentally, he tried to deceive the Americans to ensure their help. However, US postwar attitudes would not even stretch that far, enhanced by the post-nationalisation *misunderstanding* that Eden had immediately decided to settle the crisis by force. By July 1956, the *misunderstandings* between the US and Britain were in place, along with the seed-bed of pressures set to influence the Prime Minister. The events of the summer and autumn did not appear suddenly, like a rainstorm on a fine day, but rather they evolved from the misconceptions discussed in this introduction and with them the *misunderstanding* of Eden and his conduct of the Suez Crisis.

1
Nationalisation of the Canal: 26 July–3 August

Expropriation of the Canal, the First Ministerial Meetings and the Search for a Solution

The period from 26 July to 3 August 1956 comprised the initial stage of the Suez Crisis. Started by Nasser's nationalisation of the Suez Canal Company, during these eight days there was a flurry of diplomatic activity, particularly in Britain. Abhorring war and politically astute, Eden sought a peaceful solution, although he was unsure exactly how this could be achieved. Fearing the results of an escalation of tension, the Prime Minister attempted to win international support for condemnation of Nasser and his actions. Extensive support did not arrive instantaneously, and, in particular, US support was uncertain and slow. However, Eden continued to explore all possible solutions, exploiting political and economic sanctions backed from a position of strength with the possibility of military involvement in the background. He endorsed the NATO principle of 'peace through strength', hoping to employ a threat to Egypt alongside mediation with Nasser through the UN Security Council. However, misunderstandings of intention developed between the British and the Americans. This has clouded events both then and now. Confusion was increased by Cabinet's eventual decision to employ a dual-track policy, whereby a peaceful solution of the crisis would be sought, although, in the last resort, if this failed then force might have to be employed.[1]

Nasser's nationalisation of the Suez Canal on 26 July 1956 shocked Eden and the world. Less than two months before, on 10 June, the Egyptian Government had recognised the continuing validity of the concession made by the Khedive, which was to expire in 1968.[2] However, the Prime Minister remained calm despite the culmination of all his fears. He heard of the Egyptian action during dinner at Downing Street, in honour of King Feisal of Iraq, on the evening of the 26th. The Iraqis, as Selwyn Lloyd recalled, held similar fears of Nasser to those of Eden and himself, but Nuri-es-Said, the Iraqi Prime Minister, advised the British to 'hit Nasser hard and quickly'.[3]

This pressure from the Iraqis increased as the crisis deepened, channelled through the bellicose British Ambassador in Baghdad, Sir Michael Wright. However, despite Eden's surprise and the immediate aggressive advice, the Prime Minister remained calm, immediately convening an impromptu ministerial meeting to discuss his options. He suggested taking the issue to the Security Council, where world condemnation of Nasser's actions could pressure the Egyptians to reinternationalise the Canal. This sentiment of negotiation was far removed from the alleged bellicosity, although the suggestion was eventually rejected because of the threat of the Soviet veto.[4] The Prime Minister realised that the Soviets would veto any attempt to bring the UN into the dispute, and thus it was a pointless exercise at a time when a quick resolution was of an essence to appease both British public opinion and world confidence.[5] After the rejection of his own idea, Eden was keen to find a solution to the crisis. He wished to hear the opinions of his senior ministers along with those of the Leader of the Opposition, French Ambassador and the American Chargé d'Affaires. He wanted a united bloc against Nasser, both at home and abroad, to pressure the Egyptians into relinquishing their sole control of the Canal. Consequently, he summoned an eclectic group, which would provide a variety of ideas for a possible solution and also elucidate the opinions of the key countries in the dispute, notably Britain and France, whose interests were most grossly effected, and the US who acted as the world's unofficial 'executive power'. The meeting, which followed the dinner for the Iraqis, included the Lord President, Lord Salisbury, the Lord Chancellor, Viscount Kilmuir, the Secretary of State for Common wealth Relations, Lord Home, the Foreign Secretary, Selwyn Lloyd, Deputy Under-Secretary of State at the Foreign Office, Harold Caccia, Leader of the Opposition Labour Party, Hugh Gaitskell, one of the Chiefs of Staff, Lord Mountbatten, the French Ambassador to Britain, Jean Chauvel, and American Chargé d'Affaires, Andrew Foster.[6] Judging by the number and diversity of people invited, Eden had not decided on any controversial secret decisions, such as the decision to use force, that could be compromised by their foreknowledge. This was underlined by his lack of trust in people's discretion, particularly that of French officials. In addition, if he had wanted to railroad an aggressive solution past his senior advisers, it would have been more likely to succeed if he had kept the meeting as small as possible.

He sought to concert opinion and, although shocked by Nasser's actions and their possible ramifications, continued to search for a policy, as the variety of discussion at the meeting of the 26th revealed. However, as Guy Millard one of Eden's private secretaries recorded, the meeting was 'badly organised' and included discussion of possible economic and military retaliation, but nothing could be concluded.[7] Winthrop Aldrich, American Ambassador to Britain, believed that it 'reached no conclusions...other than that there must be immediate consultation with the United States at a high level'.[8] Frederick Bishop, another of Eden's private secretaries, remembered that the nationalisation 'represented an acute acceleration of a developing crisis [but] I don't think it immediately meant that some sort of armed conflict was inevitable'.[9] By the meeting's impromptu nature, and under such dramatic circumstances, it proved disorganised but gave the Prime Minister the chance to listen to a cross-section of reaction and test opinion before more detailed discussion could continue with Cabinet and the governments of France and the US.[10]

Historians have claimed that it was at this meeting that Eden decided upon the immediate use of force to settle the crisis.[11] Others have suggested that the decision was reached soon afterwards.[12] William Clark, Eden's Press Secretary, is frequently cited as in support of the Prime Minister's determination to use force.[13] However, Clark's original diary entry for 26 July was exaggerated when reproduced in his memoirs and contradicted its original conclusion. The sentence, '[t]his was the meeting at which Eden made it absolutely clear that military action would have to be taken', was added several years after the event and does not appear in the original diary entry which actually concluded that '[all] that emerged [from the meeting] was a dullish statement for use in the House'.[14] Clark, as he recorded in his memoirs, became very 'disillusioned by – and even let down by – a prime minister I had previously admired', eventually resigning over collusion.[15] This tainted Clark's record of events, particularly his memoirs, which he used to exaggerate Eden's bellicosity. In addition, Clark admitted, in later years, that his own source of information was not always reliable: 'What Ministers say in a temper or casually to me as a non-Government member, just an official, was very often very revealing of their personality, but not terribly revealing of what Government policy was going to be and that includes the Prime Minister's remarks.'[16] Despite these reservations, voiced in 1979, he contradicted his original diary entries, telling the interviewer that Eden 'made it absolutely clear that military action would have to be taken, Nasser would have to go'.[17] His contemporary diary entry showed that the meeting had concluded very little, and had not produced a commitment to force. The Press Secretary was not a member of the meeting of the 26th.[18] When pushed as to what Eden actually said at the *ad hoc* meeting, he replied: '[T]he question that Eden put perfectly clearly was when can we take military action to topple Nasser, free the Canal? Those were not, I think, his words. He was a diplomat by training. But the answers that he got were addressed to that question.'[19] Clark was unable to judge the situation correctly because, missing the majority of the meeting, he assumed that Eden had already chosen to use force, whereas the Prime Minister's enquiries were an attempt to clarify the situation and keep all 'policy' options open. Clark's own confusion and frustration were increased by the inability of the Chiefs of Staff to suggest any ways in which Britain might respond immediately.[20] Despite these contradictions historians have continued to rely on his evidence.[21]

Further speculation as to Eden and the Government's immediate decision to use force was aroused by Lloyd's comments to Andrew Foster at the meeting. This represented an opportunity for the British to use Foster to test the water with the American administration, to see what action they could suggest or support. Taking Foster to one side he told him that the only solution was for a Western consortium to take over the Canal, by force, should that prove necessary. Nevertheless, the content of Foster's telegram to Eisenhower suggested that the meeting had done little more than focus on all the possible solutions. He wrote that the British had agreed that the Western Governments must consider ways of keeping the Canal open, through economic, political or military action and regardless of any legal implications. He also reported that the Chiefs of Staff had been ordered to prepare a logistical study for a possible military operation to seize the Canal. Eden did not want Nasser 'to get away with it', but there was no suggestion that a decision to employ force had been made.[22] Eden had shown his intention to talk to the Americans in the hope that they might help provide a solution to the crisis. However, Eisenhower, with Dulles abroad, received advice from Herbert Hoover Jr., the US Under-Secretary of State, who warned that the 'British might feel compelled to move drastically' and suggested extreme caution in dealings with the United Kingdom.[23] Hoover, a consistent anglophobe, continued to portray the British attitude in the worst light.[24] The first mistake had been made and a misunderstanding developed as to British intentions, despite Eden's assurances to the President.[25] The American reaction has reinforced historians' belief that Eden had already decided to use force. However, the Prime Minister had only outlined his and the Cabinet's conclusions that a peaceful settlement would be sought, backed by the threat of force which could be employed if all other solutions failed. He continued to search for a policy to resolve the crisis, unaware of American suspicions of British belligerency, and hopeful of US assistance.

An immediate military solution was also not a practical option. Sir Frank Cooper, the Head of the Air Staff Secretariat and a member of the Egypt Committee from mid-September, recalled that the Chiefs of Staff 'made it crystal-clear that they were not going to run a quick operation'.[26] However, Earl Mountbatten of Burma, First Sea Lord, later alleged that he had offered the Prime Minister the proposal of an immediate Royal Marine Commando assault.[27] In spite of this, Mountbatten contradicted his own version of events in an account dictated a month later.[28] The minutes of the first meeting of the Chiefs of Staff after the nationalisation of the Canal revealed that despite Mountbatten's misrepresentation, the political directive was clear and pacifist. He told the other Chiefs 'that Ministers had already given consideration to the attitude the United Kingdom should adopt in the situation and had decided that until the views of other interested powers had been obtained no action should be taken which could be construed as threatening Egypt'.[29] Eden had not decided to use the military to devise an immediate forceful reaction but had only to wait to co-ordinate his efforts with the other countries most affected, to settle the crisis. At this early stage, he had not even agreed to threaten Egypt with military moves to bluff Nasser into relinquishing sole control of the Canal.

However, this scenario with Mountbatten illustrated another of the problems that Eden encountered and another area of pressure exerted upon his policy-making. Mountbatten had suggested an immediate deployment of force, which Eden had rejected, but went on to criticise the eventual launching of the military initiative in October. In November 1956 he outlined his role in a letter to Lord Hailsham: 'I had done everything in my power to carry out his orders, as in duty bound, loyally and to the full in making all the necessary naval preparations for building up a position in which we could have negotiated from strength.'[30] He believed Eden to be employing a peaceful, diplomatic solution. Despite having promoted a forceful solution, in view of the failure of force, Mountbatten pragmatically supported Eden's policy of negotiation from a position of strength. Cooper suggested that the problem with Mountbatten was that he was always 'on the make...always out for [himself]'. Reviewing the First Sea Lord's 'performance in Suez', he explained: 'he rode very successfully all the hurdles, weaving left and right and down the middle...but from the time he became First Sea Lord, nobody trusted him'.[31] Mountbatten's apparent volte-face also reflected the disillusion that many contemporaries had with collusion despite their initial backing of a forceful riposte. The Chiefs of Staff vacillated and remained divided on their choice of action. The problem did not rest solely with Mountbatten. The Chairman of the Chiefs of Staff, Sir William Dickson, spent much of the crisis away on sick leave. Of the remaining Chiefs, Templer called for 'resolute action', while Air Chief Marshal Sir Dermot Boyle, Chief of the Air Staff, was undecided.[32] At one point, Templer accused Boyle of being 'yellow'.[33] However, at this early stage in the crisis, Templer did not influence Eden, and as Richard Powell, the Permanent Secretary at the Ministry of Defence, reflected, the pressure for a military operation only 'built up after time'. As he continued, 'I would guess that Eden had it in mind that we might have to resort to force quite early on, and the Chiefs of Staff were asked to produce a plan for a military operation'.[34] Yet despite the conjecture, logistically, a forceful riposte was impossible at such short notice and the Egyptians had a number of tanks and armour deployed, capable of repelling an operation mounted with paratroopers.[35] In addition, Cabinet, whose principal members had witnessed or been central participants in the Atlantic alliance of the war years, put great faith in Anglo-American and Commonwealth co-operation. Eden, in his own words, had been 'tempered' by his wartime experiences, but emerged 'illusions intact, neither shattered nor cynical, to face a changed world'.[36] He had lost two brothers and a son during the two world wars, and another brother had been interned in a prisoner-of-war camp. Although having fought gallantly in the First World War, he held none of Churchill's imperial warrior pretensions and believed in the need for continued peace just twelve years after the Second World War.[37]

Eden set about defining a policy to reinternationalise the Canal but included seeking support at home and abroad to pressure Nasser. On the following day, 27 July, the Prime Minister met with Alan Lennox-Boyd, the Colonial Secretary, to unite colonial opinion.[38] Then, after a statement to the House of Commons, he firmly set out his line of thinking to the Cabinet, before opening the floor to discussion. He stressed the importance of the Middle East, and in particular the Suez Canal, not merely to Britain but 'the economic life of the Western Powers'. Of the seventy million tons of oil passing through the Canal, sixty million tons went to Western Europe, two-thirds of the Western European oil supply. Once again, in determining the courses of action open to the Government, the Prime Minister began by stressing the need to 'reach a common understanding... with the French, as partners in the Canal enterprise, and with the United States Government'. The French Foreign Minister, Christian Pineau, was due to arrive in London on the 29 July and Eden proposed sending 'an urgent message to the President of the United States inviting him to send a representative to take part in the discussions early in the following week'. The Cabinet agreed that every effort must be made to restore effective international control over the Canal. The Egyptians would not yield to economic pressures alone and had to be subjected to the maximum political pressure which could be applied by the maritime and trading nations whose interests were affected directly. In the last resort, this political pressure had to be backed by the threat and ultimately, if necessary, the use of force. The Chiefs of Staff were then officially instructed by Cabinet to prepare a contingency plan and timetable for military operations against Egypt that would only be employed should they prove unavoidable. This was a normal reaction and reflected the traditional principles that militaries followed and continue to follow, to safeguard all eventualities. In conclusion, Eden declared:

> It must now be our aim to place the Suez Canal under the control of the Powers interested in international shipping and trade by means of a new international Commission on which Egypt would be given suitable representation. Colonel Nasser's action had presented us with an opportunity to find a lasting settlement of this problem, and we should not hesitate to take advantage of it.

This reference to a 'lasting settlement' was particularly significant. Military intervention could not provide such a long-term solution because it would alienate Middle Eastern countries. In addition, it was unlikely that a 'lasting settlement' could be maintained without a military presence in the Canal Zone if the short-term settlement had been achieved by force. Eden knew that a military solution would require a large financial commitment which Britain could not afford. This had been the reason for the withdrawal from the Suez base. In searching for a long-term solution, Eden had to find something more diplomatic and less provocative to the Arab world than the use of force. However, while all the effort was to be centred on the diplomatic reinternationalisation of the Canal, a dual-track policy had begun.[39] If all political, economic and military pressures failed to press Nasser into relinquishing sole control of the Canal, then, as a last resort, because of the importance of the free flow of oil supplies to Western Europe, the Government believed that the use of force was justified.

In addition, Eden had broadly set out his vision for reinternationalising the Canal. In the short term he wanted to develop solidarity among the principal Canal users and use them to originate a solution to the crisis. At the same time the Americans saw the need to develop a similar line, as Eisenhower wrote to Eden on the 28th: 'We are of the earnest opinion that the minimum number of maritime nations affected by the Nasser action should be quickly consulted in the hope of obtaining an agreed basis of understanding.'[40] Both countries had simultaneously derived similar solutions to the crisis. However, the Americans were keen to use any device to, as they saw it, hold the British back from using force. Therefore, in reality, the similarities of intent were not as clear-cut and led to misunderstandings over the forthcoming Canal Users' Association. Although announced in public first by the Americans, it appeared to the British to mirror Eden's own move toward producing a solution to the crisis. Nevertheless, at this stage both countries considered ways of mobilising the political and diplomatic weight of the maritime countries in opposition to the Egyptian action.

In the interim, Cabinet decided to send a note of protest against Nasser's actions to the Egyptian Government, before more considered representations concerted with the Americans and the French could be made, as soon as possible.[41] Cabinet agreed

> that our essential interests in the area must, if necessary, be safeguarded by military action and that necessary preparations to this end must be made. Failure to hold the Suez Canal would lead inevitably to the loss one by one of all our interests and assets in the Middle East and, even if we had to act alone, we could not stop short of using force to protect our position if all other means of protecting it proved unavailing.[42]

Cabinet believed that the seriousness of the situation might require the use of force. It had condoned the planning of the contingency measures but this was a long political and moral step from starting war. In an attempt to unite British and American opinion and protect both countries' influence in the Middle East, Eden then telegraphed Eisenhower. He reiterated the earlier Cabinet conclusions, pushing for American help in the ensuing negotiations by proposing the idea of an immediate tripartite meeting.[43]

Even in private, Eden remained non-committal towards the use of force. On the 27th, he met with Iverach McDonald, Foreign Editor of *The Times*.[44] McDonald, unable to support a forceful resolution, only lost faith with Eden after 14 October, when the Prime Minister finally decided force was required.[45] This suggests that Eden, whilst agreeing with Cabinet that force might have to be used, showed no signs of resorting to such lengths at this point. In line with the dual-track policy agreed on 27 July, the crisis would be resolved peacefully unless this proved impossible. All efforts would focus on deriving a negotiated settlement. The possibility of force remained only as a final, and naturally undesirable, option. If Eden had been prepared to tell McDonald and not the Egypt Committee of his decision to use force in October, then he would also have told him of any earlier decision if he had decided earlier to invoke a military solution. He could have used *The Times* to keep public opinion polarised in favour of force until it could be deployed, as he would later expect, in October. However, he made no reference to force at the meeting with McDonald apart from the need to maintain a threat to Nasser and to protect against any further aggressive Egyptian action. The Prime Minister gave exclusive interviews with McDonald and on 27th repeated the information of Cabinet discussions, the telegram to Eisenhower, and his own thinking on the subject. 'More than once he said that if we showed weakness in the face of Nasser then all our position in the Middle East would crumble', but he countered this, believing that because the Canal Company was archaic there was potential for Nasser accepting a revised agreement for the running of the Canal.[46] Eden hoped that the international control of the Canal could be modernised and would not reflect the imperial control of the Suez Canal Company which had been established in 1856: 'There was a real chance, if Nasser would take it, of getting an up-to-date agreement.'[47] From McDonald's recollections, Eden was extremely candid with him, using him as a confidant and sounding board. Talks with McDonald and his editor, William Hayley, continued throughout the crisis, to the point that they 'were given so much secret information that they found it difficult to have the usual roundtable easy talks with [their] leader writers as a group'.[48] McDonald believed that historians misjudged Eden and that the Prime Minister's 'hopes of a wider international agreement' became stronger.[49] Eden's commitment to the first part of the dual-track policy originated in Cabinet discussion: the reinternationalisation of the Canal by broad economic, political and international pressure on Nasser. It also confirmed his desire to unite the 'maritime Powers' who used the Canal, against Egypt.[50]

On the evening of the 27th, the Egypt Committee was formed 'to keep in touch, on the Cabinet's behalf, with the situation arising from the recent action of the Egyptian Government in respect of the Suez Canal, and to formulate plans for meeting that situation'.[51] Cabinet, rather than solely Eden, had been responsible for instigating the group but it had been the

Prime Minister's advice to form a sub-committee, in exactly the same fashion as Churchill had done concerning Egypt. The committee was dominated by the hawkish Macmillan but also consisted of less impulsive members – Butler, now the Lord Privy Seal, and Walter Monckton, the Minister of Defence.[52] The group also included Eden, Lloyd, Lord Home and Lord Salisbury but varied in size and membership.[53] The committee became increasingly involved in the sensitive issues surrounding the military contingency plans but Eden never let the military timetable dominate diplomatic machinations. At this early stage both he and the committee were as concerned with implementing pressure upon Egypt and not using force. Consequently the Prime Minister ordered the freezing of Egypt's assets on the 28th, while on 30 July, he ordered a ban on the export of all further war material to Egypt.[54]

The Prime Minister also attempted to unite Commonwealth opinion, as he had discussed both with Cabinet and McDonald. On the 27 July, Eden had instructed Lord Home to talk with the Commonwealth High Commissioners. His telegram to the New Zealand Prime Minister, Sidney Holland, showed his intentions: 'If we do not [stand firm], the oil supplies of the free world will be at his [Nasser's] mercy and Commonwealth communications and trade will be gravely jeopardised ... We believe that we should seize this opportunity of putting the Canal under proper international control as a permanent arrangement.'[55] However, while the New Zealanders 'assured' full support 'to ensure that vital British rights [were] fully protected', and Robert Menzies, the Australian Prime Minister, appeared supportive, the Canadian reaction suggested problems for the future.[56] Prime Minister Louis St Laurent responded: 'I fully share your great concern ... while the matter is not of the same direct importance to Canada.'[57] This reaction suggested that the focus of the crisis was oil supply rather than communist insurgence. Eden had hoped to gain support by demonstrating a Soviet threat in the Middle East, but this letter showed the difficulty in trying to rally countries who did not have the same oil interests in this part of the world and consequently were not prepared to offer assistance in pressing Egypt. Nevertheless, the Prime Minister continued to derive support, hoping that economic and political pressure would bring Nasser to the negotiating table or create the instability that would unseat the Egyptian leader, and bring the crisis to an end.

Press reaction cemented the Government's decisions, with its condemnation of Nasser's actions. Yet, because the newspapers promoted a strong reaction to Nasser, supporting the immediate use of force, they appeared to support Eden and the Government's line. Again, this has added to the confusion concerning the Prime Minister's intentions. While Eden had not determined on a military solution, his vanity welcomed the support of the press. He read the newspapers closely every day, believing they gave important insight into public opinion.[58] In particular, he believed that *The Daily Telegraph* reflected Conservative Party opinion.[59] As Eden's Private Secretary, Bishop recalled, directly referring to press criticism, Eden 'always paid great attention to it. Almost everyone who knew him would probably say that he paid far too much attention to it.'[60] Having experienced a turbulent time with the newspapers, particularly *The Daily Telegraph*, in the early days of his government, he now welcomed their support, while, pragmatically, the publicity increased the pressure on Nasser with the threat of aggression. On 28 July, *The Times* reported: 'The seizure is an act of international brigandage', while the Populist-Conservative *Daily Mail* declared: 'The time for appeasement is over. We must cry "Halt!" to Nasser as we should have cried "Halt!" to Hitler. Before he sets the Middle East aflame, as Hitler did Europe.'[61] Even before Eden had publicly drawn any similarities between Nasser and the dictators of the Second World War, the Socialist *Daily Herald* called for 'No more Hitlers'.[62]

It was not just the press who reacted vehemently against Nasser's actions. The French Prime Minister Guy Mollet publicly charged Nasser with being a 'would-be Hitler' and Pineau had written to Eisenhower drawing parallels between Nasser and Hitler.[63] On 2 August, Gaitskell spoke to the House of Commons using similar language: 'It is all very familiar. It is exactly the same as we encountered from Mussolini and Hitler.'[64] Herbert Morrison, the former Labour Foreign Secretary, went as far as to say that, 'if the United States will not stand with us, then we may have to stand without them'.[65] Harold Macmillan believed that Nasser was an 'Asiatic Mussolini'.[66] A body of opinion, outside of Eden's control, was now favouring strong action, at least in the short term, and importantly Macmillan's own view of Nasser was cast. From this date, in his diaries, Macmillan adopted a much more belligerent attitude toward resolving the crisis. Eden remained uncommitted to a forceful solution, confident in his own leadership. Members of the Private Office noted that, even despite the hectic pace of those days, the Prime Minister 'has clearly risen to the occasion with exhilaration. He is the only member of the Cabinet who has held a position of comparable responsibility at a comparable period of crisis, and it makes him feel his superiority.'[67] At this stage Eden was not being influenced by the more bellicose, including Macmillan. However, the split of opinion was not immediately apparent because, as press polarisation suggested, the Prime Minister needed to promote a strong front against Nasser to maintain the reality of any threat. In addition, because of the importance of the Canal he had not ruled out the ultimate use of force if all other solutions failed. This apparently united front also helped to fill the policy vacuum. Economic and political pressure had been applied on Egypt and Eden hoped to define a more precise solution.

Eden had only just begun his search for a policy. He had to wait for the tripartite meetings to begin, so that a policy with international support could be divined. As a precursor to these discussions, once again, he tested the ground with the Americans, this time focusing on less aggressive support. His immediate thought was to bring about a peaceful resolution to the crisis. On 28 July, the British Ambassador to the US Roger Makins and Lord Harcourt, the Economic Minister at the British Embassy in Washington, went to see Hoover, 'to discuss possible action to protect the Suez Canal Company's assets and to block the Egyptian balances in the United States; payment of Canal dues and plans to meet possible closure of the Canal (including rationing and alternative oil supplies)'. Immediately, however, the apparent difference in attitudes of the Americans and the British toward Nasser's conduct was revealed. Hoover and his advisers raised sufficient objections to impress on Makins that they 'were weak and irresolute in the face of this crisis, and are tepid about taking any vigorous action...The State Department do not feel themselves directly involved as principals in the dispute with Egypt and are acutely aware of the domestic repercussions which strong action (e.g. involving the prospect of rationing of oil) might have.'[68] President Eisenhower then sent Robert Murphy, the Deputy Under-Secretary of State, to London as his representative. He did not recall Secretary of State Dulles from Peru, where he was attending the inauguration of the new President. The Middle East was of minor importance and 'American investments in the Canal Company were negligible.' Murphy would go to London 'to see what it's all about', carrying no other instructions than to 'hold the fort'.[69] Such orders suggested that Eisenhower, while fearful of Hoover's warnings, remained only mildly suspicious of British bellicosity. The President was unconvinced, as of 28 July, that Eden had decided upon any method to settle the crisis. The apparently benign attitude left Makins suggesting the need to frighten the Americans into providing any form of assistance.[70]

However, neither Eden nor his delegates at the meeting resorted to frightening the Americans. The Prime Minister did not have a set agenda and waited to see what suggestions or assistance the US might offer. Murphy arrived in London on Sunday, 29 July.[71] The first of the proposed tripartite meetings took place that evening, attended by Murphy, Lloyd and Pineau. Throughout the day, Eden maintained his reins on the situation, keeping in frequent touch with Foreign Secretary Lloyd from his country home.[72] Immediately Murphy was told that 'political and economic pressure was unlikely to have any effect on Nasser unless he knew that there were military sanctions in the background. It was therefore necessary to proceed with military preparations as far as possible, in case it was necessary to take military action.'[73] Immediately the British outlined their prospective policy to the Americans in the hope that they might receive support. There was no suggestion that war had been decided upon, but rather a military threat had been shown to Egypt to strengthen any negotiation with Nasser. Murphy remained unconcerned and did not believe that this reflected any British desire to start a war. He remembered that '[t]he conversation was rather restrained and I did not learn anything very specific'.[74] After the first tripartite meeting with Lloyd, there was still no suggestion that the decision had been made to invoke a forceful solution to the crisis. The Prime Minister continued to hope, as he had shown at the meeting of the 26th, that through enough discussion of opinion and options, a diplomatic answer would be found.

Macmillan then began to employ his own agenda, further confusing the American perception of Eden's intentions. After hearing Lloyd's account of the talks, the Chancellor recorded that '[i]t is clear that the Americans are going to "restrain" us all they can'.[75] Macmillan's fears were heightened by a report of a conversation between Dulles and Makins. Makins recorded that, despite Dulles's agreement that the attitude of Britain and the US should be firm, Nasser had chosen the perfect moment to nationalise the Canal. Even if the US had been disposed to 'take strong action', which at that moment it was not, they would be tied by Congressional inaction and 'probable recalcitrance during an election campaign'.[76] Dulles continued to observe that the President had no authority from Congress to use force but, despite this reticence, he reiterated that if the Egyptians refused to 'consider reasonable proposals for the international supervision of the canal and the provision of the Suez Canal Convention then the situation would be created which might call for a different approach'.[77] Nevertheless, Macmillan believed that he had the advantage over Dulles and that he understood the Americans.[78] Eden thought that Macmillan actually 'follows Dulles around like an admiring poodle and that is bad for Foster and worse for British interests in [the] Middle East'.[79] The Chancellor's appraisal proved optimistic. Reinforced by Makins, who 'impressed the need...to make a strong impression on Murphy', he overestimated his ability to affect American opinion.[80] Macmillan took his own initiative, as he lunched with Murphy and Pineau, along with Lloyd, Foster and Caccia. While the meeting showed that the 'French are absolutely solid with us', Macmillan and Pineau took the opportunity to 'frighten Murphy all we could'.[81] The Chancellor had begun to take Makins's advice. This deceived the Americans as to British intentions, and clouded historians' judgement. Macmillan was taken all the more seriously by the Americans because of his close links with them during the Second World War and because he had recently developed a rapport with the US whilst serving as Foreign Secretary.[82] The success of the British bluff gave the US the sense that Eden had already decided on war, corroborating the fear that Hoover had expressed to Eisenhower on the 27th. However, if the Prime Minister had been ready to use force it would have been counterproductive to create a crisis atmosphere by admitting his intentions. This would have made it much more difficult to employ force because of the development of passive consensus, making time for the Egyptians to build up further Soviet assistance. As the Government was in no position to fulfil such a decision this would only have led to the Egyptians gaining more time to improve their defences and arming their forces. With the consequent delay, from the decision to the possible implementation of force, it made no sense for Eden to show his hand, unless he was interested in bluffing the Egyptians to strengthen his own bargaining position and inducing the Americans into supplying diplomatic assistance to prevent war.

During the evening of the 30th, Macmillan continued in his quest to influence the Americans, furthering the confusion. He invited Murphy, an old wartime friend, to an informal dinner at Number 11. Also present were the American Chargé d'Affaires Foster, the Deputy under Secretary of State at the Foreign Office Caccia and Field Marshal Sir Harold Alexander. The discussion was calculated to remind Murphy of the wartime Anglo-American amity, and that in Greece in 1944 Macmillan and Alexander had been right to overrule the Americans and take prompt action.[83] Murphy had already developed a 'great admiration' for the two men but recalled that the conversation was 'not reminiscent of past associations'. Such was the nature of the informal discussion that Murphy, in contrast to the tripartite meeting, which Macmillan had not attended, 'was left in no doubt that the *British Government* believed that Suez was a test which could be met only by the use of force'. Furthermore, he was informed that the French 'saw eye to eye with the British' and would therefore be likely to be involved in the 'military moves' that, it was intimated, 'might start in August' and 'would not take much' to ensure that 'Nasser [was] chased out of Egypt'.[84] Macmillan reflected on the meeting: 'We went on with the good work – did our best to frighten Murphy out of his life. We gave him the impression that our military expedition to Egypt was about to set sail. (It will take at least 6 weeks to prepare it, in fact)'.[85] Murphy and the Americans were now under the illusion that not only had the decision to use force been made but that it would be implemented immediately. Shocked by these events, Selwyn Lloyd, who had been negotiating on Eden's behalf, concluded that it was this dinner party which led 'to a misunderstanding of our position, particularly by Eisenhower' as 'the Cabinet had not decided to use force without delay, as Eisenhower thought'.[86] Lloyd's reaction implied that Macmillan had taken his own initiative without involving Eden and there is no suggestion that Eden had authorised or even knew of Macmillan's meetings. Murphy's wartime links with Eisenhower and the fact that he was an 'old friend' of the President meant that his reports of British intentions were taken seriously.[87] Thoroughly alarmed, Eisenhower, urged by Hoover, ordered Dulles to travel to London, convinced that the British were ready to start a war. Macmillan's action had worked so well that Eden had no ability to influence the Americans into providing support of any variety. American fears as to British commitment to the use of force to settle the crisis were now confirmed. The US could not support the British intention to use the military threat to substantiate a diplomatic solution because it was believed that force had been chosen. Any future American involvement or assistance during the crisis would be compromised by the need to prevent war. Again, this could only undermine Eden's desire of negotiating from a position of strength, by failing to appear aggressive to Nasser and hence failing to bolster the British bluff in her dealings with Egypt. Without Eden's knowledge, his hopes for a peaceful solution to the crisis had been undercut.

Again, the actions of third parties confused understanding of Eden's intentions, for contemporaries and historians. Once more, Macmillan had acted independently, but this time the ramifications were much greater. It was assumed that Eden had sanctioned Macmillan's action. However, the Prime Minister had been consistently incensed by Macmillan's exceeding of his ministerial role and Macmillan resented the constant Prime Ministerial intrusions. Therefore, Macmillan was not asked to the *ad hoc* and hastily gathered meeting on the evening of 26 July. Later informed by Sir Norman Brook, the Cabinet Secretary, of some of the Chancellor's proposals, Eden minuted, 'Not his business anyway!'[88] Some historians have been kind enough to call Macmillan's action 'inventive independence', others have not been so sympathetic.[89] Bishop described the Eden/Macmillan relationship as 'competitive', while Millard believed the Chancellor to be 'a devious man'. Eden 'regarded Macmillan as an intriguer and somebody who was after his job', which, as his secretary remembered, 'he probably was'.[90] Eden maintained his resolve for a diplomatic solution to the crisis. At this stage Macmillan had little influence on the Prime Minister and had not convinced him to employ force. However, the rivalry between the two would have important implications when, physically and mentally weakened in October, Eden became reliant on his advice and that of other 'hawks'.

Eden limited the majority of his correspondence with Macmillan to purely economic matters. Yet this could have caused its own problems. Bishop had been recruited into the Private Office to deal with 'economic affairs'; however, as he had revealed at the interview for the position, 'I knew nothing about economics and wasn't an economist.' While Eden seldom sought advice on foreign affairs, 'he did expect to be told one's thoughts' on 'economic and domestic matters... [H]e acknowledged that he was not a great expert on economic matters, and he observed that it was on this side of things that I was supposed to deal with... ignorant though I was of economics as a technical subject.' In addition, 'He really expected his ministerial colleagues to guide him in matters of their own department, particularly Mr. Macmillan.'[91] Only time would demonstrate the problems of this deficiency and reliance. It also illustrated that Eden was a traditionalist who believed in government through collective responsibility. He could not make decisions *ex parte*, unlike Macmillan.

The Prime Minister had shown his readiness to influence the US and bring the greater American power to bear. Eden condoned Macmillan's overzealous attitude which reaped short-term benefits for the British.[92] The Chancellor's 'frightening' of Murphy, secured Foster Dulles's involvement in negotiations which appeared to signal a diplomatic victory for the British, particularly as they believed that Dulles, rather than Eisenhower, created American foreign policy. As Makins reported, 'Dulles's departure for London...was clearly decided upon at extremely short notice. I was informed only after [he] had left.' The Americans had altered their plans at the last minute as a result of Macmillan's recent actions. They now believed the situation needed greater attention, which promised the British American assistance in resolving the crisis. Makins continued: 'Hoover told my New Zealand colleague...that Mr. Dulles's visit had been undertaken on account of the anxiety of the United States Government about the danger of trying to force Nasser to rescind his action. They felt that it was important to give the most carefully considered guidance to public opinion on this issue and to avoid any precipitate action.' After the results of his previous meeting with the Americans, Makins was extremely surprised by the extent of the US action in placing under licence the Suez Canal Company's assets and Egyptian Government balances in the US, including the balances of the National Bank of Egypt.[93] Macmillan, having engineered the American higher involvement, reflected: 'It seems to me we have succeeded in thoroughly alarming Murphy. He must have reported in the sense which we worked [for], and Foster Dulles is now coming over post haste. This is a very good development.' However, the Prime Minister's acceptance of Macmillan's action misleadingly suggested an agreement between Eden and Macmillan on objectives and methods of achieving them. Force had become a probability for the Chancellor, while it still remained a last resort for the Prime Minister. Macmillan hoped to encourage American backing of force, while Eden hoped that American threats would be enough to destabilise Nasser's position. The Prime Minister took on Macmillan's initiative, because of its success, and both Eden and Lloyd continued to threaten the Americans in their meetings, although not with the same zeal as the Chancellor.

Eden continued trying to keep Nasser guessing, leaving the Egyptian leader unsure as to whether he would be attacked. Again, he hoped that this pressure might loosen Nasser's hold on the Canal. Even though it was not to be used, the Prime Minister convened a committee at the outset of the crisis, made up of former Special Operations Executive (SOE) members, to suggest to Nasser 'that some form of clandestine action was being considered'.[94] In addition, he tried to maintain a deterrent which he hoped would prevent further actions by the Egyptians. This was also in line with his and NATO's principles of 'sword and shield'; shielding British interests from aggressive action and deterring against any such action by publicising the 'sword' of heavy potential military retaliation.[95] Referring specifically to two frigates, but reflecting this 'policy', he remarked that, 'I think it important that they should be available now, and seen to be so.'[96] He believed that Nasser would expect some form of retaliation, and not at least to threaten the Egyptians would show weakness and irresolution, not simply to Nasser but also the colonies. In addition, it was impossible to gauge the extent or the consequences of the insurgent nationalism, or for the Foreign Office legal advisers to give a definitive assessment of the issues, so as Eden remarked, 'we should be strong enough to meet any calls'.[97] Eden's position was just as he had discussed with Cabinet, Eisenhower and McDonald. Millard, Eden's Private Secretary summarised: 'The Cabinet took the decision at the very beginning... [I]t was decided that, in default of other solutions, eventually there would have to be a military solution to reverse what had happened. Other solutions would be explored first, but from day one they were committed to a military solution if all else failed', a dual-track policy.[98] This remained consistent with the line he and Cabinet had agreed on 27 July.[99] At this stage, economic and psychological pressures would be used, in conjunction with the threat of force, to reverse Nasser's nationalisation of the Suez Canal. However, if the Egyptian leader continued to prove recalcitrant, then Eden and the Cabinet were prepared for a military operation. It was not inevitable that Nasser would 'hold out', or that the Government would resort to force, or that Eden would remain consistent in his attempts to procure a diplomatic settlement. The Prime Minister had begun a programme of bluffing Nasser whilst building on the bluff of the Americans. This would have disastrous effects on the crisis and its historiography. The Americans no longer believed that the British were intent on bluffing the Egyptians and as such would not support any British policy with any vigour. This suggested to historians that Eden had decided to use force. In hindsight, the knowledge that the Prime Minister eventually made the decision to use force made the earlier policy of bluff appear a charade, despite his commitment to it. However, Eden continued to build up a military threat to bolster his position of strength in the ensuing negotiations. He had already placed economic and political sanctions on Egypt and now waited in the hope that the tripartite discussions might provide a more immediate solution to the crisis.

Outwardly to Nasser, tripartite negotiations of a particularly high level were being conducted, leaving him guessing as to any resolution. Eden, not as concerned as his letters to Eisenhower suggested, continued to try and project a strong and united bloc against Egypt. Needing American diplomatic assistance, he tried to demonstrate a threat to US interests in an area that the President considered of minor importance.[100] Eden believed he could continue to maintain military support against Nasser, as he had done during 1955, but direct American diplomatic action would substantially increase the pressure on Egypt, particularly when backed by such a large military threat. This showed how Eden, while endorsing the continuation of a policy that had been at the forefront of recent British dealings in the Middle East, had the flexibility to adjust to the more serious development of Nasser's potential Pan-Arabism whilst maintaining a peaceful approach. Deference to an American lead could also show the way for other countries to condemn Nasser's actions openly, because of their recognised position as the world's leading power and moral policeman. Recognising the importance to the Americans of distinguishing the dispute from any that might arise over the Panama Canal, Eden 'found it encouraging' when Eisenhower had appeared to support his firm line in his letter of 31 July.[101] The President remained fearful of Eden's 'decision to employ force without delay or attempting any intermediate and less drastic steps'. However, despite this misunderstanding, he recognised the 'transcendent worth of the Canal', and conceded that force might have to be used as a last resort but only after 'every peaceful means of protecting the rights and the livelihood of great proportions of the world had been thoroughly explored and exhausted'.[102] Eden also believed in a peaceful solution and the power of deterrent and threat of military retaliation to reverse crises by peaceful means rather than by open declaration of war.[103]

On the following day, Dulles declared at a tripartite meeting that they would use 'force if necessary'.[104] After Eisenhower's telegram, this suggested that the Americans would support a strong line which would leave Nasser's position untenable, in much the same way as OMEGA had been intended. OMEGA had always promised, if not delivered, to go further than just economic sanctions.[105] While it had never promised military action against Egypt it threatened to destabilise the countries in the Middle East who supported Egypt, such as Syria, as well as Egypt's own economy.[106] The weakening of any international support for Egypt and the political ramifications of weakening its economy might provide enough pressure to force the relinquishing of the Canal or the creation of sufficient instability to promote Nasser's internal removal with a regime that would return the Canal to international control. The British Government's belief in OMEGA continued into October, also reflecting the potential that they saw in it.[107] The Prime Minister was unaware of the extent to which the Americans feared British bellicosity. Much of Eisenhower's and Dulles's reaction suggested that they were not concerned by potential British action. The Americans supported a peaceful solution and the British hoped that Nasser could be removed by means derived from the threat of force. Should this fail then more stringent measures would be adopted. This suggested an Anglo-American unity of opinion; as Cabinet had agreed, the use of force was only a possibility if all other solutions failed. Eden, surprised at Dulles's position, told McDonald that 'Dulles freely committed himself to the stand that the Canal should not be left in the sole control of Egypt and should be brought under an international authority.'[108] Reinternationalisation of the Suez Canal remained Eden's central tenet. The Prime Minister's policy remained consistent but he now believed that the US should not be antagonised unduly, otherwise the chance of any form of support against Nasser might be lost. This led to the taking of a much more conciliatory line. Eisenhower thought that Murphy's intervention had actually relegated 'the immediate use of force to the background', perpetuating the American misunderstanding of the British position.[109]

The Prime Minister believed that the US had made important undertakings, as he minuted on the Cabinet conclusions of 1 August.[110] Macmillan agreed, believing that '[t]he Americans have certainly moved a long way'.[111] The Foreign Secretary reported American support believing them 'anxious to help... at this juncture' and that Dulles 'had said that Egypt must be made to "disgorge" the Suez Canal'. The word 'disgorge' became central to Eden's belief that Dulles was as serious as the Prime Minister in his attempts to resolve the crisis.[112] Dulles had also 'made it clear that the United States would strongly deprecate any premature use of force to secure these objectives' and Cabinet learnt of the American desire for a conference of Canal users. Washington had seized on Eden's commitment to the uniting of the 'maritime Powers' who used the Canal to suggest the convening of a conference involving them.[113] Macmillan's diary confirmed that this sentiment was congruent with current British thinking.[114] However, the precise form that the conference would take remained in doubt.

The US wanted a conference that should be related to the Constantinople Convention of 1888. Eden agreed, having stressed the importance of the 1888 Convention to Cabinet on the 27th because of the Convention's recognition of the Canal's 'importance as an international waterway [which]... had increased with the development of the oil industry and the dependence of the world on oil supplies'.[115] However, the Americans also wanted the conference to include the Soviets because it was their intention to distinguish the Suez Canal from the Panama Canal. This move involved a risk of Russian manoeuvres on behalf of Egypt and would be repugnant to political opinion in Britain.[116] On 28 July, the Egypt Committee had feared that a conference would prove impotent without the threat of possible military action.[117] Over the next two days the Committee were won over to the idea, because '[i]t had become clear that both the Americans and the French were anxious that there should be a conference'.[118] By 31 July, such was its commitment to the idea that its members believed it necessary to sponsor the conference with the French, even if the US 'were unable to indicate their readiness' to do the same: they 'would have to summon it [the conference] and trust that the United States might later see their way to associate themselves with the conclusions of the conference'.[119] It had also become apparent how important the conference would be in uniting other countries in opposition to Nasser's act of nationalising the Canal. By bringing together the most prominent countries who used the Canal, the conference could be used to consolidate strong opinion against Nasser from the people whose trade and navigation potentially stood to suffer. Eventually, on 1 August, Cabinet agreed to the establishment of the conference.[120] However, at this stage, conference details, including a location and date, had not been agreed upon.

Believing in the NATO principle of peace through strength, Eden hoped to frighten Nasser into submission, or at least to undermine his position by confronting Egypt with a potentially aggressive bloc. 'Talking tough' might weaken Nasser's personal control and avoid more overt confrontation. Deference to Dulles's demands, over Soviet inclusion at the conference, required US agreement to a tough communiqué to be issued at the end of the tripartite talks condemning Nasser's actions, as 'the [Egypt] Committee thought it essential that the present tripartite talks should be seen to end in some tangible result...[and that] such a statement alone would not meet the needs of the present situation'.[121] This would keep a focus on the crisis, maintaining international pressure on Nasser and appeasing public demands for a solution. The Committee's 'ultimate purpose was to place the Canal under international control', but her 'immediate objective was to bring about the downfall of the present Egyptian Government'. The two were believed to be synonymous, although as the Chiefs of Staff reflected, the latter might be achieved 'by less elaborate operations than those required to secure physical possession of the Canal itself'.[122] British and French economic, political and military threats could undermine Nasser's internal position, particularly if backed by the US and world opinion. In addition, the decision to use force had not been made because a variety of possible plans were being considered by the Chiefs rather than simply defining the military solution. Eden could see the merits of holding a conference of maritime powers and supported Cabinet's opinion that steps should be taken 'to ensure that American co-operation, if it were obtained at this price, would be fully maintained and that there would be no departure from the understandings reached'. It was preferred that these 'understandings' should take the form of a written minute of agreement and Cabinet would continue 'to press our views on the time and the place of the conference'.[123] However, while backing the conference, the Prime Minister needed to demonstrate to Nasser, the British public and the Conservative Party that he held control over the crisis. This would allay fears at home and strengthen the potential of any military threat made against Egypt.

At the tripartite meeting of 2 August, Eden had Lloyd convince Dulles to hold the conference earlier rather than at the end of the month. It was convened for 16 August in London.[124] Not only was this a sign to Eden of Britain's importance, in that she could sway the Americans, but it reflected that the Prime Minister was not intent on the use of force. Initially, it had been discussed by the Egypt Committee that force might be invoked directly after the conference if Nasser refused to comply.[125] This would have given the British time to prepare for any possible aggressive action. By moving the conference date forward, Eden left time for discussion, reducing the need for any use of force. Any resolutions emerging from the conference could be backed by the threat of force, with absolutely no chance of actually using it, as it had not been, nor could be, prepared. The American insistence that the Soviets should also be allowed to attend the conference immediately weakened its resolution, because they were prepared to support the Egyptian position. However, as McDonald remembered, 'For some weeks Eden remained hopeful of diplomatic help and moral support from Dulles.'[126] Soviet attendance was a price worth paying to try to convene wider support against Nasser in the form of the conference of canal users.

American acceptance that a statement should be made setting up the conference, proved to be a short-term diplomatic victory for Eden and the British. It showed that despite the failure to develop a co-ordinated long-term policy, Eden had begun to work with the Americans and the French to resolve the crisis. The US produced a draft statement which was more than satisfactory to the British and French, but it proved impossible to reach an agreement on the terms of the statement setting out the intentions of the governments in subscribing to the tripartite policy presented in the communiqué, particularly the maintenance of their liberty of action if the policy failed. Difficulty arose in expressing this in terms acceptable to the Americans. There was not enough time to debate this question at length because Nasser's position, if left unchallenged, would strengthen with each day, while press and public would become more aggrieved at the apparent stalemate. The Prime Minister also felt the pressure, from the right-wing Conservatives and the public, not to appear inactive.[127] Lloyd suggested the solution, calling for the US to amend its draft and issue it as the US Government statement, to which the British and French Governments would make short statements expressing *general* agreement.[128] Using this as a sign of Anglo-American solidarity, Eden sent a telegram to the Commonwealth Prime Ministers, setting out his primary intention and attempting to gain support for this principle and for the conference: 'The communiqué reflects the decided view of all of us that in future the Canal must be put under an international authority.'[129] The US was more likely to encourage support against Nasser than Britain who appeared biased by her imperial pretensions, despite wanting to return control of the Canal to an international authority. It remained a British hope that other countries would follow the American lead and condemn Nasser's actions. Eden was still unaware of the US fear of British intentions and the subsequent limitation of the help that they were prepared to give. Eden's continued belief in the ability of world condemnation of Nasser's actions confirmed his commitment to resolving the crisis by peaceful methods. He had made no attempt to derive support for the use of force.

By 3 August, Eden had become even more committed to seeking a peaceful solution, buoyed by American, French and certain Commonwealth support.[130] As McDonald noted in a confidential memorandum, Eden

> was satisfied with the results of the Three-Power talks. At first the Americans had been slow in coming along... He had frankly expected Dulles to be rather negative, but Dulles began and continued very well. The talks became better after he arrived. Undoubtedly the Americans fear that we and the French might fly off the handle straightaway helped to

bring Dulles nearer and faster to our point of view. At any rate, Dulles freely committed himself to the stand that the Canal should not be left in the sole control of Egypt and should be brought under an international authority.[131]

In his private talk with McDonald the Prime Minister had shown the intention of his bluff to bring the Americans to support the reinternationalisation of the Canal. He demonstrated that he had not made the decision to use force, as the French and the British '*might* fly off the handle', but that at this stage their intentions lay as opposed to a military solution as Dulles's position. Eden emphasised that it was the bluff of force that had brought the Americans 'nearer and faster to our point of view'.[132] That Eden already knew of the American 'veto' of the use of force reaffirmed that the three countries were virtually aligned in the desire to reach a diplomatic solution. It remained for the details to be agreed.

The period 26 July to 3 August had been one of confusion for Eden and the Government as they reacted to the nationalisation of the Suez Canal. The large number of meetings, particularly those of the Egypt Committee, reflected the difficulties in the defining and the planning of a policy. During the nine days, the Cabinet met three times, the Egypt Committee ten times and there were another twenty meetings involving senior ministers either as a group or tête-à-tête. Under normal circumstances Cabinet would have met once or possibly twice and there might have been as many as three other senior ministerial meetings. These problems were accentuated by the realisation of Britain's own weaknesses and, in particular, her diminished role as a world power, but more particularly by Eden's characteristic vacillation. Eden set out to induce the downfall of President Nasser because of the threat of his personal brand of Pan-Arabic nationalism to Britain and Western Europe.[133] He hoped to achieve this in conjunction with his broader aim of returning the running of the Suez Canal to an international authority, again with a view to protecting British and European interests. He attempted to continue to derive a 'policy' from maintaining close links with the US and the Commonwealth. Because of French involvement with the Canal Company and their immediate support he was also keen to maintain a united front against further action by Nasser and in turn to threaten Nasser into submission, much as he had foreseen for the Baghdad Pact and the Soviets.[134] By 3 August, the initial furore had died down. The Egypt Committee would not meet again until 7 August, and the Cabinet, 14 August. As McDonald noted, Eden was now pleased with the situation. Public opinion supported the government line and Dulles appeared to have made a gesture in coming forward. Eden was unaware of the extent of the American fears of British bellicosity. Now the Prime Minister had to wait to see if the conference of maritime powers could re-establish international control of the Canal, either directly or by uniting world opinion against Nasser and forcing him to relinquish his control. A policy remained uncertain but the Americans appeared to be keener to find a solution to the crisis. Despite the aggressive stand of the Labour Party, the British press and Mollet, the large section of public support for the use of force and Dulles's statement calling for Nasser to 'disgorge' the Canal, Eden remained in favour of a peaceful settlement. If there was ever a time when force was acceptable to enough opinion to justify its implementation then it was in July/August, 1956. However, because of his moral objection to a military option, the Prime Minister did not yet resort to force as he still saw potential for a diplomatic solution by generating international support against Nasser.

2
Negotiation: 4 August–9 September

Tripartite Talks, the First London Conference and the Menzies Mission

Increasingly, Eden became concerned that his military preparations would be misinterpreted and prejudice his own freedom of action. Fearful 'that the bellicose Press would be too bellicose', on 31 July, he had asked his press secretary to arrange for a meeting with editors of the *Daily Express*, *Daily Mail* and *News Chronicle*.[1] Concerned that too much information regarding military preparations had been released, the Prime Minister then sent a memorandum to the First Lord of the Admiralty, Lord Cilcennin, and Mountbatten. In particular, there had been a disclosure concerning tank landing craft. Venting his exasperation, Eden wrote: 'Now the tank landing craft are on the news, on the authority of the Admiralty spokesman. Surely he can say "No Comment" and stick to it, unless specifically authorised to speak.'[2] These were precautionary measures in the nature of passive crisis management, as Eden consistently believed, and as he wrote to New Zealand Prime Minister Holland, outlining the dual-track policy: '[W]e have of course no intention of using force unless all fails.'[3] He still believed, as he had at the time of his February 1955 meeting with Nasser, that the Egyptians feared the potential of Western power.[4] Therefore, a threat posed by American, British, French and Commonwealth forces would be taken seriously by the Egyptian leader and the larger the threat, the more likely Nasser would be to comply with reinternationalisation of the Canal.

However, the Prime Minister remained worried that the American Government and, to a much lesser extent, both political and public doubters at home, might misunderstand his strategy. In addition, continued publicity of the precautionary measures might lead to Egyptian complaints to the Security Council that such actions were a threat to peace and, as Eden told the Egypt Committee, continued press speculation could easily 'prejudice the forthcoming international conference, since some countries might be led to believe that the conference was merely a façade to cover military operations which had already been planned'.[5] Consequently, in his meeting with the editors of the major newspapers on 3 August, he had asked 'for discretion in reporting and commenting on British and French troop and ship movements'.[6] McDonald noted that 'Eden seemed especially worried about well-directed speculation about the likely objectives of troops and ships.'[7] However, neither he nor Walter Monckton 'were thinking of direct censorship', eventually deciding on '[v]oluntary restraint'.[8] The Prime Minister had never been keen on any direct forms of censorship which he would have required if he had needed to hide a policy which included a military invasion of Egypt.[9]

It had been suggested that Eden deliberately invited such a large number of the press to the Downing Street meeting of 3 August to create an atmosphere of crisis to enable him to polarise press opinion in support of a forceful solution and, in the short term, to provide an acceptance of a limited form of censorship through D-notices.[10] For reasons of keeping all options open in national security, Eden would not explain the real position. He had already come under extensive press criticism for vacillating in the face of Arab nationalism and Soviet communism.[11] The Prime Minister could not *appear* weak to Nasser, whom he hoped he could threaten with bluff, or the British public, who were divided over what action they thought the Government should take. The press were beginning to oppose any planned military operation against Egypt.[12] Attempting to create an agitated and aggressive atmosphere would have alienated this broad section of opinion. In addition, if he had wanted to use force he would have only limited his support by increasing the sense of crisis. The situation had become extremely delicate for the Prime Minister. He had to appear strong in the face of the expropriation of the Canal but could not afford to lose the support of sections of the press or public either through apparent vacillation or excessive belligerency. He also had to apply as much pressure on Nasser as possible without alarming the UN Security Council or the pacifist element of the British public and international opinion who were beginning to air their opinions more vociferously.

He had quickly decided that public and press support were strong enough to justify revealing such information; indeed 'such preliminary steps...would help avert...the criticism that the Government were inactive', and there could be no consideration of a surprise invasion with a task force having to sail from so far away.[13] However, in the event of an invasion, the force would have had to operate from Tobruk, which would have required calling up as many as 2,000 specialist reservists which 'could not be done without proclaiming a state of emergency'.[14] These soldiers had not been requisitioned; Eden had not decided to mount a military operation against Egypt. This assertive posture would act as a direct threat to Nasser and, importantly, maintain public support at home. At this stage a high percentage of the public supported his maintaining the threat, reversing the nationalisation of the Canal and replacing it under international control.[15]

However, time was running out for preventing Nasser from consolidating his position and remaining unchallenged in the eyes of the Arab world. Eden used the period before the Conference to great effect, attempting to unite the 'maritime powers' against Egypt. The Prime Minister's telegram to Eisenhower of 5 August reflected his concern, typifying his extra efforts to bring the Americans on side and secure a quick and peaceful resolution to the dispute. He opened by saying that 'I do not think that we disagree about our primary objective', suggesting a common aim and continuing to show support for the ensuing conference. He hoped that the conference would 'bring such pressures upon Nasser that the efficient operation of the Canal [could] be assured for the future'. In addition, as he continued, 'if Nasser is compelled to disgorge his spoils, it is improbable that he will be able to maintain his internal position. We should thus have achieved our secondary objective.'[16] Despite the Prime Minister's hatred of the Egyptian leader, he subordinated this emotion behind the practical need to reinternationalise the Canal. Again, this showed that his reactions to events were measured by his understanding of world politics. However, for propagandistic purposes, he also evoked memories of the 1930s and 1940s, likening Nasser to Mussolini. Whereas previous imagery, largely communist, had been directed at the administration as a whole and more pointedly at Dulles, this was a direct appeal to the President, the former Supreme Allied Commander, and a number of his colleagues who had served during the Second World War. Eden remained keen to maintain what he had seen as US support. Particularly important in the letter had been the use of the word 'disgorge', which Dulles had originally used himself. On 9 August, Sir William Hayley, the Editor of *The Times*, recorded that, 'Eden placed a great deal of reliance on the word "disgorge". Dulles stuck to this. Eden was sure that this was still America's policy'[17] – a policy, as his letter to Eisenhower showed, that would be promoted through the conference. Dulles's use of the word 'disgorge' underpinned all of Eden's interpretations of US signals which meant that he believed in the American attempts to derive a settlement to the crisis.[18]

Nevertheless, while the Prime Minister believed the Americans to be in accord, the French began to create more problems for Eden. Although immediately siding with the French to promote solidarity in the face of Nasser's actions, he came under increasing pressure from them to start military proceedings. In a memorandum to Eden, on 8 August, Lloyd reported a visit he had received from the French Ambassador in an attempt to quicken British military preparations. The Ambassador had heard from Admiral Henry Michel Nomy, the French Chief of Naval Staff, and Vice-Admiral Pierre Barjot, the Deputy Allied Commander-in Chief, 'that British planning was a fortnight behind the French'. Continuing, 'he said that he was doing everything possible to prevent the idea being disseminated in France that the United Kingdom were [sic] dragging their feet.' With Britain uninterested in a military operation, Lloyd abstained from comment. However, the seeds of doubt had been sown in the minds of the French as to Eden's commitment to a forceful riposte.[19] The bluff that Eden attempted to use to reverse the nationalisation of the Canal began to create it own problems with the 'friendly powers'. As backbench MP and Suez Group member, Julian Amery, remembered: 'They [Egyptians] had no confidence in Anthony either and nor had the French or the Israelis or indeed Nuri. All the time they were wondering if he meant business.'[20] Neither Eden nor Lloyd were prepared to commit themselves at this point. In his report to Eden, Lloyd added that '[s]ince dictating this I... am proposing to see Chauvel again to discourage ostentatious moves or meetings'.[21] Britain's reluctance to keep up with French planning reflected her primary desire to achieve a peaceful solution. However, there remained a need to present as large an opposition as possible against Nasser to pressure him into relinquishing his control of the Canal. So Britain supported the French despite their bellicosity. It was also more agreeable to enlist the assistance of the countries most affected by the nationalisation of the Canal. As a major shareholder, and with the Suez Canal Company (Compagnie Universelle du Canal Maritime de Suez) being French, France had a strong cause for complaint which, along with Britain's, would have a more dynamic effect in uniting world opinion against Egypt, particularly in the UN Security Council.

However, French support had its price. Even at this early stage, the threat of Israeli military involvement in the area had become another worry for Eden, reflecting French enthusiasm for a military solution. The French wanted to involve the Israelis in any planning, and according to one source, Eden had already been approached by Premier Mollet on 27 July to collaborate with France and Israel against Egypt.[22] The Prime Minister had vehemently turned down the proposition and consequently, in his conversations with Chauvel, Lloyd had to impress 'the importance of keeping the Israelis out of this'.[23] In addition, Eden knew the volatile nature of the situation and feared lest Israel take advantage of the 'developments in the situation to move her military forces against Egypt', the consequences of which, in a Pan-Arabic context, were clear: '[W]hile working... through diplomatic processes to bring pressure to bear on Nasser, Her Majesty's Government were using the same channels to try to keep the Israeli problem separate from the Canal problem.'[24] However, Macmillan was attempting to change the minds of the Prime Minister and Cabinet, expressing his concern about aspects of the military plan and suggesting that the Government should 'make use of the immense threat to Egypt that resulted from the position of Israel on her flank. The Israelis would almost certainly take advantage of any military operations in that area and it would be desirable to ensure that their actions should be directed against Egypt rather than against Jordan.'[25] Privately, Macmillan believed that

> we *must* make use of Israel against Egypt, if the military operation is actually undertaken. The C.I.G.S. feels the same and was very grateful [for broaching the subject to Egypt Committee]. Of course, there is great danger in this. But if we make no contact with Israel and have no understanding with them, they will probably attack Jordan – which really *will* be embarrassing. Nuri Pasha could not stand to it; but I don't believe he would feel the same about an Israel attack on Egypt.[26]

Eden was 'very shocked' at Macmillan's suggestion and at a meeting held at 11 Downing Street on 3 August, it was decided, despite Macmillan's arguments, that Israeli assistance should, unless it was unavoidable, stop short of active intervention.[27]

Eden had not committed himself to a military solution, much less one that involved the Israelis. Nevertheless, Macmillan continued to believe it 'wiser to undertake an operation directly' related to overthrowing Nasser's Government:

> what worries me the most is that I feel that the directive on which the Chiefs of Staff have framed the plan is perhaps the wrong one. It is to occupy the Canal. The object of the exercise, if we have to embark upon it, is surely to bring about the fall of Nasser and create a government in Egypt which will work satisfactorily with ourselves and the other powers.[28]

Macmillan's use of 'if' in his diary entry illustrated that a military operation had not become policy.[29] He had no reason to lie or shade the truth. Any apparent weaknesses in the Government's contingency plans reflected that they had not been thoroughly considered because they were not policy. Evelyn Shuckburgh concluded, 'Eden's objective was to establish some form of international regime for the canal which would prevent canal traffic from falling under exclusive Egyptian control', not to invoke force without delay.[30] Macmillan prepared a paper concerning the military plan for the Egypt Committee meeting of 7 August, again trying to manipulate the Prime Minister.[31] Eden did want to remove Nasser, but he hoped that this could be achieved by more peaceful means in conjunction with the reinternationalisation of the Canal. The Prime Minister reacted angrily, incensed by Macmillan's interference but more importantly because Macmillan had urged Churchill to influence Eden concerning the plan: Macmillan noted in his diary that, 'Eden had no doubt thought that I was conspiring with C. against him.'[32] Warily, the Prime Minister had told Hayley that 'Churchill is convinced that the only way to settle the whole thing is to be prepared to go straight to Cairo', which 'Eden [was] not in favour of'.[33] The Prime Minister was so annoyed that he refused to allow Macmillan's paper to be circulated to the committee, or to the Chiefs of Staff.[34]

Acceptance of Macmillan's Israeli initiative would have appeased the French, who had been supplying arms to Israel despite British and American objections.[35] However, Eden remained unconvinced of the need to implicate the Israelis, or to placate the warmongering French. Evelyn Shuckburgh remembered how Churchill would often 'come out' with some reference to working militarily with Israel, but by contrast, 'this was entirely contrary to everything I had ever been brought to believe was Anthony Eden's policy'.[36] As the military preparations were contingency measures there was no need to consider Israeli involvement which could potentially ignite their hostile relationship with the Arabs. In addition, as the British Ambassador in Paris, Sir Gladwyn Jebb argued, 'Anglo-French action in the Canal Zone will probably be misrepresented, to our damage in the Arab world, as part of an imperialist plot hatched with Israel'. The ambassador strongly advised that Britain, France and the US used their influence 'to keep Israel right out of the dispute'. With the senior French commander arriving on Sunday, 5 August and the planners expected to arrive on the following Monday, the Foreign Secretary had suggested his own 'personal intervention' to prevent matters getting out of hand.[37]

The prospect of Anglo-French co-operation excited the French who began pushing the British even harder to invoke a military solution.[38] Chauvel announced that he wanted certain French troops to be moved to Malta and French and British planners to meet in Paris with 'stimulated publicity'. British fears were expressed in a telegram to Jebb, signed on behalf of the Foreign Secretary: They did not want to jeopardise the Canal conference, despite the need to make 'certain preliminary military measures'.[39] These reflected Eden's own concerns, which he had voiced to Hayley on 9 August. Talking 'freely and with no sign of tension', he described the French as 'being both good and silly... [b]ut now there was a danger of France getting a little out of hand'. He revealed that the French had privately told the British Government that they wanted to take some action for 'political reasons', including the sending of parachutists to Malta, but Eden had turned these ideas down.[40] The Prime Minister remained pacific; he had not decided on the use of force and therefore did not want to have troops in advanced positions that, while threatening Nasser, would bring open condemnation and pressure from the UN, weakening any potential negotiating position.

Eden and Lloyd tried to give the forthcoming London Conference of Canal users a chance to succeed and provide the pressure on Nasser to induce a peaceful settlement.[41] This was summarised by the Foreign Secretary's arguments, in his messages to the foreign ministers of the countries invited to the conference. The object of the conference 'was to make the Egyptian Government give way by an expression of international opinion in favour of an international system to operate the Suez Canal and that it was a genuine attempt to reach a peaceful solution'.[42] On 12 August, Eden backed his own vision for international control of the Canal and for getting the most out of the conference. In a memorandum to the Lord President and Foreign Secretary he positively assumed that the result of the Conference would be 'agreement by a large majority that some form of international control over the Canal [was] necessary'. He determined, as he had on 1 August in the Egypt Committee meeting, that the Conference should endorse a declaration 'to impose this solution', but now he specified what should be done if Egypt refused reinternationalisation: he foresaw that 'all the Powers using the Canal [would] refuse to pay dues to Nasser's company'.[43] This form of reinternationalisation by pressuring Nasser remained central to Eden's hopes for settling the crisis. However, he now conceived how this pressure could be most effectively used against Egypt. He saw the potential to invoke a heavy economic sanction against the Egyptians in the form of users of the canal withholding their transit dues. Nasser had argued that he had nationalised the Canal to help raise revenue for development within Egypt and primarily to help pay for the Aswan High Dam project, for which the Americans and British had withdrawn support in July 1956. By preventing this money from reaching Egypt, the British hoped that failure to fulfil his promises to his nation would destabilise his position within Egypt and force him either to return the Canal to international control or prompt a coup, which would replace him with a leader who would be prepared to reinternationalise the Canal.[44] In the Egypt Committee meeting of 14 August, the Prime Minister re-expressed these hopes that the US and the other maritime powers would agree to refuse to pay any transit dues to the Egyptian Government and instructed the Foreign Secretary to consult with Foster Dulles concerning the possible co-operation in 'strong economic measures to ensure the proposals agreed by the [London] conference'.[45] The Prime Minister feared that because of the 'uncertainty about Eisenhower's health' and the American 'overriding pre-occupation... with the elections' Washington's eye might not be 'on the ball'. Nevertheless, he was still sure that the US remained intent on reinternationalising the Canal, 'the main-point [of their policy] being that they were sure this could be done by way of an international conference', and he had been pleasantly surprised at the positive 'response to the invitations for the Conference'.[46] If the conference failed, then Eden believed that the precautionary measures 'should have to go a step further... [but] he didn't think the country would remain hostile which was the dependent on which the use of military action hung'. He had always been ready to maintain flexible military preparations 'to enable forceful action (should this be necessary) to follow hard upon the presentation to the Egyptian Government of any plan approved by maritime countries'.[47] However, as of 9 August, 'he was rather frightened by... [the public's] present enthusiasm for him' and, because of his apparently firm resolution, their support for the use of force.[48] If Eden had already decided to invoke a military solution he had enough support within the country, despite the shift in opinion, so that there was no reason why he should stay his hand. However, keen to derive a peaceful solution, he refused to bend to public pressure, alarmed by the bellicosity of the British people. Unlike Lloyd George in 1914, and more like Asquith, Eden did not understand the proportion of the public who favoured war. After the national experience of the two world wars, he could not reconcile their attitude. Having fought and suffered the emotional and psychological scars, in spite of victory, Eden believed that his personal experience was similar to that of the majority of the country. On a pragmatic and personal level he abhorred war, remaining confused by the extent that the public were prepared to defend British interests.

At this point the Americans appeared supportive of a resolution that could remove Nasser. To Eden there was no change or retreat from the US goal of Nasser's being made to 'disgorge' the Canal. The conference proposal had begun to look as if it would bear fruit, with regard to the number of countries attending and hence the extent of potential world pressure upon Nasser. The public and the press appeared to support the Government's line. The precautionary measures were beginning to have an effect, despite the leakage to the press 'of the postponement of certain troop movements consequent on the decision to defer the dispatch of reinforcements to Libya', which, in itself, indicated the Government's reticence to march into a war and their belief in diplomacy.[49] Nuri-es-Said, Prime Minister of Iraq reported that the 'Egyptians seemed very nervous' and that he had already had two indirect approaches for Iraq to offer to mediate, one of which was from the Chancellor of the Egyptian Embassy in London.[50] This reinforced Eden's belief in Egypt's fear of Western power and his ability to bluff them with force to ensure reinternationalisation of the Canal. The Prime Minister also remained confident that the Arab world would not hold together over the crisis and 'emphatic' that Britain was better off without the Canal Base.[51] He could now afford to wait for the results of the conference more confident than at any point to date in the crisis that he held a strong position to achieve a peaceful resolution of the dispute.

However, Eden refused to wait. He continued supplying friendly countries with arms, particularly the supply of tanks to Iraq, to maintain a united bloc against Nasser's potential Pan-Arabism. By 15 August his efforts were once again beginning to bear fruit, as the US began to fulfil their agreed commitment of offshore equipment.[52] The Prime Minister, whilst being concerned with the possibility of trouble in the Persian Gulf, was hopeful that providing a show of force would 'prevent any serious trouble and [that] there [would therefore] be no need to evacuate the British population' in the Gulf, which would have had to precede military action. As, on 8 August, the Foreign Secretary had emphasised to the Italian Ambassador, 'we did not wish to resort to force: our military moves were entirely precautionary and, indeed, essential in view of the British lives and interests at risk in Egypt'.[53] For this purpose the Prime Minister had been in contact with the First Sea Lord to make a third frigate available and to discuss further reinforcing of the area.[54] There followed a series of exchanges between Eden and the Prime Minister of New Zealand in an attempt to obtain the services of the frigate, HMS *Royalist*. This underscored the decision not to use force, as Eden sought to strengthen the visible threat to Egypt, while also maintaining a deterrent against any further Egyptian action which threatened British resources. The Egypt Committee meeting of 9 August revealed the attempt to adopt a deterrent capability: 'The Prime Minister said that he was concerned about the possibility of trouble in the Persian Gulf. However, if we could make a show of force we should be able to prevent any serious trouble.'[55] This emphasised Eden's commitment and hope that he could forestall any further additions to the crisis in the Middle East by posting a deterrent in the form of military planning, and more specifically in terms of the strategic deployment of military power, such as the *Royalist*. He had to negotiate from a position of strength. Negotiation would have a much better chance of success if Eden could back it with a serious threat.

Despite remaining in 'a "flap" about the press', and from time to time ascending to a 'highly emotional state...making life very difficult all around him', Eden did not reconvene the Egypt Committee between 10 and 14 August.[56] Despite his apparent concern and irritation over the continuation of the crisis, the Prime Minister did not see the need to summon the committee which had been created 'to formulate plans for meeting' 'the situation arising from the recent action of the Egyptian Government in respect of the Suez Canal'.[57] This reflected the superficiality of his 'flap', his tendency to overreact to events in private, particularly press criticism, and his ability to conduct foreign affairs much more pragmatically and rationally. This only increased the majority of his contemporaries' misunderstanding of his intentions, consequently clouding the historical perception of him. On the 14th, the Prime Minister demonstrated his intent, believing that 'it would be preferable to delay the final decision to launch any military operation until it was certain that such action was required'.[58] He believed in the possibility of a peaceful solution which stood before any decision to employ force. Consequently, while his address to the Egypt Committee included the suggestion that a *casus belli* might be sought, he placed the most emphasis on the possibility of further negotiation, concluding: '[t]he programme of military preparations should continue as planned, on the understanding that nothing would be done which would prejudice a decision to defer the actual date for any military operation'.[59] Eden's ultimate scenario of having to use force was thus placed in its true perspective, where it had always been, as a last resort, as he had outlined with Cabinet backing on 27 July.[60]

The Prime Minister's decision not to employ force immediately was endorsed on 15 August, when the Suez Canal Sub-Committee of the Official Middle East Committee considered the implications of military action and rejected the option. They considered that such action would lead to the closure of the Canal. Eden and Cabinet's concerns over the nationalisation had centred on the possibility that traffic through the Canal would be inhibited and this reaction would induce the very situation that they had hoped to prevent. In addition, when the Canal reopened after military action, the maritime powers would have to 'discriminate between potential users', which would violate the 1888 Convention; the overarching principle behind negotiation and the Conference of Canal users.[61] The Committee's opinion strengthened Eden's belief in the search for a peaceful settlement. Meeting with Foster Dulles on the same day, he was buoyed by the apparent American optimism. As the Prime Minister put it, '[Dulles] seemed not to exclude the possibility of [the] joint use of force.'[62] After Eisenhower's communications, it was clear that the US was not prepared to use force unless it was the last resort, if at all. While the President wrote 'last resort', commitment to peace in the post-war world, the pacifist attitude of the majority of the American public and a weakening political position meant that 'last resort' should have been interpreted as 'not at all'. However, Dulles appeared to Eden and the Cabinet to be agreeing with their position set out on 27 July. This suggested that the US were viewing the crisis with a similar sense of importance and were therefore likely to try and help resolve the issue as quickly as possible, forcing Nasser to 'disgorge' the Canal. The Prime Minister had been pleased to hear that Dulles 'seemed to like' the idea of paying the transit dues 'elsewhere', other than to Egypt. Confident of American support, Eden had passed on 'certain details of our plans, in part in order to show him where we stand' and hence identify a unity of purpose. Dulles appeared, to Eden, to be 'ready to talk joint resolution'.[63] In a conversation with Lloyd on the 15th, Dulles expressed his concerns over reports 'that there was a difference between the United Kingdom and United States position'. He had tried to correct these inaccuracies, demonstrating Anglo-American solidarity, in a broadcast and a public statement.[64] This offered more hope to Eden, reinforcing the American enthusiasm from his own meeting with Dulles. Not only were the Americans offering their support and backing to the international conference, giving it a credibility in world eyes, but they might issue a joint public statement condemning Nasser's actions, demonstrating American anger at the nationalisation of the Canal to Egypt and building international opinion in opposition to Nasser. A peaceful settlement, invoked by this pressure, continued to appear, to Eden, to be very much alive.

On the morning of 16 August, the London Conference opened at Lancaster House. Eden welcomed the delegates before Lloyd was elected as chairman.[65] The Conference itself was a very grand affair, attended by delegates from twenty-two countries. Dulles reported to Eisenhower that the atmosphere was 'on the whole ... much more composed than two weeks ago'.[66] *The Times* was surprised by the 'swift start', with procedural questions 'covered at only one short session in the morning'. Dmitri Shepilov, the Soviet Foreign Minister, and Dulles made opening speeches. While Shepilov made a 'pro-Egyptian' statement, Dulles continued to give the British hope that the Americans were backing any attempt to gain a peaceful solution to the crisis.[67] Speaking to the delegates, he challenged the Egyptian action of nationalising the Canal. He questioned the move's legality, suggesting that it breached the 1888 Constantinople Convention, which had established the rights of the Canal Company until 1968 and had protected international operating rights.[68] He then went on to outline a 'four-point plan':

(1) The operation of the canal should be the responsibility of an international board established by treaty and associated with the United Nations. Egypt should be represented, but no one Power or group of Powers should be in a position of dominance.
(2) Egypt's right to an equitable return should be recognized.
(3) Fair compensation should be paid to the [Canal] company.
(4) Any differences over compensation or the return payable to Egypt should be settled by an abitral commission.[69]

The American attitude gave every reason to believe that they would endeavour to reverse the nationalisation of the Canal, particularly since the proposals 'conformed in effect to the earlier tripartite proposals'.[70] After this formal and 'expeditious start', the conference broke down into private meetings between small groups of the twenty-two delegations, where the 'real work' would take place.[71]

The Egypt Committee members, also meeting on the 16th, confirmed their thoughts of the previous meeting that the timetable of the contingency plans was in advance of the diplomatic moves, believing that Nasser was now unlikely to provoke an early incident. The deterrent appeared to have prevented any further aggression. As a safety measure the question of whether military operations should be launched might be reviewed in eleven days' time, on the 27th. Nevertheless, the Chancellor was keen to speed the pace of the preparations and thus appeared the more committed to the use of force.[72] However, even he believed that the diplomatic moves were 'going well'.[73] This belief, by the most ardent supporter for a forceful solution within the Government, testified to the primacy of gaining a peaceful settlement and the early optimism from the conference. However, this meant passively following the American line and continuing to react to events rather than outline a policy.

On 16 August, the Chancellor had presented a lengthy memorandum, providing an in-depth study by the official working party on measures of economic pressure on Egypt. However, he noted by way of preface: 'I do not think that action is required on any of its recommendations at present.'[74] The report had concluded that any further sanctions against Egypt would have little effect without parallel efforts by at least the US and the Commonwealth. Action taken to date, principally the 'embargo on the shipment of war material' to Egypt and the blocking of Egyptian sterling assets, had begun to take effect. It had been estimated that the latter had prevented 'Egypt from using some 60 per cent of her total currency and gold reserves, and in particular has made it impossible for her to pay sterling area exporters for her purchases from them.' These measures, in combination with similar action by the French and the Americans, had left 'the Egyptian authorities... in some difficulty over the financing of a large area of their current trade'. It had been estimated that about 40 per cent of Egypt's external trade was normally financed in sterling. Now the Egyptian authorities were faced with the problem of finding suppliers who did not require payment in sterling or francs. Even if such suppliers were found, Egypt would have a problem in paying them, because it was estimated that her 'free gold, foreign currency and credit reserves [were] not likely to be sufficient by themselves to finance imports, even on a reduced scale, for more than a year at the outside assuming that Egypt were prepared to exhaust entirely her free reserves'.[75] While Soviet aid to Egypt would weaken the pressure of sanctions, and the attempts to unite wider European economic action against Egypt had drawn little support, the conference could enable the development of a more concerted effort to destabilise the Egyptian economy. This would force Nasser to reinternationalise the Canal in exchange for the lifting of the sanctions. The report concluded that wider international sanctions were needed, which would 'increasingly be felt within a matter of months'.[76] This confirmed the sense of Eden's own designs for a solution and backed his attempts to gain broader support, particularly from the US, to press Nasser to 'disgorge' the Canal. The report also supported Macmillan's belief in the potential of the present action for achieving a peaceful solution and the Government's decision to wait for the conference to unite opposition against Nasser. Even after the first day, there had been immediate support for Dulles's proposal that the Canal should be reinternationalised.[77] Macmillan feared that further economic pressure might lead Egypt to close the Canal, 'which would pose in an acute form the question of the necessity for direct military action'.[78] The Government did not develop extra economic sanctions against the Egyptians; they were not intent on a war and wanted to pursue a peaceful resolution of the crisis. A blockade of the Canal would prevent the free flow of European oil supplies, a scenario, Cabinet had concluded on 27 July, that would require a military reaction. This would have been the obvious excuse for a Prime Minister who had decided upon war to initiate a military operation. However, Eden continued to place his hope for a peaceful resolution in the pressure of the present economic sanctions and the solidarity of the user countries.

However, only some in Whitehall were prepared to sit and wait. Sir Ivone Kirkpatrick, Permanent Secretary at the Foreign Office, challenged by the Assistant Under-Secretary Harold Beeley as to the grave consequences of the use of force, replied that '[i]t seems to me easy to enunciate these views – which are sound and, I think, generally accepted here, but it is more difficult to draw up a programme which will achieve the end... I shall be grateful for ideas.'[79] Cabinet did not want to use force and were willing to cling to straws in defence of a firm but universally acceptable policy. On the 18th, the Egypt Committee invited Selwyn Lloyd to arrange for a study to be made of possible actions by the Egyptian Government which might justify forcible retaliation.[80] Here, again, Eden and the Cabinet were considering every option and negating any accusation of appeasing the Egyptians.

Macmillan continued to try to influence the Americans. By the 20 August, Eden and the Cabinet were aware that, while Dulles had recognised the value of the military preparations in evincing Britain's determination to achieve a satisfactory solution, the 'United States Government could not justify going to war over oil in the Middle East, in view of the surplus of oil supplies available in the United States'. However, Dulles had warned the Soviets that the US 'would not stand by' if Britain and France were involved in a war.[81] After his talk with the Secretary of State on 15 August, the Prime Minister surmised that this meant that in the event of hostilities the US 'would at least provide material help'.[82] While Eden did not exaggerate what the American reaction might be, Dulles's vague phraseology reflected the vagueness of much of the Anglo-American communication during the crisis and underlined the misunderstandings between the countries. Dulles's statement reinforced the extent to which Eden believed that the Americans were susceptible to manipulation by using the communist threat. Potentially, the Prime Minister could reinvoke this threat to influence the US into supplying some form of help if their assistance was unforthcoming. However, Macmillan believed that Dulles 'didn't think the Russians would press things to extremes'.[83] Earlier in the month, Eden had also concluded that 'Russia was not being too bad'.[84] Bereft of this line of argument, Macmillan's anxiety increased and he began to pressure Dulles more directly, fearing that

> 'if Nasser gets away with it', we are done for. The whole Arab world will despise us. Nuri and our friends will fall. It may well bring the end of British influence and strength for ever. So, in the last resort, we must use force and defy opinion, here and overseas.
>
> I made this quite clear to Foster who really agreed with our position. But he hopes (and may be right) that Nasser will have to yield – in the course. This again brings up the frightful problem of how to keep a military expedition, [?] together at huge cost, 'all dressed up and nowhere to go'... Mr. Governor tells me that we shall have a very big pressure on sterling, but he believes that we can hold out.[85]

Eden had not invited Macmillan to talk with Dulles. Rather, the Chancellor, fearful as his diary revealed, once more tried to quicken the pace of discussions with the Americans. This time he hoped for at least acquiescence but, preferably, support for a military solution. His line frightened Dulles, weakening the chance of American support for a diplomatic solution because of their fears of being embroiled in a war. By the next day, after a long talk with Lord Salisbury, the Chancellor of the Exchequer believed that 'Foster was getting rather "sticky". He won't help us any more with economic sanctions etc. I cannot help feeling that he really wants us to "go it alone" and has been trying to help us by creating the right atmosphere.'[86] Macmillan's fears continued to affect his judgement, particularly of Dulles, but at this stage did not confuse Eden.

Unable to reach a conclusion 'on the general situation' during the Egypt Committee meeting, Macmillan suggested that 'a few of us should meet later' because '[w]e shall very soon have to make definite and tremendous decisions'.[87] Both Eden and Macmillan could see the seriousness of the situation, along with all the interested parties. Jebb confirmed that the 'French were being very tough, because they realised how much was at stake', while '[t]he British people were unconscious of all the implications of a diplomatic defeat'. Macmillan wrote, on 20 August, that Dulles 'will be firm'.[88] However, he continued to fluctuate in his doubts over Dulles's commitment. Eden, on the other hand, believed that Dulles was aligning himself with the British. Events suggested the possibility of a settlement and even the bellicose Chancellor had recognised that '[t]here are a number of ways in which we could bring pressure on Nasser – short of force. These must be studied.'[89] Economic and political pressures continued.[90]

In the Egypt Committee meeting, Eden began to place more emphasis on the need to negotiate, delaying the necessary photographic reconnaissance of the Canal Zone in case it jeopardised the present conference. 'He recognised that this would mean a corresponding alteration in the earliest date by which an operation against Egypt could be opened' and he agreed with the balance of opinion which was in favour of putting the planning date for the earliest 'D-Day' (date of the possible implementation of a military plan) back to 19 September.[91] Even Clark, who had thought that Eden *had* decided to use force, now began to doubt the Prime Minister's bellicosity and believed that the military plans were contingency measures and unlikely to be invoked.[92] Likewise McDonald, even after conversations with Admiral Sir William Davis, the Vice-Chief of the British Naval Staff, and hearing that 'there was no doubt that he [Eden] was determined to fight, if necessary', remained convinced until the surfacing of the plans for collusion, that Eden would try to secure a peaceful solution.[93]

The French continued to accelerate the pace of military preparation, exasperating the Prime Minister. On 23 August, he became very concerned when he discovered that three French ships with approximately 600 troops and equipment were due to leave Marseilles on the 24 August, arriving in Cyprus on the 29th. He believed that these moves would be prejudicial on the subsequent diplomatic agenda, 'particularly if it were decided to bring the... situation before the Security Council'. Despite believing that the United Nations did not have the machinery 'for any means of redress for the threat which the recent Egyptian action constituted to the vital interests of the United Kingdom', he believed it the best option to take the issue to the UN 'as a means of presenting... the case before world opinion' as long as Britain's full liberty of action was preserved.[94] Impressed by the need for haste, the Prime Minister, Salisbury, Butler and Macmillan met at 3 p.m. to discuss the imminent problems, notably the UN and the recall of Parliament.[95] They met again at 4 p.m. without Eden, and Macmillan believed 'I think we may have got the germ of a plan to help us right with U.N.'[96] Sir Leslie Rowan and Sir Denis Ricketts, senior Treasury officials, then arrived to talk 'on possible new economic sanctions against Egypt, in which US and the other signatories of the Declaration might join if Nasser refuses [to comply with the resolution of the London Conference]'.[97] On the following day, 24 August, there was a meeting of officials of Britain, the US and France to discuss this aspect of continuing pressure upon Egypt.

Eden pressed on for a solution and suggested 'raising the matter... in N.A.T.O., warning them beforehand of our intention'. As he reflected, '[w]e have after all been urged many times to take Cyprus to N.A.T.O. Why not Suez, which may be geographically more distant but is even more important to the survival of the majority of its members?' Failing this, there was always the Western European Union.[98] The Foreign Secretary had received a letter from the Belgian Minister of Foreign Affairs, Paul-Henri Spaak, which had called for a 'policy of absolute firmness' and drew parallels with the 1930s. Spaak was annoyed that the issue had not been taken to the NATO Council because this would have provided the unity of the Western Alliance but, nonetheless, his letter demonstrated the support of another European country.[99] The Dutch premier had also sent a letter of support. Nevertheless, essentially for his projected policy of increasing pressure on Nasser, Eden wanted to keep the Americans on side but any support was valuable in influencing Egypt.[100]

Earlier in the month the Prime Minister had noted the Soviet acceptance of the importance of the Canal and the question of oil to Britain and it soon became clear that he was contemplating reintroducing the Communist threat into the equation to try and influence the US.[101] There was a risk that Anglo-Soviet relations could be severely affected if the Russians discovered that Eden was employing the 'Communist bogey'. However, this was a risk worth taking and reflected the seriousness of the crisis to Eden, in particular the threat to Western European oil supplies. Throughout the summer, the British Ambassador in Moscow, Sir William Hayter, had kept the Prime Minister informed of the Soviet position over Suez. Eden's lack of concern over the

Soviets was illustrated by his lunch meeting with Hayter during the autumn. Also at the dinner was Lady Hayter, who recalled the Prime Minister's lack of interest in her husband's report on the Soviets, constantly referring to Nasser and likening him to Hitler.[102] These were Eden's true fears but the comparison of Nasser to Hitler also showed how he exaggerated events to convey their importance. After his experiences as Foreign Secretary he had a very clear idea of what Hitler and Mussolini were like. He made regular reference to Nasser as a Mussolini, as had other members of the Government. This understanding reinforced the sense that any comparison between Nasser and Hitler was done for effect and to try to influence support against the Egyptian leader.

Hayter's earlier reports had already convinced the Prime Minister of Soviet docility. This gave him the chance to try to use the Communist threat to influence support, particularly from the Americans. The Prime Minister continued to hope for increased US support against Nasser, particularly after Dulles's apparent commitment to making Nasser 'disgorge'. Reacting to Khrushchev's strongly pro-Egyptian speech of 1 August, Hayter had concluded that it appeared 'like a serious attempt to take the heat out of the situation'. In fact, the ambassador suggested that the Soviet Government might be worried by 'the explosive potentialities' of Nasser's action, and in emphasising the Soviet interest in maintaining freedom of navigation in the Canal 'may have wished to convey a hint to the Egyptians that an unreasonable attitude on this point would not have Soviet support'.[103] Hayter also reported a conversation between the French Ambassador, the US Ambassador, Bulganin and Shepilov. Bulganin had asked the US Ambassador, Charles E. Bohlen, for his reaction to Khrushchev's speech, to which he replied that 'it seemed designed to calm the affair down'. Bulganin had confirmed that that had been the intention.[104] Hayter remained convinced that the Soviets were not prepared to do more than exchange words over the Middle East and, in particular, the Suez Crisis. In consultation, the French Ambassador to Moscow was in agreement.[105] Thus, the potential to influence the US had arisen again. When it became clear that taking matters to the Security Council would antagonise the Americans, instead of looking toward Europe Eden began trying to manipulate the US. This need was increased, because even after the halt of US aid to Egypt, there was still a reported $35,800,000 worth of foreign aid supplies in the pipeline, and despite foreign aid officials referring to this as '"only a trickle" of small items', it amounted to a breach of the tripartite commitment and weakened the potential that any sanctions on Egypt had of undermining Nasser's position.[106]

On 24 August the London Conference closed. It marked an important and substantial attempt, particularly by the British, to obtain support for a solution to the crisis. Between 15 and 24 August, outside of the conference itself Lloyd held 29 meetings and 12 informal discussions with delegates.[107] The results surprised Eden and were listed in the form of the Eighteen Nation Proposals. He was immediately attracted by the common Anglo-American aim of protecting the rights of the Canal users under the Treaty of 1888 and believed there existed the potential to reinternationalise the Canal. However, as the proposals revealed, there existed very little specific substance. The user countries, in particular the US, UK and France, would have to discuss and agree on the precise details with Egypt.[108] The US, as the driving force behind the proposals, supported the resolution of the conference on 23 August. The Prime Minister believed 'much more had been achieved in mobilising international opinion than could have been expected'.[109] Eighteen nations, of the twenty-two who attended, had supported the principle of international operation of the Canal, vindicating Eden's belief that an American lead would induce other countries to come out in protest at Nasser's actions.[110] However, the Prime Minister, and the British delegates to the Conference, had missed the fundamental difference between the US and UK's intentions. The British saw the need to reinternationalise the Canal, while Dulles and the Americans believed they had to restrain the UK and France from war. Nevertheless, unaware of his misunderstanding, Eden pushed on for a peaceful settlement based on solidarity with the Americans and the other user countries. In a meeting held at Number 10 Downing Street, on the same day, Eden placed the issue of taking the matter before the UN as top priority and immediately wanted to talk to Dulles and the French. The Prime Minister saw the UN as another way of providing a peaceful solution to the crisis. Either it would press Nasser directly or, more realistically, it would provide a forum from which to present the case against Egypt and unite support for reinternationalising the Canal. The possibility of provoking an incident with Egypt was considered, as a last resort, and it was agreed to recall Parliament for the 3 September to calm the 'talk of war'.[111] To discuss war at a time when the public was becoming increasingly divided could only have been counterproductive if the Prime Minister had decided to use a military solution. However, Eden was keen to dampen the existing support for war because he had not decided to use the military to resolve the crisis. The threat of war with Egypt was essential in maintaining the policy of negotiation from a position of strength, but too much 'war fever' would only prejudice wider international support and thus weaken the ensuing mediation.

Misunderstanding Foster Dulles's real concerns about Communist insurgence, and therefore overemphasising what he thought to be the concerns of the US administration, Eden wrote to Eisenhower, on the 27 August: 'I have no doubt that the Bear is using Nasser, with or without his knowledge, to further his immediate aims. These are, I think, first to dislodge the West from the Middle East, and second to get a foothold in Africa so as to dominate that continent in turn.' He continued to underscore the communist threat, not only to the British but also to US interests, notably, Wheelus

Field, a US air base in Libya. Importantly, however, he made the point that 'the firmer the front we show together, the greater the chance that Nasser will give way without the need for any resort to force'. Eden continued to seek a non-violent solution, attempting to manipulate the Americans into supporting economic and political pressure against Nasser. He could not afford to support this idea publicly because, again, it would weaken his attempted solution of the situation by showing Nasser that despite the bluster the threat of force was merely bluff, which it was. Eden then reaffirmed his thanks for Dulles's help at the conference and emphasised that the country's continued military preparations were intended to show a firm front, unified with France, and therefore act as a deterrent to any further aggression.[112]

The resolution of the London Conference had also led to the formation of a committee. The Menzies Mission, intended to meet with President Nasser to explain to him the proposals of the eighteen nations, would bargain with him for the return of control of the Canal, as laid down by the 1888 Convention.[113] The delegation, headed by Robert Menzies, Australian Prime Minister, was made up of Loy Henderson, a senior Middle East expert in the American State Department, Dr Ali Qoli Ardalan, the Iranian Foreign Minister, Ato Aklilou Hapte-wold, the Foreign Minister of Ethiopia and Osten Unden, the Swedish Foreign Minister. On the 24 August, Menzies had been granted an audience with Nasser, not in Geneva as arranged, but in Cairo on the 3 September. Menzies was sceptical of the possibility of success of the mission. He told the Lord Chancellor, 'The chances of failure are 99 to 1 but these are the chances worth taking.'[114] Eden was also sceptical, additionally so because he thought that Menzies would give too much ground to Nasser in the negotiations.[115] This was a misjudgement, as Menzies proved excessively inflexible in the subsequent discussions in Cairo, earning the nickname of 'the Australian mule' from the Egyptians.[116] However, from 9 August, Eden had believed that Menzies' involvement 'would be a rod for [his] own back but he felt it was the best thing to do'.[117] By 29 August, he had become 'rather worried over Menzies', seeing him as too soft.[118] However, his involvement provided the possibility of enlisting Commonwealth support by the inclusion of the Australian Prime Minister. On 28 August, in the first Egypt Committee meeting since the passing of the resolution by the London Conference, the Prime Minister informed members of the details and suggested the need to reconsider the timing of 'D-Day'. 'D-Day' represented the theoretical implementation of force. However, the flexibility of the plan, represented by the proposed changing of the 'D-Day', demonstrated that the decision to use force had not been made. That decision would only be made, as Cabinet had agreed, as a last resort, if all other peaceful attempts at resolving the crisis failed. This flexibility was also demonstrated by the fact that an 'H-hour' had not been discussed.[119] The committee decision to continue the search for a peaceful solution was reinforced by the promising news that Dulles was likely to agree with taking discussion of the crisis into a NATO meeting.[120] It was then concluded that the further postponement should be explained to the French and would mean that the Committee would not meet for another week.[121]

However, while this was a move forward, Eden, keen for negotiation from a position of strength, was becoming indignant at the American attitude on taking the issue to the UN, exaggerated by Dulles's procrastination. The Prime Minister's initial reaction was that they should 'mind [their] own business' but this reflected his irritation at Dulles's technical problems with his intentions. These sounded pettier than they actually were, inciting Eden further, as controversy arose over whether the crisis should be considered a 'dispute' or a 'situation'.[122] Dulles was concerned that recourse to the UN Security Council might not result in condemning Egypt, particularly as the Soviet Union and Yugoslavia were certain to vote against, and Peru, China and, possibly, Panama were not certain supporters. Makins also reported that 'Mr. Dulles was in a rather legalistic mood, and was completely non-committal.'[123] Eden remained unable to compromise on his ultimate goal of international control for the Canal. When Moore Crosthwaite, British Deputy Representative to the UN, suggested creating 'something more general' rather than a plan based on the Eighteen Power Resolution, Eden minuted, 'No – The man misses the whole point.'[124] The Egypt Committee had determined on 28 July that any solution should be derived from resolution of the Eighteen Power Conference.[125] This had been upheld by the London Conference and formed the resolution of the Canal users in their representation to Nasser. To water down that principle would make the conference pointless and show a weakening of resolve to Nasser. This was at a time when the Egyptians had begun to doubt the potency of the British policy of bargaining from a position of strength.

On 2 September, Egyptian newspapers reported that Nasser had assured his military leaders that the Franco-British mobilisation moves were all bluff.[126] However, as Sir Humphrey Trevelyan, British Ambassador to Egypt had informed the Foreign Office, there was 'little doubt that Nasser seriously underestimated the strength of Western reaction and is concerned about Western military preparations and his own future, though he is reported to have estimated the chances of invasion at 10–1 against.'[127] This began to challenge the confidence that Eden held in the ability of Western power to frighten Nasser. Trevelyan had served as the head of the Embassy in Cairo only since 1955 but his experience of the Middle East made him a reliable source of opinion.[128]

On 3 September, the American reply reached Eden. In his communiqué, the President was in full accord with the Prime Minister concerning the Soviet threat and was, himself, placing a great emphasis on the success of the Menzies Mission. In addition, he shared Eden's view that it was important 'that Nasser be under no misapprehension as to the firm interest of the nations primarily concerned with the Canal in safeguarding their rights in that waterway'. This sentiment reiterated that of Dulles at the opening of the Conference. The President continued: 'If the diplomatic front we present is united and is backed by the overwhelming sentiment of our several peoples, the chances should be greater that Nasser will give way without the need for any resort to force.' However, from this point on the letter adopted a harsher and more direct tone:

> As to the use of force or the threat of force at this juncture, I continue to feel as I expressed myself in the letter Foster carried to you some weeks ago. Even now military preparations and civilian evacuation exposed to public view seem to be solidifying support for Nasser which has been shaky in many important quarters. I regard it as indispensable that if we are to proceed solidly together to the solution of this problem, public opinion in our several countries must be overwhelmingly in its support. I must tell you frankly that American public opinion flatly rejects the thought of using force, particularly when it does not seem that every possible peaceful means of protecting our vital interests has been exhausted without result.

In the President's opinion, there were two problems. The first was the 'assurance of permanent and efficient operation of the Suez Canal with justice to all concerned', while 'the second [was] to see that Nasser [should] not grow as a menace to the peace and vital interests of the West'. These two issues were distinct and, it was said, must be resolved simultaneously. But despite the apparent severity of the communication, Eisenhower was still as ready as Eden to put his faith in a 'solution along the lines of the 18-nation proposals'.[129] The Prime Minister still believed in settling the crisis peacefully but he had hoped that military preparations, backed by US support, could, by themselves, destabilise Nasser's position. With the American rejection of any such concerted position the potential threat had been removed, weakening all of the Prime Minister's moves to date.

The letter leaked to the press in Britain and its central tenet was announced by Eisenhower at a press conference.[130] That press conference, in Washington, while a chance for the Americans to publicly maintain their passivity, had not been designed to divulge the contents of the letter. However, when specifically questioned about the use of force, the President unequivocally rejected the possibility of its implementation. This undermined the majority of the work done so far, and in particular weakened the effect of the precautionary measures, realising Nasser's charge of bluff.[131] The President's letter contradicted the Prime Minister's and Lloyd's understanding of Dulles's position, and therefore the American position, on 15 August.[132] It also appeared to Eden, to undercut his own hopes of negotiating from a position of strength. More specifically it undercut any possible success of the Menzies Mission. As Menzies put it in a message to Canberra, 'it is all very well for people to denounce the use of force, but in a negotiation of this kind, it is good sense to keep the other man guessing'.[133] Had Nasser believed that a military invasion, condoned by and possibly including the Americans, could be launched against him, there existed more chance that he might back down, agreeing to the reinternationalisation of the Canal. However, the Egyptian leader was now aware of the differences in commitment between the British and the Americans, and could guess at the potential limitations imposed on any hypothetical British action. Despite this setback, Eden's confidence in his own policy was bolstered by the hardline Kirkpatrick who was sure that 'we might [still] bulldoze [the Americans] into suitable economic and psychological measures simply by threatening that, if they did not agree, we shall have no alternative but to have recourse to force'.[134] This line had been behind all of Eden's communications to the President, many of which Kirkpatrick had drafted, and demonstrated the Prime Minister's continuity in dealing with the crisis, despite the need to react rather than follow a defined policy.

There was also hope for Eden, despite his annoyance at the special help that Nasser was receiving from the Indians, because as Trevelyan reported: 'He [Nasser] takes great risks, but he has been known to retreat, (e.g. over the Sudan), and might be prepared to do so again at the last moment or even to resign to a colleague in order to save the revolution.'[135] In the Egypt Committee meeting of 4 September, the Prime Minister suggested that Parliament be recalled 'to secure the...endorsement of a policy which had involved the taking of certain precautionary steps and would entail further measures of the same nature'. He wanted to continue with the dual-track policy initiated in July which relied on the threat of force through the 'precautionary steps' or the initiation of force in the last resort. He hoped that this would calm the 'talk of war', as he had suggested on 23 August, through the disclosure of his plans to effect a solution.[136] Parliament was therefore recalled for 11 September. In addition, the Prime Minister believed that the public should be 'fully informed of the strength of our legal case', particularly considering the possible repercussions of Eisenhower's outburst on public opinion. The Committee also considered a further postponement of 'D-Day'.[137] Trevelyan was concerned that the 3 September letter had made the US look weaker than either France or the UK and he hoped that Loy Henderson, the principal American representative in the Menzies Mission, would dispel the myth.[138] While Eden remained concerned, it was not merely the Prime Minister who had become worried by the American undermining of the potential negotiation from a position of strength. This suggested that the situation had deteriorated further and the possible solution to the crisis had received another setback.

However, these events did not represent a turning point in the way Britain dealt with the US or Egypt. This was represented in the letter from Eden to

Eisenhower of 6 September, originally drafted by Kirkpatrick but sent with Eden's amendments.[139] Despite Britain no longer being able to maintain her deterrent to Nasser, and as it appeared that the Menzies Mission would end in failure, the letter opened with conciliatory lines, suggesting a unity of purpose, and tried to eradicate the myth that they might suddenly resort to arms, without further provocation, especially while there was a joint initiative in operation. It continued:

> If the Committee and subsequent negotiations succeed in getting Nasser's agreement to the London proposals of the eighteen powers, there will be no cause for force. But if the Committee fails, we must have some immediate alternative which will show that Nasser is not going to get his way. In this connection we are attracted by Foster's suggestion ... for the running of the canal by the users in virtue of their rights under the 1888 Convention.

Eden saw the possibility of solving the crisis through the user's club to reinternationalise the Canal by pressing Nasser. He had considered a similar idea as early as 12 August but was in no position to implement policy and needed to follow an American lead. Dramatic parallels were drawn between Nasser and Hitler, and the Soviet threat was evoked, the telegram ending with Kirkpatrick's romantic but scaremongering lines: 'it seems to us that our duty is plain. We have many times led Europe in the fight for freedom. It would be an ignoble end to our long history if we tamely accepted to perish by degrees.'[140] Finishing with these lines underscored the attempt to pressure the Americans into action by moral and physical threats. Due to the nature of this letter and the specific ordering of objectives, Eden was subordinating the use of force merely to bluff backing a negotiated settlement, or ultimately as he had always seen it, as a last resort.

By 6 September, Eden realised that a new stage of the crisis had been reached. A telegram from Menzies confirmed his suspicion that the mission had failed.[141] Without the threat of force in the background, it appeared to Menzies that Nasser would not accept the proposals for reorganising the control of the Canal. On the same day, the Foreign Office passed on information to Dulles that 'the probability is that by the week-end Menzies will have to announce that his Mission is a failure'.[142] They continued to suggest the need to go to the Security Council, following Eden's wishes and 'genuinely directed towards a peaceful settlement'.[143] On 9 September, Nasser officially replied to the Menzies Committee's letter of 7 September rejecting the offer of the Menzies Mission.[144] It was thus only left for Menzies to journey to London to report his failure. Then, returning to Australia via Washington, he met President Eisenhower. Showing his disappointment with the President, for making the 3 September letter public, he waited for an explanation: 'When a press conference is held, the democratic process requires that questions should be answered', he was told.[145] Diplomatic channels had not been exhausted but Eden's use of bluff could no longer dominate his attempts to secure a solution to the crisis without a potentially more real threat and/or much wider international condemnation of Nasser's actions.

The Prime Minister had hoped to achieve success but had not believed that he should compromise over such an important set of issues, particularly as the potential for forcing Nasser to accept a 'negotiated' settlement appeared to him a real possibility. This was reflected in Menzies' telegram to Eden of 6 September. Menzies shared Eden's unrealistically high hopes and many of his fears of Nasser's intentions.[146] Despite Eisenhower's letters of 6 and 8 September, the President reflected: 'I do not differ from you in your estimate of [Nasser's] intentions and purposes.'[147] All the time there was hope for Eden that the US might be able to coax a solution out of the embroiled mess of the crisis.

However, Dulles was not moving quickly toward producing a solution. The French were still endeavouring to 'inject a note of urgency'. Dulles had not yet reached a conclusion as to the timing or formulation of the draft resolution to be presented to the Security Council. In particular, he feared that what was being proposed 'was in effect to enlist Security Council support to force upon Egypt the conclusion of a treaty bestowing new rights on the users of the Canal. This was to say the least of it, a very novel use of the Council.' Dulles wondered whether Britain and France should not agree what legal rights the 1888 Treaty had vested in them. 'If Egypt then resisted (which he felt sure she would) we should have a clear case to take to the Council.' He was non-committal on these rights but his attitude appeared positive. However, Dulles was unlikely to be able to 'go along with the operation in its present form' without 'considerable modification'. Makins reported the Secretary of State's attitude and emphasised that the US could not be counted upon to support an appeal to the Security Council. In fact, as Makins continued, such a move, without full discussion with the US Government 'would have a most unfortunate effect'.[148] Eden did not believe that he could take the issue to the UN without American support because this would undercut the whole point of going to try to unite world opinion against Nasser. However, he had seen the possibility of a solution in line with the Americans and one which he himself favoured.

Before the failure of the Menzies Mission, Lloyd had dined with Allen Dulles, Director of the CIA, and Patrick Reilly, then Minister in Paris and temporarily Deputy Under-Secretary at the Foreign Office.[149] During the conversations Lloyd informed Dulles that if Nasser rejected the 18-power proposals then military intervention would be a 'very serious possibility'. Allen Dulles later failed to acknowledge that this had ever been discussed but his brother produced his plan for a 'Users' Association' (originally named CASU or Co-operative Association of Suez Canal Users and later renamed SCUA or Suez Canal Users Association) shortly afterwards.[150] Once again the British had used the threat of force to incite the Americans into action, but this time Foster Dulles had produced a plan in line with Eden's thinking. Despite the letters of 6 and 8 September which gave the Prime Minister only limited American backing for his own concept of a users' association, Eden still thought that he held enough US support to derive a peaceful solution. The Anglo-American misunderstanding deepened. Dulles still believed that Britain remained set on starting a war. The US Deputy Under Secretary of State, Robert Murphy concluded that SCUA had only been designed to pull the British and French back from the brink of military action.[151] However, Eden saw a chance for a peaceful settlement to the crisis, which, critically, appeared to have American support. The Prime Minister, adamant in his belief of maintaining US opinion, entered a new phase of the crisis ready to inaugurate SCUA and press Nasser into reinternationalising the Canal.

However, the two countries' perceptions of a users' association were fundamentally different in structure, as well as intent; a point missed by Eden and the British Government, after Eisenhower's telegram of 28 July, the American support for the resolution of the First London Conference and now at SCUA's conception.[152] The British were impressed by the apparent similarities between the two visions for a peaceful solution to the crisis. The Prime Minister saw it as a permanent organisation established to reinternationalise the Canal either directly or by pressing Nasser into relinquishing his control by the use of economic sanctions in the form of withholding transit dues. For the Americans, SCUA was primarily a device to occupy the British and French, holding them back from war. In contrast to the British proposal they suggested 'a semi-permanent organisation of the user governments to take over the greatest practical amount of the technical problems of the Canal, such as pilotage, the organisation of the traffic patterns, and the collection of dues to cover actual expenses'. The US wanted to arrange 'coexistence' with Egypt.[153] This would protect the new-found Egyptian control and made no attempt to reinternationalise the Canal which was central to Eden's aims for resolving the crisis. There would be no pressure of withholding dues, and bearing in mind that the Canal users were experiencing virtually no 'technical problems' during transit, the American proposal would be as hands-off as possible. Dulles's apparent flexibility on the issue and his apparent willingness to talk about the details of the plan increased the British belief that they were talking virtually identical plans with minor differences over detail. They completely missed the fundamental differences of structure and intent.

During 3 August to 9 September, pressures increased on Eden. The French accelerated their attempt to goad Britain into accepting a military solution. Indirectly, Israel was also becoming involved in the wranglings of the crisis and led Macmillan to try to exert more of an influence on both government policy and American acceptance of the use of force. At the beginning of the period, there appeared to Eden to be similarities in Anglo-American outlook, specifically the dual-track policy. Both countries supported force but only as a last resort. However, this rhetoric disguised broad differences in meaning. While the US wrote to Eden discussing force as a last resort, it was effectively saying no to any military solution, a subtext the harried Prime Minister missed. This misunderstanding increased American scepticism over British intentions, limiting the extent to which the US was prepared to develop serious solutions to the crisis. This meant that Dulles had offered the American SCUA proposal, in his opinion, to bring the British and the French back from the brink of war. However, Eden continued to reject the idea of a military solution, except as a last resort, openly denigrating Israeli involvement and ignoring French desires. In an attempt to promote a diplomatic solution, he ordered Treasury officials to develop further economic sanctions against Egypt and backed the Menzies Mission. While economic sanctions had brought little reward, and the Menzies Mission promised even less, the Prime Minister could afford to chance their success because, after the London Conference, he had begun to acquire widespread support which he believed could weaken Nasser's position. He needed to maintain as much pressure as possible on the Egyptians. Increasingly, with the Americans dragging their heels (in reality their assistance had been thwarted by distrust and Macmillan's interference), Eden began to think more seriously about taking the issue to the UN to supplement the burgeoning international condemnation of Egyptian actions. This did not represent a turning from his belief in Anglo-American co-operation but reflected that the crisis had reached a new stage that required the exploration and development of other peaceful solutions.

This analysis diverges from the existing historiography in that Eden put a great faith in the London Conference to develop a solidarity amongst the Martime Powers which could be used to press Nasser into relinquishing his control of the Canal. Nor has the historiography focused on Eden's commitment to his own vision for SCUA, as this chapter has identified. In addition, therefore, there has been a failure to recognise the full British and American misunderstandings of what SCUA should be. This has led to an underestimation of Eden's commitment to the tripartite talks, the London Conference and the Menzies Mission. In reality, the Prime Minister hoped to secure an agreement for a users' association through the aforementioned meetings. Because of the misunderstandings of the various interpretations of SCUA, little headway could be made throughout this period, 3 August to 9 September. However, Eden had committed himself to developing and eventually defining the users' club. This would form the focus of all of his attempts to resolve the crisis, as his continued commitment to the idea in the face of Dulles's prevarication revealed.

3
SCUA: 10 September–21 September

Suez Canal Users Association and the Second London Conference

With the failure of the Menzies Mission and after Macmillan's initial interference in August, Dulles believed in the need to develop a new solution with which to hold Britain back from the brink of war.[1] In addition, he did not want the British to appeal to the UN. He had originated the idea of a users' club, such that users of the Canal would band together to 'hire the pilots, manage the technical features of the Canal, organise the pattern of navigation, and collect the dues from the ships of member countries'.[2] While Dulles did not foresee real potential in this, for Eden it represented the embodiment of his idea for reinternationalising the Canal and using economic sanctions, in this case the dues from the Canal users, to destabilise Nasser's political position. His commitment to it represented the clearest indication that he had not decided to use force, and that he continued to want to resolve the crisis peacefully. Despite the poor relationship between the Prime Minister and Secretary of State, both saw this as an opportunity to achieve their ends and so both tried, by their own definitions, to work together. The crisis thus moved into a much more deliberative period as both men and their administrations attempted to define a peaceful solution from a detailed and specific agreement over establishing a canal users' association (SCUA). At this stage Eden did not understand Dulles's motives, or, therefore, the reasons for the extended discussions and problems that arose out of the development of SCUA. As Murphy concluded, Dulles did not have any real intention to make SCUA work.[3] With these talks being held in private, the Prime Minister's own motives came under increased scrutiny as he appeared indifferent to a peaceful solution, while continuing his military preparations. However, he continued to search for a diplomatic settlement to the crisis, either through SCUA or the UN.

In early September, Eden began to express reservations about the military plan, 'Musketeer Revise', consistent with his distaste of war. As the name suggested, the plan had already been changed once. Neither the plan nor its aims had been fully determined and therefore, quid pro quo, the use of force had not yet been decided. In the Egypt Committee meeting of 7 September, the Prime Minister raised concerns over the 'extensive devastation and loss of life that would be inevitable'.[4] Eden also worried about the lack of flexibility of the plan. He believed that this 'was perhaps even more serious', because

> [i]f D-day was not to be postponed it meant that certain actions such as the sailing of the store ships and the requisitioning of passenger liners would have to be put in train during the next two days. Once these and subsequent decisions had been taken the margin for manoeuvre was very limited. Furthermore, these decisions would have to be made before the recall of Parliament and the preparations would inevitably be an embarrassment when we referred the dispute to the Security Council.[5]

The Prime Minister, although keen to leave the door open for negotiation or a retreat by Nasser, feared that any attempt to take the issue to the Security Council would be impaired by overt preparations. Additionally, he was sceptical of using force, particularly in view of the movement in public opinion and the Labour leadership's opinion. The support for war had waned in the eyes of the public.[6] By 11 September, a *News Chronicle*/Gallup poll found that 81 per cent of those interviewed were in favour of taking the issue to the UN, while 34 per cent favoured using a military ultimatum if the move to the UN failed, with 49 per cent opposed. In the conservative *Daily Express* poll, 49 per cent of people were satisfied with the Prime Minister's handling of the 'Suez Situation', compared with 58 per cent a month previously.[7] The Labour Party had reacted strongly against Nasser's actions and opposed his brand of 'nationalisation' which it saw as different from Labour's post-war reconstruction led by the Attlee government. However, Nasser's domestic policies appeared to reflect Labour ideals to the British electorate, increasing the numbers of people who supported the Egyptian action of nationalising the Canal company.

Eden confirmed his trepidation over the new plan and his concerns to his diary:

> saw Chiefs of Staff and [General] Keightley [Allied Commander-in Chief] and Walter [Monckton] for two hours on a paper of theirs... This included a new method for 'Musketeer'. I was not at first enamoured of it, but in discussion and as Chiefs of Staff amplified it, became more reconciled. Its advantages are obvious, but in these things one has to be... against being unduly enticed by them, especially when the advantages are largely political.

The political benefits of the new plan meant increased flexibility such that any contingency timetable could be set in motion at the latest possible date. This was in line with Eden's reactive conduct of foreign affairs and meant that a decision to use force had not been made, nor would it have to be until, as he concluded on 27 July, the last possible moment when no other option remained. After the Committee meeting, he was still doubtful about the military plan. 'Finally another long talk with Keightley this time alone. It was clear that he much preferred the second plan. I am still not... convinced.'[8] Eden could see the short-term benefits of the plan as the Cabinet minutes for 11 September illustrated, but he was also aware that a short-term reaction would not necessarily solve the crisis. He had thought that the military men wanted to see him alone because they were tentative about the plan but they were intent on manipulating the Prime Minister's decision.[9] While the Chiefs of Staff were divided as to their course of action, they were dominated by the resolute Templer, Chief of the Imperial General Staff, who took an aggressive stance reminiscent of the previous century.[10]

In an attempt to keep all his diplomatic options open and as a reflection of the public mood, Eden tried to develop French support for a possible move to the UN.[11] This did not mean that he had given up on SCUA. The Prime Minister and the Egypt Committee therefore invited Mollet and Pineau to London. The French had been opposed to going to the Security Council because in France this would be regarded 'as an alibi for failure'.[12] Eden knew of the importance to the French of being certain 'before launching the Security Council operation'.[13] However, he did not want to create the wrong impression to the Security Council or the public and suggested that their visit 'could ostensibly be on the pretext of hearing Mr. Menzies' report on the Cairo mission'.[14] Eden also wanted to tell Mollet and Pineau, who had been 'unwilling to come', 'that there was little chance of our setting out on operation Musketeer'.[15] He was also concerned with the French attitude towards the Users' Club because he believed it could be made to work. As Jebb reported on 8 September, the French were in agreement that 'not only was Mr. Dulles putting us in an incredibly exposed position, but he seemed to have no concrete proposals of his own'.[16] While Eden thought that SCUA could offer a peaceful solution to the crisis, the French did not believe that the Americans were prepared to back the British concept of a users' club. In addition, they believed that if the matter went to the UN, Nasser could ignore the US proposals and make his case to the Security Council.[17] Pineau had 'expressed the view that we are really wasting our time talking to the Americans. As he [Pineau] sees it, they will *never* authorize any action likely to provoke the fall of Nasser, at any rate until after the elections, which could mean that we should never be able to take any such action at all. In his view, it is essential that, in spite of all obstructions, our two countries should now go firmly ahead on our chosen path [move to the UN].' Pineau was also suspicious lest Dulles design a new move to prevent the departure of the Canal pilots. If this happened then he believed that Britain and France should 'dig our toes in and say firmly "no". Apart from anything else it would be a complete humiliation for us to have to beg the pilots to stay in present conditions.'[18] Pineau's attitude reflected his and the French Government's desire to resolve the crisis forcefully but at this stage Eden did not share the scepticism over American intentions for any proposed solutions and continued to believe that they could solve the crisis peacefully.

The Prime Minister also faced objection to a move to the UN from Dulles, whose opinion was regularly being sent to London by Makins. In particular, he raised issue with the text of the proposed letter of introduction to the President of the Council. The Foreign Secretary conveyed the Government's reaction to the Ambassador in Washington in what would become the first of a number of occasions when the Government expressed private disappointment that the US had appeared to retreat from support for the British position. Lloyd ended the communication by trying to influence the Ambassador 'to impress upon Mr. Dulles the urgency and gravity of the present situation and the grave dangers if we do not continue to act resolutely together'. However, the real problem was brought out in the last line: 'I feel at the moment that I do not know where the United States Government stands on any of these matters.'[19] As this line demonstrated, the British did not know what the Americans were prepared to do and so the Prime Minister vacillated, influenced by the importance of maintaining what he mistakenly believed to be American support. This was reinforced by Eden's consideration of confining himself to a simple letter which did not propose immediate UN action and therefore did not upset the US. This was in line with advice from Makins, who believed that 'to divide ourselves from the Americans in this way on this matter at this point is not only unnecessary but would have the most unfortunate consequences'. Dulles 'had never seen the President more deeply worried about anything'. 'Of course', as he continued:

> Nasser could not be allowed to win in this contest. He must be cut down, but the President did not think that either the threat of or an attempt at military action would work. Long range methods would be more effective.
>
> Economic pressures on Egypt could be maintained. The jealousies between the Arab states could be fomented. The Administration felt it was a handicap to be operating on the tight time schedule which had hitherto been imposed. It excluded what, in the United States view, were the most dependable possibilities of action. The President did not exclude the use of force in the last resort. Between us we could get Nasser down, and the United States Administration were quite determined that this should happen. If Nasser obstructed the canal and used force, they would use it too. But they did not believe that the methods and the tempo which we were advocating were the right ones.

This telegram appeared supportive, despite undercutting Eden's bluffing of the Egyptians, but matters were complicated by Dulles's attitude toward the French: '[H]e realised our [Britain's] need to collaborate closely with the French. Nevertheless this was a complication for the administration. It was much easier for them [the Americans] to work these problems out with us. They distrusted French security in general, not only from the technical standpoint.'[20] It was also clear, as Makins revealed, that Dulles had been working on his idea for an American SCUA proposal, which while still undergoing full conceptualisation, presented the only progressive option.[21]

Eden later recounted that 'the whole purpose of the Users' Club had been, by a display of unity with the United States, to avoid having to recourse to force.'[22] This proved to be his primary objective at the time, as endorsed by among others Gwilym Lloyd George, the Home Secretary, who knew of Eden's doubts over the scheme.[23] However, this undercut the similarity it held with the Prime Minister's own vision of 12 August, for peacefully resolving the crisis. Ironically, SCUA divided London and Washington, as they saw it serving different functions: Britain saw it as a way of reinternationalising the Canal, while the Americans saw it as a way of distracting the UK and France from war. The Egypt Committee was becoming less convinced over Dulles's intentions for SCUA but agreed with the need to side with the Americans while still reserving judgement: '[I]t must be first established whether the United States Government intended to pursue them with a serious determination and to attempt to enforce such a plan on the Egyptian Government, or whether the proposals were more in the nature of delaying tactics to provide time for further reflection and negotiation in an election year.'[24] This did not mean that the Egypt Committee was against negotiation, as long as the specifics of that negotiation represented an attempt to achieve a settlement rather than a device to allow the Americans politically to tread water. The greatest fear was that Dulles's proposals would mean that in the event of any blockade or disruption to traffic through the Canal, American vessels would be forced to re-route around the Cape of Good Hope.[25] In addition, Dulles had only seen the proposals as temporary, to last for, perhaps, one year.[26] If SCUA represented such a defensive measure then it could not bring any pressure to bear upon the Egyptians.

The need for US support increased the scepticism over taking the issue to the Security Council but as the Egypt Committee discussed, 'there was some risk that the United States, having advised against referring the dispute to the United Nations at this stage, would feel themselves free to support amendments of a kind which might seriously hamper our subsequent freedom of action, to the resolution which we ourselves would table if we were to decide independently to place the matter before the Security Council'.[27] Eden believed that he had to support the US resolution, particularly as 'Mr. Dulles had implied that the support of the US would be forthcoming if the matter had to be referred to the Security Council at a later stage, after an attempt had been made to seek a solution on the basis of his proposals for a 'Users' Club and had proved unsuccessful'. As the Committee concluded, '[i]n any event, the United States could scarcely withhold their support in such circumstances'.[28] The Egypt Committee believed it was in a strong position. In line with the Prime Minister and Cabinet's decision of 27 July, it pursued a peaceful solution to the crisis, now through the use of the British SCUA proposal to pressure Nasser into reinternationalising the Canal. If this failed, they would take the issue to the Security Council, believing that the US would be obliged to back such a representation. The myth that the Americans were actively trying to solve the crisis persisted in the minds of the British Government, except that of Macmillan who continued to believe that Britain's best interests would be served by employing force without delay.[29] However, Eden remained consistent in his belief in the potential of a users' club. Despite Nasser's unequivocal rejection of international control in his reply to the Menzies Mission, there was still hope for a settlement, as he believed 'that the real insulation of the Canal from politics would best be guaranteed or a renewal of the 1888 Convention. Either as we have already declared, is acceptable to us [Britain]'.[30]

Eden, seeking to keep in tune with US policy and personally sceptical about the rigidity of the contingency plan, decided to seek the Egypt Committee's approval for adjustments to 'Musketeer'. The Committee accepted the change of the military plan, which, Eden made it clear, would mean that the 'actual date for D-day must be dependent on the American "Users"' plan and, possibly, reference to the Security Council'. The 'Users plan' pertained to the as yet unpublished proposals offered by Foster Dulles 'for an association of user countries to operate the Suez Canal themselves', and 'organise as among themselves for the most effective possible enjoyment of the rights of passage given by the 1888 Convention'.[31] Military preparations were further downgraded and again placed as secondary to the pursuit of a peaceful settlement, particularly since the bluff to invade the Canal Zone had lost credibility. The lack of importance of the use of force was also revealed by the failure of the British to consult the French over the change to the plan.[32] The need to increase the flexibility of the contingency measures outweighed the need to create a more definitive military operation and there was no reason to antagonise France, where both the left- and right-wing supported an immediate aggressive solution. In redefining the plan without French interference, the British did not have to commit themselves to the use of force through a more specific plan with precise aims and timetabling. The French had begun to doubt that Britain would ever decide to use force and were concerned by the lack of commitment such an imprecise plan demonstrated.[33]

However, conflicting opinions began to blur Eden's understanding of the situation. Menzies' letter to Eden apologising for his failure began by suggesting that '[y]ou have about as difficult a task over Suez as mortal man ever had'. He continued to appraise the situation in Egypt and Nasser's personality, fuelling any distrust that Eden had already developed: 'Egypt is not only a dictatorship but it has all the earmarks of a Police State. The tapping of telephone lines, the installation of microphones, the creation of a vast body of security police – all these things are accepted as commonplace.' Of Nasser, he had at first thought him to be 'quite a likeable [sic] fellow' but after spending some time with him, considered him 'rather gauche', with 'considerable but immature intelligence'.[34] It was this latter point which was of the gravest concern to Eden and his administration, because of Nasser's unpredictability.

By the Cabinet meeting of 11 September Selwyn Lloyd informed his colleagues that the 'Egyptian Government had flatly rejected the proposals for international control of the Suez Canal'. He and the Prime Minister had been in close touch with the French and American Governments and were considering three courses of action: (a) to proceed at once with military action; (b) to offer a resolution in the Security Council supporting the conclusions of the London Conference and thus calling on Egypt to restore the rights of the maritime countries under the 1888 Convention; and (c) adoption of the US plan for an organisation to 'enable the principal users of the Canal to exercise their rights under the 1888 Convention'. In discussion, Cabinet believed that there were difficulties associated with the third option but they 'were outweighed by the great advantage that the US would be publicly involved in a plan of positive action' and '[i]f the plan succeeded, Colonel Nasser's original action would be largely frustrated: if it failed, by reason of Egyptian obstruction, the maritime Powers would have stronger grounds either for an appeal to the Security Council or for recourse to more forcible measures'. Cabinet then ratified the Users' proposal. Eden had convinced his colleagues of his own belief in this line, consistently hopeful of pressing Nasser into relinquishing his hold on the Canal.

Macmillan did not believe that SCUA could be made to work for a peaceful settlement. He re-exerted pressure on his colleagues in support of a forceful settlement of the crisis: '[I]t was unlikely that effective international control over the Canal could be secured without the use of force.' The Chancellor believed that the move to effectuate the Users' Club was 'a step towards the ultimate use of force. It would not in itself provide a solution.' He doubted that the concept could work or that, more importantly, the Egyptians could accept it. In reality the Egyptians *would* not accept the scheme but Macmillan's scepticism was not founded on this principle. He was merely keen, as he concluded, 'to bring the issue to a head'.[35] Macmillan's fears had been growing with regard to the mounting threat to the British economy.[36] He attempted to press the Cabinet by indicating the importance of a quick settlement of the crisis to the national economy, with particular reference to restoring confidence in sterling; a threat that he failed to reassert in November when, the decision to use force having been made, sterling came under increasing international and, particularly, American pressure, in an attempt to scare Britain out of her occupation of the Canal Zone.[37] Summing up Cabinet discussion, the Chancellor hoped 'that Parliament could be persuaded to give the Government a mandate to take all the necessary steps, including the use of force, to secure a satisfactory settlement of this problem'. In his diary he went further: 'The more we can persuade them [Americans] of our determination to risk everything in order to beat Nasser, the more help we shall get from them. We shall be ruined either way; but we shall be more inevitably and finally ruined if we are humiliated.'[38] This concerned Walter Monckton, the most consistent opponent to the use of force. He feared that SCUA would be regarded as a move toward the use of force, although even he 'did not exclude the possibility that, if the Canal could be brought under effective international control, the present regime in Egypt might be overthrown by means of a short war'.[39] He believed in the importance of having the US on side and of maintaining the support of public opinion at home and abroad. Monckton and Macmillan met frequently and privately throughout the crisis and the Chancellor's bellicosity distorted the Defence Minister's understanding of Government intentions, further confusing history's judgement of Eden.[40]

Eden summarised Cabinet's opinion, which remained consistent with their immediate reaction of 27 July. It was 'agreed that Egypt's disregard of her international obligations could not be tolerated and that effective international control over the Suez Canal must be re-established'. Every 'reasonable' effort should be made to achieve this peacefully but 'we should be justified in the last resort in using force to restore the situation'. Reflecting the more controversial aspect of Cabinet conclusions, he then raised questions on the possibility of military operations. He considered that it would be difficult to decide exactly when the recourse to force had become unavoidable and suggested that it would be affected by the state of public opinion in the US and the views of the French, who he said 'were increasingly impatient of delay'.[41]

The Prime Minister had not decided to use force. Consistent with his conduct of foreign affairs, he reacted to events, thus waiting until the very last moment before making any decisions, especially something as politically sensitive as the use of force. Conservative Party member, Nigel Nicolson, continued to believe that the Prime Minister intended to bluff the Egyptians, with force, into relinquishing their control of the Canal.[42] Eden's remarks reflected the line Frederick Bishop had suggested to the Prime Minister for Cabinet. Bishop's memorandum on the issue advised 'binding all your colleagues into our present policy', particularly 'the issue of using force if diplomatic methods fail to get us a satisfactory solution'. Bishop believed that this was 'of course a hypothetical question; but the question is bound to remain hypothetical for some little time'. However, Eden's passivity and belief in SCUA meant that he did not pursue Bishop's line with the same vehemence as his private secretary had suggested to him. In particular, he did not use the pressure of letting Nasser 'get away with this' to attempt to unite his colleagues in support of the use of force because, as he already implied during Cabinet, the decision to use it had not been made.[43]

Eden still placed great importance on having the Americans on side but he did not see a divergence in thinking between the two countries on the resolution of the crisis.[44] He and Macmillan appeared to share the same views about the importance of US support. Eden saw the need for American assistance in terms of using their power to directly influence and increase international pressure on Nasser to relinquish his control of the Canal.[45] The Chancellor of the Exchequer, in contrast, supported Dulles's proposals in order to gain financial backing for an increased military build-up and potential hostilities.[46] He revealed this preoccupation in his memoirs, recalling that as he was so fully employed with the financial problems of the period he could only have 'a general knowledge of the intricate but, alas, ineffective attempts to reach a peaceful solution in accordance with the claims of justice and equity'.[47] Macmillan consistently favoured force. However, Eden still maintained the reins of power.

Cabinet agreed to support the Users' Club, once again siding with a peaceful solution. Even Clark, who had concluded he was incorrect on 26 July to assume that the military option had been adopted, now doubted whether Cabinet had made any conclusions on force.[48] Eden had always favoured international solidarity as a means of increasing the pressure upon the Egyptians. He was keen to maintain allegiance with both the US and French but recognised that the French were extremely impatient. Complicating the situation was that Douglas Dillon, the US Ambassador in Paris, had on several occasions and without Eden's knowledge, repeated conversations with Pineau to Washington, which 'made it absolutely clear that the French were determined upon the use of force if reasonable terms were not arrived at about the Canal'.[49] If the Americans had had any doubts over Anglo-French intentions to use force, they were now firmly convinced of the French, and by association, British bellicosity. This weakened the possibility for the US to threaten Egypt so as to define a solution. The Americans were now even more inclined to develop skeleton solutions, which had no chance of success, but would keep the British and French from war. The chance of this manipulation appearing to work was enhanced by the fact that Eden continued to pursue a peaceful solution tied to an American lead and the fact that he did not know that any US-inspired solution had not been designed to succeed.

Britain could not act alone and would need the support of the French Government but, at the same time, Eden had been consistently fearful that France might commence hostilities to reduce domestic political pressure. He also believed that the French and particularly Pineau were warmongering and untrustworthy. Recent relations between them had prevented the creation of a stable environment for building trust.[50] In September, Eden found himself in the same position as the summer of 1956, not wishing to alienate the French despite the reservations he held over their intended policy and its timing. After the meeting it appeared that the French were in agreement over the current policy, as the Foreign Secretary informed Roger Makins. In addition, both parties believed 'that the United States... genuinely intend to do their utmost to bring the CASU [SCUA] into being, and to make it work':

> We agreed in principle to the Users' Club on the basis of United States participation and payment of dues including United States ones to the new organization forthwith. It is also our understanding that the United States Government genuinely intend to do their utmost to bring the CASU into being, and to make it work. In these circumstances we and the French would be prepared not to go to the... Security Council at the moment and would confine ourselves to a letter to the President of the Security Council... If Mr. Dulles does not agree about the Users Club we shall be obliged to bring the matter before the Security Council straight away.[51]

The British sought to evaluate the viability of SCUA whilst trying to maintain enough support to promote a peaceful solution, either through the Users' Club or the Security Council.

Lloyd had told Dulles, prior to Nasser's meeting with the Menzies Mission, 'that if Nasser rejected our proposals we ought to go to the Security Council straight away'.[52] There was a danger that the Soviets or the Yugoslavs might raise objection to the British concentration of forces as a threat to peace which would undermine all of Eden's objectives. Dulles also argued that if Nasser rejected the Users' Club, then 'we should be in a much stronger position when we went to the Security Council'. Eden had then persuaded a reluctant Cabinet to accept the British proposal for SCUA and it hoped 'the United States would be publicly involved in a plan of positive action to enforce the users' rights under the Convention'.[53] He attempted to strengthen the Anglo-American front but by 10 September it was unclear what the policy would be.[54] Even by the next day the Private Office '*still* do not know what the Americans will reply about the users' club, nor therefore what tomorrow's speech will say!' Such was the importance of Anglo-American solidarity to Eden that until the last minute the content of the speech was still undecided in deference to any possible US lead. As late as 11:30 p.m., the night before, the 'office was still vague'.[55] The Government waited as long as possible to enable the aligning of the two countries in the statement of the following day.

Matters were, again, complicated by Dulles. He informed Makins, the British Ambassador in Washington, that he was concerned that SCUA was a wholly

Western organisation and ended with the assertion that his draft proposal for the Users' Club had 'inevitably been compiled in great haste, and that it must not be taken as representing the United States government position in every detail'.[56] While Eden had backed his own proposal for SCUA because of his belief in its potential for reinternationalising the Canal, he had also expressed his support because of its American origin. This underlined the fundamental misunderstanding that the Prime Minister held of the differing intentions that the UK and the US had for the Users' Association.[57] As a US proposal it carried more weight and had greater potential for wider international acceptance. In turn, this would increase the pressure on Nasser, furthering the chance of placing the Canal under international control. Now Dulles was withholding American support from the Association proposal until more details had been worked out. This implied the need for more Anglo-American discussions to agree on the precise details of SCUA, which would extend the crisis and the duration of Nasser's hold on the Canal, at a time when Eden was coming under renewed pressure to be seen actively to be resolving the dispute. While this also suggested an understanding of the differences between the British and American proposals, it also suggests they could be compromised; a view which fails to see that they were fundamentally different in intent and structure. The Prime Minister did not have any concrete proposals to show the public, his party or Nasser. Then, adding insult to injury, it was only when Dulles had learnt that the British and French were no longer going immediately to the Security Council that he 'stressed the point that he had not opposed recourse by us [British] to the Security Council but had merely felt obliged to point out as a friendly critic what he considered to be weaknesses in our case and to make it clear that if others sought an injunction against the use of force the United States representative could not be committed to opposing it'.[58] On the same day, Dulles continued to imply support for Eden, referring to the possibility of the US joining the UK and France in sending the proposed letter to the President of the Security Council. He then supported Eden's ultimate action of using force as a last resort. The Secretary of State suggested that 'it would be preferable for the United States not in this way and at this time to create an identity of interest which might prove a somewhat embarrassing limitation on the United Kingdom and France in the future'. By way of clarification, William Rountree, the Assistant Secretary of State and through whom the message had been passed, added 'that what Mr. Dulles had in mind was of course the same point which he had been obliged to raise in relation to the proposed recourse to...the Security Council, i.e. a possible decision to use force in the future'.[59] Even the President's press conference of 11 September left room for speculation. While disassociating the US from any form of military action he declared that '[i]f, after all peaceful means are exhausted, there is some kind of aggression on the part of Egypt against a peaceful use of the Canal, you might say that we would recognize that Britain and France had no other recourse than to continue to use it even if they had to be more forceful than merely sailing through it'.[60] Rather than exciting the British, who, had they decided to use force, would have been delighted by this sentiment, concern arose that the Americans no longer believed in the Users' Association as the British had defined it.

Lloyd telephoned Makins with his doubts concerning American participation in this sort of SCUA.[61] Makins believed it necessary to write back to the Foreign Secretary with some 'afterthoughts', because, fearing he had misheard him, he did not follow Lloyd's arguments. He reviewed US actions:

> They have all worked like Trojans against time and with great energy on the political and economic aspects of their proposals. But of course much still depends on our skill in leading them along.
> ... Here, it is vitally important that the Prime Minister's statement in the House tomorrow in sense and substance, should not materially depart from the statement of the United States position, for this was approved by the President and will be the basis for Dulles's statement on Thursday. Any substantial discrepancy will of course be seized upon. I hope there is no risk of this, for in my opinion and that of my French colleague the statement gives our two Governments all that we could hope for at this stage.[62]

Thus, until the last moment, when the speech to Parliament had to be made, Eden could not be completely assured of US backing or aware of the line it was going to take. Unable to do anything without US consent, he waited for the American lead. Later he revealed that 'the words I used about SCUA [in the House of Commons] had been agreed between the three governments, ourselves, the French and the United States. Moreover, so far from being jubilant, I had had the gravest doubts as to whether we could endorse SCUA. Many, perhaps a majority of my colleagues including the Foreign Secretary, were against doing so.'[63] The Prime Minister was becoming sceptical about Dulles's intentions for the British idea for SCUA because he appeared to be emasculating it, suggesting that the withholding of dues to Egypt by the Canal users should be voluntary.[64] Dulles had set out his original plan for SCUA in a letter signed by Eisenhower and sent to Eden on 8 September. This involved promoting 'a semi-permanent organisation of the user governments' to run the Canal, organising pilotage, traffic patterns, and the collection of dues to cover actual expenses. In addition, there were 'economic pressures which, if continued, [would] cause distress in Egypt'.[65] To remove the 'collection of dues' and not replace them with the 'economic pressures' undercut the potential sanctions that Eden hoped to impose on Nasser. The sanctions were central to strengthening the users' bargaining position in any negotiation with Egypt. Not only might they induce Nasser to relinquish his control of the Canal but they might destabilise Egypt, generating the conditions for a coup which might replace Nasser with a leader more likely to reinternationalise the Canal. The fundamental differences in the UK and US proposals were finally appearing for all to see.

Eden reacted to this apparent weakening of Dulles's resolve over SCUA by taking what he believed was the American line and adopting the suggestion of strengthening the bargaining position. The Middle East Official Committee approved a Foreign Office draft for inclusion in the Prime Minister's Parliamentary statement the day before and this was ratified by the Egypt Committee.[66] In it Eden referred to 'the possibility of recourse to direct action against Egypt, should it prove impossible to reach a peaceful solution'. In his diary Eden commented: 'I was careful by agreement to make... [the] ...statement on [the] 'Users Club' in exactly the terms agreed with Foster's. We are not enamoured of the scheme but it has the great advantage of being American.'[67] While Eden had started to lose faith in Dulles's commitment to the British idea for SCUA and had taken the opportunity to maintain the pressure on Nasser by publicly strengthening his resolve to settle the crisis by force, as a last resort, he consistently aligned himself with the US. Outwardly, this increased the potential threat against Egypt because the statement appeared congruent with US policy. However, it showed Eden's continued resolve for a peaceful solution, as he followed the American lead which had offered to reinternationalise the Canal in the same way as he had envisaged in August.

The Prime Minister, remained precariously balanced, still keen on a peaceful solution, but needing to maintain a serious threat to Nasser, and prevent any criticism of his apparent lack of policy. Eden and the Egypt Committee still saw the need to work with the American proposals and the Foreign Secretary was asked to 'make the arrangements... for further international consultation on the proposed association of user countries'.[68] The Prime Minister continued to try to develop support for his SCUA proposal and build international pressure against Nasser through the Users' Club.

But the Foreign Secretary, voicing Eden's concerns, was still disturbed by the slow speed at which events surrounding the conception and implementation of either SCUA proposal were moving. As he wrote to the Ambassador in Washington: 'we cannot rest on a mere announcement of an intention'.[69] Britain needed something concrete to show Nasser, and to a lesser extent the British public, that they were working towards a solution. In addition, Lloyd was concerned that because of the talk in the Commons' lobbies of SCUA being a Dulles plan he might 'think that we are deliberately trying to saddle him with responsibility for it'. Lloyd's remark reflected that although Dulles had proposed a users' association, it was important to Dulles that he should not have to carry sole responsibility for it. This was because the Americans had not designed their SCUA proposal as a solution to the crisis but rather as a way of keeping the British and French from war.[70] The British continued to believe that the US and UK proposals for SCUA were virtually the same, bar some specific details. Lloyd thought that leaving the Americans to promote the Association would anger Dulles who had just disassociated American agreement 'on every detail' of the Users' Club. However, the British misunderstanding continued as they believed that Dulles would still promote a solution to the crisis through a users' club. In addition, they needed American support for this idea which had origins on both sides of the Atlantic and represented Eden's preferred method of resolving the situation. The Foreign Secretary was adamant when he finished with 'I do not want him [Dulles] to have any sense of grievance.'[71] The British were concerned about the time it had taken to reach this point in their deliberations with Dulles and the Americans, adding to their worries about how slowly the decision-making processes were moving. This concern and that of Eden's, increased with the news from Egypt, on 12 September, that Trevelyan, the British Ambassador in Cairo believed that Nasser's 'purpose is presumably still to drag out the negotiations while consolidating his hold on the Canal, in the hope that time is on his side and that chances of the use of military force are diminishing'. He believed that Nasser

> has probably been encouraged by President Eisenhower's statement and recent reports from Washington suggesting that there is something of a split between the Americans and our view, and he perhaps calculates, on the basis of these reports and of reports of political differences in the United Kingdom, that it will be increasingly difficult for us and the French to wage war on him. Like other dictators he listens to advice from very few, but has plenty of people round him who will tell him that he is securing a succession of diplomatic successes.

However, there was hope:

> One influence tending against compromise is if, as is likely, he believes that we and the French mean to have him out anyway, and that a deal on the Canal issue will only diminish his prestige and security in the Arab world and Egypt, without at the same time diminishing British and French hostility. But a last minute compromise is not absolutely excluded, if an obviously solid front is erected against him.[72]

Makins reported that Hoover, who had been prepared to represent the US at the forthcoming conference, had entered hospital, so Dulles did not believe he could send anyone to Europe before Monday, 17 September. This added to the problems and pressure on Eden. It was essential to maintain solidarity against Nasser and continue to divine a solution. Any apparent vacillation would strengthen the Egyptian resolve and perpetuate her sole control of the Canal. Dulles hoped he could fill the breach, although he did not specify with whom, and Makins suggested that Lloyd or the

Prime Minister should send a letter encouraging his attendance.[73] This was done and, in the end, an almost satisfactory situation was reached. Eden believed that he had shown the Americans that he was reasonable 'while retaining essential power and not disturbing our allies...U.S. is committed and Foster comes on Tuesday, but position is still much involved'.[74] Continuing to exert 'power', and hence a possible solution to the crisis, through the Americans, the Prime Minister now had agreement for Dulles's attendance at the new conference. This promised to bind world opinion together against Nasser. However, once again the Anglo-American misunderstanding lurked behind the appearance of success. Eden believed that Dulles's attendance marked an important political victory, demonstrating the American resolve to develop a solution to the crisis. But, once again, Dulles intended to draw out negotiations in an attempt to neutralise any possible aggressive action.

By the 13 September, Eden found himself under intense pressure both from the opposition and from a split in his own party.[75] The Commons debate took on a new dimension with the opposition calling for a referral to the UN. Eden had considered making the move to the UN for the previous six weeks but he vacillated because of his fears of the Soviet veto, American opposition to taking the issue to the Security Council, and American insistence that another solution could be found. He favoured the use of SCUA to procure a solution above all other options. However, now cornered by American intransigence and opposition fervour, the Prime Minister was forced to tell the House, after much avoidance of the issue, that if the Egyptian Government defaulted under the 1888 Convention 'we should take them to the Security Council'.[76] Having not made any public references to taking the issue to the UN, Eden's apparent intransigence, followed by this affirmation, emphasised the suspicion of his warmongering to contemporaries and historians. He had appeared to remain politically inactive whilst developing contingency plans for a possible invasion of the Canal Zone. Previously, this reaction had been acceptable to public and opposition, but it now carried with it the fear of war. As Laurence Cadbury, the Chairman of the *News Chronicle*, explained to the *Daily Mirror*: The Labour Party 'feel that the Government is playing a dangerous game – even if it is largely bluff – by allowing the impression to grow that it "means business".'[77] More direct criticism continued from the *Manchester Guardian* and *Daily Worker*.[78] These newspapers presumed that Eden wanted to take the issue to the UN, where he would try to justify his case, having exhausted all peaceful options for a solution, and then employ force.[79] Gaitskell, whose pressure had largely induced Eden's 'public' commitment to the UN, 'wrote a letter to *The Times* claiming that the Government's position on the use of force was contrary and obscure'.[80] The Prime Minister, immediately believing that this had undermined his position, took solace in Macmillan's advice: 'Was it necessary to tell Nasser beforehand how every card in the pack was to be played?'[81] Eden's method of maintaining limited freedom of action as well as thought, had played a prominent role in his previous attempts to deter Nasser. As Macmillan recalled, 'If P.M. were to "climb down" under Socialist pressure, it would be fatal to his reputation and position. As we *are* going to Security Council – as soon as we can rely on U.S. support there – events, not words, will justify us.'[82] Eden had shown a weakening of his resolve and had looked to the Chancellor for support. While this was only a temporary move, it showed that under pressure he would turn to Macmillan. In the depths of the crisis, in October, when the pressure on the Prime Minister had increased substantially, this would prove decisive in inducing the declaration to use force.

In a press conference, also on 13 September, Dulles, having made the agreed statement, then destroyed the last vestiges of a military threat against Nasser, by further weakening the potential of the British vision for SCUA, substantially reducing what Eden had envisaged. He had not intended to undercut the British position but simply outlined what had always been the US position with regard to the Users' Association:

> [I]f we can not work out at the working level a program for getting ships through the Canal on acceptable terms, and if physical force should be used to prevent passage, then obviously as far as the United States is concerned the alternative for us at least would be to send our vessels around the Cape [of Good Hope]. Now, of course, that would involve inconvenience, cost, delays. But we have given a very careful study to that whole problem, and we believe that it is solvable.

After a subsequent question, he went on to reiterate and reaffirm the American position:

> If force is interposed by Egypt... [w]e do not intend to shoot our way through. It may be we have the right to do it but we don't intend to do it as far as the United States is concerned... If we are met by force which we can only overcome by a shooting we don't intend to go into that shooting. Then we intend to send our boats around the Cape.

Having weakened the possibility of Nasser accepting SCUA by removing the 'position of strength', he then further denigrated SCUA: 'I am afraid that the Users' Association is not going to be in a position to quote guarantee unquote anything to anybody; we can't even guarantee anything to our own ships.'[83] This immediately realised the fears of the Egypt Committee expressed at the meeting of 10 September.[84] In addition, when asked whether this represented a divergence in American and British thinking, Dulles replied: 'I do not recall, but perhaps you do recall accurately just exactly what Sir Anthony Eden said on this point. I did not get the impression that there was any undertaking or pledge given by him to shoot their way through the canal.'[85] While Dulles was technically correct, he immediately undermined any remaining British deterrent. A good proportion of the press conference weakened or reflected the weak Anglo-French position because of complete American detachment from the issue and Dulles's removal of the threat of force.[86] Eden had consistently hoped that he could maintain a strong threat against Nasser to back any negotiation. He could achieve this more successfully if the US, with its greater superpower status, substantiated the Anglo-French threat as seriously as he had thought.[87] In combination, these factors seriously weakened the Prime Minister's position. Nevertheless, he believed he needed to align Britain with the US in the hope that the potential of the Users' Club could be fulfilled.

To maintain Anglo-American links and so possibly develop SCUA, the Prime Minister suggested making a public statement, that 'as a result of planning in recent weeks with our American friends...we were in a position, should Nasser take reckless or violent action to obstruct navigation, that the means existed to maintain the economic life of Europe'.[88] Dulles then confirmed his attendance at the Second London Conference.[89] With the Secretary of State's involvement it was believed that there would be more chance of uniting countries in favour of a powerful SCUA. Then, with a view to the forthcoming discussions and indicative of the importance Eden and the Government placed on the Users' Club, the Middle East Official Committee drew up the 'U.K. Proposals for an Association of Suez Canal Users'.[90] The Prime Minister now believed that his vision for achieving a peaceful solution had begun to take shape, despite Dulles's remarks at the press conference of the 13th that had infuriated him. Eden hoped that SCUA would reinternationalise control of the Canal, securing the free passage of ships but more specifically the transit of oil to Western Europe. By uniting the users of the Canal into an association he believed that more pressure could be exerted on Nasser at least to share control of the waterway. If the Egyptian leader remained intransigent, Eden believed that the Association could deprive him of transit dues by refusing to pay the Egyptian authority for the use of the Canal. Egypt needed the revenue from the Canal to survive, and Nasser had promised his people that the nationalisation of the Canal and the consequent money collected would pay for the Aswan Dam. Egypt was already facing financial difficulties before the expropriation of the Canal, meaning that further reduction of revenue would be felt much harder. Macmillan estimated that Egypt 'was probably in external deficit to the tune of £4m. a month just before the incident, and it was not likely that as much as one-third of this was covered by Iron Curtain arms credits, &c.'[91] Eden and the Government hoped that Egypt, financially crippled and politically weakened, would turn on its leader. This was more likely because the country had already shown itself to be unstable after the coup of 1952 and then Nasser's own removal of General

Mohammed Neguib in 1954.[92] MI6 'had good information that there were elements in Cairo ready to rise against Nasser', which suggested that if the political equilibrium could be unsettled by internal economic pressures, which were the results of empty promises, conditions might stimulate another coup.[93] The British had developed a working draft for the design of SCUA and so Eden believed that he had a chance of reinternationalising the Canal if he could gain acceptance of this idea by the Canal users themselves.

Eden knew Britain needed American support, despite Dulles's apparent duplicity, but his view had been severely tested. The Prime Minister's distress was then compounded by Nasser's speech of 15 September. The Egyptian leader had described SCUA as 'an association for waging war', whilst also condemning the British and French by suggesting that Egypt was defending herself against 'international thuggery and imperialism'. Such was the Prime Minister's anger at the speech that he ordered the document to be circulated for the next Egypt Committee meeting.[94] The next day, frustrated, he asked Lord Reading if it would be possible to 'mobilise Jewish opinion to help us take a firm line'.[95] However, this attempt to exert pressure on the US Government through the Jewish lobby did not represent an attempt to develop a separate policy and was not tried again.

There remained the possibility, as Dixon suggested, that the British could 'well complain to the Security Council on the basis that Egypt was in default under the 1888 Convention and was denying right of free passage'.[96] Eden was again interested in this proposal, and in the Egypt Committee meeting of 17 September, after discussion with the Foreign Secretary, and keen to maintain as much of an upper hand as possible, he suggested taking the initiative and referring the issue to the Security Council. Although he held hopes for a powerful SCUA, he now turned to any forum that offered the possibility of reinternationalisation without force. He hoped that 'this action would avoid giving the impression that the issue had only been referred to the United Nations as a result of outside pressure', and thus strengthen the position that the Opposition had challenged in the previous Commons debate.

Yet, once again, Eden still had to present a united front with the Americans as well as other maritime states. As Lloyd reported:

> It would be desirable... first, to reach agreement with the United States Secretary of State about the setting up of the proposed co-operative association of Suez Canal users, so that the transit dues which were at present being paid by American shipping companies in Egypt, were denied to the Egyptian authorities. Secondly, the timing of such a reference would need to take account of the risk that the Scandinavian countries might withhold support for the proposed co-operative association, pending the outcome of any reference to the Security Council.[97]

Eden feared that he did not know how SCUA would fare because 'many of the countries have got cold feet'. He believed his attempts to develop SCUA were beginning to have a destabilising effect in Egypt. Nasser had openly condemned the association. Perturbed by the apparent solidarity of the Western powers and the possibility of the issue going to the Security Council, the Egyptians sent a letter of remonstration to the President of the Security Council.[98]

Continued reports came in from Makins that Dulles's attitude had not changed and that his principal aim still remained 'to secure the maximum possible support for the Users' Association, with particular reference to Eastern countries'. Makins was concerned that Eden might be put off by the increased press speculation in the US, concerning Dulles's intentions. He remarked: 'The press here continues to be very sloppy, and the State Department have not been very successful in guiding it. I hope you are not paying too much attention to it.'[99] Makins then sent a statement from Dulles, concerning US aims in the Suez dispute, to the Foreign Office, outlining both his and Eisenhower's position with regard to SCUA. The tone was set by the initial statement that 'The United States is dedicated to seeking by peaceful means assurance that the Suez Canal will carry out the international purpose to which it is dedicated by the convention of 1888.' He listed three main points, beginning: 'Let me make certain things quite clear.' However, the overall tone reflected a resolution towards taking a firmer line:

1. The United States is dedicated to seeking by peaceful means assurance that the Suez Canal will carry out the international purpose to which it is dedicated by the convention of 1888.
2. We are not, however, willing to accept for ourselves nor do we seek from other nations acceptance of an operating regime for the Canal which falls short of recognizing the rights granted to Canal users by the 1888 convention.
3. We are not trying to organize any boycott of the Canal but we cannot be blind to the fact that conditions might become such that transit through the Canal is impractical or greatly diminished. There must always be ways to assure the movement of vital supplies particularly oil, to Western Europe.

Accordingly we are carrying out planning as a prudent precaution but our hope remains that satisfactory operating arrangements can be worked out with Egypt.

At London we will consider developments since the conference on the Suez adjourned August 23 and I hope, find a common approach to the future.[100]

Once again, Anglo-American goals appeared united and Eden could realistically hope that US pressure would yield the results he wanted without force.

The US had given a sharp directive, apparently giving 'teeth' to SCUA by promoting the defence of the Canal users' rights under the original treaty of passage. The Prime Minister could take heart from this support and the potential of the forthcoming Second London Conference to mobilise similar support, and hence pressure on Nasser.

On 18 September, Dulles flew to London for the conference. That night Macmillan dined with him at the American Embassy, and again showed his resilience and intention. Dulles's attitude towards the conference had showed hope for the Government who were now thinking in similar terms. This was an opportunity to unite Anglo-American aims:

> Foster Dulles, Lord Salisbury, the Ambassador and I had a long talk after dinner. We did our best to convince Dulles of the need to take a very firm line. But I purposely did not divert his attention from the great political issues by introducing the question of American money support, either by loan or aid. For to do so assumes that we have given up the idea of using the Canal (either by force or negotiation) and accepting the need to go round the Cape. It is vital that the Americans should not think that we are weakening, in spite of the Socialist Opposition and the other defeatist elements here.[101]

Despite appearing in tune with the Americans, the Government was keen not to appear, to its international audience, too inflexible. It was not apparent, to those outside of the decision-makers, that Eden had been pushing so hard to find a peaceful solution to the crisis, while maintaining British dignity and interests. His attempts to present a strong threat to Egypt had convinced many that he had already decided to use force. It was therefore important that he kept the British Ambassador in Cairo informed so that he could accurately help in any discussions or as an adviser to future negotiation. However, it was also important that not too much information was imparted and that Nasser did not understand the reality of the Anglo-French bluff.[102]

The French also saw the conference as 'immensely important'. But in reality, Pineau argued that 'either we got countries representing eighty per cent of the traffic going through the Canal to enter CASU (or if not to enter CASU at any rate to refuse paying dues to Nasser) or we did not'. If this was achieved then 'it was just possible that Nasser would lose enough face for us to get rid of him so to speak peacefully'. However, if this was not achieved, then, the French Foreign Minister continued,

> a very grave situation would arise. Recourse to the Security Council would (in his opinion) then be largely immaterial, except for window dressing purposes. What was material was that Nasser would clearly in the circumstances be thought to have got away with his seizure. We should

thus be left with the distressing alternative of using force or facing the fact that our two countries were 'completely finished'.[103]

This provided further pressure for the Government but Eden was pleased that HMS *Royalist* had sailed out to the Middle East, and he had 'no doubt that her presence has a strong political and stabilising effect'.[104] This was consistent with the attempt to increase the pressure on Nasser and the deterrent to any other action within the Middle East which might adversely affect British interests. In particular, he had set out the use of the *Royalist* for such a purpose as early as 4 August.[105] It also showed that the Prime Minister of New Zealand believed that Eden only had peaceful intentions for the ship because when war did eventually break out it was specifically requested by Holland that the *Royalist* should not be involved.

On 19 September the second international conference opened in London, a further attempt to unite the maritime powers against Nasser by adopting some sort of a SCUA or developing other means of peacefully reinternationalising the Canal. The eighteen nations that had endorsed the proposals of the First London Conference, and convened the Menzies Mission, met at Lancaster House. Thirteen of the countries sent their Foreign Ministers, which Lloyd, who had been elected chairman, believed meant that '[o]ur friends were taking the SCUA proposals seriously'.[106]

Dulles made a very firm speech, outlining his proposal for a users' club:

> We all want a world in which force is not used. True, but that is only one side of the coin. If you have a world in which force is not used, you have also got to have a world in which a just solution of problems of this sort can be achieved. I do not care how many words are written into the Charter of the United Nations about not using force; if in fact there is not a substitute for force, and some of these problems, inevitably the world will fall back again into anarchy and into chaos.[107]

In his statement at the First Plenary Session of the Conference he continued:

> The operation of the Suez Canal is a highly complicated, intricate affair. It offers infinite possibilities of covert violation and the practice, in obscurity, of preferences and discriminations. Lack of efficiency can be a grave hazard. It is against risks of this kind that the users can and I believe should, protect themselves in the exercise of their rights under the 1888 Treaty. The economic wellbeing of many nations and peoples is at stake, and there are no adequate sanctions against the dangers I describe.[108]

Lloyd believed, quite reasonably, 'that we were at one again'.[109] On the same day Trevelyan sent an appraisal of Nasser's position to London.

He began positively: 'The internal situation remains quiet. There is no evidence of unrest or of any excitement or anti-foreign feeling on the part of the general population. Nor, on the other hand, are there any signs of new enthusiasm for Nasser and his policies. The Press is as regimented as ever.' However, while there was a shortage of 'imported foodstuffs and other imported consumer goods' there was 'no apparent shortage of essential foodstuffs'. Small traders were suffering from an increased number of bankruptcies, and note circulation had risen, 'presumably a symptom of slight inflationary pressure'. In summary, 'though many traders are suffering, the financial restrictions have apparently not yet made any significant impact on the country's economy'. Looking politically, 'Nasser was obdurate and defiant... and has shown no signs of being willing to compromise'. However, there were 'indications that he [Nasser] is disturbed' by the initiative to form SCUA and

> has been trying to dissuade the Pakistanis from joining it... Nasser's line is still to offer negotiation without commitment while avoiding any incident which might be treated as provocation by the Western Powers... Meanwhile, propaganda against the Western Powers and C.A.S.U. continues and much is made of the alleged success of the Canal Authority in keeping the convoys going after the disappearance of the foreign pilots. This is hailed as a defeat of an attempt by the French and ourselves to sabotage the Canal.[110]

Nasser's fears supported Eden's belief in SCUA as a tool for bringing about a peaceful solution to the crisis. However, economic sanctions had not had the desired effect, to date, and needed to be increased to induce a settlement along the line that the Prime Minister consistently envisaged.

By 20 September, the pressure from the press was beginning to take its toll on the Prime Minister, but *The Times* and Iverach McDonald, although depressed by SCUA's apparent weakening, were buoyed by Eden's faith in the Users' Association and continued to back the Prime Minister's attempt to win a peaceful settlement. Eden remained hopeful. Talking alone with Macmillan, after a meeting on defence expenditure, he was unsure how it would go but 'it seems that Foster Dulles is doing his best to get it [SCUA] started'.[111] But he agreed with Clark that he should continue to rally support for the Users' Association, and he went on to say, that 'if we can make the clause on payment dues effective... it will be just worth while'.[112] This was just one of the sticking points between the British and American Governments over the working of SCUA. Eden hoped, as he believed Dulles had maintained at SCUA's conception on 7 September, that the dues from the Canal would be paid into a separate Users' Association bank account, rather than directly to the Egyptian Government. Withholding this money from Nasser would exert pressure on the Egyptians and therefore Eden could put more faith in the potential of SCUA to force the reinternationalisation of the Canal.[113]

On the same day, the Second London Conference drew to a conclusion. It resulted in the representatives of the eighteen governments believing that the proposals that had originated from the First London Conference and had been presented to Nasser by the Menzies Mission, 'still offer a fair basis for a peaceful solution of the Suez Canal problem, taking into account the interests of the user nations as well as those of Egypt'.[114] They were adamant that they would 'continue their efforts to obtain such a settlement'. The Conference delegates then approved the founding of a Suez Canal Users Association, which they saw as 'designed to facilitate any steps which might lead to a final or provisional solution of the Suez Canal problem'.[115] However, the users' proposal proved a more emasculated version than Eden favoured. In short, the Conference adopted the American vision of a users' association. Of particular concern was the fact that users of the Canal were not compelled to pay their dues to SCUA. In addition, Eden's frustration increased because the Association would only be established 'after the Delegates to this Conference have had an opportunity to consult... with their respective Governments'.[116] Clark, who along with Eden had been excited by the possibility of a peaceful solution, concluded, it had been a 'ghastly day with all the worst expectations turning up. Dulles pulled rug after rug from under us, and watered down the Canal Users' Association... till it was meaningless. Tony Moore (of the Foreign Office) came in halfway through the afternoon almost in tears about the whole thing – how could we prevent it all seeming a total disaster.'[117] It was Dulles's deliberately slow pace which 'pulled the rug' from under the British efforts to induce a solution along the lines they envisioned. The longer that he delayed any action the more likely Nasser's control of the Canal would become accepted by international opinion but still continue to threaten the free passage of ships, particularly the carriage of oil, to Western Europe. In addition, the Conference had devised a users' association which did not press members to pay transit dues to an account outside of Egypt. This emasculated the British vision for SCUA but confirmed the US view. British reaction was evidence of how little the British understood the US vision. They had hoped that the withdrawal of the payment of dues would have been a strong economic sanction against Egypt which could have forced the reinternationalisation of the Canal.

In a letter to Lloyd, Dulles confirmed the slow speed at which proceedings were moving, describing 'the steps that will be taken with our Treasury officials and with the representatives of owners of American flag vessels... with a view to perfecting this cooperation in terms of actual operating practices'.[118] Dulles believed that ten days should be allowed for the eighteen countries to join SCUA before a move to the Security Council.[119] Eden, still a firm believer in the broader potential of the Users' Club, needed a quicker move to demonstrate to Nasser, his own party and the British public that he was not vacillating but continuing to develop a solution to the crisis. The Prime Minister and Dulles had discussed 'setting up a very secret working party... in London to consider continued economic and political means of weakening and lessening the prestige of the regime of Colonel Nasser'.[120] On the 21st, Dulles and Lloyd decided to 'take the matter up immediately'.[121] However, the purpose of such a group was unclear. The Conference had concluded that 'recourse should be had to the United Nations [Security Council] whenever it seems that this would facilitate a settlement'.[122] Eden had put off any representation to the UN, but now, as his possibilities decreased, he had 18-Power backing of a move to take the issue to the Security Council. However, such a decision was not easy to make because of the implications, most notably the possible Soviet veto and American resistance.[123] Nevertheless, the option had been given serious credence and support by the very authority that Eden had believed would derive a peaceful solution to the crisis.

During the period from 10 to 21 September the US and Britain tried unsuccessfully to find common grounds from which to settle the crisis. Despite Cabinet scepticism, Eden believed in the potential of a powerful duescollecting SCUA to reinternationalise the Canal and exert enough economic pressure on Egypt to destabilise the country and bring about Nasser's downfall. However, Dulles, still convinced of Britain's warlike intentions, offered his Users' Club as a way of distracting Eden's Government from what he believed to be their true intent: war with Egypt. In reality, as the US Deputy Under Secretary of State, Murphy revealed, 'If John Foster Dulles ever was actually convinced of the possibility of organizing a Canal Users Association to operate the Suez Canal, I was not aware of it.'[124] Murphy was clearly talking about a British SCUA. Yet Eden remained unaware of Dulles's true motivation and continued to back the Users' Association. The Secretary of State's extending of discussions over SCUA infuriated Eden, but was not enough to dissuade the Prime Minister from his belief in the Association's potential for reinternationalising the Canal. Anglo-French relations had become increasingly tense because the French were impatient for Britain to join them in a war against Nasser. Nevertheless, Eden did not yet commit himself to a military solution, particularly since the suggestion of a powerful SCUA had begun to stimulate Nasser's fears. The Prime Minister had also tried to evaluate the chances of a solution by other methods. In particular, he had begun to show an interest in his own immediate reaction on 26 July, which he had quickly shelved, of taking the issue to the UN. This idea had been given further credence by recent public pressure and the conclusions of the Second London Conference. He had almost conceded to taking this line because of the opposition calls to formally deny charges of warmongering. He had played down the importance of the military preparations, delaying the possibility of the implementation of any action. However, the time Dulles had spent deliberating over the specifics of SCUA had led to public charges of vacillation. Yet the Secretary of State had represented the Americans at the Second London Conference, ensuring the creation of SCUA, which could lead to a solution of the crisis. Seeds of doubt had been sown in the Prime Minister's mind over Dulles's intentions and Eden had been disappointed by the structure of the Users' Association. Nevertheless, he continued to follow the American lead in a venture which appeared, but only appeared, to mirror his own proposed peaceful solution to the crisis.

4
Mounting Pressure: 22 September–3 October

SCUA, American Indifference and the Decision to go to the UN

During the period from 22 September to 3 October Eden continued to search for a peaceful solution to the crisis. The pressures of the crisis accentuated his vacillation. He became increasingly reliant on advice, mentally weakened by the effects of nine weeks of crisis management. Any attempts at negotiation from a position of strength were worthless in the long term, without much clearer international condemnation of Nasser's actions. Trapped, particularly by a benign and intransigent American approach, Eden had struggled to follow the US lead in divining a solution to the crisis.[1] Wary of appearing indifferent and inactive he searched for an answer, still maintaining belief in SCUA's potential, but needing a more immediate initiative to show his strength in the process of resolving the crisis. A move to the UN Security Council could peacefully reverse the nationalisation of the Canal by uniting broader international pressure against Nasser. It would also be a popular move in Britain, where it received 81 per cent support in a popular opinion poll.[2] In the face of mounting pressure from the public and Opposition, the Prime Minister, fearful of the reaction to the apparent vacillation and demise of the British vision of SCUA, and the failure of the Menzies Mission, had to decide whether he was prepared to take the issue to the Security Council or whether he could still coax a solution out of American assistance.

In a letter to Churchill, the Prime Minister reluctantly admitted that his strategy might have to change, diverging from the American line because of frustration with their impotence: 'firm is even more important than united. Foster assures me that U.S. is as determined to deal with Nasser as we are – but I fear that he has a mental caveat about November 6th. We cannot accept that.'[3] November 6th was the day of the American presidential elections and Eden believed that their delay was indicative of their lack of belief in SCUA. This was reinforced by Iverach McDonald's information that, 'Norman Robertson, the Canadian High Commissioner, had confided ... that Dulles had only produced the users' plan because' he believed that Britain and France would invade Egypt if Nasser rejected the proposals presented by the Menzies Mission.[4] It also reflected Eden's lack of faith in Dulles's offer of reimplementing OMEGA's covert political and economic destabilisation of Nasser's regime. Macmillan's frightening of Dulles into thinking that the invasion force was about to set sail, had led the Secretary of State to offer the American proposal for the Users' Association as a solution but determined that it would be an empty promise with which he could keep the British in line until after Eisenhower's re-election. Nevertheless, Eden still believed the Users' Association lay at the centre of any solution of the crisis. Consequently, he might have to abandon following the American lead, although only in the short term by going to the UN to gain wider support for SCUA which had been American in origin.

While Dulles had surprised Eden with his initial suggestion of SCUA, a false mirror of the Prime Minister's vision for a solution, Eden now realised that he would have to make SCUA work on his own.[5] Thus, despite US reservations, Eden saw the need to go to the UN to gain international support and validity for SCUA, whilst also exerting international pressure on Nasser.[6] Even without full American support, the Prime Minister still had international backing for reinternationalising the Canal. The London Conference had backed an initiative to the UN, 'whenever it seems that this would facilitate a settlement'.[7] Increasingly concerned by his own intransigence and its public perception, the Prime Minister wrote to Lloyd, expressing the need to take the issue to the UN: 'I agree strongly with you that it must be called together early next week, even if only for a preliminary meeting. Otherwise we shall appear to drift – and in fact be drifting.'[8] Eden added the last sentence by hand, stressing his personal concerns beyond the private secretary's draft.

The move to the UN had been gestating in Eden's mind since 26 July, but he was reluctant to play this card.[9] He remained adamant that a solution to the crisis should be sought within the parameters of the 1888 Convention, and placed some hope in the Conference's conclusion that the proposals of the First London Conference offered the basis for a resolution of the crisis.[10] In addition, pressure increased from the French. Pineau, in London for the Conference, 'seemed almost on the edge of dissolving the alliance'.[11] Eden told him, on his visit to Number 10, of the decision to go to the UN, well aware of France's objections to the move.[12] To keep Pineau 'sweeter' Eden agreed to visit Paris for talks on 26 September and made the UN *demarche* public.[13] However, this represented very little in terms of a commitment to the French policy which hoped to use force, because as Sir Patrick Reilly, the number two in the British Embassy in Paris, recalled, the meeting had been 'arranged *before* Nasser nationalised the Canal'.[14] Moshe Dayan, the Israeli Chief of Staff, believed that Pineau had told Eden that France might act alone, invading Egypt, and might even be aided by Israel. Eden replied that he was not opposed to this plan as long as Israel did not attack Jordan.[15] Yet

Eden was unaware of the extent of the planning and links developing between the French and the Israelis. Such was his stance over the crisis, that Dayan thought the attitude of Britain gave Israel cause for concern should she be involved in a military operation with the French. The Israeli Prime Minister, David Ben-Gurion was suspicious of Britain for the same reasons.[16] The French Military had been consistently suspicious that Britain was uncommitted to deciding upon the use of force.[17] There was no real sense of what Britain would do, so Pineau hoped to twist Eden's arm on the 26th in favour of force. A move to the UN would avoid war and Eden began to see the potential to use it to secure support for SCUA which, despite the US having refused to give SCUA the power Eden thought necessary, still offered the clearest possibility of pressuring Nasser into relinquishing control of the Canal.

Such were the pressures on Eden, particularly from American intransigence and the French, that he had written to Churchill on 21 September. The Prime Minister constantly needed private and selected sounding-boards, as both Hayter and Powell recalled.[18] The latter two were chosen to be talked *to* rather than to gain advice. With Churchill it was potentially different because Eden had always revered the former Prime Minister. Churchill had always acted as a sounding-board for Eden but there had only been limited contact between the two in mid- to late 1956, and his letters to the 'Old Man' had conveyed information, rather than personal sentiment. Eden had been keen to show his independence from Churchill by refusing to employ him in the election campaign of 1955.[19] He had tried to limit their meetings, although he had always admired Churchill's political awareness. Churchill's bodyguard, Edmund Murray, recalled that:

> Prior to his taking over the reins of power, Sir Anthony had been a most frequent visitor to wherever Sir Winston was staying. As Foreign Secretary, Sir Anthony always seemed to be hanging on to every word Sir Winston uttered... At parties and similar gatherings he would invariably leave whoever he was talking to and make straight for Sir Winston when the latter appeared on the scene. When he became Prime Minister... the visits seemed to stop abruptly.[20]

Public meetings between the two were deliberately limited. However, after the nationalisation of the Canal, he had 'much to tell' Churchill.[21] A link had been reopened that Eden would gradually tap more and more as the crisis mounted. In the end, this proved a dangerous move because Churchill began to back an aggressive line, consistent with his hardline imperial beliefs, and Eden believed that Churchill still held sway with the public.[22] The former Prime Minister's own reaction to Nasser's actions was to stand firm and potentially aggressive: 'Personally, I think that France and England ought to act together with vigour, and if necessary with arms, while America watches Russia vigilantly. I do not think that the Russians have any intention of being involved in a major war. We could secure our rights in the Arab world, and France has every reason to resent Nasser's attitude and action in Algeria.'[23] This appeared in line with Eden's own reaction. However, Churchill's doctor, Lord Moran, recorded in his diary how Churchill was so angered by Nasser's actions that he was prepared to sacrifice Anglo-American co-operation, and potentially relations, forcefully to remove the Egyptian leader:

Winston is very angry about Nasser's seizure of the Suez Canal.

Moran:	'Nasser is not the kind of man to keep his job for long?'
Winston:	'Whoever he is he's finished after this. We can't have that malicious swine sitting across our communications.' (He said this with something of his old vehemence.) 'I saw Anthony on Monday. I know what they are going to say. Anthony asked me to treat it as a matter of confidence.'
Moran:	'What will the Americans do?'
Winston snapped:	'We don't need the Americans for this.'
Moran:	'Will you speak in the House?'
Winston:	'I might. I shall dictate something and see how it goes.'[24]

However, after the debate in the House, in which he did not speak, Churchill was satisfied with the Government's line: 'The French are very sporting and it is nice to feel they are working with us, and that we and the Americans are both agreed. We have taken a line which will put the Canal effectively on its international basis, and will also make it secure until long after 1968.'[25] That his summary reported apparent Anglo-American solidarity reaffirmed that Eden had not decided to use force, because it was a reaction that the US could not and did not condone.

Eden had convened a committee to deal with the situation in Egypt, just as Churchill had in 1953. He had sided with the French and brought the Americans in, as the latter had suggested in a letter to his wife of 30 July.[26] In fact, Eden's letter to Eisenhower of the following day appeared to mirror Churchill's sentiment. This has confused the understanding of Eden's intentions during the crisis, suggesting a continuity and similarity of purpose to Churchill's aggressive imperialism.[27] However, the divergence in the opinion of the two men, as to the ultimate use of force, was reflected in Lady Churchill's reply of 1 August to her husband. There was a fear from the more aggressively minded that 'A.E. will wait for America who for the third time will arrive on the scene very late.' She went on to implore Winston: 'I hope you may be able to influence him.'[28] Yet, for all his dislike of Nasser, Eden waited, hoping that the Egyptian leader would be brought down from within. Churchill was ready, and had always been ready, to send troops into Egypt, as Shuckburgh had noted in his diary in 1953.[29] As Prime Minister he had hoped to bring American troops into Egypt, but now out of power and lost in 'reminiscences' of imperial control he advocated ignoring the US and sending an invasion force to capture the Canal.[30]

Macmillan seized on this as another opportunity to try and pressure Eden into using force. As Foreign Secretary, Macmillan had endorsed the practice of sending Foreign Office telegrams to Churchill. Sir Anthony Montague-Browne, Churchill's private secretary during his premiership, had returned to the Foreign Office after Churchill's resignation but went to see him 'two or three days a week', helping 'him with his immense correspondence' and bringing him 'a selection of Foreign telegrams'. These were part of the 'small attentions' that Macmillan was able to pay Churchill, for which '[h]e was very grateful'.[31] The practice continued throughout the crisis, with the number of telegrams increasing. Churchill's bodyguard confirmed that '[a]lthough, by then, he had been retired for well over a year, he was still closely in touch with things, and Foreign Office dispatches were still being delivered to him in ever-increasing numbers as the crisis deepened'.[32] Maintaining his favour, Macmillan urged him to influence Eden. On 5 August, Macmillan dined with Churchill at Chartwell. Talking with both his host and Christopher Soames, Churchill's son-in-law and Under-Secretary at the Air Ministry, about the contingency plan, Macmillan said that 'unless we brought in Israel, I don't think it could be done'.[33] Churchill agreed 'with all this' and decided to go to Chequers on the 6th to 'put all the results of our talk and his own thoughts before Eden'. Macmillan, realising the importance of Churchill to Eden but also of Eden's own pride, recorded, '[n]ow the fat will be in the fire'.[34] Murray recalled that Churchill was

> [s]o perturbed... by the course that events were taking that he made a special, secret trip to Chequers to talk things over with the Prime Minister... All the way there from Chartwell, a secretary sat beside him in the back of the car with a typewriter on her knees, making last minute notes. This was a procedure only followed in the most important circumstances.[35]

The need for Macmillan to use Churchill and Churchill's own concerns suggested that Eden had shown no definite commitment to the use of force to settle the crisis.

Such was Churchill's desire to convey his attitude to the Prime Minister that he set off on the next day, 6 August, from his home at Chartwell to Chequers. His haste meant that he had to take his secretary with him to transcribe his thoughts and the car had to pull in to a lay-by so that she could type out a finished copy for Eden. 'Awfully pleased' with his 'little note',

Churchill presented it to the Prime Minister.[36] It pressed Eden, threatening him with the possibility of further Soviet incursions into Egypt.[37] He also posed the 'Israeli question': 'On the other side a volte face should certainly free our hands about Israel. We should want them to menace and hold the Egyptians and not be drawn off against Jordan.'[38] Shuckburgh remembered that this was not a new idea for Churchill who had often advocated some type of co-operation with Israel.[39] In 1953, Churchill had 'growl[ed]' at Eden: 'Tell them [the Egyptians] that if we have any more of their cheek we will set the Jews on them and drive them into the gutter, from which they should never have emerged.'[40] Eden was particularly angered by Churchill's interference, although Macmillan believed that Eden was beginning to agree with Macmillan's, and therefore Churchill's, views.[41] However, this reflected the Prime Minister's acceptance of the new, more flexible, military plan, not the favouring of siding with the Israelis. Shuckburgh believed that co-operation with Israel 'was entirely contrary to everything I had ever been brought to believe was Anthony Eden's policy'.[42] Macmillan continued to meet with Churchill.[43] However, their relationship remained 'quite different' from that of Eden and Churchill and threatened to continue pressuring Eden toward the use of force.

Churchill had never been an advocate of the complete withdrawal from the Canal Base in 1954.[44] Macmillan, while he had approved of this move, was now inciting Churchill to influence Eden by playing on Britain's weakness derived from her withdrawal of troops from Egypt.[45] Churchill believed that Eden had brought the problem on himself, having organised the 'scuttle', and had no problem in telling him so.[46] He also enjoyed the semi-official nature of his task, having never been able to fully reconcile himself with his resignation in 1955. By 16 September, Churchill was much depressed by the situation: 'I don't like the way things are going...I want our people to take up a strong point on the Canal with a few troops and to say to Nasser: "We'll get out when you are sensible about the Canal"...I am afraid we are going downhill.'[47] Thus, by the time that Eden voiced his concerns to Churchill, the latter was frustrated and favoured a military solution, backed by Israel. It was only after the failure of the military operation that he declared, 'I would never have dared to do it without squaring the Americans.'[48] This mix of emotion and the fact that Churchill no longer held any direct power made him a destabilising influence on an already tired and potentially ill Eden. In spite of Churchill's aggressive attitude, the Prime Minister had not decided to use force.

By Saturday, 22 September, Clark reported that Eden was getting very 'tetchy indeed'. He had gone to Chequers for a working week-end, increasingly worried by press criticism, ringing Clark 'in a great state about something in the press (I forget what)'.[49] Pressure was mounting, not least from *The Daily Telegraph* which Eden continued to see as indicative of Conservative Party opinion.[50] To make matters worse, McDonald had made some criticism of

Eden's policy to Clark who had passed the concern on to the Prime Minister.[51] 'Challenged' by his confidant, it was a real blow for Eden, at a time when his vanity was under threat from all quarters. McDonald described him as seeming 'very tired and piano'.[52] Signs of the Prime Minister's mental and physical weakening were beginning to show.

Eden had rung Lloyd that morning to 'put to him his view that the Suez Canal dispute should be referred to the Security Council'.[53] The timing of such a move was not an easy decision for Eden. He now firmly believed, after consultation with representatives of a number of different countries, that the ability to maximise the membership of SCUA would be enhanced if Britain immediately and publicly announced her intention to go to the UN. He considered that the London Conference had been indefinite on this point, 'no doubt in deference to the United States'. A telegram to Macmillan reflected the doubts and fears surfacing in Eden's mind. As the Chancellor was in the US, and therefore in a position to make a more direct and personal appeal to US Government officials, the telegram was also a direct attempt to secure American support for wider payment of Canal dues away from Nasser, increasing SCUA's potential to bring about a peaceful solution:

> SCUA is widely held here to be more feeble in its plan for execution than was expected. This includes the subject of dues, where the United States has supported us as to their own payments. It would be good if they could follow this up with Panama and Liberia, who pay more. The truth is SCUA has been much watered down from its original conception.[54]

Eventually, according to Nutting, Eden 'was persuaded by Lloyd's arguments' to take the issue to the Security Council.[55] Eden told McDonald that '[w]hat finally decided the Government was their realization that the Users' Club was not going to have its first meeting until October 1 and would take some time to establish itself. [He] realized that public opinion was drifting badly and there was a need to pull it together.'[56] This assessment was supported by Eden's earlier fears over public opinion and the public popularity of taking the issue to the UN.[57] The decision was made and a telegram sent to the Americans and French outlining the initiative and reflecting Eden's and the Government's fears. There was a need to explain to Dulles why the British were going to the Security Council because of his reticence to back the move. Britain had to placate him, maintaining the possibility of any form of American support. It was suggested that the Soviets were also thinking of going to the UN and thus there was need to get in first. It was also thought that the British indecisiveness on the issue of whether to go to the UN, which had recently been fuelled by Dulles's disapproval, should be conveyed to Washington, along with notification that the President of the Security Council had been asked to convene a meeting for the next Wednesday,

26 September.[58] Again, this demonstrated the need for Britain to align herself with the US and keep that government informed.

However, Makins reported that Dulles had not had time to consider the move. The State Department asked the British Government to postpone her action until Dulles had 'had an opportunity to consider the question properly': '[W]e have been conducting the whole operation in common, and [Dulles] simply would not understand being faced with this at such short notice.' Makins was in complete agreement with the State Department's sentiments.[59] Dulles himself 'feared immediate recourse to the Council would make some of the 18 (notably Iran, Pakistan and Ethiopia and perhaps also Sweden and Denmark) hesitate to join S.C.U.A. until they saw how things go in the United Nations'.[60] Further pressure to halt the move came from Henry Cabot Lodge, the US Permanent Representative to the UN. In talks with the British representative, Sir Pierson Dixon, Lodge considered that there was no sense in the US that the Soviets were about to take the issue to the UN and he believed that Britain ought to 'figure our way through' before starting a Security Council operation.[61] After consultation, the Prime Minister and Foreign Secretary decided to postpone any decision until 3 p.m. the next day, to give Dulles a 'reasonable opportunity to comment on our proposed action'.[62] At 2:30 p.m. on the 23rd Lloyd decided to extend the postponement until 5 p.m., to 'enable certain posts abroad to be informed of the plans before the public announcement', and it was hoped that the Security Council would be called together for 3 October.[63]

Many observers have seen the move to the UN as an empty gesture.[64] Eden saw the UN as a much needed opportunity to unite public opinion, as well as world political condemnation and support against Nasser.[65] The decision not to rely on the newly created SCUA reflected Eden's diminished hopes for the Users' Association as formulated under American terms, but he still expected US support in the UN. Dulles had warned, through Makins, that he could not be a co-sponsor of the move to the UN because 'we might later find them [the US] applying the brakes in a way which would embarrass you and M. Pineau'.[66] While this contradicted Dulles's own earlier remarks, Eden believed that US support in the UN would preclude any need to resort to force, consistent with his belief that Dulles's ultimate goal was to make Nasser 'disgorge' control of the Canal.[67] The Prime Minister had still not decided to use force to end the crisis.

The Prime Minister wanted a firm and speedy resolution to the crisis but had vacillated since 26 July because he did not want to invoke a military solution. He knew that he could not induce wider support for SCUA, and hence a peaceful solution, without going to the UN. His advisers warned of the risks involved in such action. The Americans continued to appear to the British, sceptical of this move. Herman Phleger, the State Department's Chief legal adviser, warned 'that the Security Council is like a quick-sand; once one gets into it one can never be sure how deep it is or whether one will get out'. Eden had doubts about the Security Council's ability to deal with the situation but had now decided to refer the issue to the UN. Selwyn Lloyd summarised the meeting:

> M. Pineau and I should represent France and the United Kingdom and we should try to get M. Spaak whose views are particularly robust, to represent Belgium.
> We should endeavour to infuse into the debate the atmosphere of crisis. In other words that we want an expression of opinion from the Security Council within a week. It is not a question of lengthy procedural discussion.
> We should take the initiative in tabling a resolution emphasizing the seriousness of the situation and recommending the 18-Power solution.
> If our proceedings become bogged down in procedural wrangles and innumerable amendments, the Foreign Ministers should withdraw saying that the proceedings were futile and that the United Nations had shown itself incapable of dealing with the matter.
> American support should be sought for these tactics at the highest level, it being pointed out that the object of the exercise is to put us in the best possible posture internationally over the action which we propose to take, and that that is an objective which, in view of the great issues at stake, is very nearly as much to their interests as to ours.[68]

This memorandum showed the key element in Eden's attempts to induce US support. Britain was again trying to create an atmosphere of crisis and bluster, consciously developing a stance of strength, from which to negotiate, so that she could avoid the use of force. Eden maintained an unfailing resolve to seek a solution based on the 1888 Treaty of Constantinople and the 18-Power Proposals resulting from the London Conferences. Confirming this to McDonald, he believed that the move to the UN 'would open another door to the possibility of negotiation'. As McDonald remembered, Eden 'had, right from the beginning, said that he would pursue negotiation, if at all possible'.[69] It also revealed his belief in Anglo-American solidarity and demonstrated the Prime Minister's consistency, in terms of both his conduct of foreign relations and his attempts to achieve a peaceful solution to the crisis.

Pressure to maintain independence of action was beginning to mount from all sides. Sir Michael Wright, who had increasingly supported a forceful resolution, expressed the fears of Nuri-es-Said, who Eden respected and relied upon for support in the Middle East. Wright wrote to the Prime Minister on the 23 September, the telegram arriving on the 24th. Immediately the letter increased Eden's fears, attempting to entice him into action: 'Nasser has not yet been obliged to give way on anything and that unless and until he finds himself compelled to do so time is definitely on his side.' Wright continued to dampen Eden's hopes for SCUA, revealing that not only was it barely understood in Iraq, but that it was seen as standing 'for something less than the original agreement of the 18 Powers on the need for a form of international control'. The Second London Conference was perceived in Iraq 'to have shown less unanimity and less firmness than the first', and that as time goes by it would be more unlikely 'that pressure on Nasser can effectively be brought to bear'. Wright continued to encourage Eden to act aggressively and quickly, voicing his concerns that the 'Arab Powers' held 'misgivings' about Nasser. Nasser had taken his initial action over the Canal and then rejected the Menzies Mission without consultation with the other Arab states. This had put them in a difficult position with regard to the West because they might have to support him in a conflict or at the very least 'cut off the oil supplies on which their economies (but not Egypt's) depend'. This was a grave threat to the Prime Minister whose concerns over the crisis were founded on the need to maintain the free transit of oil supplies. It was also believed that Nasser's actions might expose the other Arab States 'to extreme peril from Israel', and, combined with his co-operation with the communists, was alienating Nasser from those Arab States, particularly the influential King Saud. Wright emphasised the need to move quickly because 'these misgivings rest on the assumption that the West is not prepared to let Nasser get away with it and may even use force against him. If at any point it becomes clear that their assumption is definitely false their misgivings will vanish, Nasser will have a clear field and support for him will increase.' He reported that the King of Iraq had said to him recently that 'the vital question was whether Nasser could be brought down within a short time. If not he would do irreparable harm to the Middle East.' The Crown Prince, he reiterated, considered 'that a weak compromise over Suez would prove no remedy to the situation'. Nuri also 'thought that time was working in favour of Nasser'. Wright concluded, by offering an estimate of the effects if Nasser 'won the game'.[70] Of particular concern to Eden, and sidelined by him, was the re-emphasised possibility that the Egyptian leader would deny Middle Eastern oil to the West. This was consistent with his fears prevalent in all his dealings with the Middle East and voiced to Cabinet on 27 July.[71]

Trevelyan's telegram of 24 September reinforced Sir Michael Wright's assessment that Nasser was not losing ground internally.[72] Because of its late arrival at the Foreign Office, 10:37 p.m., Eden did not see it until the 25th but marked it as 'urgent' for the Cabinet Meeting of the 26th. Trevelyan went further than Wright in his assessment but was much calmer with his suggested action. His latest information showed that, since the Second London Conference, 'Nasser has gained ground especially among the young'. They were, he continued, 'impressed by the new boast in the official Press that Nasser has wiped the eye of the "Imperialists"'. Eden was particularly concerned by Trevelyan's opinion that '[f]ew seem to realise that Nasser is getting less than half the dues'. The Prime Minister was concerned by the Egyptians' perceptions of SCUA which exacerbated his own fears:

SCUA is regarded as having lost its teeth at birth and as being virtually only a body to negotiate with Nasser. Time is not on our side if the situation is stabilised in its present condition, but the balance may well shift with any clear sign that Nasser has not won the game, such as if the mass of the population really begin to suffer at home or if defections from support of Egypt develop in the Arab world.[73]

Trevelyan's view attempted to counter the aggressive sentiment espoused by Sir Michael Wright.[74] However, inadvertently, Trevelyan increased the pressure on Eden. Having suggested that the Egyptian leader's popularity and standing had increased, he did not provide a solution. Wright had argued that the best way of maintaining or possibly increasing Arab disillusion with Nasser was to act ruthlessly and immediately against Egypt. The Prime Minister had spent the previous eight weeks avoiding this solution but he believed that his options were narrowing if he was to achieve a solution in accordance with the 1888 Treaty and the resolution of the First London Conference. There was, however, no suggestion that he had decided to use force.

On 24 September, such was the Prime Minister's apparent frustration and Macmillan's scaremongering, that the Minister of Defence, Walter Monckton, the most vocal opponent of force, tendered his resignation.[75] He alleged that this was because of the increasing likelihood of Britain allying herself with the French and the Israelis against Egypt.[76] This prophetic statement, however, is unsubstantiated.[77] Eden had been strongly opposed to any links with the Israelis, fearing they would invade Jordan, who was protected under treaty by Britain. As Millard, Eden's Private Secretary, remembered:

> Throughout September and October, there was a fear that the Israelis might attack Jordan because of these border incidents. Then we would be obliged under our Treaty with Jordan to go to their aid and that would have been extremely inconvenient to say the least because it would have taken the pressure from the Canal issue. We could even have found ourselves on the same side as the Egyptians fighting the Israelis.[78]

Powell also recalled that this fear went further than the Private Office: 'Within the Ministry of Defence there was a fear that we might have to go to war against Israel.'[79] The Prime Minister's frustration frightened Monckton, who believed that Eden's mood, backed by the effect of Macmillan's fears, might lead to a forceful resolution of the crisis before all peaceful attempts had been tried.

Nasser now appeared, to both Eden and the Egypt Committee, unlikely to endanger his own position by acting foolishly. Warned by Sir Michael Wright that time was on Nasser's side, the Prime Minister believed that there were few choices left. Writing to Eden on 1 October, Monckton delayed any decision to resign until after the move to the UN had been made. Monckton explained, 'as long as we do everything we can to get a satisfactory settlement by other means first, I have never excluded the use of force in the last resort'.[80] His support for the Government's policy arose from the belief that recourse to the UN was a serious diplomatic intention. In addition, Monckton had not been forced to resign.[81] He continued to sit on the Egypt Committee and in Cabinet Meetings, even after being moved to the position of Paymaster-General on 18 October, when Eden had finally decided that force would be employed and Monckton decided to resign as Minister of Defence. Yet, as Powell believed, '[i]t was his initiative I'm sure. He certainly was not moved because he was thought to be the wrong man for the job [of Minister of Defence].'[82] Even from this position, as Eden wrote to his close friend Lewis Douglas, a former US Ambassador to Britain, Monckton continued his 'daily job of co-ordinating our publicity in the present crisis'.[83] If Monckton had been so openly against Government policy, it made no sense for him to be employed in the role of maximising the public understanding of that policy. Eden was unaware of Monckton's depth of belief.

Even a hawk like Macmillan recognised that a peaceful solution was still the policy, as he confided to his diary. He believed that '[j]udging from the telegrams and the newspapers, the situation on Suez is calming down a bit, & the general opinion growing that we have chosen the right moment to appeal to the UN. But there is still a great uncertainty as to what is to come next. Can we overcome Nasser by argument & negotiation, or shall we be driven to force?' Despite his fears, Macmillan evidenced the continued attempt by Eden to achieve a peaceful settlement of the crisis through 'argument & negotiation'. He was worried by the state of the reserves and the pressure on sterling, fearful that if the situation was not resolved quickly, the country would be 'driven to devaluation or bankruptcy'.[84] However, there is no evidence to suggest that he conveyed these financial worries to Eden. At the same time, the newspapers were publicly revealing an Anglo-American split over the decision to go to the UN. *The Daily Express* led with 'Where Does Dulles Stand?', in which it reported that Dulles had not been informed of the Anglo-French decision to go to the UN on Friday 21 September (as the Government had declared) but on Saturday 22nd, and that Dulles did not 'think it would be wise to bring it up for substantive action until the Users' Association [was] formed'.[85] *The Daily Telegraph* managed to remain positive, showing Dulles's eventual support of the move to the UN and quoting him as saying that with regard to war, '[m]aybe it will have to come to that'.[86] The press, as a whole, then offered some respite for Eden, turning its attention to the defection of a Soviet ballerina.

On 25 September, the Egypt Committee met and the order of business suggested the continued priorities. SCUA was first on the agenda and during discussion Lloyd confirmed Eden's suspicions that 'the United Kingdom would have to take the main responsibility for setting up the Association'.[87]

The Committee then turned its attention to the 'possible courses of action during the debate in the Security Council'. They wanted to take a firm line, supported by the *Daily Telegraph*, whose editorial staff believed that the proposals of the Second London Conference had provided 'A Fair Basis for Peaceful Solution'.[88] However, they realised that this would lead to an immediate veto by the Soviets. In addition, as Nasser had already rejected the 18-Power Declaration, some countries would believe that 'greater freedom of manoeuvre should be allowed'. Proposals centred around the concept of the Users' Association and the arbitrary settlement of compensation, transit dues and amounts allocated for development. Egypt would be responsible for the management of the Canal but the UN would appoint 'international supervisors' for each department of the Canal's administration. A court was also suggested, 'analogous to that in existence for the Panama Canal', to settle any disputes, and finally regular meetings were suggested for a representative body of the Canal users and the Egyptian management. The Committee members considered that the new measures

> satisfied many of the minimum requirements laid down by the Western Powers. Recognition of the Canal Users' Association by Egypt would be a valuable step forward. The proposed system for controlling the transit dues would not leave this question to the sole discretion of the Egyptian Government: it would in fact provide for tighter control than was provided for under the existing Convention. Further, Egypt would be prevented from diverting revenues received from use of the Canal for other purposes. The United Nations advisers would guarantee against discrimination and interference by the Egyptian management with the ships of particular countries. Such a scheme would, however, need some effective sanctions. Thus, it would be valuable if provision could be made that, in the event of a failure by Egypt to implement a decision by the proposed independent Court transit dues would be paid to independent trustees. Provision might also be made for the agreement to be registered with the United Nations in such a way that any continuing infringement by Egypt would constitute an act justifying the use of force under Article 51 of the United Nations Charter.[89]

While this was less potent than the Government had hoped, they believed that a settlement could be achieved but not unless some sort of qualifying threat was issued with the proposals. Again, this was consistent with the attempt to negotiate from a position of strength created by bluffing the Egyptians. At the same time the Committee members were aware of the need to keep options open. Nasser had already appeared to renege on one attempt at settlement. It was also recognised that there was a need to placate the French, particularly since their internal politics were so unstable.[90] *The Daily Telegraph* had reported that Pineau was facing trouble from within his own Cabinet.[91] More important, however, was the need to show Anglo-French unity, 'since any disagreement between France and the United Kingdom about the adoption of such a plan would certainly be represented as a victory for Colonel Nasser'.[92] To show any sign of weakness to the French at this stage could have undermined all of Eden's work. Despite the implications of siding with the French, and the consequent allegations of warmongering, solidarity against the Egyptian action remained key to the Prime Minister's attempts to resolve the crisis. He continued to promote wider international support against Nasser but it was important that Britain and France, the two countries most affected by the expropriation of the Canal, maintained their grievance.[93] If they were to appear divided in their reaction to the 'take-over', then the base from which to build wider condemnation of Egypt would be weakened. Therefore, placating and allying with the French was essential so that Eden could generate support for any specific attempt to resolve the crisis, such as SCUA, or to unify pressure on Nasser through support of the resolutions of the London conferences.

Finally the Committee turned to the contingency plan. Once decided upon, operations could now be postponed for three weeks from as late as D−4 (four days before the date of invasion) because of the new plan, 'Musketeer Revise', and the Prime Minister was keen to avoid 'taking any action before that date which could be construed as giving a definite indication of our intention to take military action'.[94] This, again, demonstrated the need to deter Nasser through the threat of force, whilst recognising the need not to disrupt any negotiation passing through the Security Council. It also represented the need to keep operations secret so that in the event of a decision to use the military, the element of surprise was maintained. Butler, Lord Privy Seal, noted on his copy of these arrangements, 'V[ery] secret seems v[ery] good'.[95] As a strong if silent dove, his agreement with these arrangements suggested that they were nothing more than contingency measures. In spite of his disillusion and earlier scepticism over British intentions, Clark conceded that

> there was... military security, that was primarily it. It was also important not to let it leak out because of a feeling that it would probably be stopped in the United Nations by the US or what have you. But there was also secrecy of a different kind. We wanted to keep Nasser guessing and it was certainly the hope, right up to the end I think, that we would not actually have to draw our sword from its sheath in order to overthrow Nasser, that if we could only seem to be threatening him, seem to be rather ominously growling round the outside of his camp, he might be overthrown by his people.[96]

It was not an attempt to conceal an increase of military activity from the Americans. US officials were informed of the contingency measures until the blackout of information which followed the decision to use force. Even after the blackout, Anglo-American military channels, particularly those of the navies, were kept open.[97] Chairman of the Joint Intelligence Committee (JIC), Patrick Dean, recalled that there was an American observer who sat on weekly JIC meetings and 'had a good deal of contact with the JIC staff in the Ministry of Defence'.[98] In addition, what would actually constitute the final plans was still in doubt with the politicians, as well as the military.[99] This was a further suggestion that a plan to use force had not been decided upon, paralleled with the increase in diplomatic efforts to determine a peaceful solution. On 10 September, it had been agreed to change the terms of reference of the Egypt (Official) Committee, making it the official counterpart of the Egypt Committee, to co-ordinate policy over the crisis. Thus, despite the apparent complexity of issues and obvious timetabling pressure, the role of the Egypt Committee was reduced and it did not meet again until 1 October. It had been intended to meet on Friday, 28 September but the Prime Minister, increasingly tired, took Butler's advice and retreated to his home in Wiltshire for a long weekend.[100]

However, by the end of September Eden's diplomatic moves were reaching a stalemate.[101] Lord Home believed that '[t]he only thing that might have been done, and I think ought to have been done, would have been if Sir Anthony...had gone to see the President'.[102] Eden never wanted or tried to arrange a personal meeting with Eisenhower throughout the whole of the crisis.[103] The Government believed that Dulles directed foreign affairs and as he spent much of August and September in Britain meeting with Eden and other Government officials, they had no need to talk directly to the President. Macmillan, however, did see the President. On 20 September, the Chancellor had left for the US to attend a meeting of the International Monetary Fund (IMF). Even on the flight he said enough to suggest to David Pitblado, a former private secretary to Churchill and Eden, that 'we would have to deal with Nasser', confirming that 'he, as everybody said, was a hawk'.[104] Nevertheless, Macmillan had been sent to rally support for a united front and economic sanctions, against Nasser, from the other Commonwealth Ministers and from a short tour of the US. This remained consistent with Eden's attempts to resolve the crisis peacefully. The Prime Minister had tried to unite support against Nasser to pressure the Egyptian leader into reinternationalising the Canal. From the outset of the crisis he had attempted to induce Commonwealth opposition to Egypt, along with that from France and the US. He had then used the First London Conference to broaden this opposition, before finally deciding to make the move to the UN to develop as much support against Nasser as possible. Macmillan's mission lay within this remit reflecting a continuity in Eden's actions during the crisis, to produce a peaceful settlement.

On 25 September Macmillan was invited for a secret meeting with the President. Reminiscent of the atmosphere of his meeting with Murphy in

July he recalled that 'It was just like talking to him [Eisenhower] in the old days at the St. George Hotel in Algiers, at Allied Force [Headquarters].' However, having talked about Churchill, conversation turned to Suez: '[Eisenhower] was sure that we must get Nasser down. The only thing was, how to do it. I made it quite clear that we could *not* play it long, without aid on a very large scale – that is, if playing it long involved buying Dollar oil.' In reference to the UN, Eisenhower said that

> [w]e had created something wh[ich] was all very well as long as we could control it. But soon we might not be able to do so, even when we acted together... He was 'mad' with some of his critics. They always said what had been done wrong in the past, or made wonderful promises for the future. But they never said what ought to be done now. (That's why they were not making Suez a campaign point. Democrats had nothing to suggest.)[105]

Macmillan reported this 'half hour chat' to Eden but there were a number of conflicting reports. In his first communication he said that '[a]lthough nothing very specific emerged, I formed certain impressions, about which I will write to you. I feel sure the President understands our problems about Nasser, but he is of course in the same position as we were in May 1955.'[106] He went on to say that '[a]s usual with Ike, it was rather rambling and nothing very definite. Nevertheless, I formed certain very clear impressions.' The President was getting anxious about the election campaign. However, Macmillan believed that the most important point Eisenhower made was 'that the United Nations had destroyed the power of leadership of the great Powers, that under the cover of all these international agreements for peace, small nations like Egypt could do the most outrageous things, and that he felt that the great Powers – U.S., U.K., France and Germany – should get together to maintain order, peace and justice, as well as mere absence of armed conflict'.[107] Macmillan believed that Eisenhower understood the difficulties in 'playing it long' and 'accepted that by one means or another we much achieve a clear victory'.[108] However, Makins, who had sat through the entire conversation, was 'astounded' by its omissions: 'I was expecting Harold to make a statement, say something important on Suez – but in fact he said nothing... Nor did Ike say anything. I was amazed.'[109] Macmillan strengthened the tone of his diary in his reports to Eden, declaring that the 'next feeling I had was that Ike is really determined, somehow or other, to bring Nasser down... I explained to him our economic difficulties in playing the hand long, and he seemed to understand. I also made it clear that we *must* win, or the whole structure of our economy would collapse. He accepted this.'[110] Makins described these events as a 'failure in communication' but he already knew that the US neither could nor would consider moral or material support, much less military intervention, especially prior to the elections.[111] He had warned of this regularly and all the key British personnel, notably Eden, Macmillan and Lloyd, were aware of and had made several references to the importance of the American elections with regard to their ability to conduct policy. The British Government believed that Makins was too close to the Americans.[112] Vitally, Macmillan chastised himself for not making more of the importance of the elections to Eden, and Eden took Macmillan's reports seriously. The Prime Minister had steadily confided in 'the strong man of the Cabinet' more and more, trusting Macmillan's understanding of and liaison with the Americans, particularly as his own relationship with Dulles was so strained.[113] Macmillan was adamant that he understood the President fully, because Eisenhower 'had retained (or perhaps, regained) all his old simplicity'.[114] Eden believed Macmillan's evaluation of the US attitude, which appeared to support any method of undermining Nasser's position. Again, this was consistent with his belief in Dulles's commitment to make Nasser 'disgorge'.[115]

This was reiterated after the Chancellor met with the Secretary of State. On the same day, at 3:30 p.m., Macmillan conversed with Dulles. He was not surprised to learn of the Secretary of State's anger at the Anglo-French decision to take the issue to the Security Council but was taken aback by the intensity of Dulles's reaction: 'He really had been hurt by this action.'[116] Makins described it as 'a tense meeting...where Dulles vented his spleen'.[117] As Macmillan recalled: 'From the way Dulles spoke you would have thought he was warning us against entering a bawdy-house', but despite this reaction he later believed that he should have put more weight on Dulles's words and, in particular, the date of the presidential elections, in his advice to Eden.[118] In his telegram to the Prime Minister, Macmillan sounded particularly optimistic of US indifference, if not support: 'Some of the things he [Dulles] said were very helpful but might be dangerous to him if they got out in the electioneering atmosphere.'[119] After the general conversation, Dulles took Macmillan into his private room, kept for 'special interviews'.[120] In a note to Eden, Macmillan recorded how Dulles had gone 'on to talk about different methods of getting rid of Nasser. He thought that these new plans might prove successful.'[121] After consultation with the Chancellor, Makins remembered that these plans had been voiced at the earlier meeting and were 'in effect...a return to the OMEGA plan', whereby Nasser would be removed by the implementation of covert economic measures, or if these failed, more direct means. Dulles 'expanded further on this' in the private meeting with Macmillan 'when he indicated that the U.S. government would proceed with OMEGA after 6 November'. Yet the precise nature of the assistance that the Americans were prepared to give remained vague. Dulles continued to be deliberately evasive, as he had throughout the crisis, particularly over SCUA. He also 'warned' Macmillan that the Americans would not condone a showdown with Nasser before then [6 November]'.[122] However, Macmillan, having been told that this course would take six months, told Dulles that 'I did not think we could stand for six months, unless, of course, Nasser was losing face all the time'.[123] The British were aware, from diplomatic reports of the previous two days from Iraq and Egypt, that Nasser was not losing face but, if anything, gaining in popularity.[124] Dulles finished the private talks by hoping that peace could be preserved 'at least until Nov. 6th! But he had been careful in his broadcast to defend the vigour of Britain and France to use force, if they could not get their rights in any other way.' Then turning to Britain's economic position, he thought that, after the election, 'we should raise the question of our loan payments'.[125] At the end of the Second London Conference, on 21 September, Dulles appeared to support this policy. He had made it clear that 'it was imperative that Nasser should lose as a result of Suez'. 'War', he continued, 'would make Nasser a hero. It was better for him to "wither away".' Again, this supported his claim that OMEGA would be redeployed after the elections, and by implication Nasser would be removed, possibly by covert methods, presumably such as had been used to overthrow Mohammed Mossadegh in Iran. Thus, Macmillan's talks with Dulles reinforced the belief that ultimately the Americans wanted Nasser removed by any means.

On 26 September, the Security Council set 5 October for the British appeal and the Foreign Secretary informed the Cabinet of the results of the Second London Conference.[126] Eden and Lloyd then flew to Paris for talks. Sir Gladwyn Jebb, the British Ambassador in Paris was excluded from these private discussions, which were not attended by advisers or interpreters.[127] This promoted his suspicion and resentment of the Government's intentions. Yet, as Clark revealed in his diary, again contradicting his own earlier view of Eden's belligerence, formulated on 26 July: 'I gather since that at the meeting in Paris the French were very anxious to use force at once and the P.M. had a difficult task in persuading them to hold their hand. As a makeweight the Queen was persuaded to make a Royal visit.'[128] Lloyd recalled that

> [i]t was not an easy meeting, After a long argument we agreed that our line should be that we were prepared to listen to any proposals put forward. If Egypt still rejected the eighteen-power proposals put forward by Menzies, she should be asked to come forward with counter-proposals, but Pineau was insistent that we should not accept anything less satisfactory than the eighteen-power proposals. We discussed SCUA, its membership, organisation, headquarters and how the dues should be paid. There was then an easier discussion about European co-operation and the cleaning up of minor areas of friction between French and British policies in various parts of the world.[129]

This was substantiated by the telegram Eden sent to Butler detailing the meeting and outlining how the French were pushing hard. The level of disagreement between Britain and France, particularly over the use of force, remained high. Discussions had to continue on the following day. The French, who had been 'very disturbed at the result of the Conference', were unimpressed by the formula worked out in Cabinet and were prepared to stand by the 18-Power proposals without 'any modification of them'.[130] When they were told that there had to be some negotiations at the UN, '[t]his was received with concern'. Eventually it was agreed to work out the following four stages on the next day:

(a) the definition of a common attitude in the United Nations.
(b) willingness to act in common in certain circumstances.
(c) an effort to liquidate Franco-British difficulties.
(d) a common approach to European problems.[131]

Eden and Lloyd had already spent an hour 'in persuading the French to abandon their idea of voting against the inscription of the Egyptian item on the Security Council agenda'. Despite Mollet's own opinion that this was a folly, the French Cabinet had earlier decided on this course of action. Eventually they deferred to the British. However, as a whole they remained 'completely unimpressed as to the alleged effect of American action on Egypt' and believed 'that Dulles was now proposing...much less than he had offered in London'. Increasingly dissatisfied with the most recent London Conference, they maintained that the 'Italians were now paying all their dues to Egypt whereas previously they had paid only part of them'. The situation was deteriorating. Eden had no information to that effect. Finally, the French were adamant that the Russians were supplying reinforcements of tanks and aircraft to Egypt. Therefore, they asserted, '[e]very week that action was delayed made the military situation more dangerous for both of us'. Eden ended the telegram with a black summary of the French position and the pressure they were therefore exerting on the British:

> My own feeling is that the French, particularly M. Pineau, are in the mood to blame everyone including us if military action is not taken before the end of October. They alleged that the weather could preclude it later. I contested this. M. Mollet, as I believe, would like to get a settlement on reasonable terms if he could. I doubt whether M. Pineau wants a settlement at all.[132]

Much of the Prime Minister's line paralleled a long minute that Bishop had sent him in Paris. Bishop suggested that 'I think the main line to keep our eyes on is still the payment of dues.' He then went on to explain how, '[i]f, because he [Nasser] is not getting dues, he tries to stop shipping, that still seems to me the best way to the point at which the use of force could best be justified to the country'.[133] Even now force was not yet adopted as policy, rather Eden looked at the legality with regard to the crisis; if Nasser blocked passage through the Canal, then action under Article 51 of the UN Charter would be justified.[134] Macmillan had seen SCUA as a direct means of enabling a forceful riposte, whereas Eden had seen it as a means of reintroducing international control of the Canal, which would have destabilised Nasser's position.[135] At last Eden's plan had become coherent and clear, with the ability to fulfil all of his prerequisites: reinternationalise the Canal through negotiating from a position of strength and exerting economic pressure on Egypt, whilst maintaining American, Conservative Party and British public support, all without the need for force.

On his return from Paris, Eden was greeted by a letter from Butler: 'Welcome home, you must have had a difficult time.' The French reaction had been expected but he believed that '[y]our colleagues will have confidence in your handling of the French'. Having suggested the need for further talks about the meeting in Paris, he then suggested a 'short break'; 'We shall all be available for an Egypt C[ommit]tee whenever you get back.'[136] The strain was beginning to show on Eden. From at least 21 August he had been trying to find the time to take a holiday. Under orders from his doctors that he should try 'a slightly different regime', he wanted to put off any decision until he had recuperated on holiday and could make the decision 'in good health'.[137] Ever since his failed gall-bladder operation in 1953, Eden had suffered from recurrent high fevers, resulting from his cholangitis.[138] These fevers increased in occurrence during 1956, and their debilitating effects of weakness and lassitude were attested by Eden himself.[139] Clark believed that Eden had been 'prescribed amphetamines' by his doctors and Chester Cooper, the CIA Station Chief in London, remarked that 'as a consequence [of the illness] Eden was taking some sort of drug that apparently effected his nervous system'.[140] Eden was a severely weakened man. His wife remarked: 'Although he's much tougher than he looks his doctors had told me, even *before* Suez, that he wouldn't be able to go on.'[141] Thus, despite the proposed Egypt Committee meeting of 28 September, Eden rested in Wiltshire.[142]

Before he left for the country, Eden spent the morning of the 28th catching up on the voluminous boxes of telegrams. He was particularly interested in the message from Sir Edwin Chapman Andrews in Khartoum, minuted it for Egypt Committee attention and had it repeated to Paris. Eden was taken by Chapman Andrews's news that 'Nasser's position in his own country and in the Middle East generally has deteriorated.' The Sudanese considered that Nasser had only himself to blame for 'acting "like a mad horse"' and that the recent Arab League meeting had helped to bring 'him to his senses'. Again, of particular concern to Eden and noted by him was the report of Sudanese Ministers returning from Cairo, 'that although Nasser may be able to rely on the Army, having purged it, he is now unpopular with the people who do not want war, and have lost confidence in his leadership'. Andrews considered, therefore, that time was on Britain's side but that they should 'accept no compromise on the principle of international control'. This appealed to Eden. Andrews continued that Britain should also 'maintain our forces at the ready with discreet, but not aggressive, publicity' and 'covertly undermine Nasser's personal position by all means in our power'.[143] The interest in this telegram emphasised his agreement with Andrews that the crisis required a peaceful solution. There was, therefore, now a need to calm press propaganda, which it had been hoped would help to 'threaten' Nasser, if the UN could be made to work:[144]

> On the 28th, Eden received a threat from Soviet Prime Minister, Nikolai Bulganin:

> To try to materialise these or those plans by way of the use of force against Egypt is to put oneself in opposition to the majority of countries including those States whose interests of security are directly affected by the developments in this region and who cannot remain indifferent when a breach of peace and an aggression are in question.[145]

Eden saw this as the Soviet Government fishing 'in troubled waters', rather than an honest concern.[146] He considered writing immediately to the US President, but the telegram was not sent until his return from Wiltshire on Monday, 1 October.[147] The telegram read:

> You can be sure that we are fully alive to the wider dangers of the Middle East situation. They can be summed up in one word – Russia... There is no doubt in our minds that Nasser, whether he likes it or not, is now effectively in Russian hands, just as Mussolini was in Hitler's. It would be as ineffective to show weakness to Nasser in order to placate him as it was to show weakness to Mussolini. The only result was and would be to bring the two together... That is why we are doing everything we can to make the Users' Club an effective instrument... I feel sure that anything which you can say or do to show firmness to Nasser at this time will help the peace by giving the Russians pause.[148]

The Prime Minister tried using the 'Soviet' and 'Dictator' threats to influence the President. Anthony Nutting, Minister of State at the Foreign Office called it the 'Communist bogy', although as he justified to Iverach McDonald, in private talks, and later to the Cabinet, the Soviet threat had increased within his own concerns.[149]

Once again, Eden believed he could influence the Americans by using the communist threat. Macmillan's earlier reports, reinforced by further meetings over the weekend, had shown the possibility of using this element to encourage American moral support against Nasser. On the evening of the 29 September, Macmillan called on Robert Murphy. The Chancellor thought Murphy, the US Deputy Under Secretary of State 'very sympathetic with our difficulties in Suez'. Once again the importance of waiting until after the elections before the US could give any form of assistance was made clear but there appeared to be grounds for appeal to US sensibilities.[150] On the following day, Macmillan also visited the British permanent representative at the UN, Sir Pierson Dixon. Dixon 'was very anxious that we should really make our case in a convincing and comprehensive way... We had been very patient and we ought to gain the moral advantage of our patience.' This meant not making any other additional resolution which would impede the British freedom of action.[151]

On 1 October, the Egypt Committee discussed the possible courses of action 'in light of the recent talks... with French Ministers in Paris'. Eden, aware of the French attitude and their bellicosity, reiterated his telegram of 26 September: The French 'were convinced that, if he [Nasser] were allowed to get away with his seizure of the Suez Canal, the influence of the Western powers in the Middle East and Africa would inevitably be lost to Russia'. He also saw the possibility of tripartite agreement over the future courses of action, continuing that 'this aspect of the matter should be impressed on the United States Government', which he had tried to do in the telegram.[152] The French continued to attempt to embroil Eden in an aggressive solution. They were concerned about the timing of the possible military operations 'since the French forces could not be kept at their present state of readiness for any protracted period'.[153] However, again, while this represented a build-up of pressure on Eden it did not immediately induce a favouring of the use of force.

The French had been planning with the Israelis for a 'coordinated action... against Egypt' since the beginning of the month and pressure was brewing in 'an eve-of-war atmosphere'.[154] On 30 September, at a meeting between the French and the Israelis, Pineau said that he 'would try to convince the British that Anglo-French military measures were the only course, but he was doubtful that he would succeed'.[155] This showed the reluctance of the British to involve themselves in such a military operation and also reflected their attitude in the recent talks with the French. Such was the French suspicion of Britain's commitment to a forceful resolution that they requested that they and the Israelis 'explore possibilities of joint action'.[156] However, the problem for the French, as Moshe Dayan, Israeli Chief of Staff, realised, was that, without Britain, the Israelis would be reluctant to join the French in a military operation.[157] Likewise, the French were reluctant to enter into an operation with the Israelis without the British. This led to the French trying to 'reassure' the Israelis as to Britain's commitment and hence confusing opinion of, in particular, Eden's attitude.[158] Yet, believing that they could and had to influence Eden, they exerted greater pressure on the Prime Minister.

However, Eden believed that '[i]f Anglo-French solidarity were to be maintained during the forthcoming debates in the Security Council, we must stand firmly by the principles endorsed by the 18 Powers at the London Conference'. Again, this presented Eden's commitment to a peaceful solution consistent with his belief in keeping the bellicose French on side. The Foreign Secretary supported Eden's move reiterating the possibilities of a solution through negotiation similar to that proposed by Krishna Menon, Indian Minister without Portfolio and considered during the last meeting of 25 September. Consistent with Eden's beliefs, the Committee 'agreed that any settlement must provide for effective international control of the Suez Canal'. It was also suggested, 'as a possible solution', that to protect against the possibility of Egypt infringing upon the rights of the 'users', a new tripartite declaration should be made, reserving the right to take any steps that the three countries believed were necessary 'either within or without the United Nations'.[159] Eden and the Egypt Committee continued to seek a way of bringing world pressure to bear on Nasser to ensure the reinternationalisation of the Canal, with increasing desperation.

Within the Government the 'hawks' began to exert more pressure, despite limited resistance from the legal advisers. The legal question was particularly confused. The Egypt Committee now understood that under Article 51 of the United Nations Charter, the breach of a treaty obligation could not be seen as an 'armed attack justifying the use of force in self defence', despite the influence of Lord Kilmuir.[160] However, the Committee also believed that 'one of the purposes of the United Nations Charter was to uphold the rule of law and, in the last resort, the use of force for this purpose could be justified'.[161] This latter attitude began to dominate the thinking of committee members despite being inconsistent with advice coming from the Foreign Office Legal Advisers, who themselves were becoming more and more agitated by the Lord Chancellor's advice. Sir Gerald Fitzmaurice had written to Sir George Coldstream, the Lord Chancellor's Private Secretary, expressing his concern over the 'situation that seems to be developing' and in particular the effect of 'gun-boat diplomacy' on a world whose climate of opinion had changed so dramatically.[162] Making little headway, he then attempted to influence Sir Ivone Kirkpatrick, the Permanent Under-Secretary at the Foreign Office, grieving, 'what worries me, inter alia, is the apparent complete lack of concern amongst Ministers – and elsewhere – as to what the [situation] looks like. Yet I believe H.M.G. *will* care very much, eventually.'[163] However, Kirkpatrick, who had been pushing very hard for a legal justification to oust Nasser, showed his true colours, minuting: 'The problem remains. Should we resolve to perish gracefully because opinion thinks that this is what we should do?'[164] There is no suggestion that the consistent fears of the Foreign Office Legal Advisers actually reached Eden. Sir Frank Cooper believed that Selwyn Lloyd must be given much of the responsibility for this, because as head of the Foreign Office he had a duty to report Foreign Office opinion.[165] However, even after the decision to use force had been made, Fitzmaurice continued to blame Kilmuir for Eden's ill-founded belief in the legality of the use of a military solution: 'Throughout the Suez Crisis, the task of the legal advisers here has been rendered almost impossibly difficult due to the fact that the Cabinet and the Prime Minister were proceeding independently on the basis of private advice tendered by the Lord Chancellor.'[166] Thus, the Prime Minister's information with regard to a legal justification remained imparted by a narrow, belligerent group.

In addition, Eden was now accepting advice from Kirkpatrick and Cabinet Secretary Brook, both of whom were supporting the use of force.[167] Geoffrey McDermott, a member of the Foreign Office who had been involved in the planning of 'Musketeer', recalled that Kirkpatrick had 'appeared to participate in the enterprise with zest'.[168] Lord Sherfield remarked that Kirkpatrick, '[s]carred by his Munich experience... continued to be a strong advocate of the use of force against Nasser, whom he saw as another dictator who should not be appeased. He did not at any time advocate caution and, never having served in the United States, did not understand the American psyche and set-up and the deep-seated opposition to the use of force. This was a contributory factor, albeit a relatively minor one, to the subsequent debacle over Suez.'[169] Kirkpatrick's and Brook's advice compounded the pressure from elements of the Conservative Party, British public, media and the French to employ an immediate solution to the crisis.

On 2 October, Dulles destroyed Eden's latest hopes of a peaceful settlement. The Secretary of State made another extremely damaging statement at a Washington press conference, which, as Eden reflected, 'was likely to make Nasser believe that if he held fast, the United States would fall apart from France and Britain over the seizure of the canal'. Dulles told the world that

> The United States cannot be expected to identify itself 100 per cent. either with the colonial powers or the powers uniquely concerned with the problem of getting independence as rapidly and as fully as possible. There were, I admit, differences of approach by the three nations to the Suez dispute, which perhaps arise from fundamental concepts. For while we stand together, and I hope we shall always stand together in treaty relations covering the North Atlantic, any areas encroaching in some form or manner on the problem of so-called colonialism, find the United States playing a somewhat independent role. The shift from colonialism to independence will be going on for another fifty years, and I believe that the task of the United Nations is to try to see that this process moves forward in a constructive, evolutionary way, and does not come to a halt or go forward through violent, revolutionary processes which would be destructive of much good.

Then turning to SCUA, he said: 'There is talk about the "teeth" being pulled out of it [SCUA] but there were never "teeth" in it.'[170] This was a staggering blow to Eden who had put all his hopes into SCUA and the possibility of international control of the Canal. Once again, this reaction demonstrated the complete British misunderstanding of what the Americans had said all along. Nutting believed that this was 'for Eden the final let-down'.[171] Meeting with the Prime Minister on the following morning, Iverach McDonald found him still 'immeasurably angry and shocked'. Eden could not understand how Dulles could 'so completely misunderstand his determination to have the canal internationally controlled as to think that he was reverting to colonialism... "It was I who ended the 'so-called colonialism' in Egypt. And look at what Britain has done all over the world in giving the colonies independence".' The timing of Dulles's public declaration also angered him, 'at such a critical time': 'We have leaned over backwards to go along with him. And now look. How on earth can you work with people like that? It leaves us in a quite impossible position. We can't go on like this.'[172] McDonald summarised the importance he saw in these events:

> In the light of later events it is more than probable that it was Dulles's words on October 2, coming after all his other moves backwards and sideways, which convinced Eden into thinking that Britain and France must do as seemed best to themselves... What was clear at the time was the element of tragedy. Dulles had exploded his mine under Eden's feet just when discussions – unpromising but not entirely hopeless – were at long last about to begin.[173]

This was an important turning point for Eden during his handling of the Suez Crisis. He no longer believed that he required American support to acquire a peaceful solution, although their assistance would always be preferred.

Despite Dulles's remarks, Eden and the Government agreed not to say anything publicly, but Clark contacted *The Times*, 'which wrote a sharp leader'. The Prime Minister decided to add a piece into a forthcoming speech.[174] At 5 p.m. senior ministers met at No. 10. In a meeting with Makins, Dulles called the press conference 'a really bad blunder'. He apologised that he had been drawn into an 'undesirable line of discussion' and that 'his remarks had been given a connexion which he did not intend, between the colonial question and the Suez Affair'.[175] Despite the apology, the damage had been done. British hopes for SCUA had been emasculated by the full public withdrawal of American belief and support in its potential as a solution to the crisis beyond the weakened US version which the Second London Conference had produced. Increasingly disturbing for the British was that Dulles had not apologised because he had made a mistake in what he said but because he had said it publicly.

On the next day, Suez was only second on the agenda but there appeared to be a new and potentially aggressive atmosphere. Eden informed the Cabinet of the results of the conversations with the French of the 26 and 27 September. He appeared much more officious and terse, dominating the issue:

he was impressed by the vigour of M. Mollet's Government and their uncompromising attitude towards the Suez situation... There was indeed a risk that the Soviet Union might conclude a pact of mutual assistance with Egypt... If they [Egypt] continued to be obdurate, world opinion might be readier to support a recourse to forceful measures. If they offered to negotiate, the task of achieving a satisfactory settlement would be more difficult and more protracted.[176]

It marked a strengthening of Eden's resolve but still it did not reflect a final decision to remove Nasser by force. As Eden continued, '[i]n either event the weeks ahead would be critical'.[177] On 2 October, Eden had held a confidential meeting with McDonald where he had referred to the same issues as those of the Cabinet meeting of 3 October. He had said that '[t]he French... were clearer than he himself had been about the Russian part in the Egyptian crisis'.[178] The fear of the potential of Soviet backing for the Egyptians was beginning to play on his mind, particularly at a time when American assistance, of any variety, was looking less likely. Earlier that morning, in a meeting with Macmillan, Eden showed his fear of 'the dangers of another Nasser coup, and the possibility of a Russian intervention'.[179] Under these pressures, he reacted with a fit of pique to McDonald's assertion that 'Nasser would be quite capable of letting American ships through but stopping ours, and America would not back us'. The Prime Minister retorted that 'we should go straight in'. In later conversation he qualified and dismissed this 'by saying that he did not think that Nasser would stop any ships'.[180] Significantly, and consistent with the Prime Minister's attempts to achieve a peaceful solution, he 'hoped to get a blessing from the Security Council on the 18-Power plan as a basis for negotiation. That would allow us to talk direct to Egypt.' McDonald recorded that 'Eden indicated that he might move a little further and faster [than the French on the negotiations]. He said that he had said repeatedly that we could not leave the Canal "in the unfettered control of one man or one Government" – leaving the actual form of control rather more open.'[181] This was the opinion of one of the few people that had known and worked with Eden for the past twenty years. He still believed that Eden was keen to settle the dispute peacefully, if at all possible. It was not until later, when McDonald became aware of the plans that formed the basis of the 'collusion' with France and Israel, that he lost faith with the Prime Minister's attempts to resolve the crisis peacefully.[182]

From 20 September to 3 October, Eden continued to see SCUA as the best method of reinternationalising the Canal by economically pressuring Nasser. It was hoped that the withholding of money, vital to promised development within Egypt, would destabilise Nasser's position. Either it would force him to accept international control of the Canal in exchange for revenue from transit dues, or possibly, as MI6 had suggested, provide the spark for a coup which would replace Nasser with a leader more likely to return control of the Canal to an international body. The Prime Minister began to show signs of frustration with Dulles's denigration of British plans for SCUA and saw the need to take the issue to the UN Security Council where he believed he could develop wider international support for the Users' Association. He began to communicate more with Churchill, who strongly favoured a military invasion to recapture the Canal. There is no evidence to suggest that Churchill influenced Eden; however, a channel of advice had been opened that, in association with other pressures, would have an important and bellicose effect on Eden's decision-making in October.

At this stage, the Prime Minister decided to take the matter to the UN, a decision consistent with his belief in the value of an organisation for dealing with international crises. This was a development of his belief in, and training at, the League of Nations.[183] It was not as large a break from Anglo-American solidarity as has been assumed. Eden's motives for the appeal, to gain wider support for the Association, showed that in the long term he was actually promoting Dulles's line. However, Eden finally saw that Dulles was not prepared to make SCUA work as Britain wanted it to work. At the same time, Macmillan, who was in the US to gain support against Nasser's actions and to attend the IMF meeting, now reported that both Dulles and Eisenhower favoured Nasser's removal by any means. Nevertheless, the Prime Minister continued not to show any signs of moving from his belief in a peaceful settlement of the crisis, potentially still through SCUA. Pressure for a forceful solution continued to mount from elements of the press, notably *The Daily Telegraph*, but also and especially from the French caught in a 'catch 22' situation with the Israelis. The French Government and military wanted to use force to settle the crisis. They needed the Israelis for this and, if possible, the British. The Israelis were not prepared to embark on a military operation without the British, whose involvement had been promised by the French as a lure to the Israelis. However, the British remained undetermined to decide on force. Consequently, Israel pressed France to bring Britain into the fold, which increased an already strong commitment, on behalf of the French, to press Eden. The Prime Minister continued to receive bellicose advice and pressure from Macmillan, while Kirkpatrick and Brook also backed the strong line justified by the Lord Chancellor. Sir Michael Wright, in Baghdad, also continued to push for an aggressive solution to the crisis. Still Eden put his faith in the User's Club until Dulles's comment to the press.

Dulles's public statement, undercutting an active, powerful SCUA, and Eden's consequent reaction to American attitudes marked a watershed in the Suez Crisis. The Prime Minister continued to pursue a resolution through the UN but he no longer believed in the need for American assistance in reaching any solution. A new stage of the crisis had been reached. In addition, on 3 October, Eden informed Cabinet that '[t]he Jews have come up with an offer', although this was not recorded in the minutes.[184] While

Eden did not show any signs of accepting a military solution at this stage, he did not react as angrily to the suggestion of Israeli involvement as he had done in July and August. Pineau allegedly broached the matter of what Eden would do if Israel attacked Egypt, to which the Prime Minister made 'some inconclusive remark', before relaying the information to ministers.[185] All the influences and pressures strengthened his resolve. The Prime Minister believed that his options had narrowed, based on his maxim that a negotiated settlement had to be agreed that upheld the provisions of the 1888 Convention. Eden showed increasing signs of physical and mental deterioration. However, he continued to conduct his foreign affairs by reacting to events. The UN still provided hope for an acceptable settlement despite the mounting pressure for the use of force.

5
Transition to Force: 4 October–14 October

The Security Council, the Promise of a Settlement and the Decision to Use Force

After Dulles's press conference of 3 October, the Suez Crisis entered another phase. During this period Eden continued to seek a peaceful solution. He still hoped for US assistance and French support to end the crisis as negotiation entered the United Nations Security Council. However, the Americans were keen to maintain political distance from the British because they believed them ready to use force. Yet it was the French, who did not believe that the Security Council could offer a solution, who remained 'the driving force behind [a] policy of action'.[1] Eden was caught between the two camps, trying to arouse support for a negotiated settlement, although ready, in the last resort, to use force.[2] This period would prove critical because of the increasing pressure upon the Prime Minister, notably from the French and the right-wing Conservatives within Britain, and more importantly, the timing of this pressure. Increasingly ill, tired and frustrated, on 14 October, the French proposed that he collude with them and the Israelis in a military operation to recapture the Canal. Eden accepted this initiative.

On 4 October, Eden wrote to Makins, keen to maintain peace. He expressed his fears of the consequences of Dulles's press conference, and tried to influence the Americans through the Ambassador: 'Mr. Dulles knows that not one of us would ever want to make difficulties over Anglo-American relations. It would, however, be dishonest to pretend that the Press Conference did not give a severe shock to public opinion here.' Eden's fear intensified after confirmation from American Ambassador Aldrich. The Prime Minister continued to express his concern in the telegram to Makins: 'My anxiety is for the encouragement which this Press Conference will have given to Nasser and still more important to the Russians.' However, despite his concerns, Eden was still keen to maintain peace, stressing that '[a]nything which could be said by Mr. Dulles to redress that balance would buttress peace. Make any use of this that you think fit in talk with Mr. Dulles.'[3]

Eden's pacifism showed that Ben-Gurion was right not to 'count on British participation' in any military operation against Egypt, and supported the Israeli belief, on 4 October, that an 'operation would not take place'. In fact, by 4 October, Ben-Gurion had agreed that any 'operation should not be launched without the foreknowledge and agreement – even silent – of the British'. This implied that *at this point* the British were not expected to embark on an operation. In his memoirs, Dayan summarised the results of Franco-Israeli planning: 'There had been clarification at the meetings, and contingency decisions had been taken on what each side would do *if* it were resolved to go ahead with the campaign. But the manner in which it was to be launched, *if at all*, had not been decided.'[4] Contingency measures had been drawn up but no decision to employ them had been made and no complete operational plan had been developed. Both the French and Israelis wanted to use force but the decision had not been made because they were dependent upon Eden, who had *not* committed himself to this line, was not keen to invoke a military solution and had therefore also not decided to use force.

Makins wrote back directly to Eden, including a copy of an article by Chalmers M. Roberts in the *Washington Post* on the US attitude towards colonialism, which he believed was 'near the mark'.[5] It argued that Dulles had been trying to take both sides over the question of colonialism. He remained caught by 'the dilemma created by the inevitable passing of the 19th century colonialism and the absolute American need to maintain the Atlantic Alliance with those Western European nations which still rule in one form or another millions of colonial peoples in Asia and Africa'. The Secretary of State had had his own State Department Policy Planning Staff working on this problem and had even involved an outside organisation including Dean Rusk, President of the Rockefeller Foundation, President James R. Killian of Massachusetts Institute of Technology and former President Henry M. Winston of Brown University. Dulles remained trapped by the need for certain 'strategic' colonies to be maintained to check communism's advance and so could not completely refute colonialism.[6] Eden, reading the telegram on the 5th, reacted vitriolically, minuting: 'The article describes the most dishonest policy I ever read.' In response to Makins's observation that 'this deep seated feeling about colonialism...occasionally [wells] up inside Foster like lava in a dormant volcano', Eden, still incensed, wrote 'futile!' Makins believed that 'Foster is well aware of the damage that has been done' but that his press conference remarks 'may indirectly have a good effect in emphasising the need for three power unity in the forthcoming difficult discussions [of potential action to be taken because of the nationalisation of the Canal] in New York'.[7] Yet, Eden remained angered by the reference to colonialism, supported in his disgust by other members of the Cabinet, particularly Butler.[8] Dulles's remarks proved particularly frustrating because Eden did not hold the traditional imperial pretensions of ruling the Middle East or even Egypt.[9] He merely wanted, as he had consistently made clear to Cabinet and other colleagues, to maintain freeflowing supplies of oil for Western Europe.[10] In addition, the American attitude could affect the possibility of maintaining support against Nasser, particularly from other Middle Eastern countries who would not want to be openly associated with an imperial 'power'.

However, the Prime Minister no longer expected any direct American assistance over the Suez Crisis after Dulles's denigration of a potent SCUA in his press conference of 2 October.[11] He revealed the extent of his thinking in a minute on Selwyn Lloyd's telegram from New York: 'I think that D's purpose is different from ours. Canal is no sense vital to U.S. & his game is to string us along at least until after polling day.'[12] This confirmed Eden's recent suspicions about Dulles's lack of commitment to finding a solution and qualified his rejection of the need for American support on the 3rd. However, it also revealed an escalating insecurity within the Prime Minister, as he now sought to justify his decisions both to himself and to Lloyd, even though he had decided that American agreement was no longer vital or possible. This was why it had been such a difficult decision to make the move to the UN without US support.

On 5 October, the Security Council debate began. To many contemporaries, the move to the UN represented a commitment to a long-drawn-out 'period of fruitless negotiation', but which would also rule out the use of force.[13] *The Daily Telegraph* saw it as a 'Neutralist Move', while the Egyptians had seen the referral to the UN as ruling out the possibility of the use of force.[14] Mahmoud Fawzi, the Egyptian Foreign Minister, asked Dag Hammarskjøld, the UN Secretary-General, 'if he thought Britain and France really wanted to reach an agreement', because the Egyptians could see no point in 'wasting their time' if there was no possibility of a settlement. Hammarskjøld, replying that 'he had known...Lloyd for a long time, and had discussed the situation with him on many occasions', believed that 'Lloyd genuinely wanted to reach a peaceful solution' and that 'it was safe to rule out the possibility of Britain's using force'.[15] The Foreign Secretary had been sent to the UN to attempt to get a 'settlement [that] must provide for effective international control of the Canal'. It was hoped that this could be obtained through uniting the Security Council behind the resolution of the London conferences, which would 'establish "a definite system destined to guarantee at all times, and for all the Powers, the free use of the...Canal"'.[16] Having already discussed this with Hammarskjøld, the Secretary-General understood the hopes, goals and methods that Lloyd would bring with him to the Security Council meetings. Lloyd had already been briefed by Eden and the Egypt Committee. To ensure that the move to the UN could be productive, the Foreign Secretary had been dispatched to New York, arriving on 2 October. Over the next three days he met with a number of UN representatives from countries including Australia, Peru, Iran, Yugoslavia and Russia. He also met with Hammarskjøld, again. Britain was against having 'a negotiation about a negotiation' and Lloyd took the opportunity to test the water for the possibility of private meetings between Pineau, Fawzi and himself, with Hammarskjøld as chairman.[17] Even Dmitri Shepilov, the Soviet Foreign Minister 'appeared disposed to agree to' this plan for discussion: '[F]irst a public session of the Council with opening speeches, then a private session, then an adjournment for two or three days for private discussions.'[18] The British cards were placed on the table and Lloyd continued to work diligently in preparation for the private meetings which would start on the 9th.

The approach to the UN marked an important stage in the crisis, based on the worldwide belief in its potential to effect a solution. In Britain alone, 81 per cent of people interviewed had backed a move to the Security Council, while 67 per cent favoured reinternationalisation of the Canal.[19] The UN still carried a strong sense of being the 'agency of peace' developed after the Second World War. Expectation rose for a possible solution based on the importance of the organisation and the seriousness with which it appeared to be approaching the situation. It brought together 'the largest number of Foreign Ministers to attend any session of the Council since the United Nations began'.[20] Eight Foreign Ministers were present at the first public meeting of the Security Council and were ready to meet 'the greatest test of its efficacy since the Korea war'.[21] Such was public interest that *The Times* produced a 'Guide to Voting Procedure in [the] Security Council'.[22] The British public remained firmly behind the move to the UN, justifying Eden's decision to take the issue to the Security Council and reaffirming support for his belief in this form of international representation, previously seen through his work with the League of Nations.

Lloyd reported that Dulles believed that '[t]he potential use of force must be kept in existence'.[23] This paralleled Eden's own designs for a solution: negotiation from a position of strength with the possibility of recourse to force as a last resort. However, it also contradicted Makins's report of Eisenhower's opinion, adding to Eden's confusion.[24] On 6 October, Dulles went further in another press conference.[25] Whilst talking about 'waging peace' he turned to a 'practical illustration of the interdependence of peace and justice [in] the present Suez Canal situation'. He alluded to the possibility of having to use force to settle the crisis, should the Security Council prove ineffectual:

> No nation should be required to live under an economic 'sword of Damocles'. There has been strong worldwide sentiment against using force to right this situation. That is natural and proper. But those who are concerned about peace ought to be equally concerned about justice. Is it just, or even tolerable, that great nations which have rights under the 1888 Treaty and whose economies depend upon the use of the Canal should accept an exclusive control of the international waterway by a government which professes to be bitterly hostile? That is the issue

now before the United Nations' Security Council, and it faces that Organization with a crucial test.[26]

This reinforced the tone of Dulles's meeting with Lloyd and Pineau, suggesting that force could be used if the move to the Security Council broke down after a serious attempt to achieve a peaceful settlement had been made. This did not reflect Dulles's opinion but the British understood it to be his position.[27] Confusion over the American position continued. Dulles, Pineau and Lloyd had met during the morning of the 5th, Lloyd reporting to Eden that Dulles thought 'Nasser's prestige was declining'. Eden minuted 'Rubbish', aware that the Egyptian leader remained popular.[28] Again, the Prime Minister was frustrated by what he saw as Dulles's misunderstanding of the situation, confirming to Eden the belief that the crisis was not as important to the Americans as to Western Europe.[29] Eden no longer believed that he needed the Americans but having their support remained, however unlikely, beneficial. Any form of American support bolstered the chances of a settlement, although part of that potential had been destroyed by the previous press releases.

Nevertheless, on 5 October, at the first meeting of the Security Council, the chance of a negotiated peaceful settlement appeared high to the delegates and their governments. Britain and France immediately introduced a draft resolution which supported the proposals reached by the London Conferences. These included the establishment of an International Board for the Canal as a basis for negotiating with the Egyptians. Despite Shepilov's opposition to the resolution, Fawzi compromised on Egypt's earlier position and laid down three conditions which would affect any ensuing negotiation. Hammarskjøld, with Dulles's support, saw the possibility of an agreement and called Lloyd, Fawzi and Pineau into private sessions which would begin on 9 October. This was in line with the British hopes that Lloyd had expressed for a structure to be used to reach a solution.

Eden wrote to Eisenhower to enhance Britain's 'position of strength' in the forthcoming negotiation. Once again, he tried to influence the President and was principally concerned that the Americans could improve Britain's own potential threat used to bluff Nasser, while at the same time suggesting Anglo-American solidarity to the outside world. He did not refer to Suez. Since the 1953 Bermuda Conference, the US had supplied the British with 'technical information to enable' modification of RAF aircraft to carry 'certain types of United States atomic weapons'. The US Air Force came over to Britain to train the British aircrews in operating the weapons. Eden believed that 'some public announcement in very general terms ought to be made soon', which would 'provide helpful evidence of continuing solidarity between our two countries'.[30] In addition to broadcasting the joint Anglo-American threat to Nasser, it would reinforce the credence of Britain's own deterrent, already underscored by the exploding of a nuclear bomb on 27 September.

Unusually, Eisenhower did not reply for seven days, frustrating Eden's hopes to use this propaganda to deter Nasser and strengthen his position in the debates.

The pressure was beginning to take its toll on Eden. Clark noted, 'P.M. ...seems very tired.'[31] Eden was unwell, consulting his doctor on 4 October.[32] On the afternoon of the 5th, travelling to Chequers, he called into University College Hospital to visit his wife who was undergoing a dental examination.[33] Almost upon arrival he was taken ill with a severe fever characteristic of his illness. His temperature rose to 106 degrees, and as Eden recalled, 'I did not know much more after that for a while.'[34] Sir Horace Evans, Eden's doctor revealed that there had been a 'removal of an obstruction in the bile duct', which meant that the Prime Minister had undergone surgery. His illness had worsened.[35] He remained in hospital until Monday the 8th, and although unable to attend the Cabinet meeting or the Egypt Committee meeting that evening, had appeared, to both himself and his colleagues, to discharge his business as usual over the weekend. Clark recorded in his diary that '[i]n fact PM seemed as active as ever, sending messages via Guy [Millard] and Freddy [Bishop] at regular intervals'.[36] This proved deceptive, as Eden admitted later.[37] Clark, despite his earlier assumption that force had been decided upon in July, also realised this. Increasingly, as his diary entries revealed, the Press Secretary had begun to doubt his own instant judgement. He believed that the Government had 'dual track' intentions of threatening Nasser with the prospect of a military invasion in the hope of pressuring him into relinquishing the Canal, while maintaining the possibility of actually using force as a last resort.[38] Such was the extent and seriousness of Eden's medical deterioration in October that this was the turning point of the Prime Minister's conduct of the Suez Crisis. Clark recorded that 5 October induced a change in Eden that led to his commitment to the French and Israelis.[39] Monckton concurred.[40] On 9 October, *The Times* hedged, reporting that the Prime Minister 'has now almost recovered'. However, the newspaper appeared to be desperate to play the illness down and did not appear to be informed of the extent of the effect of the illness on Eden.[41]

The Prime Minister found himself incapable of maintaining his usual workload, and on 9 October wrote to Lloyd in New York apologising for being 'unable to help...Although the temperature is down, I am still pretty weak.'[42] With the deepening of the crisis Eden found it impossible to make time for a full rest, stealing moments at his country retreat in Wiltshire. Privately he bemoaned his own increasing exhaustion.[43] However, Eden's colleagues were not aware of the seriousness of his condition. Even today, few understand the severity of his illness, largely due to the confidentiality of his doctors and the support of a loyal wife. Lord Home believed that the pressure of the Egypt Committee meetings 'wasn't lessened because the Prime Minister was not, undoubtedly, well'.[44] Millard would not have resigned if he had been fully aware of Eden's state of health. The Private Secretary had wanted to leave the Private Office at the end of March, 1956, but had been convinced by Sir Norman Brook, the Cabinet Secretary to stay on until the end of the year. However, he was adamant that he would not have left, despite not liking the job, had he realised how ill Eden was.[45]

Despite his hospitalisation, the Prime Minister continued his attempts to achieve a peaceful solution to the crisis. Some historians have suggested that Eden recovered with a 'renewed vigour', ostensibly for a forceful settlement.[46] This was not the case, as Eden continued to believe in the possibility of a peaceful settlement, particularly through the discussions at the UN, which were showing positive signs. Any apparent vigour was the result of the demands of the media and the need to present himself as a well person to them. On 7 October, he had read an article by J. B. Slade-Baker in *The Sunday Times*, reporting that the Egyptians believed that the Suez Crisis was 'Burnt Out'.[47] One Egyptian senior official had told the reporter that 'in all seriousness... not only had the crisis burned itself out but that the problem of who is to control the Canal no longer existed'.[48] The Egyptians thought that the crisis had passed and that the nationalisation would be accepted by the international community. Angered that the 'Egyptians are very clever at dressing up minor concessions to look like reasonable propositions', the Prime Minister remained concerned that, as Trevelyan had warned on 24 September, the Egyptians were simply playing for time and using delaying tactics.[49] Consequently, he was reinforced in his own belief, that as the last resort, action would be necessary. This had been his view all along. He hoped that Nasser could be overthrown from within by destabilising Egypt's economy, and that the Canal could be reinternationalised.[50] He had shown this through his consistent commitment to a users' association and then SCUA, but as Cabinet had decided on 27 July, in the last resort, resolution of the crisis by force was justifiable because of the importance of the Suez Canal. Therefore, the Prime Minister stressed, it was 'very important that while appearing reasonable, we should not be inveigled away, in negotiation from the fundamentals to which we have held all along, and that we should not be parted from the French'.[51] These principles referred to the search for a solution based upon the rights of the 1888 Convention and the recent proposals of the two London conferences, with which Eden confidently assumed Lloyd agreed and which had formed the basis of the initial draft resolution presented to the Security Council on 5 October.[52] The hope remained that the control of the Canal would be reinternationalised through constant international pressure, maintaining freedom of navigation, particularly for oil bound for Western Europe.

On 8 October, Lloyd met again with Dulles, who 'was in full agreement with us on every point except the wisdom of the *ultimate* use of force'.[53] This immediately contradicted Dulles's position of 5/6 October.[54] However, even on that subject Dulles 'thought we had been absolutely right to make our preparations and that we were right to maintain our threat'.[55] This telegram was then shown to the Egypt Committee. Eden's views, of supporting Lloyd and maintaining French support, were passed on to Butler (chairing the meeting in Eden's absence).[56] Privately Eden told Lloyd that '[w]e have been misled so often by Dulles' ideas that we cannot afford to risk another misunderstanding. That is why a negotiating committee would be so dangerous. We should lose control of the situation and justifiably be accused by the French of betraying them.'[57] The Prime Minister had to 'walk the tightrope' of maintaining French support, without alienating them by appearing too docile. Up to this point he had managed to achieve the balance of enlisting their support without being drawn into the war that the French wanted. French support remained essential in maintaining solidarity against Nasser, because Eden knew Britain no longer had the power to act independently.[58] The telegram from Eden, a very similar communication to that of 5 October, revealed the Prime Minister's constancy despite Dulles's prevarication of supporting and withdrawing support for the joint communiqué backing the First London Conference, SCUA and, in reverse, the move to the UN Security Council.[59] Lloyd continued to agree with his Prime Minister. His private secretary, Donald Logan, remembered that 'as the Suez Crisis developed, the trust that Lloyd was prepared to put in Dulles weakened'.[60] Eden feared that time was running out. The more the crisis became protracted, the more likely that Nasser's hold on the Canal would become universally accepted. Yet Eden continued to hope that the Americans might be forced to help.[61] How this could be achieved remained unclear.

To complicate matters further, Nutting was beginning to act hawkishly. With Selwyn Lloyd in New York, he headed the Foreign Office. On 8 October he met with Menon to discuss proposals for a solution to the crisis. Despite seeing some possibilities for Britain in the package that the Indian Foreign Minister offered, he warned that it was 'unwise to treat the plan as other than a piece of Indian private enterprise'.[62] As Eden told Lloyd, on 9 October, he too was 'worried by the Menon plan', unsure whether to follow it up because, 'on the face of it', it looked very similar to the Fawzi proposals.[63] However, typical of the diplomatist, Eden did not want to ignore any chance of a settlement, within the parameters of the 1888 Convention and 18-Power proposals. Yet Lloyd was manipulating Nutting. He had already told him that '[w]e have now examined the Menon Proposals and do not consider that they offer an acceptable basis for negotiation'.[64] Having prepared the ground, Lloyd indirectly persuaded Eden to reject the Menon proposals, using Nutting to convince the Prime Minister on the morning of the 9th, which laid the ground for his communication to Lloyd that afternoon.[65] Lloyd was dissatisfied with Dulles and the US delegation at the UN. He disparaged press articles referring to splits between the British, French and Americans, allegedly spawned by the US delegation. Lloyd's remarks, while revealing British displeasure at the Americans for publicly disclosing that

Anglo-American differences existed, have to be read with some caution. Lloyd saw the machinations in the UN as a chance for personal advancement which, coupled with a mutual distrust of the US officials, led him to exaggerate his indictment of them. However, the comments also demonstrated the heightened tension of the moment, indicative of the importance of the UN for the British to try and reach a peaceful settlement of the crisis. The Foreign Secretary also commented that Dulles had told 'his inner circle of pressmen' that the British and French would have to accept Menon's proposals.[66] This provided another source of confusion over Eden's alleged hawkishness. The rejection of the Indian initiative, while it did not prevent Menon's continued presence during the Security Council meetings, severely limited his potential as a broker between the factions. However, Lloyd also 'believed that we had not yet got a common basis for negotiation'.[67] The Foreign Secretary, as his Private Secretary, Donald Logan, remembered, had been 'determined to make it [representation to the Security Council] work. He clung to it and worked extremely hard to get something out of these negotiations.'[68] However, despite this commitment, as of 9 October, he was not hopeful of his talks leading to a settlement.

Nevertheless, the Prime Minister sanctioned further discussions between Fawzi and Lloyd, because as Lloyd had written to Eden, after the first private session of the Security Council, despite some evasion and vagueness from Fawzi, 'I got the impression that he wants an agreement.'[69] After two hours of further talks this 'impression' was given further credence. Fawzi said that the Egyptians would accept the 1888 Convention, possibly with certain, as yet, unspecified amendments or a new convention. They were prepared to set aside a proportion of the revenue from the Canal for its development and discuss 'tolls for a fixed number of years'. They were also prepared to recognise SCUA and the payment of dues by its members to the Association. This represented the essence of the principles that Eden wanted as part of a settlement of the crisis.

Lloyd also raised the question of free passage for Israeli ships, definite 'that no new agreement in regard to the Canal was possible which did not clear that matter up'.[70] Unaware of Eden's and Lloyd's thinking, Abba Eban, the Israeli Ambassador to the UN, subsequently argued that 'Britain and France were merely going through the motions of diplomatic remedy.'[71] He suggested that '[i]f there was any real evidence that Egypt would use the Canal as an "instrument of unilateral national policy", it lay in the prolonged Egyptian blockade of Israeli shipping after the Security Council's resolution of 1951 had ruled the restrictions to be illegal.' Britain, France and the US did not want to turn the Canal dispute into another chapter of the Arab-Israeli dispute by including the Israeli delegate in the debate.[72] However, while Eban understood this logic, he, unexplainably, did not understand why Lloyd included Israeli rights in his discussions with Fawzi, keen as the British were to demonstrate the international basis of objection to the Egyptian action of nationalising the Canal. It has been suggested that Eden added this proviso, during the Egypt Committee meeting of 10 October, to pre-empt any conciliation by the Egyptians, but the decision to include the question of free passage for Israeli ships had already been made by Lloyd for a much different reason: reinternationalisation of the Canal remained the uncompromisable objective.[73] Dulles showed the importance he put on the issue, remarking to the press 'that there is little chance of a settlement so long a[s] it is possible for any nation to use the Canal "as an instrument of its distinct national policy"'.[74] Here was an area where Eden believed he agreed with Dulles; he wrote to Lloyd: '[w]e are surely entitled to full United States support over this'.[75] Despite the confusion over the American position during the previous few weeks, the Prime Minister believed that the two governments agreed over their ultimate objective for a peaceful resolution of the crisis, and while he had rejected the need for any US support, he preferred to keep them on side to maximise his chances of successfully resolving the crisis.

Eden's next communication to Lloyd 'endorsed [his] handling of this very difficult situation'. The Egypt Committee had particularly agreed with Lloyd's direction with regard to the payment of dues and his 'extremely guarded' conduct.[76] It was important to keep Nasser guessing to maintain the maximum pressure upon the Egyptians, particularly with negotiations continuing, so that any discussions could be conducted from a position of strength with the threat of force in the background. Eden urged Lloyd to gain Dulles's support for this line. Typically, the Prime Minister emphasised the need for speed, hoping to conclude the discussion in the Security Council by the end of the week, 14 October. In addition, he reaffirmed the close working with the French.[77] Eden had begun to realise that, as Lennox-Boyd had warned in August, the situation could bring down the Government and end his career.[78] However, the immediate problems did not come from the Egyptians, French or Israelis, but the Americans. Eden complained to Lloyd that the Americans still had not agreed to the opening of a bank account to receive dues paid to SCUA. As the Prime Minister continued, '[w]e can make no real progress until this is done'.[79] Lloyd reported that the US would not pay any dues until SCUA had an administrator. Unfortunately, the proposed candidate, a Dutch diplomat, was refusing to be put forward.[80] Once again, what little progress had been made appeared short-lived and Eden became frustrated by the bureaucracy and by Dulles's stalling.

Despite having publicly introduced a working model for a users' association, Dulles had done little to make it work. He never negotiated with the British to develop a precise strategy, as Logan recalled:

> The idea of them [Dulles and Lloyd] sitting down and working out what to do next is not quite true. The trouble with Dulles through this period was that he kept coming up with bright ideas and Lloyd would say, 'Let's have a look at this,' and then two days later we would find that Dulles

had gone off at a tangent and abandoned most of the suggestions he had made earlier. Lloyd had great difficulty on catching up with him on matters of substance and had the impression in the end that Dulles was playing for time by producing new ideas to keep us busy.[81]

The truth was not that Dulles was too much an intellectual butterfly but that the UK and US started from different assumptions as to what SCUA was supposed to be. Eden and Lloyd remained determined to make the Security Council work.[82] Lloyd suggested a temporary British administrator for SCUA, but these problems were then superseded by Fawzi's change of heart.

In the next private meeting between Lloyd, Fawzi and Pineau, chaired by Hammarskjøld, Fawzi announced dramatic changes to the Egyptian position. These immediately destroyed the apparent success of the previous Security Council meetings and put back the chances of a settlement along the lines of the 1888 Convention and resolutions of the London conferences. Most importantly, Fawzi could not accept that SCUA should be part of the administration of the Canal and that Egypt would have to maintain control of the pilotage.[83] He had shown that Eden's own vision for a peaceful solution was wholly unacceptable. Openly disappointed, Lloyd asked for answers to his points raised in discussion with Fawzi within twenty-four hours, otherwise 'there was nothing doing'. In his communication to Eden, he agreed that the Security Council operation should be wound up by the end of the week.[84] Lloyd and Eden were attempting to force the pace of the negotiation with the Egyptians but were, in reality, prepared to continue progressive discussion over any length of time. Lloyd was committed to making the Security Council work and negotiating a settlement.[85] Eden had been dubious that a suitable solution could be drawn from the Security Council meetings but when he began to see the progress being made, his telegrams to Lloyd reflected both his belief in the possibility of a UN inspired settlement, and in Lloyd as a negotiator. By 10 October, however, the chances of such a diplomatic settlement had substantially decreased.

Lloyd's and Eden's problems were increased by the French attitude, in particular that of Pineau. At first, the Foreign Secretary did not understand his position, commenting: 'I continue to act in the closest association with Pineau although he has a bad cold and his contribution during our meetings with Fawzi were [sic] limited to "je suis d'accord avec M. Lloyd".'[86] However, he soon concluded: 'I doubt whether Pineau really believes that a peaceful settlement is possible and I am not entirely convinced that he wants one.'[87] The British and the French may have been on the same side of the table but they still had very different views. Despite having gone along with events, Pineau had suddenly begun having concerns, which were being expressed by the French Ambassador, Chauvel, to the Foreign Office.[88] Logan was adamant that Lloyd had had more trouble with Pineau than Fawzi in New York.[89] The British were not the only ones to have formed this perception of

Pineau. Hammarskjøld had told Fawzi that he had pointed out to Dulles that 'the situation had deteriorated owing to Pineau's obstinacy', while Fawzi described Pineau as 'very louche – less arrogant [than before] but more mysterious'.[90] Pineau had a different agenda. During the time that the Security Council was in session, he met with General Yehoshafat Harkavi, the Israeli chief of military intelligence and General Maurice Challe.[91] In his memoirs, Pineau alleged that his behaviour reflected an attempt to make a secret deal with the Egyptians to safeguard Israeli rights of passage through the Canal and the Gulf in return for concessions over the handling of dues.[92] However, Lloyd had already made provision for Israeli navigational rights, and Pineau was trying to delay proceedings at the Security Council in an attempt to frustrate Eden into action. He continued to press Eden through Chauvel, who was ordered to express Pineau's main anxiety that Lloyd was being 'drawn away into unsatisfactory waters'.[93] Pineau's obstinacy and increased pressure, through the French Ambassador in London, demonstrated that he did not believe that Eden would make the decision to use force.

The French concerns were justified. The Prime Minister, buoyed by the optimism of Lloyd's reports with regard to Fawzi's attitude, pushed on for an agreement, whilst remaining flexible. Such was his belief in the possibility of a solution that, after a meeting held at Number 10 on the 11th, he remained convinced that negotiations should continue and that the timetable for discussion should be extended: '[t]he Foreign Secretary should be told that, provided the present pressure was maintained on the Egyptian representatives in these negotiations, he should not feel himself bound to terminate the discussions by the end of this week if at the time it appears that a satisfactory agreement would shortly be obtained.'[94] On the same day, despite Fawzi's apparent volte-face of the 10th, the Egyptian began to suggest specifics with regard to a users' association. Excited at the potential for the beginnings of a solution, Eden cabled Lloyd: 'You seem now to have some hope of securing our first sanction: the payment of dues through SCUA. That would be something in the bag. But the second sanction is vital. If you cannot secure something...we or you must think of something else.'[95] Eden still had not decided to go to war. It appeared to the Prime Minister that an acceptable peaceful settlement could be reached but he was careful not to overcompromise on his vision for a settlement which he had consistently confined within the parameters of the 1888 Treaty and the resolutions of the two London conferences. Even despite the problems Lloyd had faced during the Security Council discussions, Eden remained hopeful that a negotiated settlement could be achieved.

Lloyd's troubles with Pineau continued as the Frenchman's cold 'translated itself into a fever and his influence upon our discussions [became] almost entirely negative'. Pineau actively tried to denigrate any discussions at the UN in an attempt to prevent the chance of a peaceful settlement. '[D]eeply disturbed' by his attitude, Lloyd reported: 'I am doing my best to keep him in line, but he seems determined (a) to prevent any agreement, (b) to present our negotiations in the worst possible light, (c) to end up with an expression of opinion by the Security Council which would tie our hands.'[96] Lloyd's last comment reflected his fear that the UN provided the last substantial hope of procuring a peaceful settlement. If Pineau prevented the Security Council meetings from producing an acceptable solution to Egypt, Britain and France, then Lloyd knew that the only options left were to resort to force, as Cabinet had agreed on 27 July, or to allow Nasser's nationalisation to go unchallenged. That Pineau had to go to such lengths to try to weaken the effect of the meetings, suggested he feared that the British wanted a negotiated solution to the crisis and therefore had not decided upon the use of force. Yet, in spite of Pineau's actions, Lloyd still received concessions from Fawzi which gave him hope. 'Egypt would leave the Users to organize themselves as they wished...[and] would recognise the Association and... accept the dues paid through it.'[97] This fulfilled Eden's hopes.

It has then been assumed that on the following day Lloyd and Fawzi accepted the 'Six Principles' for operation of the Canal.[98] As Lloyd summarised them, these were:

1. That there should be free and open transit through the Canal without discrimination overt or covert.
2. That the operation of the Canal should be insulated from the politics of any one country.
3. That the level of dues should be fixed by agreement between users and owners.
4. That a fair proportion of the dues should be allotted to development.
5. That affairs between the Suez Canal Company and the Egyptian Government should be settled by arbitration with suitable terms of reference and suitable provision for the payment of sums found to be due.
6. As a sixth principle I suggested respect for Egyptian sovereignty.[99]

However, despite Lloyd's immediate optimism that 'I did not think there would be very much difficulty in agreeing upon those principles', he went on to express his fears. The problem was how to implement the principles, and here there were three 'main ingredients' over which Lloyd 'wanted more than vague statements'.[100] As he recalled, '[i]t was on that that the talks became vaguer and vaguer'.[101] The apparent agreement of the afternoon meeting belied the signs of retreat by Fawzi 'on what insulation from the politics of one country meant' and the technicalities of 'recourse, which had been the term for acts of enforcement'.[102] Despite their potential, the Security Council meetings floundered as the specific implementation of the 'Six Principles' could not be agreed.

Eden considered that there were now three alternatives on which the British might proceed. Negotiations could continue with Fawzi, possibly after an adjournment. The Prime Minister could authorise the end of negotiation and offer an amended version of the resolution, as had been suggested by Paul-Henri Spaak, the Belgian Foreign Minister. Lastly, he could suggest reverting to the original resolution and have a vote on it. Most important was that the French must be in agreement with the line of action, to the point that a weekend adjournment would be better than a split.[103] To complicate the timetable, Pineau had decided that he had to leave the next day, 13 October, and Lloyd believed that he could not continue the private discussions after Pineau had left New York.[104] Lloyd believed that a resolution put to the vote would be better than a negotiating committee, knowing that a resolution would get nine out of eleven votes in the Security Council. Spaak thought he could get the Egyptians to acquiesce with his resolution which would presumably leave no reason for the Soviets to veto it. Whatever the scenario, Lloyd believed that '[e]ven if it were vetoed the support given by a large majority in the Council for provisional measures should strengthen our position in SCUA and make it more difficult for the Egyptians to discriminate against SCUA ships'.[105] Reassured by this and Lloyd's belief that 'Pineau is not willing to stay beyond Sunday', Eden agreed that '[a] resolution is clearly the best as long as we are in line with the French'.[106] Eden grasped at the straw of maintaining any support for SCUA but had also already prepared to go to Paris on Sunday to talk with Mollet, should this be necessary.[107] Despite Pineau's spoiling of the discussions, the Prime Minister believed that he must maintain solidarity with the French to back any resolution that the Security Council might endorse. Eden understood the weakness of Britain's world position, understanding that he could not expect to press Nasser into reinternationalising the Canal without wider international support. For this reason, he maintained discussion with the French, as he had advocated on 27 July, because they were the other country most affected by the Egyptian expropriation of the Canal after Britain.[108] This would demonstrate to Nasser the solidarity of the two most affected countries and, Eden hoped, provide the base from which much wider international support could build to press Nasser into relinquishing his sole control of the Canal. However, despite Hammarskjøld's optimism, a workable agreement over control of the Canal remained a long way away and so the Prime Minister maintained the pressures on Egypt that he had adopted at the beginning of the crisis.[109]

On 12 October, Hammarskjøld announced agreement on the six principles but Lloyd was quick, both in his speech at the Security Council and in his report to London, to warn against 'exaggerated optimism'. He 'said there were wide gaps between Egypt and ourselves... [but believed] that it can fairly be acclaimed as a substantial victory for us'. He reiterated the need to get as strong a resolution as possible and that the Soviet veto was of little consequence. The next stage of the discussion would be tricky but Fawzi had 'offered to go in a day or two anywhere in Europe we like (except Paris and perhaps London)'.[110] The 'six principles' provided a serious problem for the British in that they did not cover reinternationalisation of the Canal, which had been the cornerstone of their aims for resolving the crisis. In addition, they did not provide the means to exert economic pressure on Nasser through withholding transit dues. However, the fundamental sticking point remained that there existed no agreement about how the limited principles would be implemented.[111] Lloyd also recognised that there was criticism that Britain and France had abandoned the principle for which they came to the UN. He proposed that there should be some backing of the 18-Power proposals, such as a paragraph in the resolution, even if it might lead to a Soviet veto.[112] This importance, and the importance that Eden now put on it, was reflected in the redraft of the proposed resolution produced by the French and British officials.[113] The Middle East (Official) Committee had considered the possibility of a more flexible system than the 1888 Convention. Eden filed the results of the meeting, which: 'concluded that the existing Convention should not be tampered with. If a new Convention were negotiated there was a danger that some of the existing provisions of value would be qualified and others, less favourable to us, reinforced.' This had been the Prime Minister's attitude over the previous negotiations, typified by the Menzies Mission, and justified his position. Significantly, the committee believed that '[n]o firm proposals for a settlement on Egypt's part could yet be said to exist'.[114] Independently Eden and the Middle East (Official) Committee had reached the same conclusion. It suggested that his analysis of the situation had not been exaggerated to give himself an excuse to use force, as has been insinuated. The failure to procure a settlement at this stage did not force Eden to initiate the military option and was further supported by his continued belief that a solution could be reached from the Security Council meetings, embodied in his encouragement to Lloyd and Pineau's impatience with him.

Eisenhower had also been impressed by the apparent progress at the Security Council with the potential of the six principles. On 11 October he had given another press conference during which he had unintentionally weakened the bargaining position of the British, announcing: 'There is nothing in the world that I wouldn't do to preserve peace with justice...Just to win a peace by saying, "well we won't fight right now" is not good enough although as you are talking and not fighting that is a gain. But what I am saying is, as long as you can get a peace based on justice, I would go anywhere, do anything in the effort to do so.'[115] At a time when Britain was relying on negotiating from a position of strength, and Nasser knew that Britain had no strength without the US, this further undermined the British position. This was particularly disappointing because, while the framework of an agreement had been reached, pressure was needed to induce ratification of the specifics of an accord. The President's remarks had specifically weakened the British position because Fawzi assumed them to be indicative of the American position. After Eisenhower learned that Hammarskjøld had announced agreement at the UN of the six principles, he remarked, at another press conference:

> Egypt, Britain and France have met through their Foreign Ministers and agreed on a set of principles on which to negotiate, and it looks like here is a very great crisis that is behind us. I do not mean to say that we are completely out of the woods, but I talked to the Secretary of State... and I will tell you that in both his heart and mine at least there is a very great prayer of thanksgiving.[116]

Once again, the American position was morally reasonable, and not distinct from that of the British. However, being a public, rather than a private statement, it weakened the British hope of bargaining from a position of strength, with the threat of force in the background. Lloyd was particularly 'disgusted', and 'spoke strongly to Dulles'.[117] Dulles was taken aback by Lloyd's rebuke 'and murmured something about not paying too much attention to what people said in the middle of an election campaign'.[118] However, the real effect of Eisenhower's statement came out in the continued discussions at the Security Council, where Fawzi, 'with obvious pleasure', quoted Eisenhower and 'clearly felt that the pressure was off'.[119] Any chance of an immediate agreement at the UN now seemed to have disappeared. The British negotiating position had been weakened by the Americans and the French. Pineau, in particular, had been obstructive to the private discussions under the auspices of the Security Council. His delaying tactics had protracted the talks limiting their effectiveness at a time when Fawzi had appeared, to Lloyd, to be showing signs of accepting an agreement.[120] Now the Egyptians were no longer prepared to make the compromises that would have ensured a settlement along the lines of the 1888 Convention which Eden had long sought. The British would have to settle for a resolution at the Security Council which might help unite opinion against Nasser.

Despite the apparent American optimism, amply demonstrated in Eisenhower's letter arriving 12 October, Lloyd then found himself in a very difficult position as both Pineau and Dulles began to create problems.[121] With regard to the resolution to be presented to the Security Council, Pineau 'strongly objected to [the] idea of putting the 18-Power proposals before the principles' leaving Lloyd no option but to comply to 'preserve Anglo-French unity'.[122] Only the day before, Pineau had told *The Daily Telegraph* that the talks were making no progress.[123] However, although already alerted to Dulles's attitude toward the payment of dues from an earlier meeting, Lloyd was left reporting: 'I have never seen anyone so anxious to denigrate his own child as Dulles with S.C.U.A.'[124] Privately the Foreign Secretary noted: '[W]e found ourselves in complete disagreement on the future of SCUA. He denied that he had ever intended SCUA to be a means of bringing pressure to bear upon the Egyptians. He said that he could not agree to the dues being paid to SCUA unless a very large proportion perhaps 90 per cent were handed on to the Egyptians. We ended with a flat disagreement on the matter.'[125] Nutting expressed Eden's fears at the Egypt Committee meeting of 8 October.[126] The vast differences in intent that had always been part of the SCUA proposals finally came into the open.

Pineau was also adamant about the payment of dues but when asked for further ideas replied that 'he would have to spend the whole of next week in the French Chamber and he thought that the interchanges should be resumed in two or three weeks time at some convenient place in Europe'.[127] The French Foreign Minister agreed with the British attitude toward using the withholding of the transit dues to press Nasser into reinternationalising the Canal but he refused to provide or support an argument against Dulles's position and suggested protracting the discussions. This development was a deliberate ploy by Pineau, who Eden considered to be usually 'impatient of diplomatic detail'.[128] In complete contrast, Pineau, following his own agenda, had decided to extend the time taken for the negotiations. Dulles was also 'unimpressed' and 'had taken a very poor view of Pineau'.[129] The Frenchman continued to play for time, hoping for the opportunity to use force to remove Nasser and frustrate Eden's hopes of a peaceful settlement.

The Prime Minister received Lloyd's communication, having returned to Chequers from the Party Conference, and was shocked and bemused: 'I cannot understand Pineau's objections to the proposal of my colleagues and myself... You give no reason for this attitude. I do not know the present form of the resolution but I must ask you to make every effort to meet the points we put to you this morning, even if this should involve an adjournment of the meeting.'[130] Eden continued to believe that the discussions at the Security Council still offered the best way of resolving the dispute. Eisenhower added to the Prime Minister's problems, unable to agree to a joint public statement on Anglo-American nuclear collaboration that Eden had requested on 5 October, the latest in a long series to get the UK a higher profile on this key issue.[131] However, the Security Council began to look more promising when, during the evening meeting, Pineau went even further than Lloyd 'in suggesting that further talks would be useful' and then, with another apparent change of heart, Dulles gave 'full backing to our resolution and the 18-Power proposals'.[132] With Anglo-American backing the chances of a settlement had once again increased, despite the lack of any concrete proposals. However, Pineau knew that Mollet had arranged for a 'delegation' to be sent to Eden, on the 14th, to persuade him to adopt force.[133] The Foreign Minister could now afford to appear compliant with the Security Council negotiations, having protracted them in an attempt to frustrate Eden.

On the evening of 13 October, the British and French resolution was voted on by the Security Council. Part I, the 'six principles' originated by

Lloyd, was supported by all eleven members. Part II, the 18-Power proposals, was supported by nine of the eleven countries, as predicted. The Soviet Union and Yugoslavia voted against and the Soviet veto killed the resolution.[134] Lloyd believed that this was as much as could have been expected and suggested preparation for 'further interchanges with Egypt without a time limit'.[135] The Prime Minister could have refused such a suggestion but, consistent with his belief in a peaceful solution, he pressed on for a negotiated settlement. Eden congratulated the Foreign Secretary and continued to support further mediation and discussion:

> should not we and the French now approach the Egyptians and ask them whether they are prepared to meet and discuss in confidence with us on the basis of the second half of the resolution which the Russians vetoed? If they say yes, then it is for consideration whether we and the French meet somewhere, e.g. Geneva.[136]

Eden had always backed negotiation, as long as he believed that it could be progressive. His belief in the Security Council discussions remained. Although Britain had US support at this moment, the Prime Minister could no longer rely on the Americans and so knew that he must maintain unity with the French, both in an attempt to pressure the Egyptians and to keep an ally, should a forceful resolution be required. Shortly before the meeting, he telegraphed Lloyd, unaware of the French offer:[137]

> I should have thought it desirable that we and the French should discuss all this [continued talks] fully very soon, perhaps Tuesday [16 October], and my present feeling is that I would have liked Mollet and myself to be in it with you and Pineau. I leave it to your discretion how far you have a preliminary talk with Pineau about these suggestions.[138]

Mollet had telephoned Eden on Saturday, 13 October, to arrange for a visit to Chequers by Albert Gazier, Acting French Foreign Minister, 'with a very special message from himself'.[139] Gazier consequently flew into London on the Sunday but brought a surprise companion, introduced as 'M. Challe of the Prime Minister's personal staff', who was in fact General Maurice Challe of the General Staff.[140] Eden had not foreseen what the visit was trying to achieve. Only the night before, alerted to the sudden delivery of seventy-five Mystère fighter aircraft by France to Israel, Eden, 'very worried', had believed that the French might have set the Israelis up to attack Jordan.[141] The visit remained shrouded in secrecy. The French Ambassador was instructed not to accompany the group to Chequers because, as Gazier explained, since the mission was to berate Eden about Lloyd's attitude in New York, it was unsuitable that the Ambassador should be present.[142]

By mid-afternoon the French had gone most of the way to convincing Eden to embark on a joint operation against Egypt, with France and Israel. After some debate and verbal fencing, Challe outlined a 'possible plan of action':

> Israel should be invited to attack Egypt across the Sinai Peninsula and that France and Britain, having given the Israeli forces enough time to seize all or most of Sinai, should then order 'both sides' to withdraw their forces from the Suez Canal, in order to permit an Anglo-French force to intervene and occupy the Canal on the pretext of saving it from damage by fighting. Thus the two powers would be able to claim to be 'separating the combatants' and 'extinguishing a dangerous fire', while actually seizing control of the entire waterway and of its terminal ports. Port Said and Suez. This would not only restore the running of the Canal to Anglo-French management, but, by putting us physically in control of the terminal ports – a position which Egypt had hitherto always held – it would enable us to supervise all shipping movements through the Canal and so break the Egyptian blockade of Israel.[143]

The Prime Minister remained non-committal, suggesting that he would reply early next week, probably Tuesday, 16 October.[144] That Eden did not agree immediately demonstrated that he had not already decided upon force and was not merely looking for a *casus belli*. It also represented Eden's vision of 'collective government', with the need to pass any plans before his most senior advisers, before any decision could be made. However, as Millard, who was also present, remembered, Eden was 'intrigued' by the plan, particularly after the recent American unreliability.[145] It was this interest that would lead Eden to agree to collusion and ultimately bring about his own downfall. The seeds of an alternative solution had been sown. The Prime Minister saw the Challe plan as the way forward despite his failure to commit to the French. He now required Cabinet agreement on this policy. In Eden's mind, the decision to use force had been made.

The option had never been more than a possibility but it now offered a way out for an overworked, overtired, ill and now uninspired leader. Reinternationalisation of the Canal remained imperative to the Prime Minister. SCUA had proved unsuccessful and the move to the UN had now become a dead end. For Eden, negotiation had left him staring at the same problem that he had faced in July: Nasser still controlled the Suez Canal, threatening Britain's oil supplies. Several key factors came together on the 14th to end Eden's pursuit of a peaceful settlement. Now cornered by the French, Israelis, the British public, his own party and the media, he recalled Lloyd from New York. However, this apparently open rejection of the possibility of a negotiated settlement is misleading. Lloyd had not shown any real signs of formalising an agreement with Fawzi, and as Millard recalled: 'I am not sure that Fawzi had actually accepted it in writing [or] whether he would have been able to sell them to Nasser.'[146] In his report to Eden, which arrived on 15 October, Lloyd justified the 'debit side' of the situation, proving to Eden that a settlement was not yet in sight:

> We are now committed to further interchanges with the Egyptians without a time limit and the Egyptians will now feel that the critical phase is past... The limited progress we have made here may encourage feeling of over-optimism which will make it more difficult for us to take a firm line with the Egyptians in the more difficult negotiations which are yet to come before a final settlement can be reached. The extraordinarily naive statement by President Eisenhower is the nearest example of this.[147]

The Manchester Guardian, the most pacifist and supportive of negotiation among the newspapers, had led on the 13th with one of the headlines: 'STILL BIG DIFFERENCES'.[148] Always the most ardent advocate of a peaceful solution amongst the press, the newspaper agreed with Lloyd, Eden and other editorials that a UN-inspired settlement was not possible.[149]

Eden had practical difficulties that could be quickly redressed by a military operation with the French. The military build-up had had to be maintained in case of action. This had caused strenuous and quite often unhealthy conditions for the reservists, 24 of whom had been arrested for protesting on 1 October.[150] Millard explained Eden's thinking: 'It did offer a way out of a dilemma because the military operation had been mounted and was sitting waiting to be launched. Obviously you couldn't keep that waiting for very long. Reservists couldn't be kept hanging about. They either had to go back to their jobs or be used.'[151] The supplies of the reservists had run down considerably and scurvy was breaking out.[152] Beyond that there was an increase in tension as they remained on alert for a possible conflict but without any orders or news. The tail wagging the dog was another facet of the Suez Crisis, underscoring Eden's lack of control. Britain's military were in no position to deal with this sort of dilemma: 'Britain had the capacity to deal with Mau Mau or with the Doomsday, with an atomic war, we did not have plans for a little local episode in the Eastern Mediterranean.'[153] It was not just a case of strategy: financially Britain could not keep an army including reservists up and ready for long periods.[154] On 11 October, a Staff Conference had deferred a statement concerning the military preparations and the reservists, until the next week (beginning 15 October).[155] In addition, the 'Winter Plan', developed to replace 'Musketeer Revise', was authorised by the Chiefs of Staff on 12 October, to take effect on 1 November. This meant that an invasion could not be mounted until spring of 1957.[156] Although D-day of the contingency plan had been constantly revised and remained flexible to take account of political decisions, the possibility that the crisis could continue for another three to four months was now unacceptable to Eden.

The military were on alert and ready for action. The Prime Minister believed that the nationalisation of the Canal, if not reversed, would mean the end for both himself and the Government.[157] A matter of national security, the Suez Crisis had now become a question of political survival.

The largest influence on Eden came from within the Conservative Party and, in particular, the Suez Group.[158] Their pressure had steadily increased, building to a crescendo at the party conference at Llandudno, 11–13 October. The right wing had used the media, with supporters such as Colin Coote, the editor, and Malcolm Muggeridge, the leader writer at *The Daily Telegraph*, and Randolph Churchill in the *Evening Standard* and the *Daily Express*. '[A]ll these anti-Munich people turned against Eden, thought he was hopeless... So this element in the Conservative Party began to be pro-Macmillan, looking upon him as the best hope.'[159] The Suez Group's support for Macmillan, the leading 'hawk' within the Government, demonstrated that Eden, in contrast, believed in a peaceful settlement, or was at least more reluctant to turn to force, which was unacceptable to the hardliners. In addition to Eden's problems, the Private Secretary Bishop recalled how the Prime Minister 'felt that there were others outside the Government who were deliberately trying to erode his position', while Millard believed that:

> Eden felt himself vulnerable because he had signed the agreement on the withdrawal from the Canal Zone and the right wing of the Conservative Party had said that he was throwing away our position and that this was yet another retreat from Empire. He was therefore vulnerable on Suez because it would be seen as the direct consequences of withdrawal from the Canal Zone. He felt perhaps more vulnerable on this issue than he needed to, and he attached too much importance to the opinion of people who didn't really matter very much, like the Suez Group, people like Julian Amery, Biggs-Davidson, Charles Waterhouse and so on, and also to the popular press. He was sensitive to that sort of thing.[160]

As Millard continued, he believed that there was a concerted campaign waged against Eden from within the Conservative Party by '[t]he old sort of Churchillians'.[161] Churchill privately encouraged this.[162] His attitude towards the withdrawal was summed up when he said to Lord Moran: 'It serves Anthony right. He has inherited what he let me in for.'[163] Churchill had made it quite clear 'that he was dead against what Anthony was doing', in closing down the base.[164] Churchill had sent private messages congratulating Amery, one of the unofficial heads of the Suez Group, for his attacks on Eden's position in his parliamentary speeches.[165] The former Prime Minister had begun to regret his decision to nominate Eden as his successor.[166] Those who were now pushing beyond a whispering campaign 'were nostalgic for the past and loyal to the old leader'.[167] This action increased in volume as the Suez Crisis deepened, culminating in the pressure at the party conference.

Transition to Force: 4 October–14 October   141

David Pitblado, who had served with Eden to the end of 1955, had never thought of the Suez Group as a thorn in Eden's side but by October 1956 it had become a serious problem for the Prime Minister.[168] Shuckburgh believed that Eden 'was looking over his shoulder at the party all the time, and that was one of the tragedies, which, in my opinion, largely drove him to the Suez disaster'. As he continued: 'I think Churchill has a heavy responsibility over that.'[169] In addition, eventually succeeding Churchill, Eden always had the added pressure of immediate comparison, from every member of the public and Parliament.[170] This had been the reason why the Prime Minister had not consulted or publicly used Churchill during the election campaign of 1955. He wanted to show the public that he could take the reins from Churchill and lead the country his own way.[171] In addition, he wanted to keep his policy separate from that of the belligerent Churchill.

Only the day before the visit of the French Minister for Social Affairs, the Deputy to French Chief of General Staff, Gazier, and Challe, on 13 October, Eden had been to the Conservative Party Conference at Llandudno where both he and Nutting, deputising for Lord Salisbury, had made 'rumbustious' and belligerent speeches. Referring to Eisenhower's press comment, he said, 'I agree with those words. We should all take them as our text. That is why we have always said that with us force is the last resort, but it cannot be excluded. Therefore, we have refused to say that in no circumstances would we ever use force. No responsible Government could ever give such a pledge.'[172] Amery revealed that the French had sent messages to the Suez Group 'asking us to put on the heat because they didn't think Eden would go ahead. We had a meeting and went there [to the Party Conference] determined to turn it on, which we did.'[173] Eden's toughened line led to rapturous applause, as did Nutting's speech, leaving him to write to Lloyd: 'The Party Conference went extremely well this week. I have never known our people in such good heart.'[174] Buoyed by his successful line, on the 14th Eden was handed the opportunity to turn hard words into a reality that he believed would ensure his and the Government's political survival. The dilemma of his decision to use force was also revealed by the lack of confidence that the French, Israelis and Egyptians had in him. Such had been his peaceful line that, as Amery recalled: 'They [the Egyptians] had no confidence in Anthony either and nor had the French or the Israelis or indeed Nuri. All the time they were wondering if he meant business.' This was consistent with the frequent doubts of the French military.[175] As Amery continued, by October, 'I think that all the time people who thought like me were getting worried, [wondering], "Were we going to give in again?"'[176] This reflected the earlier misjudgement and realisation of Eden's policy. The Prime Minister's development of contingency plans had given Churchill, the Suez Group and the French reason to believe that he would resolve the crisis with military action. His ultimate use of force reiterated this mistaken view. However, they quickly realised that his attempts at negotiation were sincere and forced them to pressure the Prime Minister, ensuring the solution that they wanted. If Eden had wanted to employ force before 14 October, he would have enlisted the support of these groups to implement a military solution, or at least privately allayed their fears, promising to invoke one at a suitable moment. Instead, he antagonised them with his pacifism and vacillation, only succumbing to their pressure three months into the crisis when he believed that the chances of a negotiated settlement had disappeared.

In addition to pressure from these right-wing groups, Eden's advisers either advocated the use of force or offered no alternatives. At the beginning of the crisis, Eden believed he had little need for advice on foreign policy, one private secretary remembering his surprise when one day Eden had actually asked his opinion on foreign affairs.[177] His limited channels of advice came from Kirkpatrick, and the Cabinet Secretary, Norman Brook, both believers in the use of force.[178] Kirkpatrick, despite being Permanent Under-Secretary at the Foreign Office, held violently opposite views on the use of force to the majority of the other members of the Department, while Bishop recalled that Brook 'had been in favour of that action [military operation]' and 'did not dissent as an adviser from what was being done'.[179] Principally referring to the eventual use of force, Shuckburgh revealed: 'I think Kirkpatrick favoured it all. I think [he] believed that Eden was right to stand up and be tough. I don't think he thought he was right to stop the operation, but I think he thought he was right to start.'[180] Sir Denis Wright, Assistant Under-Secretary at the Foreign Office, did not think that Kirkpatrick ever wavered in his defence of the Government policy and, shortly after the invasion, recorded in his diary: 'I can't help feeling that he [Kirkpatrick] is partly to blame for all this.'[181]

In October, when Eden was mentally and physically exhausted, he found himself surrounded by bellicose advice. The view of the Foreign Office had been 'tainted' by Kirkpatrick. Eden was adamant that he was unaware of Anthony Nutting's opposition to the use of force. He had asked Nutting to substitute for the belligerent Lord Salisbury at the Party Conference, and Nutting had reiterated the Government's firm resolution. Logan recalled that it was only much later that Eden learnt that a number of Foreign Office officials were considering tendering their resignations.[182] Little opposition to the ultimate use of force was heard. R. A. Butler, the Lord Privy Seal, remained a leading dove but silent.[183] As Powell said, referring to Butler's reaction to the plan of 14 October: 'Butler behaved in typical Butlerian manner of agonising over anything, wondering whether it was right or it wasn't. He certainly went through all that and expressed himself dubious about the thing from time to time. But that was just the make up of the man.'[184] This dismissal of Butler's reaction suggested that the Lord Privy Seal did not openly resist the move to use force, as he continued publicly to support the Government's policy. It was not until much later that he dissented from the action taken. Walter Monckton spoke out on two occasions, once in the

Egypt Committee meeting of 24 August and once in the Cabinet Committee meeting of 28 August.[185] However, despite his amenable personality, both friends and colleagues saw him as constantly complaining throughout his ministerial career.[186] He continued to sit on the Egypt Committee as Minister of Defence until 18 October, when it became clear that Eden would use the military.[187] He did not even protest about the Port Said landing, and despite disliking it, 'never firmly expressed the opinion that it was wrong'.[188] Even if his disagreement had been taken at face value, he was the only senior member of the Government to offer any adverse comments.

Eden recognised the need to provide a forceful deterrent to enable a peaceful solution. He actively sought the answer through the US. The Prime Minister hoped that it would set out a policy, but his attempt to tie himself to the American lead, reacting to events, was eventually weakened by his insecurity and the dissension within his party and the media. He became increasingly disenchanted with Nasser and the lack of American assistance.[189] From late September and early October he tied himself closer and closer to the French, unaware that they had been developing the germ of a plan with the Israelis. Increasingly ill and still not recovered from surgery, he ended three weeks of mounting doubts and vacillation over the possibility of a diplomatic solution for the quick win that he had avoided since July. This was not the same man who had been elected only 18 months earlier. His attempts at negotiation from a position of strength had worried Nasser. Yet this was worthless, in the long term, without much clearer international condemnation of Egypt's actions.

Trapped, Eden was unable to fulfil his policy and find a solution to the crisis by economic sanctions alone.[190] The Americans had offered solutions but had never ensured their implementation, undermining their own work and that of Eden and Lloyd. The most distressing example of this was SCUA, which Eden had believed could be used both as an authority to regain international control of the Canal and as an economic sanction to weaken Nasser's position. Even after Eden's realisation that the Americans would not help implement the British version of SCUA, which he thought vital, he continued to hope that they might place at least moral pressure on Nasser, but Dulles continued to frustrate the Prime Minister by constantly changing position. Confused, and now mentally weakened by recurrent bouts of fever, hospitalisation and the rigours of crisis management, he was surrounded by bellicose advice and even the threat of resignation from the belligerent Macmillan.[191] The French, who had been pushing for a military solution since the beginning of the crisis, now increased that pressure on Eden. They weakened the potential for a resolution in the Security Council debates by filibustering whilst directly entreating the Prime Minister through Ambassador Chauvel, Pineau and finally the Gazier/Challe mission. The failure of the talks with the Egyptians in New York added to Eden's frustration. The right-wing pressure from the Suez Group also became more powerful during October, culminating in the call for a much stronger resolution from the Government at the Llandudno conference. By 14 October, all these pressures weighed heavily on Eden. With national economic and strategic safety and political survival at stake, the Prime Minister succumbed to the pressure, which his sensitivity had exaggerated. Military collusion had finally been accepted as Britain's resolution of the crisis by a man no longer able to deal with the pressures about him.

6
Collusion: 15 October–25 October

From the Probability of Force to a Final Agreement

During the period 15 October to 25 October, Eden moved to a signed commitment of British troops and the final preparations for invasion of Egypt. However, this could not be reached until he had secured the backing of his senior ministers, reflecting his consistent belief in collective responsibility in government.[1] During this period there was an increase in the number of meetings of the Government's senior ministers and the further limitation of the power of the Egypt Committee. With this transition came Eden's use of force to settle the Suez Crisis. Closely following the French offer, these developments also testified to the timing of the Prime Minister's decision in favour of a military solution on 14 October.

Despite his promise to Gazier and Challe, Eden replied to the Frenchmen 'non-committally that he would give these suggestions very careful thought and would convey his reactions to Mollet early that week, after he had had an opportunity to discuss them with certain of his colleagues'.[2] This did not represent a commitment to the French, as he had already proposed to meet Mollet on the Tuesday, ignorant of the extent of Franco-Israeli planning.[3] However, it reflected his interest in the plan and, consequently, the need to have the agreement of at least his senior colleagues to unite the Cabinet; so he convened a ministerial meeting for the morning of the 16th.[4] Despite the Prime Minister's decision of 14 October, to use force to settle the crisis, the French had left Chequers almost as uncertain as to Eden's commitment to a forceful solution as when they had arrived. The sudden rise in the number of these ministerial meetings suggested that now, in mid-October, he had become intent on the use of force, as he tried to gain the support of his senior ministers and develop a plan of action. In the thirteen days between 14 October and 26 October, 1956, Eden attended nineteen high-level meetings with senior ministers (as a group), including three Cabinet Meetings, one Egypt Committee Meeting and one Defence Committee Meeting. This compared with fifty-nine in the previous seventy-nine days of the crisis.

During the same period Eden held fourteen private ministerial meetings in thirteen days, after only twelve in the preceding seventy-nine days. The Prime Minister required reassurance and advice to employ the solution that now not only appeared justifiable but had the potential machinery for its implementation.

The Security Council moves were deadlocked. Before he left, Lloyd agreed for Hammarskjøld, Pineau, Fawzi and himself to meet in Geneva on 29 October.[5] However, nothing more could be done until, Pineau said, he could free himself from his commitment in the National Assembly.[6] Eden believed that negotiations had now become too protracted, and, influenced by Pineau's inability to attend the discussions for an indefinite period, thought that they should now be deferred in favour of a more immediate solution: force.

Nutting wanted to convince Eden otherwise, but had been 'at a loss to know how to tackle him', adamant as the Prime Minister appeared in his quest to turn the meeting of the 14th into a real attempt to remove Nasser.[7] However, Nutting remained the only dissenting voice. Archibald Ross, the Assistant Under-Secretary for the Middle East at the Foreign Office, and Kirkpatrick outlined objections to the Challe plan for Nutting's benefit. Yet, this did not represent their own opinions, nor was it a representation from the Foreign Office.[8] Nutting later complained to Sir Denis Wright that Kirkpatrick was much to blame for the Suez disaster because he 'didn't support him in the crucial Cabinet meeting in mid-Oct. when the French Plan was discussed'.[9] At the crucial moment there was no opposition to the Prime Minister's interest in the Challe plan from his senior officials and ministers. Eden's mind now became set and Nutting quickly realised 'the Prime Minister was not going to be gainsaid'.[10] This contrasted with Nutting's earlier attempts to influence Eden, suggesting that until this point, he believed that the Prime Minister could be 'gainsaid' and hence that the use of force had not been definitely decided upon. From 14 October, Nutting no longer believed that he could affect Eden because the decision to use force had now been made. The change of pace, and hence the decision to act immediately, was indicated by Roger Makins, who, returning from Washington to his new appointment as Joint Permanent Secretary of the Treasury on 15 October, 'was astonished to find that neither Eden nor Lloyd nor even my new Minister, Macmillan, had wanted to see me...and to ask my assessment of the American position on Suez'.[11] Once again, the inner circle of senior ministers had retreated within its own advice and were unprepared to discuss the machinations of their meetings with civil servants, other than a selected few.[12] This increasingly narrow circle of advisers led to the development of a misunderstanding of Eden and his intentions within the historiography of the period and particularly the histories.

There had been no sign of any potential solution in a telegram from Dulles to the Foreign Secretary of 15 October. Dulles had set out very methodically, in four and a half pages, to dispel any misunderstanding of how the US saw SCUA's role. He outlined that, '[o]ur idea, made clear from the beginning, is that it was to be a means of practical working cooperation with the Egyptian authorities, which would seek to establish *de facto* international participation in the operation of the Canal'.[13] Eden minuted, 'Hardly the spirit of what he said. SCUA was to have been tougher than 18 Power proposals for Egyptians.'[14] Eden was disappointed that the British SCUA proposal could not be made to work and had been denigrated by Dulles. However, his minute also included the unlikely suggestion that the Users' Club would go further than the 18-Power proposals. This indicated that Eden had already made his decision to use force and was now keen to exaggerate the potential for a peaceful solution destroyed by the Americans and hence justify his decision to employ a military operation against Nasser. This exaggeration, particularly in his memoirs, was so great as to leave Brook asking Eden to soften his comments about the US, particularly Dulles, because of 'the effect which publication might have on Anglo/American relations'.[15]

On the morning of 16 October, the group of ministers met at No. 10.[16] The 'six principles' of Anglo/French/Egyptian co-operation over the Canal were discussed but rejected because they could not offer a quick resolution. The problems of the 12 October remained: the principles could not provide for reinternationalisation of the Canal nor could agreement be sought over their possible implementation.[17] The meeting could see no way of making SCUA work. Macmillan and Kilmuir strongly supported the Challe plan, while Nutting reiterated his fears and Monckton, somewhat subdued, evinced his own concerns.[18] Nutting had been sitting in for Lloyd who was travelling from New York. When the Foreign Secretary arrived Nutting told him of the Challe plan, to which he responded, 'We must have nothing to do with the French plan.'[19] However, Lloyd had received Dulles's letter of 15 October which destroyed any hope that the Americans were prepared to use the payment of dues to SCUA as a sanction against the Egyptians. It has also been alleged that on 16 October Eden received a communication from Eisenhower 'of a reassuring character'. In it, the President said that if the British and French waited until after the US elections, of 6 November, an agreement could be arranged.[20] With this knowledge and virtually no hope in the proposed meeting in Geneva, Lloyd had little with which to oppose Eden's, Macmillan's and Kilmuir's desire to accept the Challe plan.[21] Lloyd believed that Nasser should not be allowed to get away with his actions. He did not want Egypt to 'gain both the management of the Canal and the lion's share of the dues', and believed that Nasser could not be trusted 'to honour any commitment'.[22] He had already written to Dulles, fearful of the apparent 'divergence between us on the purposes of SCUA'. With the arrival of Dulles's letter, which crossed his own communication, his fears that 'SCUA will prove to have been still-born, and the prospects of a peaceful settlement with Egypt will be gravely diminished' were realised.[23] Even Lloyd, viewed by historians and contemporaries as a pacifist, now believed that force was the only option: the need to use the last resort had arisen.[24]

Faced with this position, Eden and Lloyd flew to Paris on the afternoon of the 16th, accompanied by Millard. While the French goal of removing Nasser remained the same, they had become increasingly impatient with Eden and the British. Mollet and Pineau flatly rejected any talk of negotiation.[25] They were not aware of Eden's decision to use force and and in previous discussions between the two countries, the Prime Minister had given no suggestion that he believed in a forceful resolution of the crisis, continuing to favour negotiation from a position of strength. The French impatience with Eden was reflected in their terse summary of the talks:

> The French summed up our discussions by formulating two questions. In answer to the question whether we would fight to defend Nasser, Eden said that he thought the answer was 'No'. As to the second question, whether we would intervene to safeguard the Canal and limit hostilities, he thought the answer was 'Yes', but he would have to obtain the approval of his Cabinet colleagues for both those answers.[26]

As Eden's answer showed, he neither could nor would act without the backing of his senior ministers. The French, irritated by the continuing delay, thought that Eden would be prepared to use force because he had initiated the contingency plans in July. However, their need to convene the meeting of the 14th and the subsequent Anglo-French meetings suggested that Eden would not be as compliant as assumed. The difference between military preparations and going to war had become clear.

In a post-dated minute, Lloyd set out to show his passivity at the meeting, disclosing his attempt to renew negotiations with Fawzi. This reflected Lloyd's own disassociation from the responsibility of the Cabinet decision of 18 October to intervene 'should' war break out between Israel and Egypt.[27] The Foreign Secretary's attitude and actions after Suez suggested his dissatisfaction with the way events were handled, although he never publicly stated his position. Lloyd never remonstrated over the military plan or collusion, despite many of the *dramatis personae* not believing it sound or practical. He reported that if the Egyptians offered a suggested negotiation based on the second set of principles, '[i]t would be inexpedient to reject such a suggestion'. He then qualified this faint possibility: 'We should not, however, entertain any proposals for negotiation which were inconsistent with that resolution.'[28] While he would have preferred a peaceful solution, the Foreign Secretary reconciled himself to the fact that this would not provide a satisfactory solution, and as such force remained the only option. He had reached the same conclusion as the Prime Minister, but in later years did not want to be tarnished with the same failure that Eden had to carry.

Eden discussed the meetings of the 14th and 16th with Iverach McDonald, but failed to discuss the proposed plan during the Egypt Committee meeting on the following day, 17 October.[29] Again, this indicated the level to which McDonald was privy to 'secret' information and the extent to which the Egypt Committee had no significant role to play in the resolution of the crisis. On 18 October, Eden prepared the Cabinet for the use of force by outlining the Challe Plan, in very simple terms. However, Eden was considerably more direct with the Cabinet than the minutes reveal, asking that in the event of hostilities between Egypt and Israel 'we should go in with the French to separate the combatants and occupy the Canal'.[30] Then as Lloyd wrote in a memorandum: 'Eden wanted to know whether the Cabinet differed from that point of view. There was no adverse comment.'[31] Cabinet endorsed Eden's proposed action, despite Butler's proclivity to hedge his bets, and Lloyd's fears of the effects on Arab opinion.[32] This did not fulfil the support that Eden required, because as Lloyd recalled, there 'was by no means a full attendance [of Ministers]'.[33] However, the Prime Minister sent a minute to those not in attendance, summarising his report.[34] He remained cautious, despite the offer of tripartite action made by Mollet at their previous meeting, typical of his diplomatic training.[35] He wanted to embark on a military operation against Egypt but he still believed that he needed Cabinet support or at least its acquiescence.

Franco-Israeli talks again reflected their distrust because of Eden's former caution. Mollet wrote to Ben-Gurion on the 18 October, inviting the Israelis to Paris for talks concerning the possible military operation against Egypt. As with their earlier discussions, it was decided to continue talks without the British.[36] The French could not see the British supporting a resolution other than had already been outlined by Eden. It had taken the Prime Minister eleven weeks to accept the use of force and then only under the condition of the Challe plan. This did not suggest that he would be flexible over changes to the outline of an agreed military operation. The Israelis were not keen to support this plan and so the French tried to bring them into line through intensive talks.

On the evening of 18 October, Eden received a number of telegrams from Dixon, the UK Permanent Representative at the UN in New York, bolstering his resolve. They reported that Hammarskjøld now hoped that 'in view of the progress he was making with Dr. Fawzi', the British should not 'press on with plans for payment of dues to S.C.U.A.'. He believed that this would ruin the chances of progress at any future meeting. Even despite his decision for a forceful resolution, Eden minuted 'Rubbish' on this, remaining consistent in his belief that any possibility of a negotiated settlement could only be made with the threat of economic sanctions, with the payment of dues to SCUA and not Egypt, in the background. Hammarskjøld then annoyed Eden further by suggesting that 'if we exerted new pressures in the form of deflection of dues... this would so to speak be an infringement of the status quo'.

Eden could only minute this comment with exclamation marks. The Prime Minister agreed with Dixon's view that this argument appeared to have come from Fawzi and thus carried even less weight because of Fawzi's bias.[37] Dixon's final telegram of the evening proved to be the last nail in the coffin of any possible negotiated settlement through the Security Council. He confirmed to Eden that '[t]he Secretary General seems already to have made his mind up that it will be his duty to summon the French and ourselves to another meeting whether or not we consider that Fawzi's plan offers a good enough basis for resumption of talks'. Dixon continued, suggesting that Eden might wish him to slow Hammarskjøld and suggest that the British would have to have time to consider the final plan for co-operation with Egypt. As Dixon concluded, again with which Eden agreed, '[w]e obviously cannot be bounced into a meeting on an unsatisfactory basis'.[38] On the following day Dixon wrote again with a message from Hammarskjøld raising a number of points concerning Fawzi's proposals which required answers from Egypt.[39] As Lloyd recalled: 'It was clear to us that if he had found it necessary to raise a number of points on Fawzi's paper, it must be pretty vague.'[40] As far as Eden and Lloyd were concerned, the Security Council had failed to show any sign of providing a solution by 14 October. These messages from Dixon merely reaffirmed this opinion.

On the evening of the 18th, Eden had also seen a telegram from Trevelyan, the British Ambassador in Cairo. While most of it demonstrated that '[t]he situation here has perhaps somewhat improved from our point of view', Eden remained reticent and highlighted the Ambassador's conclusion. Trevelyan, keen not 'to overstress these factors', believed that '[t]here is still no sign of Nasser climbing down on his major point, i.e. his objection to international operation as means of isolating the Canal from politics'.[41] Nasser remained completely intransigent and Eden's will to carry out the Challe Plan strengthened.

The Prime Minister then met with the French on 20 October in Paris, where he handed over 'a two-paragraph written declaration' of his intent.[42] This meeting is unsubstantiated but there is evidence of a letter sent by Eden to the French backing the Challe plan, and dated 21 October.[43] Eden had met with senior ministers at Chequers on the 21st.[44] This meeting decided to send Lloyd to meet with the French and the Israelis. Eden believed that he had enough agreement to send an outline of the proposed plan to the French, possibly even direct agreement, judging by the importance that he now placed on the opinion of his senior colleagues. Dayan recalled:

> The first paragraph stated that Britain and France would demand of both Egypt and Israel that they retire from the Canal area, and if one side refused, Anglo-French forces would intervene to ensure the smooth operation of the Canal. The purpose of this paragraph was to provide the

legal, political, and moral justification for the invasion of Egypt by Britain and France. The second paragraph declared that the British would not go to the aid of Egypt if war broke out between her and Israel. But this was not the case as regards Jordan, with whom Britain had a valid defense treaty. This paragraph was apparently designed to assure us that Britain would not turn her guns on us – even if Egypt asked her to... Ben-Gurion... did not regard this declaration as a basis for joint action.[45]

The Israelis were due to fly to Paris on the evening of the 21st. Such was the French motivation to settle the dispute by force and their relief at finally bringing Eden and the British on board, that they quickly attempted to foreclose discussions with the Israelis and bring them into the Franco-British plan. Consequently, the French sent an aeroplane for the Israelis which arrived on the morning of the 21st, enabling two French delegates to start negotiating before the British arrival at the Paris meeting.[46]

On 22 October, the French, Israelis and British met at a villa in Sèvres, on the outskirts of Paris.[47] The French and Israelis had been in discussion long before the British arrived, but on their arrival, Lloyd and Logan, Eden's assigned representatives, were informed by Pineau of the substance of the day's Franco-Israeli talks.[48] However, this did not help to remove any suspicion that the French and Israelis had been conspiring together and were, as Logan recalled, keen 'to get us on the hook'.[49] In addition, Lloyd's attitude at the meeting increased the Israeli distrust of the British, and the fear that they did not want to be involved in a military operation.[50] Mordechai Bar-On, Ben-Gurion's secretary, could not get on with the 'aloof' Lloyd, who he believed representative of the snobbish British, looking 'as if something stinks under his nose all the time'.[51] Ben-Gurion, too, distrusted the Foreign Office and Eden's apparent exploitation of the Israelis.[52] This was another example of Israeli scepticism of British intentions indicative of Eden's earlier passivity.

Having sent the letter of 21 October to Pineau, Eden believed that the meeting at Sèvres would simply be a formality to iron out any fine details. As Logan recalled: 'It became apparent to me that much of the detail had already been discussed between the French and the Israelis and between the French and the British Ministers.'[53] Despite this, the British delegates were immediately confronted by Ben-Gurion with a proposition 'that the three governments ought to concert their policies to form some sort of grand design for the Middle East'.[54] Lloyd ignored the suggestion.[55] However, pressure mounted from both sides to involve the British in some form of direct action against Egypt. Despite his decision to use force, Eden had not openly committed himself to the French. They remained reluctant to believe in any possible British commitment to force, especially after the previous thirteen and a half weeks of passivity and negotiation. The French continued to demonstrate their determination to remove Nasser, that had been consistent throughout the crisis, but they would not act without the British. As Logan continued, the French 'were determined to go ahead and do something. They were determined to find a way of involving us', and the Israelis did not want to go ahead with only the French as allies, because of the need for a strong air-force.[56] Lloyd explained to the other delegates that he had come to discuss the actions that the three governments might take if Israel attacked Egypt. He then reiterated the basis of the plan that had emerged on the 14th and to which Eden had agreed orally and in the written communication. Ben-Gurion was unimpressed, and after further discussion, 'looked depressed'. It was the French who 'tried to keep the talks going', again indicative of their commitment, throughout the crisis, to a forceful resolution.[57] Talks foundered on Lloyd's inability to agree to advancing the RAF attack on the Egyptian Air Force, also indicative of the remit that he had been given by Eden and thus that the Prime Minister had expected the meeting to be near a formality. The British then returned to London, undertaking to report to Cabinet, potentially returning with a reply on the following day.[58] Lloyd telephoned Eden to tell him that Ben-Gurion had been very truculent.[59] He did not foresee any room for agreement at this stage, telling Nutting that it appeared as though the plan would not 'come off'.[60]

On the following morning the senior ministers met at No. 10.[61] Lloyd described this meeting as 'in effect the Egypt Committee'.[62] However, this inner circle was much smaller than the Cabinet Committee, and represented the secretive move towards a forceful solution that had begun after 14 October. It was therefore an opportunity to bring the policy-makers up to date. At the Cabinet meeting immediately afterwards, Eden tried to keep the probability of using force in the near future alive, despite Israel's apparent intransigence at Sèvres.[63] He argued:

> When the Cabinet had last discussed the Suez situation on 18th October, there had been reason to believe that the issue might be brought rapidly to a head as a result of military action by Israel against Egypt. From secret conversations which had been held in Paris with representatives of the Israeli Government, it now appeared that the Israelis would not alone launch a full-scale attack against Egypt. The United Kingdom and French Governments were thus confronted with the choice between an early military operation or a relatively prolonged negotiation.

Lloyd, still looking for a diplomatic solution in the face of support for a forceful settlement, said that he would not exclude the possibility that we might be able to reach, by negotiation with the Egyptians, a settlement which would give us the substance of our demand for effective international supervision of the Canal'. However, he then qualified this with 'three serious objections'. First, the French were no longer prepared to back such a policy (if they had ever been). Second, any necessary relaxation of the military preparations would weaken the British bargaining position. And third, and most important, 'he saw no prospect of reaching such a settlement as would diminish Colonel Nasser's influence throughout the Middle East'. In conclusion, Eden demonstrated the main problem, both for the Cabinet's decision and more significantly for his own devices:

> [G]rave decisions would have to be taken by the Cabinet in the course of the next few days. For the present, however, the discussion could not be carried further until the attitude of the French Government was more clearly known. The French Foreign Minister had been asked to come over to London for consultations that evening; and the result of those consultations would be reported to the Cabinet on the following day.[64]

This statement reflected the Prime Minister's consistent belief in collective government, but also suggested that, despite the obvious French belligerency, he had not formalised an agreement over any military operation.

Pineau arrived that evening, aware of the need to move quickly. It had taken three weeks to press Eden into using force, and he did not want a reversal now. He had decided to fly to London for direct talks with Eden, rather than being asked to come, hopeful of influencing the Prime Minister to consort with the French and Israelis.[65] Lloyd had realised, early that morning, that he would be unable to reply on the question of the timing of the RAF bombardment of the Egyptian Air Force that day. Consequently he had sent Logan to Paris to keep Pineau informed.[66] Thus, Pineau flew into London at 7:30 p.m. Logan has argued that Pineau probably believed that he could make more headway by talking directly to Eden. However, Pineau dined and talked with Lloyd for an hour and a half before they were joined by Eden at approximately 10 p.m.[67] As Logan surmised, the three men reached an agreement over the use of the RAF. Eden accepted the plan that Dayan had developed earlier in the day.[68] They quickly dismissed the possibility of US intervention and rejected any further discussions because of 'their preoccupation with the election campaign and the generally unsatisfactory nature of our exchanges with Mr Dulles about US action of any character'. This effectively ended the possibility of American involvement on any level, had it ever existed.[69] However, Lloyd feared that Pineau 'might make more of our talk than was warranted' and so he wrote to the Frenchman making it clear that the British had not asked Israel to take action: 'We merely asked ourselves what our reactions would be in the event that certain events transpire.'[70] It was important to the British, as Eden later demonstrated, that the world should not see Britain as colluding with the French and especially not with the Israelis. If this leaked to the Arabs, or the Americans, the British might lose all influence in the Middle East, and so threaten Western European oil supplies. This was why Eden remained so keen to conceal the collusion, despite the consequences of his appearing to have backed a planned military solution from July.

During the morning of the 24 October, the Cabinet was informed of the consultations with Pineau, held the previous evening. Again, the ground was set for the probability of the use of force, as possible questions reflecting dissent were met with prepared answers. Eden was looking for the *casus belli*, or 'Jenkins' ear', as Macmillan had called it. However, in contrast, Macmillan had first sought this solution on 9 August.[71] Eden had only recently decided to use force. As the Prime Minister argued:

> [U]nless early action could be taken to damage Colonel Nasser's prestige, his influence would be extended throughout the Middle East to a degree which would make it much more difficult to overthrow him. It was known that he was already plotting *coups* in many of the other Arab countries; and we should never have a better pretext for intervention against him than we had now as a result of his seizure of the Suez Canal. If, however, a military operation were undertaken against Egypt, its effect in other Arab countries would be serious unless it led to the early collapse of Colonel Nasser's regime. Both for this reason, and also because of the international pressures which would develop against our continuance of the operation, it must be quick and successful.

The Cabinet then considered the possibility of resolving the crisis through further diplomacy. However, it believed that, even by following this course of action, force would have to be used. If the Egyptians accepted negotiation, then they would slowly produce unsatisfactory proposals that would lead to a stalemate. Thus, negotiation could be used to provide a deadlock that could only be resolved by force. Summarising, Eden 'said that the choice before the Cabinet was now clear', but '[b]efore their final decision was taken, further discussions with the French Government would be required'.[72] Eden had decided upon the use of force but only within the parameters of the Challe plan. He needed to define that plan more specifically, hence the need to meet with the French again. He was not prepared to adopt any far-reaching changes to the outline that he had been offered on the 14 October. From this date, he remained consistant with the agreed plan, which suggested that he had not used this opportunity to initiate a prearranged military operation but had been stricken by the French suggestion of collusion and now saw the use of force as the only solution.

On the morning of the 24th, Patrick Dean, Assistant Under-Secretary at the Foreign Office, was called to see Eden where he was instructed to go to Sèvres with Logan to continue discussions.[73] His briefing only lasted about fifteen minutes. Eden said that it might be necessary for the French and Israeli governments to 'take action if the Canal were further threatened by Nasser or as a result of hostilities between Israel and Egypt'. Britain might have to intervene 'but only if there was a clear military threat to the Canal and Israeli forces had advanced towards the Canal. After a public warning, British and French forces would then intervene between the Israelis and the Egyptians to ensure the safety of the Canal. Discussions had taken place along these lines and it must now be made absolutely clear, before final decisions were taken, that British forces would not move unless the Israelis had advanced beyond their frontiers against Egypt and there was a clear military threat to the Canal.'[74] All this was new to Dean, but Eden wanted to send someone who would not have the flexibility to agree to anything beyond his well-defined remit. While Eden wanted to remove Nasser, he did not want to agree to a solution that openly demonstrated his compliance with the French and Israelis. Logan informed Dean of the substance of the previous meetings during their journey to Paris. On arrival, Dean handed Lloyd's letter to the French and then several hours of attempted clarification and discussion ensued before the French produced three copies of a document recently typed in an adjoining room.[75] The paper, which became known as the Sèvres Protocole, summarised the results of the discussions between the three governments. That the dates were not typed on the original documents but left blank and filled in by hand after further discussion, indicated that while Eden had appeared positive in his earlier communications, he had not firmly committed himself, particularly to the timetable of events. Once again, the Prime Minister had refused to commit himself to more than the agreement of the 14th. There was no room for flexibility on this issue. While the specific details had not been agreed, Eden did not want to make broader changes to the basis of the plan. Asked to sign the document, Dean was at first unsure, but after consultation with Logan it was decided that, as it appeared 'accurate, and also useful in recording the precision which had been sent to obtain... could be signed as such'. He was, however, careful to state that he was signing it *ad referendum*.[76] The French had wanted a solid commitment that would also appease the Israelis who distrusted the British. This distrust was such that the French and Israelis signed their own separate protocol, committing themselves to each other.[77]

On his return to London, Dean reported to a ministerial meeting at No.10, which decided to recommend 'the plan' to the Cabinet of the 25th.[78] After the Cabinet meetings of 18, 23 and 24 October, members had shown that they were willing to back force, if amply justified. Although Eden did not reveal the collusive details of the Sèvres Protocole, 'the substantive matter was placed before Cabinet' as he outlined the proposed plan of action should Israel invade Egypt.[79] He warned that '[w]e must face the risk that we should be accused of collusion with Israel'.[80] Cabinet was not unanimous in accepting 'the plan', but Eden, reinforced by Macmillan's belief that the Americans would remain at least indifferent to any British operation, remained firm.[81] After discussion, members

Agreed in principle that, in the event of an Israeli attack on Egypt, the Government should join with the French Government in calling on the two belligerents to stop hostilities and withdraw their forces to a distance of ten miles from the Canal; and should warn both belligerents that, if either or both of them failed to undertake within twelve hours to comply with these requirements, British and French forces would intervene in order to enforce compliance.[82]

Cabinet had sanctioned war, ending the Prime Minister's eleven-day search for support.

Eden failed to tell the Cabinet in any detail about the importance of the 'secret conversations...in Paris', and hence their relevance to the 'contingency plan' finally backed by the Cabinet.[83] Therefore, he came under criticism for misleading ministers and civil servants. In addition, he was also accused of deceiving the Americans and the British public. Eden was ill and tired. His collapse at the beginning of October had shown that his health had worsened, due to the build-up of stress with the development of the crisis, and the long hours that the Prime Minister worked, lengthened by the recent dealings with the Security Council in New York, where their day would have been Eden's night.[84] Monckton believed that the illness had transformed the Prime Minister, telling Nutting, 'that Eden was a very sick man. He had always been excitable and temperamental, but in the last few months he had seemed to be on the verge of a breakdown.'[85] Richard Powell, who only saw Eden during October, supported this view.[86] Other of Eden's friends and acquaintances could not believe that the illness had not contributed to the decision to escalate the crisis and enter into the collusion.[87] By mid-October he had made the decision to go to war.

During the period 15 to 24 October, Eden seized the opportunity to bring the Suez Crisis to an end. While the French plan, proposed on the 14th, had appeared to offer the solution, the Prime Minister did not believe that he could accept it until he had considered it in more detail and it had been endorsed by his senior colleagues who could carry the Cabinet with them. From this point, he increased the number of meetings with his senior ministers, taking the decision-making away from the Egypt Committee and Cabinet. The Prime Minister placed further restrictions on information, keen to maintain security and prevent the emergence of the truth about collusion. Such were the levels of security that as Mountbatten told Lord Hailsham upon his arrival at the Admiralty, 'the Prime Minister's express permission was required' just to be informed of the 'precautionary measures'.[88] Eden had known about opposition to the use of force since August and yet it was now that he chose to limit the distribution of documents and other information, as the probability of a military solution became a policy.[89] Decisions were now being made by a much smaller group of seven cabinet ministers (excluding Eden) and six civil servants.[90] The Egypt Committee had been much larger, with a higher circulation of documents and information. Documents had been distributed to at least thirty-seven individuals, including the Queen. In addition, in total, forty-six people sat on the Committee (fifty-three including the secretariat). Eden failed to reveal any details of the 'secret conversations' to the Egypt Committee on 17 October, and the group did not meet again before 1 November, never having discussed the final plan to invade Egypt with the French. The committee broke down into a smaller 'inner circle'. Despite Selwyn Lloyd referring to these ministerial meetings as Egypt Committee meetings with a severely curtailed membership, they were as distinct by their smaller membership as by their purpose. The Egypt Committee had been established to discuss the possible British response to the nationalisation of the Canal, and was dominated by the development of the military precautions, which appeared to be the only way of weakening Nasser's position, through threat or possible implementation. This did not mean that force *would* be employed. The informal 'inner circle' of ministers which had always existed, in that its members conferred over prominent issues, lay dormant as a policy-making elite until October 1956. Then, on 14 October, when Eden decided that the use of force had turned from a possibility discussed by the Egypt Committee, to a probability within his own mind, the 'inner circle' took on an executive role, if still appearing to be the same discursive group of senior ministers. Now committed to the use of force, he needed support to carry his plan through Cabinet. He also wanted to maintain security both for himself and for the operation. Eden even deceived the military, maintaining that the original military plan remained operative. He imparted enough information so that Musketeer Revise was not replaced by the 'Winter Plan', but so little that the armed forces remained on the alert for possible action against Israel.[91] The sudden increase in secret meetings and covert diplomacy, matched by increased interest from the French, confirmed that Eden had now decided to go to war. This move, in mid-October, from the communication of a plan to the British on 14 October to the written commitment of 21 October, signalled Eden's attempts to develop support to implement the decision of the 14th.

7
Finale: 26 October 1956– 9 January 1957

Implementation of Force, Ceasefire, Illness, and Retirement

As agreed at Sèvres, hostilities began with the Israeli invasion on 29 October, the issuing of the ultimatum on the 30th, an Anglo-French air bombardment on the 31st, followed by an airborne invasion on 5 November and an amphibious landing on the 6th. The level of apparent conviction with which Eden entered this phase of the crisis, suggested, as Millard and Clark had argued, that he believed that he was now fighting for the Government's and his own political survival. The importance of the decision was never lost on Eden during the ensuing weeks. It had taken him three months to decide to employ force to resolve the crisis. Powell remembered that the Prime Minister 'was very jumpy, very nervy, very wrought up, there's no doubt about it. He regarded almost the destiny of the world as resting on his shoulders I think. There's no doubt about that. And he was very anxious... very communicative of his views to everybody.'[1] He had vacillated because of the weakness of his position and the desire for a peaceful solution. Having now decided to use force he demonstrated the resolution and commitment that he continued to display when he had made his mind up on an issue.

Eden had expected that the Americans would acquiesce over the Anglo-French action. However, on 2 November, the UN passed Resolution 997 (ES-1), through which both the Americans and Soviets condemned British actions and demanded a ceasefire from all combatants.[2] This was the first time that the UN had ever met in emergency session, and significantly, despite the Soviet invasion of Hungary, the US deemed it necessary to side with the communist states on this issue. Further pressure then came from the British representative at the UN. Dixon warned Eden that the British position at the United Nations 'will become untenable... if we bomb open cities with resulting loss of civillian [sic] life or engage in battle with Egyptian forces'.[3] Some British bombers had already missed their targets of the military airfields near Cairo, hitting Cairo International Airport, an exclusively civilian airfield.[4]

However, despite constant fears, Eden's resolve held, as he reiterated his convictions to the British people on the 3rd.[5] Support began to mount again and the Prime Minister took heart from that support.[6] Churchill remained resolute.[7] He issued a public statement supporting the Government and encouraging the Americans to understand the action taken.[8] Eden was pleased when this message was then published in the press.[9] On the following morning, 4 November, both Eden and Lloyd 'were in complete agreement that having got thus far, it would be wrong to call off the operation'.[10] Again, this reiterated the commitment to seeing the solution through, now that the decision had been made, in contrast to the vacillation of the previous three months. However, despite this commitment and support, the international reaction had already begun to affect opinion.

Cabinet met later that evening, and after lengthy discussion favoured 'allowing the initial phase of the military operation to go forward as planned'.[11] Cabinet were 'allowing' the military operation to proceed. This ignored the fact that there now emerged open division among its members. The Prime Minister had 'invited each of his colleagues to indicate his view', consistent with his belief in collective responsibility. While the majority of the Cabinet advocated the decision

> two Ministers were inclined to favour the third course of deferring further military action indefinitely; but they made it clear that, if a majority of the Cabinet favoured a different course, they would support it. *The Paymaster-General* [Monckton] said that he remained in favour of suspending further military action indefinitely and that, if this course did not commend itself to his colleagues, he must reserve his position.[12]

At this stage twelve ministers were for going on, Butler, Kilmuir and Heathcoat Amory were for postponement, and Salisbury, Buchan-Hepburn and Monckton were for stopping. Of the three Service Ministers, only Hailsham was for continuing.[13] Eden recoiled under this split, surprised that such opposition existed, but was concerned enough that he 'wrestled for hours with Cabinet'.[14] Butler recalled that this 'seemed to nonplus the Prime Minister. He said he must go upstairs and consider his position. If he could not have united support, the situation might arise in which someone else might have to take over from him'.[15] Lady Eden recorded in her diary that her husband took Butler, Macmillan and Salisbury aside and told them that 'if they wouldn't go on then he would have to resign. Rab said if he did resign then no one else could form a Government', to which Macmillan and Salisbury agreed.[16] In particular, this was a 'brutal *volte face*' by Salisbury at such a key time.[17] Salisbury had been a key advocate of a military solution, and despite having tendered his resignation on a couple of occasions because of his fear of the Government's appeasement of the Soviets, had remained a supporter of the military option.

In addition, Macmillan had begun to show the first signs of his infamous change of heart that led to Harold Wilson's dubbing him, 'first in, first out'. On 1 November he acknowledged his own incorrect estimation of the American attitude. Clark recorded that the Chancellor 'was very worried about the American reaction, which was much worse than he had expected; he had written to Secretary [of the Treasury, George] Humphrey, hoping to put him right'.[18] During the second Egypt Committee meeting of the day, a telegram had arrived from Dixon, reporting that the UN had been discussing oil sanctions.[19] At this point Lloyd recalled, 'Macmillan threw his arms up in the air and said, "Oil sanctions! That finishes it."'[20] The Chancellor's commitment to a forceful solution had come to an end, although it took another five days before he openly rejected it in Cabinet and pressed for the withdrawal of Anglo-French troops from the Canal Zone. He had taken the advice of the Bank of England and the Treasury and deferred a move to request funds from the IMF.[21] However, the full realisation of the consequences of this deferral would not occur until 6 November.

Nevertheless, until this point, Eden had continued to expect US support or acquiescence. Military links remained good. The Americans passed on photographs, taken by their U-2s, of the first few RAF bombing runs. This then continued 'on a discreet basis'.[22] On 3 November, Robert Amory, the American Deputy Director of Intelligence, told Chester Cooper to '[t]ell your friends to comply with the God-damn ceasefire or go ahead with the God-damn invasion. Either way, we'll back them up if they do it fast. What we can't stand is their God-damn hesitation, waltzing while Hungary is burning.' Cooper made the 'suggestion' to the JIC adding 'I'm not speaking without instructions.'[23] Eisenhower, privately, condoned the Anglo-French action as long as it was conducted quickly, but by 2 November he was impatient at the delay. He drafted a telegram accepting an Anglo-French move into the Canal Zone, but it was never sent.[24] Eden continued to enjoy cordial relations with Eisenhower, and Macmillan also believed that 'the President was more sympathetic' than the majority of the State Department.[25] On the 3rd, Dulles had been taken ill and hospitalised, with cancer of the colon, leaving him inactive for the rest of the Suez Crisis. This meant that more anti-British, or at least not pro-British, officials would be influential under Hoover and Assistant Secretary William Rountree.[26] Dulles had 'indicated' to the British that the US would issue a firmer riposte to Nasser after the 6th, with the reintroduction of OMEGA's economic sanctions, covert destabilisation of support for Nasser and, if this failed, unspecified hardline moves.[27] On 17 November, he had had another of his changes of view, even going on to say to Lloyd: 'Why didn't you go through with it and get Nasser down?'[28] This supported Dulles's earlier suggestion that he would have condoned the use of force and possibly provided US assistance after Eisenhower had been re-elected. However, Hoover, Rountree and Phleger urged caution. They convinced Eisenhower to wait before sending his telegram to Eden, which had been intended 'to keep the channel open', and in the end the message was never sent.[29] Eden had tried to influence the President on 5 November, again referring to Soviet intentions within the Middle East, and directly to the predictions in his 6 September letter to Eisenhower.[30] He then invoked the image of Nasser as a 'Moslem Mussolini' with his potential Pan-Arabism, before making a personal appeal to the President in an attempt to reignite the wartime amity.[31] However, the appeals fell on deaf ears. Eden blamed Eisenhower's change of heart on Dulles, but the Secretary of State no longer affected policy.[32]

Pressure continued to mount from the UN, as Dixon warned against continuing to refuse to accept a ceasefire, concerned that Britain would alienate the other major countries. In particular he feared: 'They [UN] will be in a very ugly mood and out for our blood and I would not be surprised if the Arab–Asian and the Soviet blocs did not try to rush through some resolution urging collective measures of some kind against us. Between them they might well cook up an appeal by the Arabs to the Soviet Union to come in and help them.'[33] As the UN was placing Britain 'in the same low category as the Russians in its bombing of Budapest', Bulganin sent a thinly veiled threat to Eden, that the Soviets might use 'rockets' against Britain and France.[34] However, Eden remained consistent in his belief that the Soviets were unlikely to play a more direct military role in the Middle East. He did not take the threat seriously, although the military were concerned that the Russians might send troops to the Middle East or increase weapons shipments. Hayter remained undecided: 'Though there is an element of bullying bluff...[but]...I am afraid there is no doubt that the Soviet Government are working themselves up into a very ugly mood.'[35] Such was the military concern that a signal was sent to General Keightley: '[Y]ou should know that Russia has just indicated readiness to intervene with force in the Middle East. United States has warned Russia that any attempt to use Russian forces in the Middle East would encounter American opposition.'[36] However, this instruction was quickly superseded when the Chiefs of Staff concluded that Russian intervention was unlikely.[37] In the end, the events of 6 November annulled the issue, although Chester Cooper told the JIC, at the same time that Cabinet was meeting, that intelligence suggested that the Russians would stand down.[38]

Cabinet met on 6 November to unite opinion as to the next move. By this point, sterling had begun to face strong pressure. Since the ultimatum there had been heavy selling of sterling in New York. Macmillan telephoned the US Secretary of the Treasury, Humphrey, in Washington, but only a ceasefire before midnight on 6 November would secure American support for an IMF loan. This information was confirmed by a telegram from Humphrey which arrived during the Cabinet meeting of the 6th. Lloyd recalled that before the Cabinet meeting he had spoken to Macmillan who had told him 'that in view of the financial and economic pressures we must stop'.[39] Macmillan then told Cabinet that he could 'not anymore be responsible for Her Majesty's Exchequer' unless there was a cease-fire.[40] For the second time during the crisis, Macmillan threatened to resign, and Cabinet agreed to the ceasefire.[41] The Cabinet conclusions made no reference to the financial crisis but it was believed that Britain had done as much as it could. The majority of the writers/ commentators adopted this view. Britain could hand over responsibility to the United Nations Emergency Force (UNEF) and start to rebuild Anglo-American relations.[42] However, Eden maintained his attempt to settle the crisis, if realising the failure of employing a policy without the agreement of the Americans. Even the day after the ceasefire was announced, the Prime Minister minuted: 'It is clear we cannot now carry this through alone, with French. We *must* therefore get U.S. support... Our aim w[oul]d be to get them to tackle an Anglo-U.S. policy for a long-term settlement in M/East.'[43] However, even the chance of any form of US support had been alienated and the Prime Minister was left with the decision of agreeing to a ceasefire, having only just committed himself to a military solution. As Eden explained in 1959, while writing his memoirs: 'Why we stopped is going to be more difficult to explain than why we started.'[44] This comment reflected the complexity of the issues surrounding the decision to call the ceasefire, as well as the need to justify himself.

Lloyd believed, without laying blame, that Macmillan's financial fears were a substantial reason which influenced Eden.[45] Many have seen Macmillan's evidence as a principal factor in the Cabinet's decision, not least the 1957 Government report on the crisis, and Macmillan's official and sympathetic biographer, Alistair Horne.[46] Anthony Head recalled of Macmillan's apparent volte-face:

> I could never believe it was just the US threat to withdraw money from us. It wasn't naked ambition, though if you had a nasty mind, you might have thought so. I didn't. And the 'fire was out' excuse must have been likely to be untenable before the operation actually began... It's the big mystery... But Harold was very strong in his warning of what the US would do... he put the fear of God into the Cabinet on finances, as Chancellor. The Treasury must have got at him, from every direction... but I simply could not believe that the US could wreck us, or would want to wreck us, in two days.[47]

Yet there is no evidence to suggest that Macmillan had received any warnings from the Treasury since 29 September and no protective measures had been taken against an economic crisis.[48] If this was not the case then the Chancellor had grossly miscalculated. He told Cabinet that Britain's gold reserves 'had fallen by £100 million over the past week – or by *one eighth* of their remaining total'.[49] The correct figure was only £31.7 million.[50] Significantly, Macmillan wrote in his memoirs that while the 'losses were great' they were 'by no means disastrous'.[51] According to 'one reliable source, Macmillan now believed that Eden was "playing ducks and drakes" with the country and had to be halted – even perhaps overthrown'.[52] Those close to Eden were quick to be critical and fearful of the Chancellor.[53] Millard reflected a more moderate opinion, believing that Macmillan and then the Cabinet 'panicked' under the pressure on sterling, exacerbated by the miscalculation of the American attitude.[54] It is therefore possible that Macmillan exaggerated the figures to ensure the panic, or had miscalculated the figures and frightened himself. Regardless, it was his recognition of his failure to understand and predict the American reaction to an 'invasion' which led to his own self-reproach and retreat. Makins thought that the senior ministers 'were still running with blinkers', while Lord Home believed that 'what really turned the scale and made the Chancellor of the Exchequer... so terribly anxious was the American action in really putting the Sixth Fleet alongside us in the Mediterranean, for all the world to see, and therefore announcing in effect that America was totally against us.'[55] While the exact cause of Macmillan's attitude remains clouded, it was this attitude which finally induced a change of policy by Cabinet and by Eden.

Within the Cabinet Eden led a small group who wished to continue with the operation, which included Head, Thorneycroft and Lennox-Boyd.[56] James Stuart, the Scottish Secretary, argued that the job would be only half done and went on to criticise this aspect of the crisis management.[57] Lord Home inadvertently summarised the Cabinet position when he answered the question about whether he agreed with Eden's desire to continue: 'It would have been better. No, I felt that the argument for getting out at this point of time did prevail.'[58] Many politicians felt this dilemma but followed Macmillan's lead. As Millard suggested, panic ensued. Significantly, those agreeing with Macmillan included the Government's senior ministers, Butler and Salisbury, along with Lloyd and Home, all of whom had previously appeared to Eden to support the military action.[59] Nutting's resignation had been announced on the 5th, Edward Boyle, Economic Secretary at the Treasury, had resigned, and on the 6th, William Clark also tendered his resignation. Eden's support had disappeared, and more significantly, opposition had arisen. The Prime Minister demonstrated the same belief in the importance of a united Cabinet, and in particular the support of his senior ministers, that he had held throughout the crisis, notably during the intensive meetings of mid- to late October, as well as throughout his career. He could not continue in the face of such division.[60] This was reinforced by his deteriorating health and excessive tiredness.[61] Eden managed very little sleep at this time, a point he emphasised to the US Ambassador Winthrop Aldrich, and made worse by the discharging of business at late hours, because of the difference in time between London and Washington.[62] Templer, Chief of Imperial General Staff remarked: 'Once the operation was launched it became quickly apparent that his [Eden's] health would collapse unless the matter could be brought to an early solution.'[63] The Cabinet minutes show that the issue was not argued at length.[64] Undercut by Macmillan's retreat which carried with it the base of Eden's support, the Prime Minister was forced to accept the Cabinet's decision to order a ceasefire.

Despite this fulfilment of his obligation to Cabinet, even though he did not complain at the time Eden later felt very hurt by the volte face of his senior ministers who had supported his decision to use force, and in Macmillan's case, had led the pressure for a military operation. His reaction showed his surprise at their change of face. In his memoirs, he wrote: 'There are always weak sisters in any crisis and sometimes they will be found among those who were toughest at the outset of the journey.'[65] The 'weak sisters' referred to Macmillan and Salisbury, but his disillusion went further. He continued to hold great contempt for Butler, telling Hugh Massingham, 'I do not care who it [my successor] is going to be but I shall make absolutely certain that it isn't Rab.'[66] In private meetings after Suez, Eden continued to bemoan his lack of support at the vital moment, a complaint supported by the Cabinet Secretary, Brook and the War Minister, Head.[67]

After the meeting Eden telephoned Mollet to inform him of the Cabinet's decision. The French reaction reflected their position throughout the crisis. Exceptionally disappointed, they desperately wanted to enforce a solution upon Nasser, preferably by removing him. Mollet personally remained more restrained, but Pineau and Bourges-Manoury wanted to continue without the British, while the military considered ways of eliminating Nasser.[68] Despite Mollet's concession that the ceasefire would be delayed until midnight, it was officially ordered at 5 p.m., GMT.[69] Eden had returned to his old maxim of favouring US support, under the pressure of an economic embargo but also because, once again, he saw the possibility of securing a solution by following the American lead.

As of the 6th, Anglo-American relations did not appear irreparable to Eden and he believed, as did Lloyd, that he held 'a gage' in Port Said.[70] The Prime Minister had received support from Eisenhower in a telephone conversation of 6 November, and trying to salvage anything out of the situation now saw the Anglo-French occupation of Port Said as a strong bargaining position in terms of world opinion on events.[71] He could now hand over control to UNEF, having theoretically separated the combatants and seen Israel agree to cease fire. This had been discussed by Cabinet.[72] Eisenhower gave the idea credence, telling Eden that 'when Hammerskjøld [sic] comes along with his people you ought to be able to withdraw very quickly'. This offered some hope that Eden could still achieve his objective of reinternationalising the Canal, even if he no longer had direct control of proceedings.

However, this limited success was only obvious to a few because of the Prime Minister's apparent capitulation. The period after 6 November was one of humiliation for Britain, and Eden in particular.[73] The failure to derive any political success out of the achievements of the armed services alienated the remaining diehard supporters within the public, military and government. The military, in particular, were deeply offended. Cabinet had agreed to the ceasefire without consulting the Chiefs of Staff.[74] They had learned of developments from the BBC news bulletin.[75] Sir Frank Cooper, then Head of the Air Staff Secretariat, recalled: 'We felt very let down by the politicians.'[76] They were 'shocked' and 'astounded', particularly as they had troops on the ground, including casualties and fatalities.[77] One British commander summarised opinion by complaining that Eden had 'obstinately decided like a girl to scratch out the eyes of his opponent but hadn't quite thought of what would happen next'.[78] Such was Templer's reaction that, writing to Stockwell to thank him for his gift of a Russian rifle, he said: 'If I could use it, I'd give my first attention to certain politicians in New York and London, and I'd have run out of ammunition before I could spare a round, even for Nasser.'[79] He had felt let down by those who had led the withdrawal. Eden had been caught in a no-win situation. He lost support because he had ordered a military operation against Nasser and because he had brought it to an early conclusion.

By 7 November, the situation worsened. After Cabinet, Eden telephoned Eisenhower, and received another positive reception before the President returned the call, agreeing to a tripartite summit on the Middle East, with the French.[80] Yet Hoover, who had entered the President's office during the telephone conversation, objected. He had already shown his fear that concessions to the British would threaten US policy in the Middle East.[81] After the telephone calls, Hoover, along with Chief of Staff Sherman Adams, Staff Secretary Colonel Andrew Goodpaster and Humphrey convinced Eisenhower to cancel the meeting.[82] Eisenhower had been won over by the majority 'but he accepted it with reluctance and impatience'.[83] From this point the US virtually ended communication with Eden until his departure to Jamaica on 23 November.[84] On 19 November, Lloyd explained the situation to Eden: 'The plain fact is that, as Bedell [Smith] said, the President is the only man who matters and there is no one round him to give advice who is of the slightest use. That the future in the Middle East should be at the mercy of Hoover and Lodge is a tragedy.'[85] This only heightened Eden's exasperation with the Americans because he now believed that, with Dulles in hospital, the President would be receiving advice from more anglophobic diplomats.

Eden's own political position became increasingly unstable, as his health deteriorated. On the same day, 19 November, late in the evening, it was announced that, under advice from his doctors, the Prime Minister must take 'a complete rest'.[86] Nutting recorded that

> The strain of the last three weeks and of acting a part so completely out of character had by now caught up with him [Eden]. The bouts of fever induced by his bile-duct trouble... had weakened him to the point of total exhaustion, and his doctors insisted that he could not carry on under the strain of office unless he now took a few weeks' rest.[87]

Evans told Butler that 'Anthony could not live on stimulants any more'.[88] Eden announced on 21 November that he would be leaving the country for three weeks' rest. However, he continued to emphasise that the decision had been made for him by his doctors. Again, he appeared to underestimate his own illness. Writing to Lloyd, on 19 November, he explained: 'Although there is nothing wrong with me apart from strain, I feel that I must follow his [Evans'] orders.'[89] The damage was far more serious than he realised, forcing him to extend his recuperation in Jamaica by one week.[90]

Politically, Macmillan had begun to build a power-base of support at a time when there was a division of opinion as to when, and even if, Eden would return. Churchill, in conversation with Moran, demonstrated the position:

> 'I should not have done half the work he has been doing. I'd have got others to do it. He let them wake him up at all hours of night to listen to news from New York – our night is their day.'
> Moran: 'Will Anthony be able to take over when he returns from Jamaica?'
> Winston (*hesitating*): 'I am very doubtful. I'd like to see Harold Macmillan Prime Minister, but they may ask Lord Salisbury. I cannot understand why our troops were halted. To go so far and not go on was madness.'[91]

The hardliners increased their support for the Chancellor despite his leading the retreat, and the remoteness of Eden's place of stay meant that he was no longer fully in touch with the machinations in the Government.[92] His residence did not even possess a telephone.[93] This proved politically dangerous for the Prime Minister at a time when Macmillan had begun to manoeuvre towards Number 10.[94]

On 16 November, believing that the Americans could not continue to support friendly Anglo-American relations with Eden as Prime Minister, Macmillan, calling himself 'Eden's deputy', visited Aldrich and suggested that he travel to Washington for talks. Such was Macmillan's manner that Aldrich was left pondering 'whether this might not be a hint that some sort of movement is on foot in the Cabinet to replace Eden'.[95] In his report to Washington, the Ambassador was more conclusive, writing that Macmillan had told him that the Cabinet would be completely 'reshuffled and ... Eden [was] going out because of sickness'.[96] Macmillan confirmed this, reiterating that Eden had suffered 'a physical breakdown and [would] have to go on vacation immediately ... and this [would] lead to his retirement'.[97] This background information set the tone for the ensuing talks between London and Washington. The Americans believed that Eden no longer held any form of power within the Government, and the Prime Minister himself had become isolated. Macmillan, while the front runner, had also been joined by Butler and Salisbury in seeking to repair Anglo-American relations and resolve the crisis. However, even the President favoured Macmillan's succession.[98]

The Chancellor seized this opportunity to exploit Eden's absence. To ensure at least a token British withdrawal from the Canal Zone, he kept quiet about his soundings of the Americans, and threatened petrol rationing even if the Americans supplied the oil previously agreed.[99] Eisenhower circumvented the State Department to enable dealings with the British, leaving Macmillan to win Cabinet over.[100] However, the Americans required a full withdrawal of Anglo-French troops from the Canal Zone, something which many in the Cabinet feared would lead to a backbench revolt.[101] On 29 November, Macmillan revealed a loss of $450 million, since September, of which $270 million had disappeared in November.[102] In reality, the situation was far worse, artificially supported by a 'forward' sale of sterling, and the sale of short-term US bonds.[103] Unsurprisingly, once again the Cabinet were united by financial fears, and agreed to a full withdrawal.[104] The reasons for Macmillan inducing this decision remain unclear. His misrepresentation of Britain's economic position to Cabinet may have been deliberate to protect his own career.[105] While he had exaggerated the economic malaise on 6 November, he underestimated the depth of the situation on 29 November.[106] That he had miscalculated the figures, but in two very different ways, suggested that either he, or the Treasury, had distorted the figures for their own ends.

Eden wrote to London on 29 November to learn how the situation was developing and offer himself for consultation.[107] However, Butler and Brook were actively trying to stop Eden's interference. Brook, replying to the Prime Minister, told him: 'Do not attempt to break your isolation. There is no major issue, i.e., Anglo-American policy at the moment.'[108] Eden remained convinced that Britain should stand up to the American use of the IMF loan as a bully stick, and wrote to Bishop, expressing his opinions.[109] These views were already well known to Butler, who after discussion with Macmillan, Salisbury and Heath, replied: '[W]e believe that the policy on which we have decided is consistent with the course which you set for us. We hope you will feel that we have taken the right direction.'[110] On the following day, he added: 'We of course considered very anxiously whether it was our duty to suggest to you that you should return. We concluded that you ought not to interrupt your rest.'[111] Finally, Eden wrote: 'I fully agree and will now pipe down.'[112] This failure to involve himself in events meant that when all the key decisions were taken he was absent, forfeiting leadership to either Butler or Macmillan, at the time of Anglo-American reconciliation.

By 7 December, Brendan Bracken believed that Macmillan's 'real intentions are to push his boss out of No.10'.[113] However, Macmillan realised that Eden could not continue as Prime Minister, both because of ill health and because of his political alienation.[114] As Millard observed on whether Eden could have continued as leader or resisted Macmillan: 'No, I don't think so. His health had been affected by Suez, and I don't think he would have been fit to carry on. Also his position in the Party was too badly damaged.'[115] Macmillan seized the opportunity to take the leadership not from Eden, whom he no longer believed to be in a position to continue, but from Butler, the other leading candidate.[116] This was best illustrated by his use of the 1922 Committee meeting of 22 November. Butler gave a basic speech, while Macmillan once again seized the opportunity and dynamically addressed the meeting for thirty-five minutes, focusing on future policy.[117] In terms of Macmillan's succession, Julian Amery believed this to be the turning point.[118] Conservative Whip Philip Goodhart, recalled: 'Rab was not on his best form, whereas Harold was at his most ebullient and managed to win the day, not only on the merit of what he said... but also physically in that his expansive gestures nearly caused poor Rab to fall backwards from the adjacent seat.'[119] This meeting induced many former supporters of Butler to switch their loyalties to Macmillan.[120] Despite his volte-face the Chancellor's more dynamic, forthright approach and his direct confrontation of the future appealed more to the Conservative Party than Butler's prevarication and caution.

Eden returned to Britain on 14 December, receiving a lukewarm reception.[121] He was met by a deputation at Downing Street, led by Butler and Salisbury, telling him: 'that, while the Cabinet were willing to carry on under his leadership until Easter, if it was then clear that his health was not fully restored they felt that a new head of Government would be necessary'.[122] However, Eden then put the last nails in his own political coffin. On 17 December, he admitted to lying over Anglo-French/Israeli action to a meeting of the 1922 Committee, and then on 20 December, lied to the House of Commons 'that there was not foreknowledge that Israel would attack Egypt'.[123] While Eden refused to admit to collusion, fearful that it would bring down the Government, Macmillan recognised the country's desire to look to the future, rather than stagnate in its own failure. To this end the Chancellor circulated a memorandum, without consulting the Prime Minister, which said that 'Suez had been a gamble which failed. Now we must go on as if it had never happened.'[124] Macmillan had observed in 1952: 'I like both Butler and Eden. They both have great charm. But it has been cruelly said that in politics there are no friends at the top. I fear it is so.'[125] Now in 1956, the Chancellor finally deserted the Prime Minister when the concept of collective responsibility was usurped by political opportunism.

By late December, Eden's health had also taken a turn for the worse, with the recurrence of fevers forcing an extension of his convalescence.[126] The Prime Minister began to ask associates whether he should resign.[127] Visited daily by his doctor, Sir Horace Evans, from 1 January, 1957, he was finally informed, on 7 January, that his health would deteriorate if he continued in office. Consequently, on the 9th, he announced his resignation, not simply as Prime Minister but also from his parliamentary seat.[128] Politically, for Sir Anthony Eden the Suez Crisis was over. Personally, it would continue for another twenty years.

Conclusion

By 14 October 1956, Eden had decided to use force to settle the Suez Crisis. After Dulles's press conference of 2 October, which finally destroyed the already slim chances of SCUA's success, force turned from a possibility discussed by the Egypt Committee to a probability discussed by an executive 'inner circle' of ministers. Formalised on 24th at Sèvres, collusion was not the fulfilment of a policy initiated in July 1956. Pressed by the French on the 14th, it offered a solution for an overworked, overtired and now uninspired leader.

Cabinet members and civil servants have compounded condemnation of Eden by suggesting that they were not consulted or that they were left out of the chain of command and the distribution of documents. As the Chairman of the JIC, Dean commented, while he himself did not feel betrayed: 'I knew a certain number of people were worried about it *ex post facto*'.[1] This affected the historiography of the Suez Crisis because it was this group who formed the basis of the confidential sources of most works and whose private papers were consulted. Mountbatten has often been cited as indicating the Prime Minister's warlike intentions.[2] Others involved in the contingency preparations, such as Sir Dermot Boyle, are also similarly used.[3] Butler maintained that he had known nothing of the details of the Sèvres meetings.[4] However, he had attended the debriefing of Dean after the second Sèvres meeting, and with other ministers had recommended the idea of the 'contingency plan' to Cabinet on 25 October, in the knowledge that this was intended as a cover for collusion.[5] Eden, annoyed by Butler's post-Suez attitude, later wrote that he 'never once made any criticism of substance at the cabinet nor even to me privately, as he could have done at any time'.[6] Clark noted in his diary '[t]he way Rab has turned and trimmed'.[7] Macmillan accepted some of the responsibility for the decisions made but, as Lloyd wrote to Eden, he 'got the wind up about how to deal with Suez' in his memoir, *Riding the Storm*:

> I share to the fullest extent the responsibility of all the decisions, not merely from the normal responsibility of a Cabinet Minister, but because I was one of the circle of colleagues whom Eden consulted. Naturally, as

I was fully employed with my own problems from the financial point of view, I could have only a general knowledge of the intricate but, alas, ineffective attempts to reach a peaceful solution in accordance with the claims of justice and equity.[8]

Macmillan, who had been the leading 'hawk' within the Government, benefited the most from the crisis, having gained support for his 'strong' line and then for his influence which ended the war and his subsequent efforts to rebuild Anglo-American relations before becoming Prime Minister.[9]

Norman Brook supported the Government's use of force but was quick to disassociate from the stupidity of such a naive plan. In November 1956 he told Clark that 'he realised that no intelligent man could support the policy', and described the invasion as 'folly' to Shuckburgh.[10] He was not alone in this assessment of the plan and its implementation.[11] Many agreed with the intention and the motives, if not the method.[12] They wanted Nasser removed and hoped this would free Britain from the threat on her interests, particularly oil supplies. It was feared that Egyptian control of the Canal would disrupt transit to Western Europe. However, they did not want to be associated with the failure of such a transparent plan. Brook suggested that Millard's 'official history' of the crisis should not have a wide circulation within Whitehall.[13] How much this was an attempt to protect himself as much as the Prime Minister is unclear, but such action only increased suspicions and inflamed reaction. The attempted cover-up, followed by the disassociation of the majority of the policy-makers from 'collusion' made Eden appear the more aggressive and dominant in the quest to use force, particularly when they involved themselves in the historiography of the crisis.

In 1967, Nutting, who had resigned on 31 October 1956, published *No End of a Lesson*, over which Eden considered taking legal action because of the inaccuracies, which he listed at length.[14] Nutting had given political reasons to Lloyd for his dissatisfaction and resignation but others were aware of personal problems which had also helped to force his hand.[15] Lloyd told Eden that Nutting had twice told friends, in September 1956, that he had 'just got to get out of this bloody Government somehow'. One of these friends was John Hope, Joint Parliamentary Under-Secretary of State for Foreign Affairs, who believed that the reason was not political but 'entanglements elsewhere', the implication being of a marriage which was breaking down. Eden could never reconcile these actions, either at the time of the crisis or afterwards.[16] Nutting had been Eden's protegé and had become disillusioned with his Prime Minister.[17] While Nutting's evidence is treated with some caution, he is still cited by historians to suggest Eden's bellicosity. Similarly to Nutting, William Clark, having seen Eden as a 'boyhood hero' became disenchanted and finally resigned over the Government's action.[18] This opposition from those who had been so close to and had admired Eden led to an exaggerated condemnation of the Prime Minister's actions. Both Nutting and Clark tried to demonstrate Eden's belligerence from an early stage of the crisis which confused the understanding of other contemporaries and historians toward Eden's intentions for resolving the crisis. He continued to back a peaceful solution until ill in October, as Clark noted in his diary but refused readily to admit publicly.[19]

Aside from Clark and Nutting, others chose to back Eden's decision. Watkinson and Reginald Maudling, Minister for Supply, wrote supportively in their autobiographies.[20] Lord Home defended the decision on 12 December 1956 in the House of Lords and maintained this stance throughout his life.[21] Likewise, Lord Kilmuir remained convinced of the validity of the Government's stance.[22] Millard concluded:

> [O]ne felt very worried about it [invasion] as clearly this was a very high-risk policy. But the risks on either side seemed to be very great. The fate of the government by this time was at stake, Eden certainly felt that, and his own career was at stake, too. On either side there were appalling risks. All I felt about it was that it was very high risk but one only hoped that it would come off.
>
> There is a lot of humbug about Suez quite honestly. People forget that the policy at the time was extremely popular. It only became slightly less popular when it failed.[23]

Suez was a divisive event, generating opinion and emotion amongst politicians, civil servants and public alike.[24] Sides were taken and honour defended, confusing the reality. While a sense of collective responsibility may have prevented a far greater reaction against the Government's decision it also promoted a smouldering contempt and distrust, which was exacerbated by Eden's eventual decision to limit information.[25] Again, this distrust was reinforced by the increasing post-war use of sub-committees, *ad hoc* committees and the suspicion of a Prime Minister who appeared to control all departments. This led to an extremely opinionated group within Westminster and Whitehall. Bereft of many facts and inundated with conspiratorial assumptions, this group generated its own history which gradually permeated into the historiography of Suez. They either believed or maintained that Eden had dominated the conduct of foreign relations, immediately deciding to reinternationalise the Canal by using force to retake control. In addition, many of those cited did not actually work with Eden until the point of increasing pressure in late September/October and were therefore unable to comment accurately on the previous period.[26] This can be seen in Richard Powell's evidence.[27] Powell did not work with Eden until 4 September, when he sat on the Egypt Committee. He then only attended one more meeting, 7 September, before finally working at length with Eden, in October, when the Prime Minister had decided on force.

Eden attempted to disguise the truth in his memoirs as he unconvincingly justified his action. Because of subsequent events, particularly the assassination of the Iraqi Prime Minister Nuri Said in 1959, this became easier to do and therefore easier to accept, because Nuri's death was seen by many British contemporaries and commentators as a result of Nasser's increasing power and influence. The reality was much different, the history of which has failed to represent the long complicated and at times confused efforts to negotiate a settlement, which finally ended on 14 October 1956. Eden did not help himself by the nature of his defence. By insisting that continuity existed from the period of facing the dictators through to Suez, reinforced by his naming the Suez memoir *Full Circle*, Eden implied that the decision to collude with the Israelis was only an extension of his own military plans and, therefore, the Cabinet decision made on 27 July 1956. This implied that, from the outset of the crisis, he was intent on removing Nasser by force. However, Eden actually tried to demonstrate the continuity that, the final invasion represented the fulfilment of the contingency plans that he had had drawn up in July, and had represented to Cabinet in October. This attempt to conceal the collusion merely enlarged the image of Eden's warmongering. Norman Brook wrote to Eden in May 1958, worried that the chapter dealing with Suez in Eden's memoirs passed 'rather lightly over the considerations which ultimately led the Government to intervene'. He was concerned that the record should show that both he and the Prime Minister had not made the decision to use force wantonly or, therefore, immediately after the nationalisation of the Canal.[28] Yet Eden was prepared to accept this representation, particularly as it answered one of the most frequent criticisms of him, that of indecisiveness, which had been so strongly portrayed by the press and had led to the French antipathy towards him.[29] This played into the hands of the many officials and ministers who were looking for absolution. Despite recognising some of these problems, both Kyle and Lucas continued to use sources such as Mountbatten and, in particular, Clark.

In addition, the Egypt Committee, which has been seen as a 'war committee', waiting to supply an excuse, did not make the decision to go to war, again demonstrating its own vacillation and hence impotence.[30] Historians believed that it was this inner group and its discussion of the military contingency plans that has given evidence of Eden's bellicosity. However, it was the even smaller, more exclusive, 'inner circle' of ministers which agreed the final course of action. Always in existence, such that its members conferred over prominent issues, it lay dormant as a policy-making elite until October 1956. Then, when Eden decided, on 14 October, that the use of force had turned from a possibility discussed by the Egypt Committee, to a probability within his own mind, the 'inner circle' took on an executive role, if still appearing to be the same discursive group of senior ministers. Thus, at the time that Eden needed the most advice and support, he had narrowed his advisory group to maintain security. This group consisted of hardliners:

Macmillan, Salisbury, Kilmuir, Kirkpatrick and Brook. However, by their lack of public support for the military operation in November, they left Eden isolated and defending what now appeared, to historians and some contemporaries, to be his decision alone, which they believed he had made in July.

From their misinterpretation of the importance of the Egypt Committee, it has been argued that the Prime Minister merely went through the motions of diplomacy, represented by the tripartite talks, the London Conferences and the Menzies Mission. Consequently, Eden's military contingencies were perceived to have been initiated as soon as possible. However, the Prime Minister tried to bluff the Egyptians with threats, whilst maintaining US support to replace nationalisation with international control of the Canal. A firm and potentially aggressive front against Nasser, backed by economic sanctions, was central to his plan to lay the foundations for a strong bargaining position in the ensuing negotiations. However, what he saw as American and Egyptian intransigence left his policy with little chance of success, finally to be overtaken and subverted by other Cabinet colleagues, French impatience and weaknesses in his own character exposed through press, party and public opinion. Despite his own assertions, the policy he had initiated before July and had continued to employ until October was not the same as that finally used to break the diplomatic deadlock. This was simply because Eden was not the same man in October as he had been in July, 1956, and, under increased pressure, agreed to the use of force to resolve the crisis.

Much of the historiography recognises Eden's illness but fails to discuss its severity and its influence on the timing of the decision to use force. Affected by their conviction that Eden had decided to use force in July, they recognised a worsening of his illness in October but did not see any correlation between this and the subsequent condoning of the Challe/Gazier plan, other than, as Lucas believed, it gave the Prime Minister 'renewed vigour' to militarily remove Nasser.[31] Eden had been ill since 1953, and his health had gradually deteriorated. In addition, three months of transatlantic crisis management, with long working hours exaggerated by the time differences between Washington and New York, Cairo and London, hastened his mental and physical decline. In combination, these factors meant that by October 1956 the Prime Minister had begun to suffer from bouts of pain, lack of sleep and high fevers, which incapacitated him for several days, first by confining him to bed and then by a lingering lassitude. Neither Eden nor his doctors fully appreciated the extent of this illness, and despite the influence of Lady Eden, he continued to work the usual long hours, further weakening himself, until in November he was forced to take the rest that his doctors had been insisting on for three months. This ignorance not only ensured further damage to Eden's health but also meant that contemporaries and historians have been unable to understand the significance of his illness. In addition, the Prime Minister's doctors believed that they 'had a duty to keep...[Eden] on the road', prescribing him painkillers.[32] These drugs, particularly in the high doses prescribed in the 1950s, also complicated the picture. The initial euphoria they produced gave Eden a false sense of his own condition, while their side-effects exaggerated his personality traits, increasing his insecurity and vanity. They also clouded Eden's perception of himself. However, the Prime Minister would be able to continue taking such high quantities of stimulants for only a limited time, as Evans revealed in November 1956.[33] Eden's treatment merely masked his physical collapse. His rapid decline in health after relinquishing his office, marked by stronger and more recurrent bouts of fever, confirmed the fears that after the late diagnosis of Eden's complaint and its exaggeration by the fateful operations in 1953, the rigours of leadership would hasten the deterioration of his health.[34] This weakening made him more susceptible to the demands for a quick resolution, which increasingly became embodied in the use of force.

Many of the pressures which finally compelled Eden to condone the use of force were already in place in July/August 1956. However, it was not until weakened and insecure, that in October these pressures combined with the failure of the American effort to initiate a settlement, finally forcing the Prime Minister to admit that his own policy had failed, and that he must resort to his and Cabinet's last option, which he had been avoiding. The method that Eden employed to settle the Suez Crisis, until October 1956, had its roots in the years before Nasser nationalised the Canal. During 1955, Eden refined the 'policy' of maintaining close links with the US. It involved trying to manipulate the Americans and asserting British power through them. This is a consistency that contradicts the common historiographical debate, which believes that Eden's past affected him in the opposite way. It concludes that his dealing with the dictators made him more likely to act aggressively against Nasser, increased by the need to demonstrate strong leadership having eventually acceded to power.[35] However, during his term as Prime Minister, he found his 'foreign policy' restricted by the country's decline as a world power, as he had begun to understand while Foreign Secretary after the war. He would have liked to play a freer role but reconciled himself to developing relations with the US and the Commonwealth. However, these ties with the US were not made out of preference. Despite being more an Atlanticist than a European, he did not fully trust the US. He had attended many of the Second World War conferences, including Tehran and Yalta, and witnessed Britain's decline as a world power and the rise of the US. Eisenhower's election in 1952 compounded the problem because of the emergence of John Foster Dulles. Dulles and Eden did not trust each other. By the time of the Suez Crisis, Anglo-American channels of communication were already compromised.[36] This led to an American misunderstanding of Eden's intention, which Macmillan made worse by frightening the US into believing that Britain had already decided to use force. This American reaction clouded historians' perceptions of Eden and his policy. The Prime Minister had hoped that the US could stand by the

British, presenting a strong and potentially aggressive front against Nasser. However, there was an immediate divergence of opinion between the British and American leaders. Eisenhower understood the situation but had his hands tied by a variety of bonds, including the coming election and Congressional opinion. This underscored the Americans' essentially passive role and provided the seeds for Eden's eventual frustration with their limited efforts to provide a solution to the crisis. Adamant that the British were intent on using force, the Americans continued to offer superficially attractive solutions to the crisis. This attempt at consuming Britain's interest and delaying the implementation of force was finally confirmed by Dulles's press conference of 2 October, which convinced Eden that he was no longer required to follow the US lead.

The Prime Minister had resorted to trying to influence the US, to counter its 'isolation'. Eden had consistently used the Soviet threat, prior to 1956, to derive non-military American aid. During 1955, as he attempted to develop the Baghdad Pact, he had asked the Americans to join, knowing they could nor would not. He increased the pressure upon them by reminding them of the Soviet threat, although he was then doubtful that the Soviets would cause serious problems in the Middle East. He used a strong position to ensure a compromise from the Americans. This manifested itself in terms of financial and material aid, which Eden employed to maintain influence in the region, and which was more acceptable to the Americans. In late 1955, MI6 undermined the Prime Minister's position, using its contact to suggest that President Nasser had developed much closer links with the Soviets. After Sir Dick White's move to head SIS, his deputy, George Young, tried to increase his own influence. A rabid anti-communist, he hoped that Eden would reassert Britain's presence in the Middle East to counter any attempted Soviet infiltration. However, Eden merely hoped to induce continued financial, material and moral support from the US. After little success, the Prime Minister then tried more direct communication with Washington. This yielded little in terms of American diplomatic assistance but fostered the misunderstanding that both the British and the Americans now held similar views of Nasser and his potential Pan-Arabism. However, Eden still did not trust the Americans who, he believed, had weakened and thus prevented the Arab-Israeli peace plan, ALPHA, from bearing fruit. When the American efforts to effect a solution failed, they reopened Anglo-American channels to support the covert measures embodied in OMEGA, to remove Nasser, who they saw as an obstacle to peace in the Middle East.[37] Once again, Eden did not trust the Americans, but Anglo-American co-operation resulted in the continued material support of important Middle Eastern countries, including those friendly to Britain.

After the nationalisation of the Suez Canal, Eden maintained a similar policy until late September/October 1956. This similarity has been ignored by historians. The Prime Minister hoped that he could maintain influence over the Americans, so that as a compromise they would offer moral support that might undermine Nasser's position in the eyes of both Egyptians and other Arab nationals. They had already backed economic moves to destabilise Nasser's regime, and potentially more sinister covert measures, through OMEGA. Eden knew that he would have to coax American support and was unable to influence Nasser on his own. In addition, the Prime Minister could not employ a more direct policy, as he continued to vacillate, unsure as to the real threat of Nasser's nationalism, a problem increased by the initial inability of the Foreign Office legal advisers to give a definitive assessment of the issues, and by his own moral beliefs.[38] During the early stages of the crisis, the Prime Minister had no legal or personal justification for employing a military solution to resolve the crisis.

His indecision resulted from more than Britain's increasingly exposed weaknesses. Eden's personality led him to vacillate. His decision-making had always taken lengthy periods of time. Combined with his own tendency to compromise, this led to 'charges of weakness' and accusations of the appeasement of both Soviets and Arabs.[39] Conflicting assessments of Nasser increased the uncertainty and continued throughout the crisis. This fed Eden's insecurity, and resulted in strong, often aggressive outbursts but no action. He had faced strong press criticism before and had reacted in exactly the same way. As contemporaries remembered, all that he really wanted to do was sound off about the accusations or the situation: 'He didn't want anything done', as when King Hussein had removed Glubb.[40] Then on 26 July, Eden reacted angrily in private. The Prime Minister, it was widely agreed, could be 'short tempered and could be irritated'. This reflected the same immediate reaction to events that Shuckburgh had witnessed in the years before Eden took over as Prime Minister. It did not represent, on this occasion, a move to a more independent policy of using force to settle the crisis and was at variance with his personality and character at the time of the decision to use force, when he remained calm and serene.[41] These events carried severe ramifications, but the Prime Minister's decisions reflected measured and rational deliberation based on a reaction to events. In the initial days of the crisis, after the nationalisation of the Canal, there was international confusion over what would be the immediate reaction to Nasser's actions. Eden vacillated, restricted by Britain's weakness as a 'power'. He did not make a decision to use force in late July/August. He remained unsure of any form of American support but convinced of the importance of reinternationalising the Canal and protecting Western European oil supplies. At this stage, economic and psychological pressures would be used, in conjunction with the threat of force to reverse Nasser's nationalisation of the Suez Canal. However, if the Egyptian leader continued to prove recalcitrant, Eden and the Cabinet were prepared to invoke a military operation. A decision to use force, which the historiography assumed had been taken, remained a giant step from this point.

The Prime Minister believed that in conjunction with the Americans, he could widen support against Nasser, pressing him to relinquish his control of the Canal. With this in mind, he hoped that the First London Conference would unite opinion in condemnation of Egypt. He was buoyed in this belief by the number of countries who sent representatives to the Conference and by its conclusion that the Canal should be returned to international control. However, how this solidarity could be translated specifically into peacefully removing Nasser remained unclear to Eden. This confusion led many historians to believe that Eden had decided to use force and was merely waiting for his excuse. It reflected the difficult decisions needed to effect a peaceful solution to the crisis, while maintaining US and French support. A committee was convened, under the chairmanship of Robert Menzies, and sent to Nasser to communicate the conclusions of the conference and press for reinternationalisation of the Canal. Eden did not expect that the Menzies Mission would be successful. The Prime Minister's doubts were born out of Nasser's intransigence and because of concerns over Menzies' abilities.[42] Yet there was a chance that the Egyptians might return control of the Canal. The possibility of a peaceful solution continued, but, after Macmillan's meetings with both Murphy and Dulles, the Americans continued to believe that the British were committed to the use of force.

Nevertheless, the Prime Minister continued to hold his traditional faith in diplomacy. He had spent the formative years of his political career working with Austen Chamberlain, Gustav Streseman and Aristide Briand for the League of Nations. He saw the need for an international organisation to enable the preservation of 'peace through strength'. In this way he had proposed rearmament during the late 1930s to act as a deterrent to the expansionist aims of Nazi Germany. In the post-1945 world, NATO offered to prevent Soviet expansion but could not involve itself in the Middle East. Therefore, Eden wanted to develop a solidarity among countries in opposition to Nasser's nationalisation of the Canal to increase pressure on Egypt to reinternationalise the waterway. In addition, he needed to use threats in order to bluff the Egyptians into believing that he would not tolerate their action. In this way he hoped to continue supporting his principle of 'peace through strength' and derive a peaceful solution to the crisis. Eden's actions until late September and early October 1956 reflected a consistent approach to foreign affairs which involved conciliation, negotiation and, in the last resort, threat. Even in the late 1930s he had advocated rearmament as a means of threatening Germany rather than taking the stronger, more forceful Churchillian line.

However, by October 1956 Eden had narrowed his own channels of advice, following the Churchillian tradition. In the early stages of the crisis this did not cause any serious problems. The Egypt Committee had been established to consider the British response to the nationalisation of the Canal, dominated by the development of the military precautions, which appeared to be the best way of weakening Nasser's position, through threat or possible implementation. The plan which the Committee approved suggested that while force might be employed, its execution and its goals had not been explored.[43] It changed three times. In addition, the hypothetical 'D-Day' was altered twice. Sir Patrick Reilly believed that '[t]he whole way in which Eden ran the affair prevented any proper thought being given to the problem'.[44] Eden was more intent on threatening Nasser than actually invading Egypt. Even Clark, who had alleged that Eden had decided to use force on 26 July, finally saw the truth.[45] Nasser expected some form of retaliation. Eden had to keep the Egyptian leader guessing, while also preparing for any further eventualities. The contingency plans were not the only example of this, as a committee had been openly established to be seen by Nasser to be discussing possible covert actions against him, and the Treasury had been asked to consider further ways of increasing economic pressure on Egypt.[46] However, outwardly, as Harold Nicolson recorded, 'the Government have shown their [sic] accustomed irresolution and confusion of purpose'.[47] This gave the impression to historians and certain contemporaries that Eden did not have a policy, and merely waited for a pretext to use force. However, internally, because of its exclusivity, the Egypt Committee prevented information reaching those trying to help to provide ideas for a solution and generated much of the mistrust that would later cloud history's judgement of Eden. Eden's secrecy prevented his intentions from being known. Clark realised this and, while still angry at the outcome of Suez, revealed:

> I was very much at the centre of affairs with my office at the end of the corridor leading down to the Prime Minister's office... and I had access to virtually all the papers that went to the Prime Minister. So, I knew all that and I frequently found that I was quite misinformed about what had happened because there had been a telephone conversation, a casual meeting in the House of Commons between some of the senior ministers.[48]

This was also compromised, as Clark continued, because of the 'fairly deliberative' nature of Government; what a Minister or even a Prime Minister might say to him 'was very often very revealing of their personality, but not terribly revealing of what Government policy was going to be'.[49] Nevertheless, even the most recent historians have put their belief in Clark's references to comments by Eden. A traditionalist, Eden believed in the collective responsibility of Government. In addition, while Clark saw the Prime Minister quite often, '[h]e did not have access to all the details of Cabinet and Cabinet Committee discussions or other confidential matters'.[50] This left Clark trying to glean information from other sources, as with the meeting of the evening of 26 July, not all of which were necessarily reliable, or themselves informed. This led to inaccurate understandings of Eden which suggested that he had decided, almost immediately after the expropriation of the

Canal, to resolve the issue forcefully. In reality, the Prime Minister, believing in the importance of maintaining free transit of oil for Britain, had to steer a path between pacifist American, militaristic French and, later, Israeli aspirations, in order to protect British interests, while maintaining pressure on Nasser and a positive face to the public and the Party. All this, dominated by the search for a peaceful solution.

This meant the continuation of supporting American initiatives for a settlement of the crisis, while maintaining amicable relations with the French. However, Eden did not blindly follow the American lead. The Second London Conference, reiterating the conclusions of the earlier conference, resulted in international condemnation of Nasser's actions. While the Prime Minister remained sceptical of the success of this form of representation without a much stronger threat, he hoped that in combination with his own pressure it would undermine the Egyptian leader's position. This was represented by Eden's hope, albeit slight, for the Menzies Mission but also his disillusion when the committee sent to inform Nasser of the conclusions of the First London Conference was undermined by the American statement publicly revealing their passivity, and Menzies' own inflexibility. Yet, while Nasser had made an unequivocal rejection of international control in his reply to the Menzies Mission, Eden still thought that Nasser believed in a reaffirmation or renewal of the 1888 Convention, which would mean the protection of British and European rights of passage by international treaty.[51] Despite the American weakening of Britain's attempts at bargaining from a position of strength, Eden continued to favour a peaceful resolution of the dispute.

In addition, he firmly believed in the British SCUA proposal, which he had conceived as early as 12 August.[52] Historians have recorded neither Eden's belief in the Association nor his proposal of a British SCUA, evidence for which lies in the significant differences between the US and British proposals for a users' association. This has meant that they could not understand, nor therefore believe, that Eden remained true to his faith in his own vision for SCUA and its potential to promote a peaceful solution to the crisis until October 1956. The Prime Minister had hoped that it would enable the reintroduction of international control of the Canal, by increasing support against Nasser and by exerting economic pressure on Egypt through the Association's withholding of Canal dues from the Egyptians. Initially the Americans had appeared to Eden and the Egypt Committee to support this use.[53] Even when Dulles undermined this proposal with his own different proposal under the same name, such was Eden's commitment and belief in it that the Prime Minister believed that it could be made to work. Only in October, when Dulles had made yet another public statement weakening SCUA's potential, did Eden decide to take the matter to the UN, in the hope of presenting the dispute before world opinion, and promoting greater world representation against Nasser. He still hoped that this could be made through a users' association which would solicit world opinion to reinternationalise the Canal. Despite the move being against Dulles's wishes, Eden was not rejecting American assistance, as he tried to fulfil both his and Dulles's plans for a users' association. For the Prime Minister, the hope he placed in the Security Council was consistent with his belief in the potential of an international organisation policing the world. This was part of Eden's mindset, generated by his work around the League of Nations in the 1920s, and explained his commitment to the 1888 Convention. However, while Eden had envisaged SCUA pressing Nasser by economic sanction, Dulles did not believe that user countries should *have* to pay transit dues outside of Egypt. Suddenly, the difference in American and British attitudes toward SCUA and their commitments to a solution became clear. The long-standing confusion that had begun on 28 July had finally been cleared. Reinternationalisation, which had been central to the Prime Minister's aim for resolving the crisis, was not part of the American proposal for a users' association. Eden now realised that the US had been convinced, falsely, of his bellicosity and had offered their proposal as an attempt to interest the British and French, drawing them back from the brink of war. As such the American vision for SCUA had never been intended to resolve the issue of control of the Canal and hence could not peacefully resolve the crisis for the British.

Eden finally lost faith with Dulles and the Americans.[54] Ill and disillusioned with his own policy, the Prime Minister began to bend under the pressure for a forceful resolution. From late September he had begun to show a weakening of his resolve, under particular pressure from the French, who were themselves pressed by the Israelis. Increasingly he turned to others for advice, including Churchill. The French were concerned that Eden would not be resolute and, fearful of an imminent political collapse, increased their efforts to involve the British in an operation against Egypt, because of the need for British air power. The Israelis did not want to act against Egypt without the British and this increased French pressure on Eden. Right-wing Conservative Party pressure, which had originated when Eden led the withdrawal from the Canal Zone in 1954, also began to affect the Prime Minister. This had been voiced through the press, particularly *The Daily Telegraph*, but now took on a more dynamic form, in terms of a forceful resolution at the Party Conference, on 12 October. Its timing was also significant, coming only two days before Franco-Israeli pressure finally resulted in the direct presentation of the Gazier/Challe initiative of 14 October and four days after Eden had left hospital after a further worsening of his illness and corrective surgery. Surrounded by few advisers, who all advocated the use of force, Eden, weakened by his medical complaint, exhaustion, and the increasing pressure for a military solution to the crisis, changed from seeking a negotiated solution to one achieved by force. Eighty days of ineffectual crisis management and the search for a peaceful solution had been suddenly ended.

Notes

PMPM Prime Minister's Personal Memorandum
PMPT Prime Minister's Personal Telegram

Introduction

1. W. Scott Lucas, *Divided We Stand: Britain, the US and the Suez Crisis* (London, 1991), 142–3; Robert Rhodes James, *Anthony Eden* (London, 1987), 454; Paul Johnson, *The Suez War* (London, 1957), 43; Richard Lamb, *The Failure of the Eden Government* (London, 1987), 198; David Dutton, *Anthony Eden: A Life and a Reputation* (London, 1997), 388; Geoffrey McDermott, *The Eden Legacy: and the Decline of British Diplomacy* (London, 1969), 132; Tony Shaw, *Eden, Suez and the Mass Media: Propaganda and Persuasion during the Suez Crisis* (London, 1996), 8 and 108–9; Leonard Mosley, *Dulles: A Biography of Eleanor, Allen and John Foster Dulles and their Family Network* (New York, 1978), 405–6; Anthony Gorst and Lewis Johnman, *The Suez Crisis* (London, 1997), 56; Cole C. Kingseed, *Eisenhower and the Suez Crisis of 1956* (Baton Rouge, 1995), 42–3; Keith Kyle, *Suez* (London, 1992), 137 and 148–52; Hugh Thomas, *The Suez Affair* (Harmondsworth, 1970), 62; Alistair Horne, *Macmillan, Volume I, 1894–1956* (London, 1988), 396 and 399.
2. Thomas, *op. cit.*, 28. I have focused on Thomas, Kyle and Lucas throughout the historiographical debate because they represent the most detailed and comprehensive coverage of the crisis. Thomas's work was the first real historical discussion of the events and involved the anonymous contributions of many of the participants of the crisis, including Selwyn Lloyd. Despite the occasional factual inaccuracy, this work is still widely respected by historians. Both Kyle's and Lucas's work represents the most recent attempts to deal with the Suez Crisis. They have benefited from the release of many of the relevant public and private papers, as well as the co-operation of many of the participants; in Lucas's case over fifty in number. Others, such as Diane Kunz and Tony Shaw, have also written recently, with similar benefits, but their work has been much more specific, focusing on the economic and media/propagandistic side respectively. In particular, both Kyle's *Suez* and Lucas's *Divided We Stand* are currently considered by historians to be the greatest contributions to an historical analysis of the Suez Crisis.
3. Douglas Jay, *Change and Fortune: A Political Record* (London, 1980), 261 remarked, 'a case not so much of collusion as confusion'.
4. PRO: CAB 128/30. CM(56) 54, 27 July, 1956.
5. David Dutton, *Anthony Eden: A Life and a Reputation* (London, 1997).
6. Harold Wilson, *A Prime Minister On Prime Ministers* (London, 1977), 303.
7. Avon (1960), 523 and 532. Eden went on to say that '[t]he same plan that had been intended to deal with Nasser's seizure of the canal fitted equally well with our new objective'.
8. *Ibid.*, 523.
9. For example, see Avon Papers (hereafter referred to as AP) 22/44/35–37.

182 Notes

10 Erskine Childers, *The Road To Suez: A Study of Western–Arab Relations* (London, 1962), dust-jacket.
11 AP 23/44/51. Eden to Lloyd, 13 November, 1959.
12 Lucas (1991), *op. cit.*, 155. Eden (1962), *op. cit.*, 437.
13 For further discussion of this issue, see Chapter 1.
14 AP 23/56/1. Brook to Eden, 29 May, 1957; AP 23/56/9A. Eden to Brook, 5 November, 1957: Eden did not think the memorandum should have a wide circulation in Whitehall; AP 23/56/10. Brook to Eden, 8 November, 1956: Brook agreed that it would not be circulated in Whitehall, only 'available for consultation in the Foreign Office'.
15 Interview with Sir Guy Millard, 25 February, 1998. For a contrast, see Selwyn Lloyd's copy, kept in FO 800/728, or Eden's, kept in AP 33/9iii, to the original kept in CAB 21/3314.
16 Edward Heath, *The Course of My Life: My Autobiography* (London, 1998), 177.
17 Suez Oral History Project (hereafter referred to as SOHP): Interview with Sir Douglas Dodds-Parker. Dodds-Parker had learnt this information from Philip de Zulueta, Eden's private secretary attached to the Foreign Office.
18 SOHP: Interview with Sir Douglas Dodds-Parker.
19 Terence Robertson's *Crisis: The Inside Story of the Suez Conspiracy*, published in 1965, devoted a chapter to the 'Treaty of Sèvres', 'based upon the recollections of Pineau, Bourgès-Maunoury, and Abel Thomas': see chapter 8, 157–74.
20 Peter Hennessy in conversation with Lord Thomas of Swynnerton, 30 May, 1987, cited in Hennessy, *Whitehall*, 165.
21 Dr. Thorpe, *Selwyn Lloyd* (London, 1989), 210.
22 SELO 237(3).
23 AP 23/44/86. Lloyd to Eden, 29 June, 1967.
24 McDermott, *op. cit.*, 148–9. Compare his reconstruction of the Sèvres meetings with those of Logan or Dayan.
25 McDermott, *op. cit.*, 11.
26 *Ibid.*, 146.
27 For example, see Lucas (1991), *op. cit.*, 146–7.
28 For a more in-depth study, see Keith Sainsbury, *The Turning Point: Roosevelt, Stalin, Churchill, and Chiang-Kai-Shek, 1943 – The Moscow, Cairo and Teheran Conferences* (Oxford, 1986), which sees the turning point in Britain's position as 1943.
29 Such as Sir Ivor Jennings, *Cabinet Government* (Cambridge, 1965) and J. P. Mackintosh, *The Government and Politics of Britain* (London, 1970).
30 For example, see: Kyle, *op. cit.*, 11; Thomas *op. cit.*, 46.
31 He had stood for Parliament in 1922, unsuccessfully contesting the Labour seat at Spennymoor.
32 For further discussion of Eden's role in these settlements, see: Rhodes James, *op. cit.*; David Carlton, *Anthony Eden* (London, 1986) and David Dutton, *op. cit.* Eden attended all the major wartime conferences: Tehran, Casablanca, Quebec, Cairo, Moscow, Washington, Yalta and Potsdam. He also led the British delegation at San Francisco in May 1945, where the final shape was put on the UN Charter.
33 PRO: PREM 11/636. Eden to Hankey, February 1953.
34 Anthony Eden, 16 February, 1953, cited in Lucas (1991), *op. cit.*, xiv.
35 For Eden's belief in the need to protect oil interests, see his speech to the 1922 Committee cited in Nigel Nicolson, *Long Life: Memoirs* (London, 1997), 160.

36 Anthony Nutting, *No End of a Lesson: The Story of Suez* (London, 1967), 20.
37 AP 20/27/4. T(E) 14/53, No. 2139. Eden to Eisenhower, 5 May, 1955.
38 The Suez Base Agreement was formalised on 27 July, 1954, and 'provided for the withdrawal of British forces within twenty months, the upholding of the 1888 Canal Convention, and for part of the Base to be kept in efficient working order and capable of immediate use in the event of armed attack upon Egypt or any other members of the Arab League': Selwyn Lloyd, *Suez 1956, A Personal Account* (London, 1978), 24, and *Agreement between the Government of the United Kingdom of Great Britain and Northern Ireland and the Egyptian Government regarding the Suez Canal Base* (Cairo, 19 October, 1954). This in itself was a fulfilment of the basic pledge of withdrawal that had accompanied the 1936 Treaty with Egypt negotiated by Eden.
39 Sir Anthony Eden, *The Eden Memoirs: Full Circle* (London, 1960), 370. In addition, Eden was also perturbed by the 'growing size of our bill for imports': AP 20/20/47. PMPM M(E) 47/55, 17 August, 1955; AP 20/20/48. PMPM M(E) 48/55, 17 August, 1955; AP 20/20/52. PMPM M(E) 52/55, 19 August, 1955, an 8-page minute to the Chancellor of the Exchequer. For further references to Eden's concern over the 'Economic Crisis', see: The Papers of Lord Stockton (Harold Macmillan) (hereafter referred to as MP)MS.Macmillan.dep.d.22. Diary entries for 1 and 2 September, 1955; MP.MS.Macmillan.dep.d.23. Diary entries for 4, 5, 6 and 14 September, 1955.
40 AP 20/22/159. PMPT T(E) 184/55 No. 1301. Eden to Macmillan, 28 September, 1955.
41 Although as Thomas, *op.cit.*, 35; fn.36, reflected, not necessarily right-wing on domestic issues.
42 SOHP: Interview with Julian Amery.
43 *Ibid.*
44 Horne, *op.cit.*, 367. MP.MS.Macmillan.dep.c.16. Diary entry for 31 July, 1954.
45 Anthony Nutting, 'Sir Anthony Eden' in Herbert Van Thal (ed.), *The Prime Ministers: Volume Two; From Lord John Russell to Edward Heath* (London, 1975), 339. Anthony Sampson, *Macmillan: A Study in Ambiguity* (Harmondsworth, 1968), 115.
46 *Daily Telegraph*, 3 January, 1956.
47 James Margach, *The Abuse of Power: The War between Downing Street and the Media from Lloyd George to James Callaghan* (London, 1978), 106. Margach was a political correspondent with the *Sunday Times*.
48 *Ibid.*, 106–7. See also Shaw, *op.cit.*, 19.
49 *Ibid.*
50 This was apparent with his final agreement to withdraw from the Canal Base.
51 PRO: PREM 11/91. PMPM M21/52, Churchill to Eden, 30 January, 1952. Churchill continued: 'I think we should be very careful lest in our desire to have an easier settlement in Egypt we do not take account of the degree of atrocity committed by the Egyptians in the murders and massacres in Cairo.' PREM 11/91. Eden to Churchill, 10 March, 1952: Eden, as Foreign Secretary, had believed that: 'If I cannot impose my will, I must try to negotiate. This is the best government we have yet had with which to do so.' Hansard, column 748, 29 July, 1954.
52 Shuckburgh, *op.cit.*, 122. Diary entry for 17 December, 1953.
53 PRO: CAB 128/30. CM(56) 19, 6 March, 1956.
54 *Ibid.*
55 For instance see: Lucas (1991), *op.cit.*, 54; Nutting, *op.cit.*, 25–6; Lamb (1987), *op.cit.*, 3; Kyle, *op.cit.*, 67.

56 MP.MS.Macmillan.dep.c.15. Diary entry for 29 December, 1953.
57 Cf. Introduction, 7–10.
58 Shuckburgh, *op. cit.*, 74–8. Diary entry for 20 January to 27 February, 1953.
59 *Ibid.*, 75. Diary entry for 20 January, 1953 and p. 78. Diary entry for 26 February, 1953.
60 Lucas (1991), *op. cit.*, 160–1.
61 Thomas, *op. cit.*, 58, 88–9.
62 Kyle, *op. cit.*, 173–4.
63 A. R. Peters, *Anthony Eden at the Foreign Office 1931–1938* (New York, 1986), 352; N. Thompson, *The Anti-Appeasers: Conservative Opposition to Appeasement in the 1930's* (Oxford, 1971), 142; Duff Cooper, *Old Men Forget* (London, 1957), 210. Duff Cooper, later Lord Norwich, was First Lord of the Admiralty.
64 Earl of Avon, *The Eden Memoirs: Facing the Dictators* (London, 1962), 552; John Harvey (ed.), *The Diplomatic Diaries of Oliver Harvey 1937–40* (London, 1970), 17. Diary entry for 25 February, 1937. Peters, *op. cit.*, 322.
65 Avon (1962), *op. cit.*, 560. Lord Birkenhead, *Halifax, The Life of Lord Halifax* (London, 1965), 377. AP 8/1/9, Eden's notes made at the time of his resignation. AP 8/1/1, Letter of resignation, 20 February, 1938.
66 Hansard, columns 48–49, 21 February, 1938.
67 David Reynolds, 'Eden the Diplomatist, 1931–56: Suezide of a Statesman', *History*, February, 1989.
68 For a discussion of the negotiations see: SOHP: Interview with Sir Evelyn Shuckburgh, PRO: CAB 128/29. CM(55) 15, 16 June, 1955. For further details of ALPHA, see: CAB 129/75. Memorandum by Macmillan, 11 June, 1955. The land to be ceded was specifically:

> two small triangles, one to Egypt with its base on the Egypt–Israel frontier and one to Jordan with its base on the Jordan–Israel frontier, in the extreme South of the Negeb, a few miles North of Elath. The points of the two triangles would meet on the Israeli Road from Beersheba to Elath; and at this junction, which might need mixed or international supervision, a road from Egypt to Jordan under complete Arab control could pass over (or under) the road to Elath, which would remain under complete Israeli control. (*Ibid.*)

69 Shuckburgh, *op. cit.*, 304. Diary entry for 22 November, 1955.
70 AP 20/22/173. PMPT(E) 198/55, No. 4485. Eden to Macmillan, 2 October, 1955. PRO: CAB 128/29, CM(55) 34, 4 October, 1955. The Pact had originated from a treaty between Turkey and Iraq, in January, 1955. Britain and Pakistan had joined later in April of the same the year, and Iran joined in October, 1955.
71 Kevin Ruane has argued that Eden 'contrary to traditional opinion, did not suffer from delusions of grandeur but had a considered programme for offsetting Britain's post-war decline'; Kevin Ruane, 'Eden, the Foreign Office and the War in Indo-China: October 1951 to July 1954' (Ph.D. thesis, University of Kent, 1991).
72 Shuckburgh, *op. cit.*, 281. Diary entry for 26 September, 1955.
73 John Colville, *The Fringes of Power, 10 Downing Street Diaries 1939–1955* (London, 1986), 686. Part of a conversation between Eisenhower and Colville, December, 1953.
74 MP.MS.Macmillan.dep.d.24. Diary entry for 13 November, 1955. The CIA, through their Middle East expert, Kermit Roosevelt, had helped Nasser to power, advising and funding the coup against the British-backed monarchy of

King Farouk. 'To the Dulles brothers [Allen was now head of the CIA]...British attempts to hold onto colonial prototypes were more than an invitation to communist nationalists; they were a directive': John Ranelagh, *The Agency: The Rise and Fall of the C.I.A.* (London, 1987), 297n. See also Lucas (1991), 13–16. While British involvement in Egypt had decreased, their diplomacy often remained reminiscent of the archaic colonialism that had incensed the US on both moral and practical grounds. For an in-depth study of the coup, see Joel Gordon, *Nasser's Blessed Movement: Egypt's Free Officers and the July Revolution* (New York, 1992).

75 Parliamentary Private Secretary to Austen Chamberlain, 1929–31. He had attended the Assembly of the League of Nations as a British delegate in 1932, whilst Parliamentary Under Secretary to the Foreign Office. Minister for League of Nations Affairs, 1935.
76 Thomas, *op. cit.*, 46; Kyle, *op. cit.*, 11; Lucas (1991), *op. cit.*, 23.
77 Kingseed, *op. cit.*, 27.
78 Shuckburgh, *op. cit.*, 274. Diary entry for 29 July, 1955.
79 AP 20/1/31. Diary entry for 2 October, 1955.
80 In particular, see MP.MS.Macmillan.dep.d.23. Diary entry for 23 September, 1955.
81 Kyle, *op. cit.*, 154 and 155, and Lucas (1991), *op. cit.*, 150.
82 Thomas, *op. cit.*, 56–8.
83 Emmet John Hughes, *The Ordeal Of Power* (London, 1963), 1. Hughes was Eisenhower's principal speech writer.
84 Stephen Ambrose, *Eisenhower, The President 1952–1969* (London, 1984), 64. The letter was sent on 23 January, 1953. Dulles had publicly to demonstrate anti-communist beliefs because of his endorsement of Alger Hiss as director of the Carnegie Endowment and his subsequent offer of a deposition on Hiss's behalf at his trial.
85 See, for example: Herman Finer, *Dulles Over Suez: The Theory and Practice of His Diplomacy* (Chicago, 1964), 30, 34, 79 and 171; Townsend Hoopes, *The Devil and John Foster Dulles: The Diplomacy of the Eisenhower Era* (Boston, 1973), 321, 322, 432 and 439.
86 Department of State Bulletin, 5 March, 1956: 'Appraising Soviet Policies: Address by the Secretary of State (Dulles) before the *Philadelphia Bulletin* Forum, Philadelphia, February 26, 1956', quoted in *Documents on American Foreign Relations 1956* (hereafter referred to as *DAFR*.) (Council on Foreign Relations, New York, 1957), 196–201.
87 *Ibid.*
88 Shuckburgh, *op. cit.*, 281. Diary entry for 27 September, 1955.
89 Archie Roosevelt, *For the Lust of Knowing; Memoirs of an Intelligence Officer* (London, 1988), 433 and 443.
90 AP 20/20/58. PMPM M(E) 58/85, Eden to Macmillan, 19 August, 1955.
91 AP 20/27/37. T28/56, No. 244. Eden to Eisenhower, 16 January, 1956. AP 20/27/40, Eden to Eisenhower, 1 February, 1956.
92 Shuckburgh, *op. cit.*, 17.
93 Nutting, *op. cit.*, 21.
94 PRO: FO 371/115492/V1073/289. No. 269. Cairo to F.O., 21 February, 1955. Eden (1960), *op. cit.*, 221.
95 Eden (1960), *op. cit.*, 221; Lloyd, *op. cit.*, 27: Eden confirmed his annoyance to Lloyd.
96 Nutting, *op. cit.*, 21.
97 *Foreign Relations of the United States* (hereafter referred to as *FRUS*) 1955–7 xiv, 71.

98 Mohammed H. Heikal, *Cutting the Lion's Tail: Suez Through Egyptian Eyes* (London, 1986), 61–5. Mohammed H. Heikal, *Nasser, The Cairo Documents: The Private Papers of Nasser* (London, 1973), 76–9. Lucas (1991), *op. cit.*, 40–1. Kyle, *op. cit.*, 60–1. Lloyd, *op. cit.*, 27.

99 DDE. Ann Whitman Series, DDE Diaries, Box 13, March 1956 Diary, Foster Dulles memorandum, 28 March, 1956; DDE, John Foster Dulles Papers, Subject, Alphabetical, Box 10, Israeli Relations 1951–7 (4), Foster Dulles's longhand notes, 27 March, 1956; DDE. Ann Whitman Series, DDE Diaries, Box 13, March 1956 Diary, White House meeting, 28 March, 1956.

100 Wilbur C. Eveland, *Ropes of Sand* (New York, 1980), 169–72; Lucas (1991), *op. cit.*, 109 and 116; Kyle, *op. cit.*, 84 and 102.

101 Shuckburgh, *op. cit.*, 305. Diary entry for 28 November, 1955.

102 Private information. For a fuller discussion of MI6's role during the Suez Crisis, see: Nigel West, *The Friends: Britain's Post-War Secret Intelligence Operations* (London, 1990); Christopher Andrew, *Secret Service, The Making of the British Intelligence Community* (London, 1985); Brian Lapping, *End of an Empire* (London, 1986); Private Papers of Sir Denis Wright (hereafter referred to as WP). Note made by Wright re: the obituary of George Young, in *The Independent*, 14 May, 1990, on the same day; SOHP: Interview with Sir Evelyn Shuckburgh.

103 For example, see Lucas (1991), *op. cit.*, 116 (Lucas believed that MI6 finally convinced Eden to conduct a more aggressive policy), and Kyle, *op. cit.*, 150.

104 A favourite story of Macmillan's, that illustrated the problems some British had in understanding the President, was recorded by Shuckburgh:

> Eisenhower had told Bedell Smith that he had been invited to run for President by both the Democrats and the Republicans and asked B. S. which he thought he should choose. B. S. asked whether he was a Republican or a Democrat. E. said his father was a Republican but his politics are democratic. But he decided to stand as a Republican because the system would only work if both parties had a turn. The country needed a change of party. (Shuckburgh, *op. cit.*, 289. Diary entry for 2 October, 1955. See also MP.MS. Macmillan.dep.d. 23. Diary entry for 2 October, 1955.)

This story was misinterpreted as showing Eisenhower as apolilitical, even stupid. There was also much talk of the President's penchant for playing golf and that he spent more time on holiday than actually working.

105 Lord Moran, *Churchill* (London, 1968), 462 and 536, entries for 19 July and 7 December, 1953.

106 Dimbleby, 'BBC 1 interview with Sir Philip de Zulueta', quoted in David Dimbleby and David Reynolds, *An Ocean Apart* (London, 1988), 206.

107 Interview with Sir Frederick Bishop, cited in *The Suez Crisis*, BBC TV, 1996.

108 SOHP: Interview with Sir Evelyn Shuckburgh.

109 *Ibid*. See also Shuckburgh, *op. cit.*, 312. Thorpe, *op. cit.*, 167: Lloyd, acting as a conciliator between the American and Indian delegation at the UN, discussing Korea, backed and, by his support, helped secure the acceptance of the Indian Resolution which left Acheson saying angrily: 'It does not pay to win victories over your friends' (Thorpe's private information).

110 SOHP: Interview with Sir Evelyn Shuckburgh.

111 *Ibid*.

112 Interview with Chester Cooper, cited in *The Suez Crisis*, BBC TV 1996.

113 For example, Lucas (1991), *op. cit.*, 24 and 142; Kyle, *op. cit.*, 10–11 and 136; Thomas, *op. cit.*, 46.
114 Some historians and commentators have seen 1 March, 1956 as the turning point in Eden's policies and ultimately in his relationship with Nasser: e.g. Thomas, *op. cit.*, 28; Lucas (1991), *op. cit.*, chapter 7: 'The Turning Point – London'. Nutting, *op. cit.*, 32, believed that:

> from now on Eden completely lost his touch. Gone was his old uncanny sense of timing, his deft feel for negotiation. Driven by the impulses of pride and prestige and nagged by mounting sickness, he began to behave like an enraged elephant charging senselessly at invisible and imaginary enemies in the international jungle.

115 AP 20/32/64. Telegram No. 344. Eden to Amman, 1 March, 1956; AP 20/32/65. No. 285. Amman to F.O., 2 March; AP 20/32/66. No. 289. Amman to F.O., 2 March; AP 20/32/69. No. 319. Amman to F.O., 4 March; AP 20/32/71. No. 324. Amman to F.O., 4 March; AP 20/32/73. No. 364. 7 March, 1956. See also Eden (1960), *op. cit.*, 347–53; AP 20/32/66. Duke to FO, 2 March, 1956.
116 Nutting, *op. cit.*, 30–2.
117 AP 33/8. Biographer's file.
118 For example, Thomas, *op. cit.*, 43; Lucas (1991), *op. cit.*, 53; Kyle, *op. cit.*, 68–9.
119 Shuckburgh, *op. cit.*, 14. AP 20/1/32. Diary entry for 7 September, 1956.
120 Shuckburgh, *op. cit.*, 35. Diary entry for mid-February, 1952.
121 SOHP: Interview with Sir William Hayter.
122 SOHP: Interview with Sir Evelyn Shuckburgh.
123 SOHP: Interview with Sir Frederick Bishop.
124 SOHP: Interview with Sir Guy Millard.
125 *Ibid.*
126 Shuckburgh, *op. cit.*, 9. Macleod cited in C. Sulzberger, *The Last of the Giants* (New York, 1970), 405.
127 R. A. Butler, *The Art of the Possible: The Memoirs of Lord Butler* (Harmondsworth, 1973), 195.
128 Interview with Sir Guy Millard, conducted by the author, 25 February, 1998.
129 AP 23/5/10B. Eden to Aldrich, 3 May, 1967.
130 Robert H. Ferrell (ed.), *The Eisenhower Diaries* (New York, 1981), 319. Diary entry for 13 March, 1956. Eisenhower wrote: 'The economy of European countries would collapse if those oil supplies were cut off. If the economy of Europe would collapse, the United States would be in a situation of which the difficulty could scarcely be exaggerated.'
131 *Ibid.* Diary entry for 8 March, 1956.
132 Eisenhower (1966), *op. cit.*, 25.
133 Shuckburgh, *op. cit.*, 17.
134 Dulles to Hoover, 16 December, 1955, cited in Diane Kunz, *The Economic Diplomacy of the Suez Crisis* (Chapel Hill, 1991), 56.

1 Nationalisation

1 For a fuller discussion of the dual-track policy, see Introduction, 1–2.
2 The Khedive was the title accorded to the Viceroy of Egypt.

3. Lloyd, *op. cit.*, 74.
4. Philip Williams (ed.), *The Diary of Hugh Gaitskell, 1945–56* (London, 1983), 552–3.
5. Selwyn Lloyd raised this issue again in the Cabinet of 27 July, but ministers rejected the proposal for the same reasons as the Prime Minister: Lloyd, *op. cit.*, 84. PRO: CAB 128/30. CM(56) 54, 27 July, 1956.
6. Papers of William Clark (hereafter referred to as WCP).MS.William Clark.160. Diary entry for 26–27 July, 1956. M. Jacques Georges-Picot, the Chairman of the Suez Canal Company was invited by M. Chauvel but remained outside and unconsulted: see Jacques Georges-Picot, *The Real Suez Crisis: The End of a Great Nineteenth Century Work* (New York, 1978), 74–5. The Americans were represented by their Chargé because the Ambassador, Winthrop Aldrich, had left for the US that afternoon: see Kilmuir, *op. cit.*, 268. Interview with Sir Guy Millard, 25 February, 1998: Macmillan was simply not invited to the meeting because his ministerial concerns were not affected. Mountbatten alleged that Sir Gerald Templer was also present but Templer denied this in a letter to Eden: AP 33/6. Templer to Eden, 21 August, 1976.
7. WCP.MS.William Clark.160. Diary entry for 26–27 July, 1956.
8. Winthrop Aldrich, 'The Suez Crisis: A Footnote to History', *Foreign Affairs* (April, 1967), 542.
9. SOHP: Interview with Sir Frederick Bishop.
10. Eisenhower (1966), *op. cit.*, 35. PRO: FO 800/726. T3358, Eden to Eisenhower, 27 July, 1956.
11. Lucas (1991), *op. cit.*, 142–3; Rhodes James, *op. cit.*, 454; Lamb, *op. cit.*, 198; Dutton, *op. cit.*, 388; McDermott, *op. cit.*, 132; Shaw, *op. cit.*, 8 and 108–9; Mosley, *op. cit.*, 405–6; Gorst and Johnman, *op. cit.*, 56; Kingseed, *op. cit.*, 42–3.
12. Kyle, *op. cit.*, 137 and 148–52; Thomas, *op. cit.*, 62, and Horne, *op. cit.*, 396 and 399, believe that on 2 August the Government decided to use force if negotiations broke down. However, they both suggest that Eden wanted and had decided that force would be employed.
13. Lucas (1991), *op. cit.*, 142–3; Kyle, *op. cit.*, 136; Gorst and Johnman, *op. cit.*, 56; Shaw, *op. cit.*, 8 and 108–9; Mosley, *op. cit.*, 405–6.
14. William Clark, *From Three Worlds: Memoirs* (London, 1986), 166. In the memoirs this entry appears as a diary entry. WCP.MS.William Clark.160. Diary entry for 26–7 July, 1956.
15. Clark, *op. cit.*, 146.
16. *Ibid.*
17. *Ibid.* See also similar allegations attributed to Clark in Mosley, *op. cit.*, 405. Clark verified these remarks to Rhodes James, *op. cit.*, 454.
18. WCP.MS.William Clark.160. Diary entry for 26–7 July, 1956. This entry suggests that he was receiving secondhand information. In 'Suez 1956: Neither War Nor Peace At 10 Downing Street', Clark explains that he was in and out of the meeting. This was also revealed by his misrepresentation of Eden's own choice of words. Clark specifically said, in his memoirs, that Eden's immediate reaction to the nationalisation, at the meeting of 26 July, was that Nasser could not be allowed 'to have his hand on our windpipe'. See Clark, *op. cit.*, 166. In his interview with Michael Charlton he referred to the same phrase as: Nasser could not be allowed to be 'in a position where his thumb was on our jugular vein': see Clark cited in 'Suez 1956: Neither War Nor Peace At 10 Downing Street'.
19. Clark cited in 'Suez 1956: Neither War Nor Peace At 10 Downing Street'.

20 *Ibid.* Clark, *op. cit.*, 166.
21 Clark remains a reliable source of evidence for events and machinations within or involving the Private Office, particularly with which he was most involved. However, he was never privy to the inner circle in which Eden confided and, as such, has proved both uninformed and misinformed as to the mindset of the Prime Minister. For details of those closest to Eden and the narrowness of his circle of friends, see Introduction, 16–17.
22 The Papers of Dwight D. Eisenhower (hereafter referred to as DDE), Ann Whitman Series, Dulles-Herter, Box 5, London to State Department, Cable 481, 27 July, 1956, cited in Lucas (1991), *op. cit.*, 142.
23 Eisenhower (1966), *op. cit.*, 35.
24 In particular, as Murphy recorded, Hoover 'couldn't stand' Eden: Murphy, *op. cit.*, 468.
25 Eisenhower (1966), *op. cit.*, 37.
26 SOHP: Interview with Sir Frank Cooper.
27 Philip Ziegler, *Mountbatten: The Official Biography* (London, 1985), 537–8; AP 33/6. Templer to Eden, 21 August, 1976: Templer exchanged post-Suez correspondence with Eden concerned about Mountbatten's allegations. Templer adamantly denied that such a suggestion had been made by Eden to the Chiefs of Staff commenting that Mountbatten's behaviour had left 'an unpleasant taste in my mouth'.
28 The Papers of Earl Mountbatten of Burma (hereafter referred to as BA) N106. Personal and Confidential Note dictated by First Sea Lord, 7 or 8 September, 1956, cited in Ziegler, *op. cit.*, 537–8.
29 PRO: DEFE 4. COS (56) 73, Confidential Annex, 27 July, 1956.
30 PREM 11/1090. Mountbatten to Hailsham, 4 November, 1956.
31 SOHP: Interview with Sir Frank Cooper; Interview with Sir Frank Cooper, conducted by the author on 2 April, 1998.
32 Ziegler, *op. cit.*, 539–41.
33 *Ibid.*, 541.
34 SOHP: Interview with Sir Richard Powell.
35 Lord Kilmuir, *Political Adventure* (London, 1964), 430. AP 33/7i. Biographer's file. Conversation between Anthony and Clarissa Eden, witnessed by Anthony Head; AP 23/37/24B. Head to Eden, 3 May, 1962.
36 Anthony Eden, *Another World 1897–1917* (New York, 1977), 168. See also Anthony Nutting, 'Another Eden', *The Spectator*, 1 May, 1976: a review of *Another World* (originally published in 1976).
37 Cf. Introduction, 5–8 and 17.
38 AP 20/30/1. Prime Minister's Engagement Diary. Diary entry for 27 July, 1956.
39 Cf. Introduction, 1–2.
40 *US Declassified Document Reference System* (Washington, DC, 1976–90) (hereafter referred to as US DDRS), US81 384B; DDE, Ann Whitman Series, International, Box 19, Eden, Eisenhower to Eden, 28 July 1956, cited in Lucas (1991), *op. cit.*, 147.
41 The note was delivered by Harold Caccia to the Egyptian Embassy in London on 27 July, 1956.
42 All quotes from PRO: CAB 128/30. CM(56) 54, 27 July, 1956, unless otherwise stated.
43 PRO: FO 800/726. T3358, Eden to Eisenhower, 27 July, 1956.
44 James Margach, political correspondent of *The Sunday Times*, described McDonald as 'Eden's closest friend': Margach, *op. cit.*, 107.

45 In conversation with Mr. Iverach McDonald, 24 February, 1998. See also Iverach McDonald, *A Man of The Times: Talks and Travels in a Disrupted World* (London, 1976), 147.
46 *The Times* Archive (hereafter referred to as TNLA). Secret Memorandum From Foreign Editor [McDonald] to Editor [William Hayley], 27 July, 1956. See also: McDonald (1976), *op. cit.*, 144, and Iverach McDonald, *The History of the Times, Volume V: Struggles in War and Peace 1939–1966* (London, 1984.), 261–2.
47 The original concession to build the Canal and set up the Canal company had been granted on 15 November, 1854 but was replaced by a more formal agreement in January, 1956. McDonald (1976), *op. cit.*, 144.
48 McDonald (1984), *op. cit.*, 263.
49 In conversation with Mr. Iverach McDonald, 24 February, 1998. McDonald (1976), *op. cit.*, 144; TNLA. Suez Canal July–August 1956 Confidential Memoranda, 'Talk With the Prime Minister', 3 August, 1956.
50 PRO: FO 800/726. T3358, Eden to Eisenhower, 27 July, 1956. See also CAB 128/30. CM(56) 54, 27 July, 1956.
51 PRO: CAB 134/1217. EC(56) 1, 28 July, 1956; CAB 134/1216. EC(56)1, 27 July, 1956; CAB 128/30. CM(56) 54, 27 July, 1956.
52 Butler was ill and missed the first two Egypt Committee Meetings but eventually attended 32 of the 46 meetings, chairing 2 of them: See PRO: CAB 134/1216.
53 Attendances out of 46 meetings by the leading personnel: Eden: 44; Macmillan: 40; Lord Home, Secretary of State for Commonwealth Relations:42; Peter Thorneycroft, President of the Board of Trade: 37; Antony Head, Secretary of State for War and later Minister of Defence: 37; Lloyd: 35; Lord Salisbury, Lord President: 34; Harold Watkinson, Minister for Transport & Civil Aviation: 34; Butler: 32; Walter Monckton, Minister for Defence and later Paymaster-General: 28; Lennox-Boyd: 28; Dickson: 22; Lord Kilmuir, Lord Chancellor: 15; Kirkpatrick: 14; Templer: 11; Mountbatten: 10; Lord Hailsham, later First Lord of the Admiralty: 9. There were a total of 43 different members, 53 including the secretariat.
54 Nutting, *op. cit.*, 48. France froze Egyptian assets in France on 29 July and the US followed suit two days later. These were the only sanctions employed to date. Further specific sanctions could not be agreed upon.
55 AP 20/25/1. PMPT T341/56, No. 7. Eden to Sidney Holland (in San Fransisco), 28 July, 1956.
56 AP 20/25/2A. PMPT T342/56, No. 2. Sidney Holland to Eden, 28 July, 1956.
57 AP 20/25/3. PMPT T345/56, M. Louis St. Laurent to Eden, 31 July, 1956.
58 SOHP: Interview with Sir Evelyn Shuckburgh: Shuckburgh believed that Eden 'read every newspaper he could find... It was the News Department's job to supply the cuttings to him, but I think he read a lot of papers before he came into the office.'
59 SOHP: Interview with Sir Frederick Bishop.
60 *Ibid.*
61 *The Times*, 28 July, 1956; *The Daily Mail*, 28 July, 1956.
62 *The Daily Herald*, 27 July. For aggressive reactions also see: *The Times*, 27 July; *The Star*, 27 July; *News Chronicle*, 28 July; *Daily Express*, 27 July; *Daily Sketch*, 27 July; *The Daily Telegraph*, 28 July. *The Manchester Guardian* stood alone in promoting a non-aggressive solution. (All dates in 1956)
63 *New York Times*, 31 July, 1956: 'Premier Mollet charges Nasser is would-be Hitler.' Eisenhower (1966), *op. cit.*, 36.
64 Hansard, 2 August, 1956, column 1613.

65 *Ibid.*, 2 August, 1956, column 1660. Morrison did go on to add, 'I ask the Government not to be too nervous.'
66 MP.MS.Macmillan.dep.d.27. Diary entry for 27 July, 1956. Macmillan's remark was made in response to Nasser's nationalisation speech. He was later asked to remove the quote from his diary but refused: AP 23/48/112. Macmillan to Eden, 26 October, 1971.
67 WCP.MS.William Clark.160. Diary entry for 29 July, 1956. See also SOHP: Interviews with Sir Frederick Bishop and Sir Guy Millard.
68 Lord Sherfield, *op. cit.*, 25.
69 Robert Murphy, *Diplomat Among Warriors* (London, 1984), 461.
70 Lord Sherfield, *op. cit.*, 25.
71 MP.MS.Macmillan.dep.d.27. Diary entry for 30 July, 1956.
72 Eden (1960), *op. cit.*, 433.
73 Murphy, *op. cit.*, 462. PRO: FO 371/119081/JE 14211/121G.
74 Murphy, *op. cit.*, 462.
75 MP.MS.Macmillan.dep.d.27. Diary entry for 30 July, 1956.
76 PRO: FO 371/119080/JE 14211/87/G. No. 1613. Makins to F.O., 30 July, 1956.
77 *Ibid.*
78 MP.MS.Macmillan.dep.c.24. Diary entry for 26 October, 1955.
79 AP 20/1/31. Diary entry for 2 October, 1955.
80 Lord Sherfield, *op. cit.*, 25.
81 MP.MS.Macmillan.dep.d.27. Diary entry for 30 July, 1956.
82 Macmillan had served with both Eisenhower and Murphy during the Second World War at Allied Headquarters in Algiers and had enjoyed much better relations with Dulles, while Foreign Secretary, than Eden had or could.
83 Horne, *op. cit.*, 397.
84 Murphy, *op. cit.*, 463.
85 MP.MS.Macmillan.dep.d.27. Diary entry for 30 July, 1956. Macmillan's diaries were written in a relaxed, informal style, often with poor grammar. The use of 'will', therefore, did not mean that the decision had been made but rather that Macmillan wanted the decision to be taken and reflected his hope.
86 Lloyd, *op. cit.*, 91–2.
87 Murphy, *op. cit.*, 130–40: chapter 7, 'Secret For Eisenhower (1942)'. During the Second World War Murphy had been seconded to Eisenhower to discuss the possibility and the implications of an invasion of North Africa. Dwight D. Eisenhower, *The White House Years: Mandate For Change: 1953–1956* (New York, 1963), 183–4.
88 PRO: PREM 11/1098. Brook to Eden, 2 August, 1956. Macmillan's meddling had a history: even as Minister of Housing, he had written foreign policy memoranda: Thorpe, *op. cit.*, 190.
89 Thorpe, *op. cit.*, 190. For less sympathetic attitudes, see Anthony Sampson, *Macmillan: A Study in Ambiguity* (Harmondsworth, 1968), 117–18.
90 Interview with Sir Guy Millard conducted by the author, 25 February 1998 and SOHP: Interviews with Sir Frederick Bishop and Sir Guy Millard.
91 SOHP: Interview with Sir Frederick Bishop.
92 TNLA. Suez Canal July–August 1956, Confidential Memoranda, 'Talk With the Prime Minister', 3 August, 1956.
93 PRO: FO 371/119081/JE 14211/114/G.
94 Dodds-Parker, *op. cit.*, 102–3. The committee included Douglas Dodds-Parker, his former wartime chief of SOE, Charles Hambro, Geoffrey McDermott (as its secretary)

and 'two others who had been specially employed and had since held high responsibility outside government'.
95 Terms coined by Norman A. Graebner, *Cold War Diplomacy: American Foreign Policy 1945–75* (New York, 1977), 47.
96 AP 20/21/164. PMPM, M174/56, Eden to Monckton, 29 July, 1956.
97 PRO: FO 800/747. A. W. Snelling (Commonwealth Relations Office) to Lloyd, 1 August, 1956.
98 SOHP: Interview with Sir Guy Millard. 'Dual-track policy' was a term suggested by the interviewer (Anthony Gorst) and agreed to by Millard.
99 Cf. Chapter 1, 25–6; PRO: CAB 128/30. CM(56) 54, 27 July, 1956.
100 Murphy, *op. cit.*, 461.
101 Eden (1960), *op. cit.*, 435. Confirmed in AP 20/1/32. Diary entry for 15 August, 1956.
102 PRO: FO 800/726. T346/56, Eisenhower to Eden, 31 July, 1956.
103 Dodds-Parker, *op. cit.*, 103. Even during the period of Appeasement in the 1930s he had begun by advocating negotiation and then rearmament, but never war (see 36). As one contemporary broadcaster said, Eden had been the 'arch-opponent of aggression during a time when one of the major pieces of aggression was in progress without successful impediment'. As Eden admitted, he was not a pacifist but had been repulsed by war: hence he was convinced, as in 1938–9, that 'pacifism on our part would not prevent war': Avon (1962), *op. cit.*, 4.
104 PRO: FO 800/726. Eisenhower to Eden, 31 July, 1956. FO 800/725. Secretary of State's Memorandum on the Diplomatic Exchanges and Negotiations from the Egyptian Nationalisation of the Suez Canal Company on July 26, 1956 to the Outbreak of Hostilities between Israel and Egypt on October 29, 1956. Lucas saw this as a stimulant to Eden's continuing pressure for a military solution.
105 DDE. Ann Whitman Series, DDE Diaries, Box 13, March 1956 Diary; Foster Dulles memorandum, 28 March, 1956. DDE, John Foster Dulles Papers, Subject, Alphabetical, Box 10, Israeli Relations 1951–7 (4); Foster Dulles's long-hand notes, 27 March, 1956. DDE. Ann Whitman Series, DDE Diaries, Box 13, March 1956 Diary; White House meeting, 28 March, 1956.
106 DDE. Ann Whitman Series, DDE Diaries, Box 13, March 1956 Diary; Foster Dulles memorandum, 28 March, 1956: There was a suggestion that covert planning should begin with the British to 'change the Government in Syria to one more friendly to Iraq and the West'.
107 PRO: PREM 11/1102. Macmillan to Eden, 'Note of a Private Talk with Mr. Dulles', 25 September, signed 26 September, 1956; Lord Sherfield, *op. cit.*, 33.
108 McDonald (1984), *op. cit.*, 265.
109 Eisenhower (1966), *op. cit.*, 38.
110 PRO: PREM 11/1098. CM(56) 56, Confidential Annex, 1 August, 1956.
111 MP.MS.Macmillan.dep.d.27. Diary entry for 2 August, 1956.
112 Cf. Chapter 2, 44.
113 Cf. Chapter 1, 42; PRO: FO 800/726. T3358, Eden to Eisenhower, 27 July, 1956. See also CAB 128/30. CM(56) 54, 27 July, 1956.
114 MP.MS.Macmillan.dep.d.27. Diary entry for 31 July, 1956; Shuckburgh, *op. cit.*, 361; PRO: CAB 134/1216. EC(56) 6, 31 July, 1956; CAB 128/30. CM(56) 56, 1 August, 1956.
115 PRO: CAB 128/30. CM(56) 54, 27 July, 1956.
116 PRO: CAB 128/30. CM(56) 56, 1 August, 1956.

117 PRO: CAB 134/1216. EC(56) 2, 28, July, 1956.
118 PRO: CAB 134/1216. EC(56) 4, 30 July, 1956.
119 PRO: CAB 134/1216. EC(56) 6, 31 July, 1956.
120 PRO: CAB 128/30. CM(56) 56, 1 August, 1956.
121 *Ibid*.
122 PRO: CAB 134/1216. EC(56) 3, 30 July, 1956.
123 PRO: CAB 128/30. CM(56) 56, 1 August, 1956.
124 PRO: PREM 11/1098.
125 PRO: CAB 134/1216. EC(56) 2, 28, July, 1956.
126 McDonald (1984), *op. cit.*, 265.
127 PRO: CAB 134/1216. EC(56) 2, 28 July, 1956; EC(56) 4, 30 July, 1956 and EC(56) 6, 31 July, 1956.
128 PRO: FO 371/119080/JE 14211/90. Commonwealth Relations Office to U.K. High Commissioners, W. No. 313, 2 August, 1956. FO 800/725. Private Papers of the Secretary of State for Foreign Affairs: Secretary of State's Memorandum on the Diplomatic Exchanges and Negotiations from the Egyptian Nationalisation of the Suez Canal Company on July 26, 1956 to the Outbreak of Hostilities between Israel and Egypt on October 29, 1956.
129 AP 20/25/4. PMPT T348/56, No. 3551. Eden to Menzies, 3 August, 1956; AP 20/25/5. PMPT T349/56, No. 125. Eden to Prime Ministers of Canada, New Zealand, South Africa, India, Pakistan and Ceylon, 2 August, 1956.
130 McDonald (1976), *op. cit.*, 144.
131 TNLA. Suez Canal July–August 1956 Confidential Memoranda, 'Talk With the Prime Minister', conducted by Iverach McDonald, 3 August, 1956.
132 *Ibid*. Author's italics.
133 For Eden's patriotism, see SOHP: Interview with Sir Frederick Bishop. McDonald (1976), *op. cit.*, 147.
134 Cf. Introduction, 9–11.

2 Negotiation

1 WCP.MS.William Clark.160. Diary entry for 31 July, 1956. The issue had been raised by Peter Thorneycroft, The President of the Board of Trade. (Because of his proximity to events that included him in the decision-making, Clark is a much more reliable source over factual issues to do with Eden's relationship with the media.) See also PRO: CAB 134/1216. EC(56) 4, 30 July, 1956 and PREM 1162: File on Security of the Press. Eden also had to worry about the 'awkward repercussions following such an approach' not least the attention it would bring to the precautionary measures.
2 PRO: PREM 11/1162. PMPM M176/56, Eden to First Lord of the Admiralty (Lord Cilcennin) and the First Sea Lord (Mountbatten), 3 August, 1956.
3 AP 20/25/7. PMPT T351/56, No. 653. Eden to Holland, 4 August, 1956.
4 Cf. Introduction, 12.
5 PRO: CAB 134/1216. EC(56) 10, 3 August, 1956.
6 McDonald (1976), *op. cit.*, 146.
7 TNLA. Suez Canal July to August 1956 Confidential Memoranda, 'Talk With the Prime Minister', recorded by Iverach McDonald, 3 August, 1956. See also PRO: CAB 134/1216. EC(56) 4, 30 July, 1956; EC(56) 9, 2 August, 1956 and EC(56) 10, 3 August, 1956.

194 Notes

8. TNLA. Suez Canal July to August 1956 Confidential Memoranda, 'Talk With the Prime Minister', recorded by Iverach McDonald, 3 August, 1956; PRO: PREM 11/1162. Note from William Clark to Eden, 2 August, 1956. Eden had never been keen on the idea of any form of censorship: see CAB 134/1216. EC(56) 4, 30 July, 1956. The decision was made after discussion with William Clark.
9. CAB 134/1216. EC(56)4, 30 July, 1956. The decision was made after discussion with William Clark.
10. Shaw, *op. cit.*, 49. For further discussion of the D-notice system, see Annabelle May and K. Rowan (eds), *Inside Information: British Government and the Media* (London, 1982).
11. Cf. Introduction, 7–8.
12. *The Times*, 7 August, 1956: 'RESOLVING SUEZ CRISIS: USE OF FORCE NOT JUSTIFIED', by Dennis Healey and Douglas Jay; 9 August, 1956: 'BRITAIN NOT SEEKING SUEZ SOLUTION BY FORCE' and 'HOPES FOR A PEACEFUL SOLUTION OF SUEZ CRISIS'; *The Observer*: 5 August, 1956: 'US FIRM AGAINST USING FORCE'; 12 August, 1956: 'UK UNDER OBLIGATION NOT TO USE FORCE'; *The Daily Telegraph*: 3 August, 1956: 'USE OF FORCE – NEED FOR CARE'; 6 August, 1956: 'INDIAN POLICY OVER SUEZ AVOIDING FORCE'; 9 August, 1956: 'WRONG WAY USE OF FORCE' by Mr Nehru; *The Daily Worker*: 3 August, 1956: 'FORCE IN EGYPT WILL GET US NOWHERE'; 4 August, 1956: 'KEEP SANE OVER SUEZ' and 'NO NEED FORCE, ALL SAY'; 7 August, 1956: 'STOP THIS "BRINK OF WAR STUFF"'; 8 August, 1956; 'MP'S RIGHT AND LEFT, OPPOSE THREATS'; *The Daily Mail*: 11 August, 1956: 'NO FORCE' by Alfred Robens.
13. PRO: CAB 134/1216. EC(56) 2, 28 July, 1956.
14. *Ibid.*
15. PRO: PREM 11/1123. *News Chronicle* Gallup Poll, reported 10 August, 1956.
16. PRO: FO 800/726. No. 3568. Eden to Eisenhower, 5 August, 1956.
17. TNLA. 'Secret': Memorandum from the Editor (William Hayley) to McDonald, 9 August, 1956.
18. Cf. Chapter 1, 37.
19. PRO: FO 800/731. PM /56/166, Lloyd to Eden, 8 August, 1956.
20. SOHP: Interview with Julian Amery.
21. PRO: FO 800/731. PM /56/166, Lloyd to Eden, 8 August, 1956. The addition was made on the original copy of this memorandum filed in PREM 11/1099.
22. Mollet had succeeded Pierre Mendès-France in February, 1956.
23. PRO: FO 800/731. PM /56/166, Lloyd to Eden, 8 August, 1956; Henri Azeau, *Le Piège de Suez, 5 Novembre* (Paris, 1964), 124.
24. PRO: CAB 134/1216. EC(56) 3, 30 July, 1956. FO 800/725. Secretary of State's Memorandum on the Diplomatic Exchanges and Negotiations from the Egyptian Nationalisation of the Suez Canal Company on July 26, 1956 to the Outbreak of Hostilities between Israel and Egypt on October 29, 1956.
25. PRO: CAB 134/1216. EC(56) 10, 3 August, 1956.
26. MP.MS.Macmillan.dep.d.27. Diary entry for 3 August, 1956.
27. Eden quote cited in Victor Rothwell, *Anthony Eden: A Political Biography 1935–1977* (Manchester, 1992), 216. PRO: CAB 134/1217. Record of a meeting held at 11 Downing Street on 3 August, 1956. The meeting was attended by: Macmillan, Lord Salisbury, Sir Leslie Rowan, Sir Gladwyn Jebb, Mr C. H. Johnston, Mr E. M. Rose, Mr J. H. A. Watson and Mr J. A. Wilson.
28. PRO: CAB 134/1216. EC(56), 11, Confidential Annex, 7 August, 1956. CAB 134/1217. EC(56) 8, 7 August, 1956.

29 Macmillan did not expect his diary to be read by the public for many years, if at all. The 'fifty-year rule' still covered sensitive political papers.
30 Shuckburgh, *op. cit.*, 361.
31 PRO: CAB 134/1217. EC(56) 8, 'Action Against Egypt': Note by the Chancellor of the Exchequer, 7 August, 1956.
32 MP.MS.Macmillan.dep.d.27. Diary entry for 7 August, 1956.
33 TNLA. 'Secret': Memorandum from the Editor to McDonald, 9 August, 1956.
34 *Ibid.* Although as the Chancellor revealed, 'the Minister of Defence had of course had copies made for them already!'
35 PRO: CAB 128/29. CM(55) 30, 5 September, 1955.
36 SOHP: Interview with Evelyn Shuckburgh. Shuckburgh was referring directly to the eventual collusion with Israel. For Churchill's attitude to Egypt, see Introduction, 8.
37 PRO: FO 371/118996/JE 11924/9/G. IMO/74, Major-General J. H. N. Poett (Director of Military Operation) to Major-General W. G. Stirling (Ministry of Defence), 5 August, 1956.
38 PRO: FO 371/118996/JE 11924/17/G. No. 248. Graham (Tripoli) to F.O., 8 August, 1956.
39 PRO: FO 371/118996/JE 11924/18/G. No. 582. J. H. A. Watson on behalf of Foreign Secretary to Gladwyn Jebb, 8 August, 1956.
40 TNLA. 'Secret': Memorandum from the Editor to McDonald, 9 August, 1956. On a subsidiary note, it was also feared that security in the French Embassy in Cairo was so poor that the 'Egyptians will be presented with a first class political and propaganda point': PRO: FO 371/118996/JE 11924/33/G. Trevelyan to J. H. A. Watson (F.O.), 7 August, 1956.
41 For details of the development of the conference, see Chapter 1, 37–41.
42 PRO: FO 800/725. Secretary of State's Memorandum on the Diplomatic Exchanges and Negotiations from the Egyptian Nationalisation of the Suez Canal Company on July 26, 1956 to the Outbreak of Hostilities between Israel and Egypt on October 29, 1956.
43 PRO: PREM 11/1099. Bishop to A. H. K. Slater (Lord President's Office), 12 August, 1956. Bishop note to P.M., n.d. Frederick Bishop, Eden's private secretary, later sent the Prime Minister a copy of this memorandum with an attached minute, reinforcing Eden's intent: 'This is a copy of the note you did as long ago as Aug 12, which you sent to one or two of your colleagues (L[or]d. Pres.[ident] And For.[eign] Sec[retar]y). It is remarkable how the "Users Club" proposal carries out the thought of this "historic document".'
44 Before the nationalisation, the Americans, and in particular Hoover, had seen the possibility of replacing Nasser and offering the new leader the financing of the Aswan Dam as a sign of friendship.
45 PRO: CAB 134/1216. EC(56) 15, 14 August, 1956, Confidential Annex, Minute 1.
46 TNLA. 'Secret': Memorandum from the Editor to McDonald, 9 August, 1956.
47 PRO: CAB 134/1216. EC(56) 2, 28 July, 1956.
48 TNLA. 'Secret': Memorandum from the Editor to McDonald, 9 August, 1956.
49 PRO: CAB 134/1217. EC(56) 17, 13 August, 1956. CAB 134/1216. EC(56) 13, Message from Monckton, 9 August, 1956.
50 PRO: CAB 134/1217. EC(56) 12, 8 August, 1956. Record of a conversation between Lloyd, the Crown Prince of Iraq and Nuri Pasha on 3 August, 1956.
51 TNLA. 'Secret': Memorandum from the Editor to McDonald, 9 August, 1956. It has often been assumed that Eden, regretting his decision to effect the

196 Notes

withdrawal from the Canal Base, decided to use force to regain control of the Canal Zone.
52 AP 20/21/171. PMPM M181/56, Eden to Reginald Maudling (Minister of Supply), 12 August, 1956 and AP 20/21/174. PMPM M184/56, Eden to Lloyd, 15 August, 1956.
53 PRO: FO 800/725. Secretary of State's Memorandum on the Diplomatic Exchanges and Negotiations from the Egyptian Nationalisation of the Suez Canal Company on July 26, 1956 to the Outbreak of Hostilities between Israel and Egypt on October 29, 1956.
54 PRO: CAB 134/1216. EC(56), 12, 9 August, 1956.
55 *Ibid.*
56 MP.MS.Macmillan.dep.d.27. Diary entry for 9 August, 1956. Information from Monckton to Macmillan.
57 Cf. Chapter 1, 27–8; PRO: CAB 134/1217. EC(56) 1, 28 July, 1956; CAB 134/1216. EC(56) 1, 27 July, 1956; CAB 128/30. CM(56) 54, 27 July, 1956.
58 PRO: CAB 134/1216. EC(56) 15, 14 August, 1956, Confidential Annex, Minute 1.
59 *Ibid.*
60 Such was the air of passivity that the Chief of the Air Staff was going on a fortnight's caravanning holiday in North Wales: MP.MS.Macmillan.dep.d.27. Diary entry for 7 August, 1956. This actually pleased Nigel Birch who thought it 'on the whole, a good thing, as his Deputy was better!': *Ibid.*
61 PRO: CAB 21/3094. Mr Darracott's Papers, Malcolm Widdup to Paul Odgers, 15 August, 1956. Re: ME(O)(SC)(56) 12.
62 AP 20/1/32. Diary entry for 15 August, 1956.
63 *Ibid.*
64 PRO: PREM 11/1099. JE 14211/796. Record of Conversation Between The Secretary of State and Mr. Dulles On August 15, 1956.
65 Lloyd, *op. cit.*, 115. Twenty-four countries were invited to the Conference, the top 16 users and the original signatories of the Convention of Constantinople in 1888. Egypt and Greece rejected the invitation, leaving the following 22 countries to attend: Australia; Ethiopia; The Federal Republic of Germany; Japan; New Zealand; Persia [Iran]; USSR; Spain; Portugal; India; Ceylon [Sri Lanka]; Indonesia; Netherlands; Pakistan; Norway; Denmark; Sweden; Italy; Turkey; Britain; France and USA. For the development of the Conference, see Chapter 1, 37–40 and Chapter 2, 47–8.
66 *FRUS XVI*, Doc. 86, 16 August, 1956, 210–11.
67 *The Times*, 17 August, 1956.
68 Lloyd, *op. cit.*, 115–16.
69 *The Times*, 17 August, 1956.
70 *Ibid.* Lloyd, *op. cit.*, 116.
71 *The Times*, 17 August, 1956. See PRO: PREM 11/1099. JE 14213/142. Summary Record Of Meetings Between The Secretary Of State For Foreign Affairs And Other Delegates To The Suez Canal Conference In London, August 1956. See also FO 800/714. Secretary of State for Foreign Affairs, Engagement Diary for August, 1956.
72 PRO: CAB 134/1216. EC(56) 16, 16 August, 1956, Confidential Annex, Minute 3.
73 MP.MS.Macmillan.dep.d.27. Diary entry for 17 August, 1956.
74 AP 20/28/1. EC(56) 23, 16 August, 1956. 'Economic Pressure On Egypt', Note by the Chancellor of the Exchequer.
75 Original footnote on the memorandum:

> Our rough calculations are that Egypt's total free reserves (gold, foreign currency and credits) can hardly be more than £45 million and that her adverse

balance of payments will run at such a level that these may well be exhausted in a matter of months unless they are replenished by external aid.
76 AP 20/28/1. EC(56) 23, 16 August, 1956. 'Economic Pressure On Egypt', Note by the Chancellor of the Exchequer. The areas considered for wider sanctions were: oil and petroleum products; wheat; fertilisers; pharmaceuticals; iron and steel products; machinery and spare parts; tea and tobacco; shipping; and even a possible naval blockade. None of these could be developed at this stage for specific reasons but especially, as Macmillan concluded, because of the possibility of the Egyptians closing the Canal which would lead to the blocking of European bound oil.
77 *The Times*, 17 August, 1956.
78 AP 20/28/1. EC(56) 23, 16 August, 1956. 'Economic Pressure On Egypt', Note by the Chancellor of the Exchequer.
79 PRO: FO 371/119128/JE 14211/1390G.
80 PRO: CAB 134/1217. EC(56) 26, 18 August, 1956.
81 PRO: CAB 134/1216. EC(56) 18, 20 August, 1956, Confidential Annex, Minute 2.
82 *Ibid*.
83 MP.MS.Macmillan.dep.d.27. Diary entry for 18 August, 1956. After a dinner with Dulles, Herman Phleger, the State Department's chief legal officer, and American Ambassador to France, Douglas Dillon.
84 TNLA. 'Secret': Memorandum from the Editor to McDonald, 9 August, 1956.
85 MP.MS.Macmillan.dep.d.27. Diary entry for 18 August, 1956. [?] could not be made out on the original.
86 *Ibid*. Diary entry for 19 August, 1956.
87 *Ibid*. Diary entry for 20 August, 1956.
88 *Ibid*.
89 *Ibid*.
90 Cf. Chapter 2, 52–3.
91 PRO: CAB 134/1216. EC(56) 19, 22 August, 1956, Confidential Annex, Minute 6.
92 See WCP.MS.William Clark.160. Diary entries for: 30 October, 5 November, 1956.
93 TNLA. Memorandum from McDonald to the Editor, 16 August, 1956, after talk with Admiral Sir William Davis. Iverach McDonald in conversation with the author, 24 February, 1998.
94 PRO: CAB 134/1216. EC(56) 20, 23 August, 1956, Confidential Annex, Minute 1.
95 MP.MS.Macmillan.dep.d.27. Diary entry for 23 August, 1956.
96 *Ibid*.
97 *Ibid*.
98 AP 20/21/181. PMPM M191/56, Eden to Lloyd, 26 August, 1956.
99 PRO: CAB 134/1217. EC(56) 39, 29 August, 1956. Letter from Mr Paul-Henri Spaak (Belgian Minister of Foreign Affairs) to Lloyd, dated 21 August, 1956.
100 PRO: PREM 11/1100. Makins to F.O., No. 1754, 28 August, received 29 August, 1956.
101 AP 20/1/32. Diary entry for 16 August, 1956. Meeting with Shepilov before Conference.
102 Lady Hayter in correspondence with the author, 11 October and 30 October, 1997.
103 PRO: PREM 11/1170. Telegram No. 1051. Hayter to F.O., 1 August, 1956.
104 PRO: PREM 11/1170. Telegram No. 1053. Hayter to F.O., 2 August, 1956.

105 PRO: PREM 11/1170. Telegram No. 1054. Hayter to F.O., 2 August, 1956.
106 PRO: FO 371/118934/JE 11015/1. Reports by the Commercial Department, British Embassy, Cairo to The African Department at the Foreign Office, taken from an Associated Press telegram from Washington dated 23 August and *The Egyptian Gazette*, 24 August, 1956.
107 PRO: PREM 11/1099. JE 14213/142. Summary Record Of Meetings Between The Secretary Of State For Foreign Affairs And Other Delegates To The Suez Canal Conference In London, August, 1956. See also FO 800/714. Secretary of State for Foreign Affairs Engagement Diary for August, 1956.
108 'The Eighteen Nation Proposals', 23 August, 1956, cited in J. Eayrs, *The Commonwealth and Suez* (Oxford, 1964), 102–3:

1. They affirm that, as stated in the Preamble to the Convention of 1888, there should be established 'a definite system destined to guarantee at all times, and for all the powers, the free use of the Suez Maritime Canal'.
2. Such a system, which would be established for due regard to the sovereign rights of Egypt should assure;
    (a) Efficient and dependable operation, maintenance of the Canal as a free, open and secure international waterway in accordance with the principles of the Convention of 1888.
    (b) Insulation of the operation of the canal [sic] from the influence of the politics of any nation.
    (c) A return to Egypt for the use of the Suez Canal which will be fair and equitable and increasing with enlargements of its capacity and greater use.
    (d) Canal tolls as low as is consistent with the foregoing requirements and, except for c above, no profit.
3. To achieve these results on a permanent and reliable basis there should be established by a convention to be negotiated with Egypt:
    (a) International arrangements for co-operation between Egypt and other interested nations in the operation and maintenance and development of the Canal and for harmonising and safeguarding their respective interests in the Canal. To this end, operating, maintaining and developing the Canal and enlarging it so as to increase the volume of traffic in the interests of world trade and of Egypt, would be the responsibility of a Suez Canal Board. Egypt would grant this Board all rights and facilities appropriate to its functioning as here outlined. The status of the Board would be defined in the above-mentioned convention.

    The members of the board, in addition to Egypt, would be other states chosen in a manner to be agreed upon from among the States parties to the Convention, with due regard to use, pattern of trade and geographical distribution; the composition of the board to be such that its responsibilities would be discharged solely with a view to achieving the best possible operating results without political motivation in favour of, or in prejudice against, any user of the Canal.

    The Board would make periodic reports to the United Nations.
    (b) An Arbitral Commission to settle any disputes as to the equitable return to Egypt or other matters arising in the operation of the Canal,
    (c) Effective sanctions for any violation of the Convention by any party to it, or any other nation, including provisions for treating any use or threat of force to interfere with the use or operation of the Canal as

a threat to the peace and a violation of the purposes and principles of the United Nations Charter.
(d) Provisions for appropriate association with the United Nations and for review as may be necessary.

109 PRO: FO 800/725. Secretary of State's Memorandum on the Diplomatic Exchanges and Negotiations from the Egyptian Nationalisation of the Suez Canal Company on July 26, 1956 to the Outbreak of Hostilities between Israel and Egypt on October 29, 1956.
110 Cf. Chapter 1, 38–9. The 18 were: Australia; Denmark; Ethiopia; France; the Federal Republic of Germany; Iran; Italy; Japan; the Netherlands; New Zealand; Norway; Pakistan; Portugal; Sweden; Turkey; Britain; Spain; the USA. Those against were: India; Ceylon [Sri Lanka]; Indonesia; the USSR.
111 PRO: PREM 11/1100. Record of Meeting held at No. 10 Downing Street on Thursday, 23 August, 1956.
112 PRO: FO 800/726. Telegram No. 3913. Eden to Eisenhower, 27 August, 1956. However, despite the attempt, Eden was unable to affect the Americans. On 30 August, Dulles used the Communist threat to justify American opposition to force. The President was himself in agreement on the 'basic analysis': US DDRS, US85 000276. Yet this information was not imparted to Eden.
113 This committee, headed by Australian Prime Minister Robert Menzies, also included a representative from each of the following four countries: Ethiopia, Sweden, Persia [Iran] and the United States.
114 Kilmuir, *op. cit.*, 269.
115 The press believed that the meeting was unlikely to provide a settlement because Nasser dogmatically refused to compromise his position: Interview with Mr Aleco Joannides, Reuters correspondent during the Suez Crisis, 25 March, 1999.
116 Heikal (1986), *op. cit.*, 149.
117 TNLA. 'Secret': Memorandum from the Editor to McDonald, 9 August, 1956.
118 TNLA. Memorandum from the Editor to McDonald, 29 August, 1956, 'talk with the P.M. in morning'.
119 'H-hour' was a precise hour that a plan would be started.
120 Confirmed in PRO: PREM 11/1100. Makins to F.O., No. 1754, 28 August, received 29 August, 1956.
121 PRO: CAB 134/1216. EC(56) 23, 28 August, 1956, Confidential Annex, Minute 1.
122 This would have affected their voting position.
123 PRO: PREM 11/1100. Makins to F.O., No. 1761, 29 August, received 30 August, 1956.
124 PRO: PREM 11/1100. Croswaite [sic] to F.O., No. 633, 29 August, 1956.
125 PRO: CAB 134/1216. EC(56) 2, 28 July, 1956. A point developed in EC(56) 3, 30 July, 1956.
126 Sir Robert Menzies, *Afternoon Light: Some Memories of Men and Events* (London, 1970), 164.
127 PRO: PREM 11/1100. Trevelyan to F.O., No. 1788, 30 August, 1956.
128 Trevelyan had worked his way up through the Indian Civil and Political Service before serving with the Foreign Office as Councellor of Embassy in Baghdad during 1948–50, economic adviser to the High Commissioner in Germany, 1951–53, as well as Chargé d'Affaires in Peking, 1953–55. The recognition for his services up to 1955 was: OBE (1941), CIE (1947), CMG (1951) and KCMG (1955).

129 PRO: PREM 11/1177. Telegram No. 4060. Eisenhower to Eden, 3 September, 1956.
130 PRO: PREM 11/1165. Leak of letter from Eisenhower to Eden, 3 September, 1956: The Foreign Office having 'pursued enquiries as far as they can... have come to the conclusion that, as the leak appears to have occurred on the evening of September 6, on which day the P.M. read the message to the Cabinet, they can take the matter no further'. Enquiries came in from the *Daily Express*, *News Chronicle* and the *Daily Telegraph*, concerning a 'high source' or a 'well informed person'. Menzies, *op. cit.*, 165; Morgan (ed.), *op. cit.*, 509. The source of the British leak was probably Walter Monckton, who had passed information concerning the crisis to Hugh Cudlipp and Cecil King, which they discussed on 5 September, 1956, with Richard Crossman, Harold Wilson and Sydney Jacobsen (Cecil King did not attend this meeting).
131 Cf. Chapter 2, 60.
132 Cf. Chapter 2, 50–2.
133 Menzies, *op. cit.*, 166.
134 PRO: FO 371/119154/JE 14211/2127. Kirkpatrick to Lloyd, 4 September, 1956. Sir Ivone Kirkpatrick was due to retire in 1957.
135 This 'special help' manifested itself in terms of economic subsidies and political support on the world stage, and saw the beginnings of a long-running distrust of the Indians and, in particular, their Foreign Minister, Krishna Menon, by Eden. Nasser believed that time was on his side and it was considered that he would try to prolong negotiations probably with the basis being the Menon proposals. This was perpetuated by Menon's secrecy. As Trevelyan remarked on 31 August: 'He [Menon] was giving nothing away.' PRO: PREM 11/1100. Trevelyan to F.O., No. 1814, 31 August, 1956; PREM 11/1100. Trevelyan to F.O., No. 1788, 30 August, 1956.
136 Cf. Chapter 2, 58; PRO: PREM 11/1100. Record of Meeting held at No. 10 Downing Street on Thursday, 23 August, 1956.
137 PRO: CAB 134/1216. EC(56) 24, 4 September, 1956 and Confidential Annex, Minute 4.
138 PRO: PREM 11/1100. Trevelyan to Foreign Secretary, No. 1868, 3 September, 1956.
139 WCP.MS.William Clark.160. Diary entry for 5 September, 1956. Clark went on to say that Kirkpatrick's letter was 'supported by long analogies with the Rhineland 1936 episode'.
140 PRO: PREM 11/1177. No. 4061. Eden to Eisenhower, 6 September, 1956. Eden had already said that Nasser was no Hitler, see PRO: FO 800/726. No. 3568, Eden to Eisenhower, 5 August, 1956.
141 AP 20/25/31. PMPT T388/56, No. 1942. Trevelyan to P.M., 6 September, 1956; WCP.MS.William Clark.160. Diary entry for 6 September, 1956.
142 PRO: PREM 11/1100. No. 4062. F.O. to Washington, 6 September, 1956. PREM 11/1100. Trevelyan to F.O., No. 1814, 31 August, 1956: As early as 30 August, Nasser in conversation with US Ambassador Henry Byroade, 'presumed the Menzies mission might take two days to give him their views. It would only take him one hour to give his... [because] when a man fell in love with somebody else's wife a compromise was difficult without a divorce. He had no intention of arranging to divorce the Canal from Egypt.'
143 PRO: PREM 11/1100. No. 4063. F.O. to Washington, 6 September, 1956. The need to go to the Security Council was particularly because of pressure at home.

144 Eden received this news on 10 September. WCP.MS.William Clark.160. Diary entry for 10 September.
145 Menzies, *op. cit.*, 168. For Press Conference cf. Chapter 2, 60–2.
146 AP 20/25/31. PMPT T388/56, No. 1942. Trevelyan to Eden, 6 September, 1956.
147 PRO: PREM 1177. No. 1839. Eisenhower to Eden, 8 September, 1956.
148 PRO: PREM 11/1100. No. 1823. Makins to F.O., 7 September, 1956.
149 No official record of the dinner remains. Patrick Dean was on holiday.
150 Thorpe, *op. cit.*, 222, gives no source for the evidence from the meeting. Allen Dulles was an important contact of Lloyd's at the time. Thorpe believes that Lloyd was the 'indirect cause of activity in others'. Lloyd, *op. cit.*, 145: CASU 'turned out to be a dirty word in Portuguese. Various other combinations were tried. Almost all of them meant something revolting, usually in Turkish. Eventually SCUA survived all tests and the Suez Canal Users' Association came into being.'
151 Murphy, *op. cit.*, 470. McDonald told William Clark, 'that Norman Robertson, the Canadian High Commissioner, had confided in him that Dulles had only produced the users' plan because we [Britain and France] had said that unless Egypt accepted the Menzies plan we would invade': WCP.MS.WilliamClark.160. Diary entry for 20 September, 1956.
152 Cf. Chapter 1, 26 and Chapter 2, 61–3.
153 PRO: PREM 11/1177. No. 1839. Eisenhower to Eden, 8 September, 1956.

3 SCUA

1 For the failure of the Menzies Mission, see Chapter 2, 61–3. For Macmillan's interference, see Chapter 1, 30–3.
2 Lloyd, *op. cit.*, 126.
3 Cf. Chapter 2, 64; Murphy, *op. cit.*, 470.
4 PRO: CAB 134/1216. EC(56) 25, 7 September, 1956. See also SOHP: Interview with Sir Richard Powell.
5 PRO: CAB 134/1216. EC(56) 25, 7 September, 1956.
6 Particularly reflected in PRO: CAB 128/30. CM(56) 56, 11 September, 1956.
7 PRO: PREM 11/1123. The report argued that the *Daily Express* poll 'gave a more accurate forecast of the result of the last General Election than any other similar organization'.
8 AP 20/1/32. Diary entry for 7 September, 1956.
9 AP 20/21/184. PMPM M195/56, Eden to Macmillan, 5 September, 1956.
10 In a conversation with Douglas Dodds-Parker, friends from their days in SOE, Templer remarked: 'I could beat the Egyptian Army with a good brigade, like Tel–el–Kebir in '84 [1884].': SOHP: Interview with Sir Douglas Dodds-Parker.
11 WCP.MS.William Clark.160. Diary entry for weekend, 7–9 September, 1956.
12 French Ambassador in Washington in conversation with Roger Makins; PRO: PREM 11/1100. Makins to F.O., No. 1827, 7 September, received 8 September, 1956.
13 PRO: PREM 11/1100. Eden minute on Dixon to F.O., No. 647, 7 September, received 8 September, 1956.
14 PRO: CAB 134/1216. EC(56) 25, 7 September, 1956.
15 WCP.MS.William Clark.160. Diary entry for 10 September, 1956.
16 PRO: PREM 11/1100. Jebb to F.O., No. 290, 8 September, 1956.
17 AP 20/1/32. Diary entry for 12–13 September, 1956.
18 PRO: PREM 11/1100. Jebb to F.O., No. 295, 9 September, 1956.

19 PRO: PREM 11/1100. F.O. to Washington, No. 4102, 8 September, 1956.
20 PRO: PREM 11/1100. Makins to F.O., No. 1840, 8 September, received 9 September, 1956. The undercutting of the bluff had been made of even less importance/consequence by the recent American press conference and the divulgence of the Eisenhower/Eden correspondence: Cf. Chapter 2, 60–2.
21 AP 20/25/34. No. 1838. Makins to Eden, 8 September, 1956.
22 Eden (1960), *op. cit.*, 484.
23 AP 33/7iii: He wrote in the margin of his copy of *Full Circle*, next to a reference to S.C.U.A., 'As Eden said to me, Cockeyed idea but if it means the Americans are with us then I think we can accept it.' Information supplied by Mr Abraham Rosenthal in August 1976.
24 PRO: CAB 134/1216. EC(56) 26, 10 September, 1956.
25 *Ibid.*
26 AP 20/25/34. No. 1838. Makins to Eden, 8 September, 1956.
27 PRO: CAB 134/1216. EC(56) 26, 10 September, 1956.
28 *Ibid.*
29 MP.MS.Macmillan.dep.d.27. Diary entry for 9 September, 1956; PRO: CAB 128/30. CM (56) 56. 11 September, 1956.
30 PRO: PREM 11/1100. Trevelyan to F.O., No. 2010, 9 September, 1956. Nasser's reply to Menzies.
31 PRO: CAB 134/1216. EC(56) 26, 10 September, 1956, and Eden (1960), *op. cit.*, 477. Dulles had proposed his idea of the Users' Club to Roger Makins in Washington on 4 September: AP 20/25/34. No. 1838. Makins to Eden, 8 September, 1956.
32 Beaufre (1967), *op. cit.*, 28.
33 *Ibid.*, 44.
34 PRO: PREM 11/1101. Copy of a Private Letter dated 9 September, 1956 from Menzies to Eden.
35 PRO: CAB 128/30. CM(56) 56, 11 September, 1956.
36 Horne, *op. cit.*, 415.
37 'At the ICBH/IHR [Institute of Contemporary British History/Institute of Historical Research] seminar, Sir Guy Millard, who handled the paperwork flowing across Eden's desk on Suez matters, said: "I'm not sure Eden saw the Treasury warnings. I didn't see them. Macmillan saw them, but he was a hawk"': quoted in, Peter Hennessy and Mark Laity, 'Suez – What the Papers Say', *Contemporary Record* (vol. no. 1, Spring 1987), 5.
38 MP.MS.Macmillan.dep.d.27. Diary entry for 9 September, 1956.
39 PRO: CAB 128/30. CM(56) 56, 11 September, 1956.
40 See MP.MS.Macmillan.dep.d.27. Diary entries for 1956. Both men had been at Balliol College, Oxford at the same time.
41 PRO: CAB 128/30. CM(56) 56, 11 September, 1956.
42 Nigel Nicolson (ed.), *Harold Nicolson Diaries 1945–1962* (London, 1971), 284. Diary entry for 12 September, 1956.
43 PRO: PREM 11/1100. Bishop to Eden, undated, but the subject of the memorandum dates it as before the Cabinet Meeting of 11 September, 1956. It was specifically written for advising with regard to the said Cabinet Meeting.
44 All information on the Cabinet Meeting from PRO: CAB 128/30. CM 56(56), 11 September, 1956, unless otherwise stated. This was reinforced in his diary, on 12 September: AP 20/1/32. Diary entry for 12–13 September, 1956.
45 For instance, see Introduction, 9–13; Chapter 1, 23, 26–7, 33–5 and 38–40 and Chapter 2, 44, 50–1, 56–7 and 64–5.

46 Cf. MP.MS.Macmillan.dep.d.27. Diary entry for 9 September, 1956.
47 Macmillan (1971), *op. cit.*, 106–7.
48 WCP.MS.William Clark.160. Diary entry for 13 September, 1956.
49 AP 33/7iii. Conversation between Winthrop Aldrich and Eden, 14 July, 1970.
50 See PRO: PREM 11/1344. No. 415. Karachi to F.O., 8 March, 1956; PREM 11/1344. No. 136. Makins to F.O., 19 January, 1956. Amended distribution from Shuckburgh, 21 January, 1956; PREM 11/1344. No. 124. Jebb to F.O., 19 March, 1956; PREM 11/1344. No. 67. Jebb to F.O., 20 March, 1956, and Shuckburgh, *op. cit.*, 274.
51 PRO: PREM 11/1101. Lloyd to Washington, No. 4159, 11 September, 1956.
52 Lloyd, *op. cit.*, 122.
53 *Ibid.* PRO: CAB 128/30. CM(56) 56, 11 September, 1956.
54 WCP.MS.William Clark.160. Diary entry for 10 September, 1956. Here, again, Clark is a more reliable source because of his proximity to events. He had to know the contents of the speech, and therefore the intended 'policy', to co-ordinate the press, particularly the Lobby correspondents.
55 *Ibid.* Diary entry for 11 September, 1956.
56 PRO: PREM 11/1101. Makins to F.O., No. 1875, 11 September, 1956.
57 Cf. Chapter 2, 64–5.
58 PRO: PREM 11/1101. Makins to F.O., No. 1878, 11 September, 1956.
59 PRO: PREM 11/1101. Makins to F.O., No. 1882, 11 September, 1956.
60 PRO: PREM 11/1101. Makins to F.O., No. 1891, 11 September, received 12 September, 1956. Transcript of President Eisenhower's press conference of 11 September, 1956.
61 PRO: PREM 11/1101. Makins to F.O., No. 1892, 11 September, received 12 September, 1956. Re: telephone conversation Lloyd to Makins.
62 PRO: PREM 11/1101. Makins to F.O., No. 1896, 11 September, received 12 September, 1956.
63 AP 33/7ii. Notes made 14 January, 1969.
64 This was also revealed in the Egypt Committee meeting of 12 September: PRO: CAB 134/1216. EC(56) 27, 12 September, 1956.
65 PRO: PREM 11/1177. No. 1839. Eisenhower to Eden, 8 September, 1956.
66 PRO: PREM 11/1101. ME(O)(56) 15, 11 September, 1956.
67 AP 20/1/32. Diary entry for 12–13 September, 1956. See also PRO: CAB 134/1216. EC(56) 27, 12 September, 1956.
68 PRO: CAB 134/1216. EC(56) 27, 12 September, 1956.
69 PRO: PREM 11/1101. F.O. to Washington, No. 4187, 12 September, 1956.
70 Cf. Chapter 3, 73–4; PRO: PREM 11/1101. Makins to F.O., No. 1875, 11 September, 1956.
71 PRO: PREM 11/1101. F.O. to Washington, No. 4203, 12 September, 1956.
72 PRO: PREM 11/1101. Trevelyan to F.O., No. 2068, 12 September,1956.
73 PRO: PREM 11/1101. Makins to F.O., No. 1902, 12 September, received 13 September, 1956.
74 AP 20/1/32. Diary entry for 12–13 September, 1956. The author could not make out the word 'power' which was suggested by Mrs Chris Penney, the Head Archivist at the University of Birmingham.
75 Macmillan (1971), *op. cit.*, 125: the extremes were represented by the Waterhouse–Amery militant wing and the moderates, attitude was demonstrated by R. A. Butler's pledge for 'no force, without recourse to U.N.' For a discussion of the Suez Group, see Introduction, 7.

76 Hansard, 13 September, 1956, column 305. WCP.MS.William Clark.160. Diary entry for 13 September, 1956: William Clark asserts that Eden actually said that he would have to go to the Security Council 'immediately', but 'the last word was lost in shouts and when *Hansard* asked what he had said de Zulueta said he did not know so "Interruption" is what appeared'. Clark was in the House of Commons at the time of the speech.
77 *The Daily Mirror*, 4 September, 1956.
78 *The Manchester Guardian*, 30 August, 1956; *The Daily Worker*, 31 August, 1 September, 3 September, 4 September, 6 September, 7 September, 8 September, 11 September, 1956 (etc.). In contrast, *The Daily Telegraph* pushed for force with recurrent justification: in particular, see: *The Daily Telegraph*, 1 September, 7 September, 1956.
79 AP 20/34/3c. See, for example, David Astor's piece in *The Observer*, 2 September, and *The Daily Mirror* headline of 4 September, 1956: 'The Time Has Come For Eden To Tell The Nation'.
80 MP.MS.Macmillan.dep.d.27. Diary entry for 15 September, 1956.
81 *Ibid*.
82 Macmillan (1971), *op. cit.*, 125.
83 PRO: PREM 11/1101. Makins to F.O., No. 1917, 13 September, received 14 September, 1956. Authorised official transcript of Dulles's Press Conference of 13 September, 1956.
84 PRO: CAB 134/1216. EC(56) 26, 10 September, 1956: Cf. Chapter 3, 71.
85 PRO: PREM 11/1101. Makins to F.O., No. 1917, 13 September, received 14 September, 1956. Authorised official transcript of Dulles's Press Conference of 13 September, 1956. Eden (1960), *op. cit.*, 483.
86 PRO: PREM 11/1101. Makins to F.O., No. 1917, 13 September, received 14 September, 1956. Authorised official transcript of Dulles's Press Conference of 13 September, 1956.
87 Cf. Chapter 2, 58.
88 PRO: PREM 11/1101. Makins to F.O., No. 1869, 11 September, 1956; PREM 11/1101. Makins to F.O., No. 1847, 9 September, received 10 September, 1956: Dulles had produced figures on 9 September to show that Western Europe could be supplied with crude oil in the event of the Suez Canal becoming unavailable. Production would be increased in the US and Venezuela to meet the requirement of 480,000 barrels a day.
89 PRO: PREM 11/1101. Makins to F.O., No. 1926, 13 September, received 14 September, 1956.
90 PRO: PREM 11/1101. ME(O)(56) 16, 13 September, 1956.
91 TNLA. 'Notes on Talk With the Chancellor of the Exchequer On September 20, 1956 Immediately Before His Departure for Washington'.
92 Nasser had been one of the principal powers behind the 1952 coup which had replaced King Farouk with Neguib. He had taken control from Neguib in April, 1954 before assuming presidential powers in November of the same year. It was not until June, 1956 that he was finally and officially elected president.
93 Sir Patrick Reilly in correspondence with the author, 12 February, 1998. Sir Patrick learnt this from his 'old friend' Sir Dick White, then the new Head of MI6.
94 PRO: PREM 11/1101. Trevelyan to F.O., No. 2150, 15 September, received 16 September, 1956.
95 AP 20/21/187. PMPM M198/56, 16 September, 1956, P.M. to Lord Reading. Reading did not think this possible.
96 PRO: PREM 11/1101. Dixon to F.O., No. 683, 15 September, 1956.

97   PRO: CAB 134/1216. EC(56) 29, 17 September, 1956.
98   PRO: PREM 11/1102. Dixon to F.O., No. 689, 17 September, received 18 September, 1956. Dixon was worried by Louffi's, the permanent representative of Egypt at the UN, letter and the effect it could have on UN opinion.
99   PRO: FO 371/119193/JE 14216/85. Makins to F.O., No. 1948, 17 September, 1956.
100 PRO: FO 371/119193/JE 14216/76. Makins to F.O., No. 1953, 17 September, 1956, received 1:03 a.m., 18 September, 1956.
101 Macmillan (1971), *op. cit.*, 128.
102 Trevelyan complained, after the crisis, that he had not been kept informed and was unaware of the decision to use force. In fact, the Ambassador was briefed up until the decision was made and was then kept in the dark. Once again, this indicated, in conjunction with the other evidence, that the decision was not made until October.
103 PRO: FO 371/119193/JE 14216/80G. Jebb to F.O., No. 318, 17 September, 1956.
104 AP 20/25/29, PMPT T401/56, No. 745. Eden to Sidney Holland, 18 September, 1956.
105 Cf. Chapter 2, 49–50.
106 Lloyd, *op. cit.*, 143.
107 *Ibid.*, 144.
108 PRO: FO 371/119195/JE 14216/153. Statement by Dulles at the First Plenary Session of the Second London Conference on 19 September, 1956.
109 *Ibid.*
110 PRO: PREM 11/1102. Trevelyan to F.O., No. 2208, 19 September, 1956.
111 MP.MS.Macmillan.dep.d.27. Diary entry for 20 September, 1956.
112 WCP.MS.William Clark.160. Diary entry for 20 September, 1956.
113 Clark cited in 'Suez 1956: Neither War Nor Peace At 10 Downing Street'.
114 PRO: FO 371/119197/JE 14216/198. Statement issued by the Second London Conference on the Suez Canal, 21 September, 1956. See also: Declaration Providing For The Establishment Of A Suez Canal Users Association.
115 *Ibid.*
116 *Ibid.*
117 WCP.MS.William Clark.160. Diary entry for 21 September, 1956.
118 *DAFR* 1956, 335. Dulles to Lloyd, 21 September, 1956.
119 PRO: PREM 11/1102. Record of a conversation between Dulles and Lloyd at Lancaster House on 21 September, 1956.
120 DDE. John Foster Dulles Papers, Subject, Alphabetical, Box 11, Miscellaneous Paper – UK(4), Foster Dulles Memorandum, 21 September 1956, cited in Lucas (1991), *op. cit.*, 217.
121 *FRUS*. 1955–7 xvi, 549.
122 PRO: FO 371/119197/JE 14216/198. Statement issued by the Second London Conference on the Suez Canal, 21 September, 1956.
123 At this time Dulles saw the possible move as an attempt to derive support for a forceful solution.
124 Murphy, *op. cit.*, 470.

4   Mounting Pressure

1   See the weakening of SCUA's potential through the failure to insist that SCUA members withhold payment of dues to Egypt and the drawing out of discussions which stabilised Nasser's hold on the Canal: Cf. Chapter 3, 78.

2 PRO: PREM 11/1123. *News Chronicle*/Gallup poll for 11 September, 1956. Cf. Chapter 3, 68.
3 AP 20/33/26a. Eden to Churchill, 21 September, 1956.
4 WCP.MS.William Clark.160. Diary entry for 20 September.
5 McDonald (1984), *op. cit.*, 265 and 267.
6 PRO: PREM 11/1102. No. 1979. Makins to F.O., 22 September, 1956; AP 20/25/44. PMPT T406/56, No. 4414. Eden to Macmillan (in US), 23 September, 1956. As the US Joint Chiefs of Staff concluded: 'The deflation of the Users' Association left an appeal to the UN Security Council as virtually the only remaining hope for a peaceful solution': National Archives, College Park (hereafter referred to as NACP). RG218. Unpublished Joint Chiefs of Staff History: The Joint Chiefs of Staff and National Policy Volume VI, 1955–56, Chapter X, 'The Suez Canal Crisis', 332.
7 PRO: FO 371/119197/JE 14216/198. Statement issued by the Second London Conference on the Suez Canal, 21 September, 1956.
8 AP 20/21/192. PMPM M203/56, Eden to Lloyd, 21 September, 1956.
9 Cf. Chapter 1, 21.
10 PRO: FO 371/119197/JE 14216/198. Statement issued by the Second London Conference on the Suez Canal, 21 September, 1956. Cf. Chapter 2, 56–8, for results of the First London Conference.
11 *Ibid.*
12 PRO: PREM 11/1100. Makins to F.O., No. 1827, 7 September, received 8 September, 1956, and PREM 11/1100. Eden minute on Dixon to F.O., No. 647, 7 September, received 8 September, 1956.
13 WCP.MS.William Clark.160. Diary entry for 21 September, 1956.
14 Sir Patrick Reilly in correspondence with the author, 11 October, 1997. Sir Patrick's emphasis.
15 Moshe Dayan, *Story of My Life* (London, 1976), 155. Moshe Dayan in conversation with M. Bourges-Manoury, the French Minister for Defence.
16 *Ibid.*, 157.
17 Beaufre (1969), *op. cit.*, 29, 44 and 63.
18 SOHP: Interviews with Sir William Hayter and Sir Richard Powell.
19 Cf. Introduction, 8–9.
20 Edmund Murray, *Churchill's Bodyguard* (London, 1988), 223.
21 Churchill Papers (hereafter referred to as CP). Letter from Churchill to Clementine Churchill, 30 July, 1956, cited in Martin Gilbert, *Never Despair: Winston S. Churchill 1945–1965* (London, 1990), 1201.
22 Cf. Introduction, 7.
23 CP. Letter from Churchill to Clementine Churchill, 30 July, 1956, cited in Gilbert, *op. cit.*, 1201.
24 Lord Moran, *Winston Churchill: The Struggle for Survival 1940/1965* (London, 1968), 735. Diary entry for 1 August, 1956.
25 Spencer-Churchill Papers (hereafter referred to as SCP). Churchill to Clementine Churchill, 3 August, 1956, cited in Gilbert, *op. cit.*, 1202.
26 CP. Letter from Churchill to Clementine Churchill, 30 July, 1956, cited in Gilbert, *op. cit.*, 1201.
27 Cf. Introduction, 7–8.
28 CP 1/55. Clementine Churchill to Winston Churchill, 1 August, 1956, cited in Gilbert, *op. cit.*, 1201.
29 Shuckburgh, *op. cit.*, 122. Diary entry for 17 December, 1953. Cf. Introduction, 8.

30 Shuckburgh, *op. cit.*, 29. Diary entry for 16 December, 1951.
31 MP.MS.Macmillan.dep.d.22. Diary entry for 5 August, 1955.
32 Murray, *op. cit.*, 223.
33 MP.MS.Macmillan.dep.d.27. Diary entry for 5 August, 1956.
34 *Ibid.*
35 Murray, *op. cit.*, 223.
36 Gilbert, *op. cit.*, 1203, and Interview with Doreen Pugh conducted by Martin Gilbert, 18 June, 1987, cited in *ibid*.
37 A threat that already been made by MI6: Cf. Introduction, 13–14.
38 CP 2/130. Note by Churchill, 6 August, 1956, cited in Gilbert, *op. cit.*, 1203–4.
39 SOHP: Interview with Sir Evelyn Shuckburgh.
40 Shuckburgh, *op. cit.*, 29. Diary entry for 16 December, 1951.
41 MP.MS.Macmillan.dep.d.27. Diary entry for 7 August, 1956.
42 SOHP: Interview with Sir Evelyn Shuckburgh.
43 Murray, *op. cit.*, 224.
44 SOHP: Interview with Lord Amery.
45 MP.MS.Macmillan.dep.d.27. Diary entry for 5 August, 1956. Meeting of Churchill and Macmillan at Chartwell on 5 August, 1956.
46 Lord Moran, *op. cit.*, 736. Diary entry for 8 August, 1956.
47 *Ibid.*, 738–9. Diary entry for 16 September, 1956.
48 Gilbert, *op. cit.*, 1222.
49 WCP.MS.William Clark. 160. Diary entry for 22 and 23 September, 1956.
50 SOHP: Interview with Sir Frederick Bishop.
51 WCP.MS.William Clark. 160. Diary entry for 22 and 23 September, 1956. McDonald could not recall what this criticism had been: McDonald in correspondence with the author, 2 March, 1999.
52 TNLA. Memorandum for Editor, 'Talks with the Prime Minister and Foreign Secretary'. Recorded on 24 September, 1956.
53 PRO: PREM 11/1102. Note by Guy Millard, 'Reference of Suez Canal Dispute to the Security Council – September 23', 1956.
54 AP 20/25/44. PMPT T406/56, No. 4414. Eden to Macmillan (in US), 23 September, 1956. All these ideas were voiced to Iverach McDonald on 23 September: TNLA. Memorandum for Editor, 'Talks with the Prime Minister and Foreign Secretary'. Recorded on 24 September, 1956.
55 Nutting, *op. cit.*, 66; WCP.MS.William Clark. 160. Diary entry for 22 and 23 September, 1956; PRO: PREM 11/1102. No. 4389. F.O. to Washington, 22 September, 1956; PREM 11/1102. No. 1859. F.O. to Paris, 22 September, 1956.
56 TNLA. Memorandum for Editor, 'Talks with the Prime Minister and Foreign Secretary'. Recorded on 24 September, 1956.
57 Cf. Chapter 3, 68.
58 PRO: PREM 11/1102. No. 4389. F.O. to Washington, 22 September, 1956.
59 PRO: PREM 11/1102. No. 1975. Makins to F.O., 22 September, 1956.
60 PRO: PREM 11/1102. No. 1979. Makins to F.O., 22 September, 1956.
61 PRO: PREM 11/1102. No. 715. Dixon to F.O., 22 September, 1956.
62 PRO: PREM 11/1102. No. 883. F.O. to Dixon, 22 September, 1956.
63 PRO: PREM 11/1102. Note by Guy Millard, 'Reference of Suez Canal Dispute to the Security Council – September 23', 1956. Nutting, *op. cit.*, 67.
64 For example: Lucas (1991), *op. cit.*, 208; Thomas, *op. cit.*, 81; Nutting, *op. cit.*, 66; Lamb, *op. cit.*, 217; Kyle, *op. cit.*, 254, does not go as far but implies the same.
65 TNLA. Memorandum for Editor, 'Talks with the Prime Minister and Foreign Secretary'. Recorded on 24 September, 1956.

66 PRO: PREM 11/1102. No. 1979. Makins to F.O., 22 September, 1956.
67 Cf. Chapter 2, 44 and 65.
68 PRO: CAB 21/3314 and PREM 11/1100: Undated memorandum on 'The United Nations and Suez'.
69 TNLA. Memorandum for Editor, 'Talks with the Prime Minister and Foreign Secretary'. Recorded on 24 September, 1956.
70 All quotes from PRO: PREM 11/1102. No. 1088. Sir Michael Wright to F.O., 23 September, received 24 September, 1956. Wright was described as a 'wild man' by his namesake, Sir Denis Wright, Assistant Under-Secretary of State at the Foreign Office, and seen as one of the key pressures on Eden to resort to force: Interview with Sir Denis Wright conducted by the author, 26 March, 1998. Sir Denis Wright recalled: 'I was worried by telegrams from our bellicose Ambassador in Baghdad...reporting that Nuri Pasha...as urging us to act quickly against Nasser': Sir Denis Wright, *op. cit.*, 302.
71 Cf. Chapter 1, 25–7.
72 PRO: PREM 11/1102. No. 1088. Sir Michael Wright to F.O., 23 September, received 24 September, 1956; PREM 11/1102. No. 2294, Trevelyan to F.O., 24 September, 1956.
73 PRO: PREM 11/1102. No. 2294. Trevelyan to F.O., 24 September, 1956.
74 Sir Michael Wright's telegram had been repeated to Cairo.
75 For Macmillan's scaremongering and effect on Monckton, see Chapter 3, 71–2.
76 Lord Birkenhead, *Walter Monckton: The Life of Viscount Monckton of Benchley* (London, 1969), 307. Personal note undated but written after the events of the autumn of 1956.
77 Eden did not favour, at this point, an arrangement and was more concerned that Israel might attack Jordan. It is not clear on whose authority, but Anthony Head, the Minister for War, suggested that as Robert Henriques was travelling to Israel and wanted to be of assistance, he might pass the following to Ben-Gurion: 'At all costs, Israel must avoid war with Jordan, but if, when Britain went into Suez, Israel were to attack simultaneously, it would be very convenient for all concerned. Britain would denounce Israel's aggression in the strongest possible terms, but at the peace negotiations afterwards, Britain would help Israel to get the best possible treaty': Robert Henriques, *The Spectator*, 6 November, 1959, 623, and 4 December, 1959, 823. However, Ben-Gurion's disbelief of the proposal and Eden's own views and fears suggest that this directive did not come from the Prime Minister.
78 SOHP: Interview with Sir Guy Millard.
79 SOHP: Interview with Sir Richard Powell.
80 Monckton to Eden, 1 October, 1956, cited in Lord Birkenhead, *op. cit.*, 309.
81 SOHP: Interview with Sir Richard Powell.
82 *Ibid.*
83 AP 20/26/42. PMPT T575/56, No. 60. Eden to Lewis Douglas, 18 November, 1956.
84 MP.MS.Macmillan.d.27. Diary entry for 24 September, 1956.
85 *Daily Express*, 24 September, 1956.
86 *Daily Telegraph*, 24 September, 1956. Dulles was also recorded as showing the economic dangers of a war in the Middle East to both Britain and France.
87 PRO: CAB 134/1216. EC(56) 31, 25 September, 1956.
88 PRO: CAB 134/1216. EC(56) 31, 25 September, 1956. *Daily Telegraph*, 22 September, 1956. For the proposals of the Second London Conference, see Chapter 3, 89.

89 PRO: CAB 134/1216. EC(56) 31, 25 September, 1956. Confidential Annex, Minute 2.
90 *Ibid*: 'The position of the French Government was precarious and they would be unlikely to survive any public retraction from the stand they had taken on the Suez Canal issue.'
91 *Daily Telegraph*, 22 September, 1956.
92 PRO: CAB 134/1216. EC(56) 31, 25 September, 1956. Confidential Annex, Minute 2.
93 Britain was the largest shareholder of the Suez Canal Company, and the company itself was French: Cf. Chapter 1, 21.
94 PRO: CAB 134/1216. EC(56) 31, 25 September, 1956. Confidential Annex, Minute 3. These decisions had been made at a Staff Conference held at No. 10 on 19 September, at 11:00 a.m. At the Chiefs of Staff Committee Meeting (C.O.S.(s)(56)5) on 24 September, Eden indicated that a decision to employ the plan would be made on D−11. Thus, even if the decision was made he had the flexibility up to nearly four weeks before any invasion had to be unleashed: PRO: PREM 11/1104.
95 CAB 134/1217. EC(56) 53, 25 September, 1956. 'Political Directive to the Allied Commander-in-Chief'.
96 Clark cited in 'Suez 1956: Neither War Nor Peace At 10 Downing Street'.
97 PRO: FO 371/119886/JE 11924/47. No. 3984. F.O. to Washington, 1 September, 1956. The State Department believed that they ought to have been consulted over French troop movements. However, Selwyn Lloyd reported that Dulles had already told Eden and himself, on 24 August, 'that it would be an embarrassment to the United States Government if they were given this information'. The CIA were fully aware of the situation. As Allen Dulles, the Head of the CIA, later said, 'we had the Suez operation perfectly taped': Allen Dulles in conversation with Andrew Tully, cited in Andrew Tully, *Central Intelligence Agency: The Inside Story* (London, 1962), 111. Foster Dulles said to his brother that the British and the French were 'deliberately keeping us in the dark'. He lacked 'any clear picture' but as the CIA Director replied, he was 'fairly well' informed of their intentions in Egypt: telephone call of 18 October, 1956, between John Foster and Allen Dulles, quoted in Christopher Andrew, *For The President's Eyes Only: Secret Intelligence and the American Presidency From Washington to Bush* (London, 1995), 228. For a fuller discussion, see NACP. RG263. Wayne G. Jackson, 'Allen Welsh Dulles As Director of Central Intelligence 26 February 1953–29 November 1961: Volume V, Intelligence Support of Policy', Chapter 1: 'Warning of the Suez Crisis of 1956', 1–38.
98 SOHP: Interview with Sir Patrick Dean. The American was only permitted to sit in for certain discussions: see PRO: CAB 159/24 and 25. JIC minutes for July–December, 1956. See also interview with Sir Frank Cooper conducted by the author on 2 April, 1998.
99 PRO: CAB 134/1225. E(O)C(56) 7, 24 September, 1956. Annex. The Egypt (Official) Committee was set up on 24 August, 1956, to 'determine that broad principles which should govern handling of civil affairs in Egypt in the event of military action by the United Kingdom and France to establish international control of the Suez Canal': CAB 134/1225, E(O)C(56) 1, 24 August, 1956. The Egypt (Official) Committee had been part of the contingency measures, set up in case force was decided upon. Now its remit was much more clearly focused toward helping to determine a peaceful solution to the crisis.

100 PRO: PREM 11/1102. Butler to Eden, 27 September, 1956. For the weekend before, Eden's engagement diary revealed that 'the Prime Minister dealt only with very urgent matters and tried to rest as much as possible over the weekend': AP 20/30/1. Prime Minister's Engagement Diary. Diary entry for 21 September, 1956.
101 PRO: FO 800/725. Private Papers of the Secretary of State for Foreign Affairs: Secretary of State's Memorandum on the Diplomatic Exchanges and Negotiations from the Egyptian Nationalisation of the Suez Canal Company on July 26, 1956 to the Outbreak of Hostilities between Israel and Egypt on October 29, 1956.
102 'A Canal Too Far', 3.
103 Eden did try to arrange a meeting with Eisenhower on 7 November, 1956, after the invasion had been committed: PRO: PREM 11/1177. PMPT T537/56, No. 5254. Eden to Eisenhower, 7 November, 1956. See also: PMPT T540/56, No. 5274. Eden to Eisenhower, 8 November, 1956 and PMPT T545/56, No. 5321. Eden to Eisenhower, 11 November, 1956.
104 SOHP: Interview with Sir David Pitblado.
105 MP.MS.Macmillan.d.27. Diary entry for 25 September, 1956.
106 AP 20/25/47. PMPT T411/56, No. 2004. Macmillan to Eden, 25 September, 1956.
107 PRO: PREM 11/1102. Private letter from Macmillan to Eden, 26 September, 1956.
108 Macmillan (1970), *op. cit.*, 135.
109 Interview between Lord Sherfield (Sir Roger Makins) and Alistair Horne, cited in Horne, *op. cit.*, 421. See also, Lord Sherfield, *op. cit.*, 32–3.
110 PRO: PREM 11/1102. Private letter from Macmillan to Eden, 26 September, 1956. The word *must* was underlined in manuscript. Compare with MP.MS. Macmillan. d.27. Diary entry for 25 September, 1956.
111 Interview with Lord Sherfield conducted by Alistair Horne, cited in Horne, *op. cit.*, 422. Horne, Macmillan's official biographer, believed that Macmillan's advice was key in its timing and hence its effect on Eden.
112 Dr Saul Kelly, 'Sir Roger Makins', *British Officials and the Suez Crisis Conference*, University of Westminster, 10 December, 1996.
113 Quote from Thomas, *op. cit.*, 163, and Horne, *op. cit.*, 422.
114 MP.MS.Macmillan.d.27. Diary entry for 25 September, 1956.
115 Cf. Chapter 1, 37 and 41.
116 MP.MS.Macmillan.d.27. Diary entry for 25 September, 1956.
117 Lord Sherfield, *op. cit.*, 33. Also at the meeting were Dulles's advisers: Herbert Prochnow, Herman Phleger, Francis Wilcox and C. Burke Elbrick.
118 Macmillan (1970), *op. cit.*, 136.
119 AP 20/25/46 and PRO: PREM 11/1102. PMPT T410/56, No. 2003, 25 September, 1956.
120 Lord Sherfield, *op. cit.*, 33.
121 PRO: PREM 11/1102. Macmillan to Eden, 'Note of a Private Talk with Mr. Dulles', 25 September, signed 26 September, 1956.
122 Lord Sherfield, *op. cit.*, 33.
123 PRO: PREM 11/1102. Macmillan to Eden, 'Note of a Private Talk with Mr. Dulles', 25 September, signed 26 September, 1956.
124 PRO: PREM 11/1102. No. 1088, Sir Michael Wright to F.O., 23 September, received 24 September, 1956 and PREM 11/1102. No. 2294. Trevelyan to F.O., 24 September, 1956.
125 MP.MS.Macmillan.d.27. Diary entry for 25 September, 1956.

126 PRO: CAB 128/30. CM(56) 67, 26 September, 1956.
127 Thorpe, *op. cit.*, 226.
128 WCP.MS.William Clark.160. Diary entry for 24–30 September, 1956.
129 Lloyd. *op. cit.*, 150.
130 PRO: PREM 11/1102. No. 4389. F.O. to Washington, 22 September, 1956. Lloyd, *op. cit.*, 151.
131 Eden noted in the telegram that he did not know what (c) meant but that 'the experts are to get to work at once upon it'.
132 PRO: PREM 11/1102. No. 337. Paris to F.O., 26 September, received 27 September, 1956. Lloyd, *op. cit.*, 151.
133 PRO: PREM 11/1102. Bishop to Eden, 26 September, 1956.
134 This view was expressed by Kilmuir and received academic backing from Professor Arthur L. Goodhart, then Master of University College, Oxford and an expert in jurisprudence. In *The Times*, on 11 August, Goodhart had written a letter justifying the use of force when a vital interest was at stake.
135 Cf. Chapter 2, 64–5.
136 PRO: PREM 11/1102. Butler to Eden, 27 September, 1956.
137 AP 20/1/32. Diary entry for 21 August, 1956. Eden had an indefatigable faith in the healing powers of the sun.
138 For details of the operations, see: Eden (1960), *op. cit.*, 51–2. Rhodes James, *op. cit.*, 362–6. 'Anthony Eden and Harold Macmillan: from Suez to Blackpool', in Hugh L'Etang, *The Pathology of Leadership* (London, 1969), chapter 12.
139 Eden (1960), *op. cit.*, 568–9.
140 Clark, *op. cit.*, 160. Interview with Chester Cooper, in *The Suez Crisis*, BBC TV, 1996.
141 Interview with Lady Avon, cited in Russell Braddon, *Suez: Splitting of a Nation* (London, 1973), 85.
142 As he had once said and now hoped, '[f]orty-eight hours at the cottage were worth a week's holiday to me': Eden (1960), *op. cit.*, 433.
143 PRO: PREM 11/1102. No. 724. Chapman Andrews to F.O., 26 September, 1956.
144 AP 20/25/48. PMPT T416/56, No. 1932. Head to Eden (Paris), 26 September, 1956. Head was particularly worried by the *News Chronicle* and the *Daily Herald*.
145 PRO: PREM 11/1170. Bulganin to Eden, 28 September, 1956.
146 Eden (1960), *op. cit.*, 498.
147 *Ibid.*
148 PRO: FO 800/726. T4540. Eden to Eisenhower, 1 October, 1956.
149 Nutting, *op. cit.*, 69. TNLA. Memorandum from the Foreign Editor to the Editor, 2 October, 1956; PRO: CAB 128/30. CM(56) 68, 3 October, 1956.
150 MP.MS.Macmillan.d.27. Diary entry for 30 September, 1956. A deferred entry from 29 September.
151 *Ibid.* Diary entry for 30 September, 1956.
152 PRO: CAB 134/1216. EC(56) 32, 1 October, 1956. Confidential Annex. FO 800/726. T4540; Eden to Eisenhower, 1 October, 1956.
153 PRO: CAB 134/1216. EC(56) 32, 1 October, 1956. Confidential Annex.
154 Dayan, *op. cit.*, 151 and 158.
155 *Ibid.*, 159.
156 *Ibid.*
157 *Ibid.*, 186–7.
158 *Ibid.*, 155 and 159.
159 PRO: CAB 134/1216. EC(56) 32, 1 October, 1956. Confidential Annex.

212 Notes

160 *Ibid*.
161 *Ibid*.
162 PRO: FO 800/747. Fitzmaurice to Coldstream, 6 September, 1956.
163 PRO: FO 800/749. Fitzmaurice to Kirkpatrick, undated.
164 PRO: FO 800/749. Fitzmaurice to Kirkpatrick, 4 September, 1956. Kirkpatrick minute dated 4 September.
165 Interview with Sir Frank Cooper, conducted by the author on 2 April, 1998.
166 PRO: FO 800/749. Fitzmaurice to Denis Laskey (Lloyd's Principal Private Secretary), 5 November, 1956. See also PRO: FO 800/747. Fitzmaurice to Kirkpatrick, 5 November, 1956.
167 In unpublished memoirs, Lord Sherfield (Roger Makins) and Sir Denis Wright have shown the role of Kirkpatrick to be more influential than has previously been considered. For other contemporary attitudes supporting Brook and Kirkpatrick's bellicosity, see: SOHP: Interviews with Sir Evelyn Shuckburgh, Sir Denis Wright, Sir Guy Millard, and especially Sir Frederick Bishop.
168 McDermott, *op. cit.*, 146.
169 Lord Sherfield, *op. cit.*, 36–7. See also SOHP: Interview with Sir Denis Wright.
170 PRO: PREM 11/1174. No. 2046. Makins to F.O., 2 October, received 3 October, 1956. Dulles's Press Conference. See also: Eden (1960), *op. cit.*, 498–9.
171 Nutting, *op. cit.*, 70.
172 McDonald (1984), 268. This memorandum was not in the *Times* Archive when the author visited on 2 April, 1998, nor could be found subsequently by TNLA staff.
173 *Ibid*.
174 WCP.MS.William Clark.160. Diary entry for 2 October, 1956.
175 AP 20/25/51. PMPT T425/56, No. 2052. Makins to Eden, 3 October, 1956.
176 PRO: CAB 128/30. CM(56) 68, 3 October, 1956.
177 *Ibid*.
178 TNLA. Memorandum from the Foreign Editor to the Editor, 2 October, 1956.
179 MP.MS.Macmillan.d.27. Diary entry for 2 October, 1956.
180 TNLA. Memorandum from the Foreign Editor to the Editor, 2 October, 1956.
181 *Ibid*.
182 In conversation with Iverach McDonald, 24 February, 1998.
183 Cf. Introduction, 10–11.
184 Horne, *op. cit.*, 427. Thomas, *op. cit.*, 96–8: In his 1970 edition, Thomas wrote that '[t]wo English Cabinet Ministers read through the relevant paragraphs of an earlier draft of this work ... [and] though raising other matters of correction, did not venture to criticize the dates.'
185 McDermott, *op. cit.*, 145; Dayan, *op. cit.*, 155.

5 Transition to Force

1 Dayan, *op. cit.*, 150.
2 For example, cf. Introduction, 1 and Chapter 1, 25–6.
3 AP 20/25/52. PMPT T426/56, No. 4592. Eden to Makins, 4 October, 1956.
4 Dayan, *op. cit.*, 167 and 170. Author's italics.
5 PRO: PREM 11/1174. Makins to Eden, 4 October, 1956; Chalmer Roberts, 'Colonialism headache: Dulles' Suez Remark – A Freudian Slip?', *The Washington Post*, 4 October, 1956.
6 PRO: PREM 11/1174. Makins to Eden, 4 October 1956.

7 PRO: PREM 11/1174. Makins to Eden, 4 October, 1956.
8 Lord Butler, *The Art of the Possible: The Memoirs of Lord Butler* (Harmondsworth, 1973), 192.
9 Cf. Introduction, 6–7.
10 Cf. Introduction, 6: For Eden's belief in the need to protect oil interests, see his speech to the 1922 Committee cited in Nigel Nicolson, *Long Life: Memoirs* (London, 1997), 160; p. 6: PRO: CAB 128/30. CM(56) 19, 6 March, 1956; p. 8 and p. 21. Eisenhower also saw the threat to European oil supplies: Robert H. Ferrell (ed.), *The Eisenhower Diaries* (New York, 1981), 319. Diary entry for 13 March, 1956; Chapter 1, p. 31: PRO: CAB 128/30. CM(56) 54, 27 July, 1956; p. 32; p. 35: AP 20/25/1. PMPT T341/56, No. 7. Eden to Sidney Holland (in San Fransisco), 28 July, 1956. See also MP.MS.Macmillan.dep.d.27. Diary entry for 4 October, 1956.
11 Cf. Chapter 4, 115–16.
12 PRO: PREM 11/1102. PMPT T435/56, No. 785. Lloyd to Eden, 5 October, 1956. Once reconciled to the Anglo-French move to the UN, Dulles also believed that it would delay any moves until at least after the US elections.
13 Lester Pearson, *Memoirs Volume II, 1948–1957: The International Years* (London, 1974), 236. Pearson was Canadian Secretary of State For External Affairs, 1948–1957.
14 *The Daily Telegraph*, 5 October, 1956. Dulles in conversation with Lloyd, 5 October, 1956, cited in Lloyd, *op. cit.*, 154.
15 Heikal (1986), *op. cit.*, 162. Hammarskjøld also believed that the French 'had enough internal problems to keep them busy'.
16 PRO: CAB 134/1216. EC(56) 32, Confidential annex, minute 1, 1 October, 1956. Quote from PREM 11/1099. Draft of Declaration: London Conference On The Suez Canal. The 'inner quote' was deliberately taken from the original 1888 Convention.
17 Lloyd, *op. cit.*, 153–4.
18 *Ibid.*, 154.
19 PREM 11/1123. *News Chronicle* Gallup Poll, 11 September, 1956. These figures showed a polarisation of political groups on the subject of 'going to the UN'. Cf. Chapter 3, 68.
20 *The Times*, 4 October, 1956.
21 *Ibid.*, 6 October, 1956. The eight Foreign Ministers were: Dulles, Lloyd, Pineau, Fawzi, Shepilov, Spaak, Menon and Koca Popovic of Yugoslavia.
22 *The Times*, 5 October, 1956.
23 PRO: PREM 11/1102. Record of a Conversation with Mr Dulles and M. Pineau in Mr Dulles's Apartment (New York), 5 October, 1956.
24 Lord Sherfield, *op. cit.*, 34. Makins met for a 'farewell interview' with Eisenhower on 5 October. He reported that the President 'could not see how the affair would end if force were attempted. In his opinion it could scarcely fail to lead to a chaotic situation in the Middle East, which would encourage further Soviet penetration.'
25 The Press Statement was actually released on 5 October, 1956.
26 PRO: FO 371/119155. No. 525, 5 October, 1956. Future release of an address by John Foster Dulles before a special convocation, Williams College, Williamstown, Massachusetts, 6 October, 1956.
27 Dulles believed that force would be useless and might actually bring the UN down. See NAW, RG59, CDF, 974.7301/10–556, Lodge memorandum, 5 October, 1956, cited in Lucas(1991), *op. cit.*, 219.

28 PRO: PREM 11/1102. Record of a Conversation with Mr Dulles and M. Pineau in Mr Dulles's Apartment (New York), 5 October, 1956. For reference to Eden's lack of belief in Nasser's decline in prestige, see Chapter 4, 97–8. *The Times* reported on 4 October, 1956: 'WESTERN "BLOCKADE FOILED"'. Egyptian Minister of Finance, Dr Abdel Moneim Kaissouni, had tried to explain, in some detail, how the Western economic and trade sanctions had had little effect on Egypt.
29 Cf. Chapter 5, 110.
30 AP 20/27/84. PMPT T432/56, No. 4612. Eden to Eisenhower, 5 October, 1956.
31 WCP.MS.William Clark.160. Diary entry for 5 October, 1956.
32 AP 20/30/1. Engagement diary entry for 4 October, 1956.
33 *The Times*, 9 October, 1956.
34 Eden (1960), *op. cit.*, 568.
35 *The Times*, 8 October, 1956.
36 WCP.MS.William Clark.160. Diary entry for 6 and 7 October, 1956.
37 Eden (1960), *op. cit.*, 568–9.
38 Cf. Introduction and Chapter 1, 25–6 and 28.
39 WCP.MS.William Clark.160. Diary entry for 4–5 November, 1956.
40 Conversation between Monckton and Nutting, 29 October, 1956, cited in Nutting, *op. cit.*, 107.
41 *The Times*, 9 October, 1956: 'The Cabinet meeting over which Mr. Butler presided last night was one that had been arranged before Sir Anthony Eden became indisposed on Friday.'
42 PRO: PREM 1102. PMPT T447/56, No. 1086. Eden to Lloyd, 9 October, 1956.
43 AP 20/1/32. Diary entry for 12–13 September, 1956. Iverach McDonald noticed and recalled this physical and mental deterioration in conversation with the author, 24 February, 1998.
44 'A Canal Too Far', 2. However, Lord Home did not think that it 'clouded his [Eden's] judgement'. For the diversity of opinion, see SOHP: Interviews with Sir Frederick Bishop, Sir Guy Millard, Sir William Hayter and Sir Richard Powell. See also Dutton, *op. cit.*, 422–4; Rhodes James, *op. cit.*, 523–4; David Carlton, *Anthony Eden: A Biography* (London, 1986), 428.
45 Interview with Sir Guy Millard conducted by the author, 25 February, 1998.
46 See Lucas (1991), *op. cit.*, 220. Kyle, *op. cit.*, 277, implies the same, recording that the illness was 'sinister news', despite then introducing Rhodes James's argument.
47 *The Sunday Times*, 7 October, 1956. See also a cutting of the article in PRO: PREM 11/1102.
48 *Ibid.*
49 *Ibid.* PRO: PREM 11/1102. No. 2294. Trevelyan to F.O., 24 September, 1956.
50 For example, cf. Chapter 1, 25 and Chapter 2, 42–4.
51 PRO: PREM 11/1102. PMPT T440/56, No. 1070. Eden to Lloyd, 7 October, 1956.
52 *Ibid.*
53 Author's italics.
54 PRO: PREM 11/1102. Record of a Conversation with Mr Dulles and M. Pineau in Mr Dulles's Apartment (New York), 5 October, 1956 and FO 371/119155. No. 525, 5 October, 1956. Future release of an address by John Foster Dulles before a special convocation, Williams College, Williamstown, Massachusetts, 6 October, 1956.
55 PRO: PREM 11/1102. PMPT T444/56, No. 801. Lloyd to Eden, 8 October, 1956.

56 PRO: PREM 11/1102 and CAB 134/1216. EC(56) 33, 8 October, 1956. Eden's views were passed on by Bishop. Butler chaired the Cabinet as the number two in the Government.
57 PRO: PREM 11/1102. PMPT T445/56, No. 1078. Eden to Lloyd, 8 October, 1956.
58 Cf. Introduction, 5–6.
59 Cf. Eden's minute on PRO: PREM 11/1102. PMPT T435/56, No. 785. Lloyd to Eden, 5 October, 1956. Cf. Chapter 1, 38–9; Chapter 3, 67; Chapter 4, 98–100.
60 SOHP: Interview with Sir Donald Logan.
61 PRO: PREM 11/1102. PMPT T445/56, No. 1078. Eden to Lloyd, 8 October, 1956.
62 PRO: PREM 11/1102. No. 1075. Nutting to Lloyd, 8 October, 1956.
63 PRO: PREM 11/1102. PMPT T447/56, No. 1086. Eden to Lloyd, 9 October, 1956. This did not mean that Eden did not want to try and find agreement over Fawzi's proposals, rather that if they were the same as Menon's, it was a waste of time to be conducting two discussions about the same set of ideas, particularly as Menon was not negotiating directly on behalf of the Egyptians.
64 PRO: FO 371/119154/JE 14211. Lloyd to Nutting, 8 October, 1956.
65 PRO: PREM 11/1102. PMPT T447/56, No. 1086. Eden to Lloyd, 9 October, 1956. See also PREM 11/1102. No. 1106. Nutting to Lloyd, 10 October, 1956. Nutting made no references to the Menon proposals or his influencing of Eden, in his memoirs.
66 Lloyd, *op. cit.*, 155.
67 PRO: PREM 11/1102. No. 812. Dixon to F.O., 9 October, received 10 October, 1956.
68 SOHP: Interview with Sir Donald Logan.
69 PRO: PREM 11/1102. PMPT T448/56, No. 813. Lloyd to Eden, 9 October, received 10 October, 1956.
70 PRO: PREM 11/1102. PMPT T449/56, No. 814. Lloyd to Eden, 9 October, received 10 October, 1956.
71 Abba Eban, *An Autobiography* (London, 1979), 208. Nutting shared this view: Nutting, *op. cit.*, 72–80.
72 Eban, *op. cit.*, 208–9.
73 Lucas (1991), *op. cit.*, 222. PRO: CAB 134/1216. EC(56) 34, 10 October, 1956. Despite allegations to the contrary, Eden gave his Foreign Secretary scope for his own initiatives. Bishop believed that Eden respected Lloyd's opinions: SOHP: Interviews with Sir Frederick Bishop, Sir Guy Millard, Sir Richard Powell and David Pitblado.
74 PRO: FO 371/119154/JE 14211/2125. No. 2098. Makins to F.O., 10 October, received 11 October, 1956.
75 PRO: PREM 11/1102. PMPT T455/56, No. 1125. Eden to Lloyd, 11 October, 1956.
76 PRO: CAB 134/1216. EC(56) 34, 10 October, 1956, and PREM 11/1102. PMPT T450/56, No. 1103. Eden to Lloyd, 10 October, 1956.
77 PRO: PREM 11/1102. PMPT T450/56, No. 1103. Eden to Lloyd, 10 October, 1956.
78 PRO: PREM 11/1152. SOHP: Interview with Sir Guy Millard.
79 PRO: PREM 11/1102. PMPT T450A/56, No. 1107. Eden to Lloyd, 10 October, 1956.
80 PRO: PREM 11/1102. No. 816. Lloyd to F.O., 10 October, received 11 October, 1956, and No. 817. Lloyd to F.O., 10 October, received 11 October, 1956.
81 SOHP: Interview with Sir Donald Logan.
82 *Ibid.*
83 PRO: PREM 11/1102. PMPT T452/56, No. 819. Lloyd to Eden, 10 October, received 11 October, 1956.

84　PRO: PREM 11/1102. PMPT T453/56, No. 820. Lloyd to Eden, 10 October, received 11 October, 1956.
85　Lloyd, *op. cit.*, 152–3; SOHP: Interview with Sir Donald Logan; Thorpe, *op. cit.*, 227–9, in particular, 228; Kyle. *op. cit.*, 281; Lucas (1991), *op. cit.*, 220–3; Nutting, *op. cit.*, 76.
86　PRO: PREM 11/1102. PMPT T453/56, No. 820. Lloyd to Eden, 10 October, received 11 October, 1956.
87　PRO: PREM 11/1102. PMPT T454/56, No. 821. Lloyd to Eden, 11 October, 1956.
88　PRO: FO 371/119154/JE 14211/2153A. No. 1132. F.O. to Lloyd, 11 October, 1956. The French Ambassador to Britain had informed Sir Ivone Kirkpatrick of Pineau's concerns that (a) we had embarked on a negotiation with Fawzi without any agreed terms of reference, and (b) the principle of international management was not guaranteed. See also PREM 11/1102. PMPT T455/56, No. 1125. Eden to Lloyd, 11 October, 1956.
89　SOHP: Interview with Sir Donald Logan.
90　Heikal (1986.), *op. cit.*, 174.
91　Eban, *op. cit.*, 209.
92　Christian Pineau, *1956 Suez* (Paris, 1976), 118–19.
93　DDF 1956 II, Doc. 263, 10 October, 1956, pp. 556–7, cited in Kyle, *op. cit.*, 283; PRO: FO 371/119154/JE 14211/2153A. No. 1132. F.O. to Lloyd, 11 October, 1956. Chauvel had already reported that the French delegation was 'rather uneasy': see PREM 11/1102. PMPT T455/56, No. 1125. Eden to Lloyd, 11 October, 1956.
94　PRO: PREM 11/1102. Meeting held at No. 10 on 11 October, 1956. Eden, Monckton, Brook, Watkinson, Kirkpatrick, Ross and J. M. Wilson (secretary) were present.
95　PRO: PREM 11/1102. PMPT T455/56, No. 1125. Eden to Lloyd, 11 October, 1956.
96　PRO: PREM 11/1102. PMPT T459/56, No. 829. Lloyd to Eden, 11 October, received 12 October, 1956. Lloyd had already warned of the possibility of (c) in PREM 11/1102. PMPT T454/56, No. 821. Lloyd to Eden, 11 October, 1956.
97　PRO: PREM 11/1102. PMPT T459/56, No. 829. Lloyd to Eden, 11 October, received 12 October, 1956.
98　Lucas (1991), *op. cit.*, 223; Kyle, *op. cit.*, 286. Kyle suggested that Fawzi had 'some scruples over the meaning of the insulation of the Canal from politics ... but it was clear that more time was required for detailed negotiation'.
99　PRO: PREM 11/1102. No. 830. Lloyd to F.O., 11 October, received 12 October, 1956.
100　*Ibid*. These ingredients were: 'First of all cooperation between the user and the Egyptian board. Secondly an international content among the employees of the Egyptian board together with provision of "verification" of what was going on. Thirdly, recourse.'
101　Lloyd, *op. cit.*, 159.
102　*Ibid*. PRO: PREM 11/1102. No. 831. Lloyd to F.O., 11 October, received 12 October, 1956.
103　PRO: PREM 11/1102. No. 1144. Nutting to Lloyd, 12 October, 1956. Eden had considered Lloyd's reports before leaving for the Conservative Party Conference in Llandudno.
104　PRO: PREM 11/1102. PMPT T461/56, No. 834. Lloyd to Eden, 12 October, 1956.
105　PRO: PREM 11/1102. PMPT T461/56, No. 834. Lloyd to Eden, 12 October, 1956.
106　PRO: PREM 11/1102. PMPT T463/56, No. 835. Lloyd to Eden, 12 October, 1956, and PMPT T464/56, No. 1156. Eden to Lloyd, 12 October, 1956.

107 PRO: PREM 11/1102. Eden to Nutting (telephoned through the stationmaster at Watford), 12 October, 1956, and No. 1144. Nutting to Lloyd, 12 October, 1956.
108 Cf. Chapter 1, 34 and Chapter 2, 44–6.
109 Cf. Chapter 1, 25–7.
110 PRO: PREM 11/1102. PMPT T465/56, No. 839. Lloyd to Eden, 12 October, received 13 October, 1956.
111 Cf. Chapter 5, 132.
112 PRO: PREM 11/1102. PMPT T466/56, No. 843. Lloyd to Eden, 12 October, received 13 October, 1956.
113 PRO: PREM 11/1102. No. 845. Dixon to F.O., 12 October, received 13 October, 1956; PMPT T468/56, No. 1172. Eden to Lloyd, 13 October, 1956 and PMPT T469/56, No. 1173. Eden to Lloyd, 13 October, 1956.
114 PRO: PREM 11/1102. ME(O)(56) 25, 10 October, 1956.
115 PRO: FO 371/119154/JE 14211/2135 or PREM 11/1102. No. 2108. Coulson to F.O., 12 October, 1956. For an earlier soundbite of the press conference, see PREM 11/1102. No. 2103. Makins to F.O., 11 October, 1956. Makins left the British Embassy in Washington on 11 October, at 10 a.m., to take over his new role as Joint Permanent Secretary at the Treasury, and hence the name of the Chargé d'Affaires, John Coulson, appears on the telegrams from this point.
116 Lloyd, *op. cit.*, 160.
117 PRO: PREM 11/1102. PMPT T472/56, No. 852. Lloyd to Eden, 13 October, received 14 October, 1956.
118 Lloyd, *op. cit.*, 160.
119 *Ibid.*, 161.
120 Cf. Chapter 5, 129–33.
121 AP 20/27/85. PMPT T460/56. Eisenhower to Eden, 11 October, received 12 October, 1956.
122 PRO: PREM 11/1102. PMPT T470/56, No. 847. Lloyd to Eden, 13 October, 1956.
123 *Daily Telegraph*, 12 October, 1956: 'NO PROGRESS, SAYS M. PINEAU'.
124 PRO: PREM 11/1102. PMPT T470/56, No. 847. Lloyd to Eden, 13 October, 1956. See also No. 846. Lloyd to Nutting (scrambled to Eden at Chequers), 13 October, 1956.
125 PRO: FO 800/728. Personal Papers of Selwyn Lloyd. M. Pineau and Mr Dulles in New York, notes dated 18 October, 1956. Lloyd, *op. cit.*, 168–9.
126 PRO: CAB 134/1216. EC(56) 33, 8 October, 1956.
127 PRO: PREM 11/1102. PMPT T470/56, No. 847. Lloyd to Eden, 13 October, 1956.
128 Eden (1960), *op. cit.*, 435.
129 Lloyd, *op. cit.*, 54.
130 PRO: PREM 11/1102. PMPT T471/56, No. 1190. Eden to Lloyd, 13 October, received 14 October, 1956.
131 AP 20/27/86. PMPT T467/56. Eisenhower to Eden, 12 October, received 13 October, 1956.
132 PRO: PREM 11/1102. PMPT T472/56, No. 852. Lloyd to Eden, 13 October, received 14 October, 1956. This change of heart by Pineau also suggests that he was now aware of the Gazier/Challe mission which had been arranged for the 14th. He no longer needed to stall events. Mollet had telephoned Eden on 13 October, to ask his permission to send a couple of delegates to see him on Mollet's behalf. Eden had agreed and so the French plan to persuade Eden to accept a military operation was set.
133 Cf. Chapter 5, 137–8.

134 Lloyd, *op. cit.*, 162.
135 PRO: PREM 11/1102. No. 854. Lloyd to Eden, 14 October, 1956. Lloyd, *op. cit.*, 162–3.
136 PRO: PREM 11/1102. PMPT T474/56, No. 1194. Eden to Lloyd, 14 October, 1956 and PMPT T475/56, No. 1198. Eden to Lloyd, 14 October, 1956.
137 The fact that it was attempted to remove Gazier's and Challe's names from the Chequers' engagement diary also suggests that Eden had been unaware of the significance of the visit of the Frenchmen, prior to their arrival: See AP 20/30/2. Chequers' Weekend Diary. Diary entry for 14 October, 1956.
138 PRO: PREM 11/1102. PMPT T475/56, No. 1198. Eden to Lloyd, 14 October, 1956.
139 Kyle, *op. cit.*, 295. Kyle does not attribute a source for the quote.
140 *Ibid.*, 296.
141 Nutting, *op. cit.*, 89.
142 Jean Chauvel, *Commentaire Volume III: 1952–1962* (Paris, 1973), 194–5, cited in Kyle, *op. cit.*, 296. This move by the French to limit the disclosure of information beyond the highest levels also suggested that they had decided to present the 'plan' of collusion before Eden.
143 Nutting, *op. cit.*, 93.
144 *Ibid*. Nutting recalled that Eden had to do 'his best to conceal his excitement'.
145 SOHP: Interview with Sir Guy Millard.
146 *Ibid*.
147 PRO: PREM 11/1102. PMPT T476/56, No. 854. Lloyd to Eden, 14 October, received 15 October, 1956.
148 *Manchester Guardian*, 13 October, 1956. See also: *The Observer*, 14 October, 1956: 'SUEZ DIFFERENCES STILL WIDE'. For the differences, see Chapter 5, 133.
149 *The Daily Telegraph*, 13 October, 1956: 'ACCORD NOT REACHED ON IMPLEMENTATION'; *The Times*, 13, October, 1956, noted that agreement on the six principles had been reached but was quick to point out that discussions would have to continue. For Lloyd's attitude, cf. Chapter 5, 132.
150 PRO: WO 32/16709. Middle East Rear Command to War Office, No. 78719/PSZ, 3 October, 1956 and Troopers to Forces, No. 06161/AG, 10 October, 1956.
151 SOHP: Interview with Sir Guy Millard.
152 Lloyd, *op. cit.*, 170.
153 Clark cited in 'Suez 1956: Neither War Nor Peace At 10 Downing Street'.
154 Frank Cooper, Head of the Air Staff Secretariat, saw 1956 as a 'watershed because the whole thing became increasingly dominated by resource considerations. Costs were escalating. We knew a great deal about what was possible in a technical sense, but no one knew how to control costs and the real world began to break in.': SOHP: Interview with Sir Frank Cooper. Such was the realisation that the Defence White Paper of the following year ultimately ended call-up and conscription as a direct result of Suez, while altering the planning bedrock from which British defence strategy was organised: John Baylis, *British Defence Policy: Striking the Right Balance* (Basingstoke, 1989), 61–2; Michael Dockrill, *British Defence Since 1945* (Oxford, 1988), 65–6 and 127; Kyle, *op. cit.*, 560–3; Alistair Horne, *Macmillan: 1957–1986 Volume II* (London, 1989), 45–54; Richard Lamb, *The Macmillan Years 1957–1963: The Emerging Truth* (London, 1995), 98 and 282–4; G. Wyn Rees, 'Brothers in Arms: Anglo-American Defence Co-operation in 1957', in Anthony Gorst, Lewis Johnman and W. Scott Lucas (eds), *Post-war Britain, 1945–64: Themes and Perspectives* (London, 1989), 203–20; Sampson, *op. cit.*, 133.

155 PRO: PREM 11/1102. Minutes of a Staff Conference held at No. 10 on 11 October, 1956. Those in attendance were: Eden, Monckton (still Minister of Defence), Anthony Head, Mountbatten, Boyle, Powell, Hailsham, Dickson, Templer, Keightley and Admiral Sir Guy Grantham, Commander in Chief Mediterranean.
156 PRO: PREM 11/1102. COS(56) 380, 12 October, 1956.
157 SOHP: Interview with Sir Guy Millard.
158 Cf. Introduction, 7.
159 SOHP: Interview with Lord Amery.
160 SOHP: Interviews with Sir Frederick Bishop and Sir Guy Millard. For a more in-depth look at the decision to withdraw from the Canal Base and the hardline reaction, see William Roger Louis, 'Churchill in Egypt', in Roger Blake and William Roger Louis (eds), *Churchill* (Oxford, 1994), chapter 27, and Henry Pelling, *Churchill's Peacetime Ministry, 1951–55* (Basingstoke, 1997), 111–13.
161 SOHP: Interview with Sir Guy Millard.
162 SOHP: Interview with Sir Evelyn Shuckburgh.
163 Lord Moran, *op. cit.*, 736. Diary entry for 8 August, 1956.
164 SOHP: Interview with Julian Amery. See also John Colville, *The New Elizabethans: 1952–1977* (London, 1977), 23; Churchill to Eisenhower, 21 June, 1954, cited in Pelling, *op. cit.*, 225; Hansard, 531, column 820, 29 July, 1954, and MP.Macmillan.dep.d.27. Diary entry for 5 August, 1956.
165 Rothwell, *op. cit.*, 210.
166 See Colville (1985.), *op. cit.*, 706: Diary entry for 29 March, 1955. See also, John Colville, *The Churchillians* (London, 1981), 170–1; Lord Swinton in conversation with James Margach cited in Margach, *op. cit.*, 105–6; Montague Browne, *op. cit.*, 132 and 182; SOHP: Interview with Sir Evelyn Shuckburgh.
167 SOHP: Interview with Sir Guy Millard. Colin Coote went on to write two books about Churchill: *Sir Winston Churchill: A Self Portrait* (with P. D. Bunyan) and *Maxims and Reflections of Sir Winston Churchill*.
168 SOHP: Interview with David Pitblado.
169 SOHP: Interview with Sir Evelyn Shuckburgh.
170 The Queen encapsulated the dilemma in her letter to Churchill, upon his retirement: '[I]t would be useless to pretend that either he [Eden] or any of those successors who may one day follow him in office will ever, for me, be able to hold the place of my first Prime Minister': Squerryes Lodge Archive (hereafter referred to as SLA). Queen Elizabeth II to Churchill, 11 April, 1955, cited in Gilbert, *op. cit.*, 1126–7.
171 Cf. Introduction, 8–9.
172 Speech at the Conservative Party Conference, Llandudno, 13 October, 1956, cited in Eden (1960), *op. cit.*, 508.
173 SOHP: Interview with Julian Amery.
174 PRO: PREM 11/1102. PMPT T475/56, No. 1198. Eden to Lloyd, 14 October, 1956.
175 For example, cf. Chapter 2, 44–5 and Chapter 4, 94.
176 SOHP: Interview with Julian Amery. Cf. Chapter 4, 95–6.
177 SOHP: Interview with Sir Frederick Bishop.
178 For opinions of Kirkpatrick, see SOHP: Interview with Sir Evelyn Shuckburgh; Lord Sherfield, *op. cit.*, 36–7; Shuckburgh, *op. cit.*, 360. Diary entry for 24 September, 1956. Peter Hennessy, *Whitehall* (London, 1990), 166.
179 SOHP: Interview with Sir Frederick Bishop. Other historians and civil servants have seen Brook as disapproving of the final plan but compliant with

Government policy: SOHP: Interview with Sir Richard Powell. It was only either much later or in private that they aired any negative views on the subject: Richard Powell, cited in Hennessy (1990), *op. cit.*, 166–7. Brook described the invasion as 'folly', Shuckburgh, *op. cit.*, 366. Diary entry for 5 December, 1956. As one 'very senior figure' put it, Brook was 'in a very difficult position. He had to be loyal to his Cabinet *and* the repository of people's worries in Whitehall': cited in Peter Hennessy, 'Suez 30 years on: the secrets which will stay secret for ever', *The Listener*, 11 September, 1986.
180 SOHP: Interview with Sir Evelyn Shuckburgh.
181 SOHP: Interview with Sir Denis Wright. Sir Denis Wright, *op. cit.*, 306–7. Notes actually made on paper in lieu of diary.
182 SOHP: Interview with Sir Donald Logan.
183 Anthony Howard, *RAB: The Life of R. A. Butler* (London, 1987), 232. Howard concludes that Butler never formally opposed the use of force.
184 SOHP: Interview with Sir Richard Powell.
185 PRO: PREM 11/1152. SOHP: Interview with Sir Richard Powell.
186 See in particular William Clark's and Harold Macmillan's diaries: WCP.MS. William Clark.160 and MP.MS.Macmillan.dep.d.27.
187 Colville believed that Monckton was 'unable to make up his mind about the rights and wrongs of Suez': Colville (1981), *op. cit.*, 183. Asked by the Editor of *The Observer*, David Astor, why he did not resign, Monckton replied: 'I owe my position to Anthony. It would be an act of betrayal. I can't be the person who knifes him and brings him down': Interview between David Astor and Andrew Roberts, 10 November, 1992, cited in Andrew Roberts, *Eminent Churchillians* (London, 1995), 277.
188 Selwyn Lloyd in conversation with Lord Birkenhead, cited in Birkenhead, *op. cit.*, 309. Monckton's position was best illustrated by a memorandum he wrote on 7 November: cited in *Ibid.*, 309–10. AP 23/53/10: Eden to Monckton, 20 July, 1959: Eden asked Monckton to proof-read his chapters on Suez for his memoirs.
189 The Americans maintained intransigence while struggling to offer a solution to a country they believed had decided upon the use of force.
190 Heikal (1973), *op. cit.*, 100–1.
191 Thomas, *op. cit.*, 103. Clark cited in 'Suez 1956: Neither War Nor Peace At 10 Downing Street'. Interview with Sir Douglas Dodds-Parker, 5 January, 1998. Harold Wilson, *A Prime Minister on Prime Ministers* (London, 1977), 312.

6 Collusion

1 Central to this group had become: Macmillan, Butler, Lloyd and Head. Also included were Home, Kilmuir and Salisbury (when in good health). Eden expected agreement as these members backed the decision to use force.
2 Nutting, *op. cit.*, 93–4.
3 PRO: PREM 11/1102. PMPT T475/56, No. 1198. Eden to Lloyd, 14 October, 1956.
4 Nutting, *op. cit.*, 95.
5 PRO: PREM 11/1102. PMPT T470/56, No. 847. Lloyd to Eden, 13 October, 1956.
6 *Ibid.*
7 Nutting, *op. cit.*, 94.
8 Lord Sherfield, *op. cit.*, 37. Lord Sherfield directly challenged the assumption, by Lucas and Louis, that Ross and Kirkpatrick 'strongly objected to the French plan

on the grounds that it would undermine Britain's position in the Middle East, the U.N., the U.S.A. and the Commonwealth'. In particular, he believed that this was not a change of position by Kirkpatrick: see page 36. For another argument see Lucas (1991), *op. cit.*, 238. For Nutting's argument, see Nutting, *op. cit.*, 96–7.

9. WP. 1957: Belgium and Luxembourg June 22–30: Notes for 29 June, 1957. Wright had met Nutting at pre-lunch drinks at a lunch given by Brian Heddy, a member of the British delegation to the Iron and Steel Community.
10. Nutting, *op. cit.*, 94–5.
11. Lord Sherfield, *op. cit.*, 36. Interview with Lord Sherfield, conducted by W. Scott Lucas, cited in Lucas (1991), *op. cit.*, 250. Interview with Lord Sherfield, conducted by Alistair Horne, cited in Horne, *op. cit.*, 431.
12. Advice which ignored the importance of the American attitude. On 28 October Makins told Macmillan about the importance of keeping the US in line: 'I think I did give him a jolt by telling him what Suez would do to Anglo-American relations': Interview with Lord Sherfield, conducted by Alistair Horne, cited in Horne, *op. cit.*, 434. The selected few were: Brook, Bishop, Kirkpatrick, Dean, Logan and Millard.
13. PRO: PREM 11/1103. Dulles to Lloyd, 15 October, 1956. SOHP: Interview with Sir Donald Logan.
14. PRO: PREM 11/1103. Dulles to Lloyd, 15 October, 1956. Nutting, *op. cit.*, 66, confirmed that SCUA 'was not going to turn out as Eden had hoped.'
15. AP 23/56/15A. Brook to Eden, 14 May, 1958.
16. PRO: FO 800/728. Foreign Secretary's Engagement Diary: Lloyd described it as a Ministerial Meeting at No. 10. No official records of the meeting remain. Those in attendance were: Eden, Macmillan, Kilmuir, Lennox-Boyd, Monckton, Nutting and the Chiefs of Staff: See evidence of a Cabinet Minister, cited in Thomas, *op. cit.*, 113. Nutting did not mention the attendance of Macmillan but added that of Thorneycroft and Head: Interview with Nutting conducted by Richard Lamb, cited in Lamb (1987), *op. cit.*, 231 and 233.
17. Cf. Chapter 5, 133–4.
18. Evidence of a Cabinet Minister, cited in Thomas, *op. cit.*, 113. Interview with Nutting conducted by Richard Lamb, cited in Lamb (1987), *op. cit.*, 233.
19. Nutting, *op. cit.*, 97.
20. Randolph S. Churchill, *The Rise and Fall of Sir Anthony Eden* (London, 1959), 295. See also Erskine B. Childers, *The Road to Suez: A Study of Western-Arab Relations* (London, 1962), 238. No solid evidence of this letter exists, although when asked if he knew of it, Donald Logan, the one civil servant who attended all of the clandestine meetings from 16 October, believed that this 'might explain the paper that Eden told Guy Millard to make sure to take to that meeting [16 October]'.
21. Evidence of a Cabinet Minister, cited in Thomas, *op. cit.*, 113.
22. Nutting, *op. cit.*, 98.
23. PRO: PREM 11/1103. Lloyd to Dulles, 15 October, 1956.
24. For Lloyd's pacifism see SOHP. Interview with Sir Donald Logan; Thorpe, *op. cit.*, 208–68 (chapter 9: 'Suez').
25. PRO: FO 800/728. Lloyd minute, 18 October, 1956.
26. Lloyd, *op. cit.*, 175.
27. PRO: CAB 128/30. CM(56) 71, 18 October, 1956.
28. PRO: CAB 134/1216. EC(56) 35, 17 October, 1956.

29 Iverach McDonald in conversation with the author, 24 February, 1998. PRO: CAB 134/1216. EC(56) 35, 17 October, 1956.
30 Butler, *op. cit.*, 193; Lloyd, *op. cit.*, 177.
31 PRO: FO 800/728. Personal Papers of Selwyn Lloyd, 1956–59. Memorandum by Lloyd, undated.
32 Butler, *op. cit.*, 193; Lloyd, *op. cit.*, 177. There has been criticism of Eden for not keeping the Cabinet fully informed but the Prime Minister had conveyed the basis of the plan to them.
33 PRO: CAB 128/30. CM(56) 71, 18 October, 1956; Lloyd, *op. cit.*, 176. In attendance were Eden, Butler, Lloyd, Macmillan, Kilmuir, Home, Monckton, Sandys, Heathcoat Amory, Eccles, Buchan-Hepburn, Head and Heath. Missing were: Salisbury, Lloyd-George, Stuart, Lennox-Boyd, Thorneycroft, Macleod and Selkirk.
34 Robert Shepherd, *Iain Macleod* (London, 1994), 116.
35 PRO: CAB 128/30. CM(56) 71, 18, October, 1956.
36 Dayan, *op. cit.*, 174.
37 PRO: PREM 11/1103. No. 882. Dixon to F.O., 18 October, 1956.
38 PRO: PREM 11/1103. No. 883. Dixon to F.O., 18 October, 1956.
39 PRO: PREM 11/1103.
40 Lloyd, *op. cit.*, 178.
41 PRO: PREM 11/1103. No. 2495. Trevelyan to F.O., 18 October, 1956.
42 Dayan, *op. cit.*, 174.
43 Ben-Gurion's diary for 26 October, 1956, cited in Kyle, *op. cit.*, 567. The diary reveals that an Israeli Ministry of Defence representative in Europe, Artur Ben-Natan, arrived in Israel with '[a] photocopy of the letter from Eden to Mollet which read: "HMG have been informed of the course of the conversations held at Sèvres on 22–24 October. They confirm that in the situation there envisaged they will take the action described. This is in accordance with the declaration enclosed with my communication of 21 October."' In an addendum to his statement given to the PRO, Sir Donald Logan recorded, in 1997, that he had spoken to a French Journalist, Vincent Jauvert, writing for *Nouvel Observateur*, who had seen a letter, signed by Eden on 10 Downing Street paper with a date after the middle of October, 1956, in the Papers of Christian Pineau (in the possession of Mme Pineau). This letter confirmed Eden's agreement to the outlines of the later document (24 October: see above). Logan believed that Eden must have sent the letter by private or secret means and not through the Foreign Office. As Logan continued, 'To have refused to sign a record of agreement still open to the three governments to confirm ("ad referendum") could by increasing suspicion of British reliability have prejudiced the operation to which Eden attached such importance': cited in SOHP: addendum to Interview with Sir Donald Logan.
44 SOHP: Interview with Sir Richard Powell. AP 20/30/2. Chequers Weekend Diary. Diary entry for 21 October, 1956: Those in attendance were Eden, Macmillan, Kilmuir, Head, Butler, Home, Lloyd, Brook, Powell and Keightley.
45 Dayan, *op. cit.*, 174.
46 *Ibid.*, 174–5.
47 Those present were Mollet, Pineau, Abel Thomas (of the French Ministry of Defence), Bourges-Manoury, Challe, Ben-Gurion, Dayan, Shimon Peres (Director-General of the Israeli Ministry of Defence), Mordechai Bar-On (Ben-Gurion's Secretary), Lloyd, and Logan.
48 PRO. Donald Logan, 'Suez: Meetings at Sèvres, 22–25 October, 1956' (unpublished, 24 October, 1986), 3; Dayan, *op. cit.*, 177–9. Lloyd, *op. cit.*, 181.

49 SOHP: Interview with Sir Donald Logan.
50 Logan cited in 'A Canal Too Far', 13. Dayan, op.cit., 180, recalled: 'Britain's Foreign Minister may well have been a friendly man, pleasant, charming, amiable. If so, he showed near-genius in concealing these virtues. His manner could not have been more antagonistic. His whole demeanour expressed distaste – for the place, the company, and the topic. His opening remarks suggested the tactics of a customer bargaining with extortionate merchants.'
51 Mordechai Bar-On cited in *The Suez Crisis*, BBC TV (1996). Lloyd's aloofness was undoubtedly due to his reservations about colluding with the French and Israelis over such a transparent plan. However, possibly through deference to Eden's experience in foreign affairs, he perpetuated the deception and did not voice any criticisms before the operation was launched.
52 Ben-Gurion's diary for 26 October, cited in Kyle, op.cit., 567. Dayan, op.cit., 179–81. Ben-Gurion had been particularly suspicious of Eden since he had announced the need to adjust Israel's frontiers, in his Guildhall speech of November, 1955, which, in itself, had enhanced his early reputation as a pro-Arabist. Ben-Gurion had also been alarmed over Eden's reaction to the Israeli raids into Jordan and the possible implementation of Operation Cordage: see Nutting, op.cit., 86–7. Sir Harold Beeley, Assistant Under-Secretary for the Middle East at the Foreign Office, suggested that Eden had been as pro-Arab as the majority of the Foreign Office, only appearing pro-Israeli in 1956, 'when he found it useful to make use of Israel', cited in 'A Canal Too Far', 15. This is supported by Nutting, op.cit., 22, and the fact that it was only after the invasion that remonstrance was made with regard to Egyptian treatment of Jews in Egypt: see PRO: FO 371/119265.
53 Logan (1986), op.cit., 4.
54 *Ibid.*, 3.
55 SOHP: Interview with Sir Donald Logan.
56 *Ibid.* See also Mordechai Bar-On, 'David Ben-Gurion and the Sèvres Collusion', in William Roger Louis and Roger Owen (eds), *Suez 1956: The Crisis and Its Consequences* (Oxford, 1989), 155–60.
57 Logan (1986), op.cit., 4.
58 *Ibid.*
59 Clarissa Eden's diary, 23 October, 1956, cited in Thorpe, op.cit., 240.
60 Nutting, op.cit., 101–2.
61 PRO: FO 800/716. Foreign Secretary's Engagement Diary for October, 1956.
62 Lloyd, op.cit., 185.
63 The Cabinet Meeting had a much higher attendance than that of 18 October, but the record of Eden's and Lloyd's reports, in the Confidential Annex, had a narrower distribution: See PRO: CAB 128/30. CM(56) 72. Confidential Annex, 23 October, 1956 and Shepherd, op.cit., 117, fn. 39.
64 PRO: CAB 128/30. CM(56) 72, Confidential Annex, 23 October, 1956.
65 Dayan, op.cit., 182; SOHP: Interview with Sir Donald Logan; Lloyd, op.cit., 186; Logan (1986), op.cit., 5; Pineau, op.cit., 134. Nutting, op.cit., 104, suggested that Eden asked Mollet to send Pineau to London so that he could press the French into making another attempt to bring the Israelis into line. This does not coincide with the other records.
66 Lloyd, op.cit., 185; Logan (1986), op.cit., 5.
67 PRO: FO 800/716. Foreign Secretary's Engagement Diary for October; Logan (1986), op.cit., 5; Lloyd, op.cit., 186.

68 Dayan, *op. cit.*, 181.
69 PRO: FO 800/725. Minute by Lloyd, 24 October, 1956. From 16 October, it had been anticipated that the US would at least be indifferent: see FO 800/728. Lloyd's undated minute re: meeting between Eden, Lloyd, Mollet and Pineau, 16 October, 1956.
70 Lloyd, *op. cit.*, 186; Pineau, *op. cit.*, 137; SELO 253(2).
71 MP.Macmillan,dep.d.27. Diary entry for 9 August, 1956.
72 PRO: CAB 128/30. CM(56) 73. Confidential Annex, 24 October, 1956.
73 Logan (1986), *op. cit.*, 5; Lloyd, *op. cit.*, 187.
74 Logan (1986), *op. cit.*, 5.
75 *Ibid*; Pineau, *op. cit.*, 137.
76 Logan (1986), *op. cit.*, 5; Lloyd, *op. cit.*, 188; SOHP: Interview with Sir Donald Logan.
77 The separate protocol was signed by Bourges-Manoury on 24 October, 1956 and was intended to appease the Israelis who were concerned that an invasion of Egypt might lead to bombing reprisals carried out against her cities. This had been a constant fear (Dayan, *op. cit.*, 181; Logan (1986), *op. cit.*, 4). She had hoped that Britain would either destroy Nasser's bombers or be on hand to intercept any raids on Israel. However, still unconvinced that Britain would partake in the operation, she signed a separate agreement with France to protect herself. The protocol read:

> The French Government undertakes to station on the territory of Israel to ensure the air defence of Israeli territory during the period from 29–31 October 1956 a reinforced squadron of Mystères IV A, a squadron of fighter bombers. In addition two ships of the Marine Nationale will during the same period put into Israeli ports. (Cited in Pineau, *op. cit.*, 154.)

78 PRO: FO 800/716. Foreign Secretary's Engagement Diary for October. Those in attendance were Eden, Macmillan, Butler, Lloyd, Head and Mountbatten: Lloyd, *op. cit.*, 188. Dean confirmed that the group was larger than just Eden and Lloyd. Kirkpatrick knew all about the Sèvres meetings because Dean reported to him: SOHP: Interview with Sir Patrick Dean. Logan (1986), *op. cit.*, 6–7. However, while Eden appeared satisfied with the contents of the protocol, he was 'taken aback' by the fact that three copies of a written record of the collusion existed. Dean and Logan were then sent back to Paris, on the 25th, to ask the French to destroy any copies of the agreement. After many hours, with the Britons waiting in a locked room at the Quai d'Orsay, Pineau rejected Eden's proposal. The Prime Minister, dismayed at the news, had all his copies and their translations destroyed.
79 PRO: CAB 128/30. CM(56) 74, 25 October, 1956; Thorpe, *op. cit.*, 244.
80 PRO: CAB 128/30. CM(56) 74, 25 October, 1956.
81 *Ibid*; Lucas (1991), *op. cit.*, 249.
82 PRO: CAB 128/30. CM(56) 74, 25 October, 1956.
83 PRO: CAB 128/30. CM(56) 72, Confidential Annex, 23 October, 1956; CAB 128/30. CM(56) 74, 25 October, 1956.
84 AP 23/5/10B. Eden to Aldrich, 3 May, 1967. Churchill told Lord Moran: 'I should not have done half the work he [Eden] has been doing. I'd have got others to do it. He let them wake him up at all hours of night to listen to news from New York – our night is their day': Moran, *op. cit.*, 743. Diary entry for 26 November, 1956.
85 Nutting, *op. cit.*, 107.

86 SOHP: Interview with Sir Richard Powell. Powell's reflections also cover the later period of the crisis. He only attended two Egypt Committee meetings (on 4 and 7 September, 1956), but when the decisions were transferred to the smaller, 'inner circle', in October, he was a regular attender, and in a position to see, first hand, Eden's state of health and mind.
87 Lady Hayter and Iverach McDonald in conversation with the author, 24 February, 1998; Dr Richard Cattell, cited in Kyle, *op. cit.*, 557.
88 Lord Hailsham, *op. cit.*, 288.
89 PRO: PREM 11/1152.
90 These were the officials who knew of the details of the Sèvres meetings: Macmillan, Butler, Lloyd, Home, Kilmuir, Head, Lennox-Boyd and Millard, Bishop, Kirkpatrick, Brook, Powell and Dean.
91 PRO: DEFE 4/91. COS (56) 103, 18 October, 1956. ADM 205/137. Mountbatten to Durnford-Slater, 18 October, 1956.

7 Finale

1 Interview with Sir Richard Powell, conducted by Peter Hennessy, cited in 'A Canal Too Far', 15.
2 UN General Assembly. Official Records, 1st and 2nd Emergency Special Sessions, 1956, 561st and 562nd Plenary Meetings, 1–2 November, 1956. Resolution 997 (ES-1), cited in Royal Institute of International Affairs (hereafter referred to as RIIA), *Documents on International Affairs: 1956* (London, 1959), 270.
3 PRO: PREM 11/1105. Dixon to Eden, 3 November, 1956.
4 PRO: AIR 20/10746. Air Marshall Barnett, 'Summary of Operations During Operation *Musketeer*. Appendix D. Bomber Participation', cited in Kyle, *op. cit.*, 383. Robert Jackson, *Suez: The Forgotten Invasion* (Shrewsbury, 1996), 70. The Egyptians had been warned to keep away from these areas: Roy Fullick and Geoffrey Powell, *Suez: The Double War* (London, 1990), 109.
5 Anthony Eden, 'Government Policy in the Middle East', in *The Listener*, 8 November, 1956. Originally broadcast on 3 November, 1956.
6 For example, AP 14/4/162. Lord Montgomery of Alamein to Eden, 1 November, 1956; AP 14/4/72. Timothy Eden to Eden, 2 November, 1956.
7 He had suffered a stroke on 29 October.
8 Churchill's statement of 3 November, 1956, cited in Gilbert, *op. cit.*, 1221.
9 For example, see *The Manchester Guardian*, 5 November, 1956; CP. 2/216, Eden to Churchill, 5 November, 1956, cited in Gilbert, *op. cit.*, 1221.
10 Lloyd, *op. cit.*, 205.
11 PRO: CAB 128/30. CM(56) 79, 4 November, 1956.
12 *Ibid.*
13 Rhodes James, *op. cit.*, 566–7. Rhodes James does not cite his source, but writes: 'another record was being kept, which has been made available to me'.
14 AP 20/2/5. Diary entry for January, 1957.
15 Butler, *op. cit.*, 194.
16 Clarissa Eden's diary, cited in Rhodes James, *op. cit.*, 567.
17 See Carlton, *op. cit.*, 451. That Carlton defends Eden suggests the severity of Salisbury's action and timing.
18 WCP.MS.William Clark.160. Diary entry for 1 November, 1956. In later years Macmillan said he had been 'absolutely amazed' by the American reaction, 'not just [the] lack of support but [the] bitter violent lining up with the

Kremlin': Alistair Horne in conversation with Macmillan (1979–1986), cited in Horne, *op. cit.*, 445. As Assistant Cabinet Secretary, Burke Trend, recalled: '[I]t never occurred to him that the old wartime relationship could be in danger': Interview with Burke Trend, conducted by Alistair Horne, cited in Horne, *op. cit.*, 445.
19 PRO: CAB 134/1216. EC(56) 37, 1 November, 1956.
20 Lloyd, *op. cit.*, 206. Lloyd also recorded that '[t]wo of those present remember this'.
21 Horne, *op. cit.*, 443.
22 SOHP: Interview with Sir Frank Cooper.
23 Cooper, *op. cit.*, 181.
24 DDE. Ann Whitman Series, International, Box 17, Eden, Eisenhower to Eden draft, 5 November, 1956, cited in Lucas (1991), *op. cit.*, 287.
25 WCP.MS.William Clark.160. Diary entry for 1 November, 1956. In reality many in the State Department were anglophiles. Eden continued to have a relatively close relationship with Eisenhower after the Suez Crisis, and the President made his surgeon available to Eden in 1957: See AP 23/29. Eden/Eisenhower correspondence post-Suez.
26 Lloyd, *op.cit.*, 202 and 221; Lucas (1991), *op.cit.*, 282. Cf. Chapter 1, 22–3. Finer, *op.cit.*, 398; Goold-Adams, *op. cit.*, 242; Thomas, *op. cit.*, 159. For other evidence of Hoover's and Rountree's anti-British feeling, see: Lord Sherfield, *op. cit.*, 9; Lloyd, *op. cit.*, 78. Dulles had actually instructed that 'Hoover take charge of all policies in the Department, except Suez': see Townsend Hoopes, *The Devil and John Foster Dulles: The Diplomacy of the Eisenhower Era* (Boston, 1973), 380–1. Rountree, as the expert on the Middle East, would help to fill the void left by Dulles.
27 PRO: PREM 11/1102. Macmillan to Eden, 'Note of a Private Talk with Mr. Dulles', 25 September, signed 26 September, 1956. Lord Sherfield, *op. cit.*, 33.
28 Lloyd, *op. cit.*, 219. See also Finer, *op. cit.*, 446–7, although it is reasonable to assume that Lloyd probably reported the meeting to Finer. Dulles's sincerity was supported by his own admission 'that he had been wrong over Suez', on his deathbed, to the Head of the Walter Reid Hospital: AP 33/6. Sir William Pike to Caccia, 28 June, 1972.
29 DDE, Ann Whitman Series, DDE Diaries, Box 19, November 1956 Diary, Staff Memoranda, Goodpaster memorandum, 3 November, 1956; DDE. Ann Whitman Series, International, Box 17, Eden, Eisenhower to Eden draft, 5 November, 1956. Both cited in Lucas (1991), *op. cit.*, 287.
30 AP 20/27/96. PMPT T520/56, No. 5181. Eden to Eisenhower, 5 November, 1956; PRO: FO 800/726. No. 4061, Eden to Eisenhower, 6 September, 1956.
31 AP 20/27/96. PMPT T520/56, No. 5181. Eden to Eisenhower, 5 November, 1956.
32 AP 23/58/77. Note by Eden.
33 PRO: PREM 11/1105. No. 1071. Dixon (New York) to F.O., 5 November, 1956.
34 Copies of the letter were also sent to Mollet, Ben-Gurion and Eisenhower: RIIA, *op. cit.*, 288–94.
35 PRO: PREM 11/1105. Hayter to F.O., 5 November, 1956. As Hayter was writing this telegram the Embassy was being besieged by demonstrators. It was not until afterwards that he realised that they had been organised, literally pulled out of the factories. When he asked them when they were leaving they replied 'in 20 minutes'. Thus, at the time he wrote the telegram, Hayter was caught up in an aggressive atmosphere which may well have led him to exaggerate the Russian threat. See Sir William Hayter, *A Double Life: The Memoirs of Sir William Hayter* (London, 1974), 146, Private Papers of Sir William Hayter (hereafter referred to as HP);

Lady Hayter's Diary: entries for 5 and 6 November, 1956, and Lady Hayter in conversation with the author, 24 February, 1998. Clark believed that Hayter's telegram, in conjunction with the Soviet threat, changed the Government's policy: WCP.MS.William Clark.160. Diary entry for 6 November and HP. Clark to Hayter, undated. Hayter later played down the importance of the threat: SOHP: Interview with Sir William Hayter.

36 PRO: AIR 8/1940. COS to Keightley, Cable COSKEY 41, *FLASH* 060536Z.
37 PRO: AIR 28/9890. COS to Keightley, Cable COSKEY 48, 6 November, 1956.
38 Cooper, *op.cit.*, 200. Ministers intent on a ceasefire cited the possibility of a Soviet invasion of Syria, 'or some other area in the Middle East, and possibly a direct Soviet attack on the Anglo-French forces in the Canal area', in the Cabinet Meeting of 6 November, while other Ministers appeared to have dismissed the threat: PRO: CAB 128/30. CM(56) 80, 6 November, 1956.
39 Lloyd, *op.cit.*, 209.
40 Evidence of a Minister, cited in Thomas, *op.cit.*, 163. Macmillan 'vigorously' refuted this, declaring 'it was not my style': Alistair Horne in conversation with Macmillan (1979–1986), cited in Horne, *op.cit.*, 440.
41 PRO: CAB 128/30. CM(56) 80, 6 November, 1956.
42 Eden (1960), *op.cit.*, 557; Macmillan (1971), *op.cit.*, 166; Lloyd, *op.cit.,op.cit.*, 210.
43 PRO: PREM 11/1105. Eden minute, 7 November, 1956.
44 AP 33/3. Eden to A. Hodge, 27 October, 1959. Argument as to the reason for the Cabinet's decision continues.
45 Lloyd, *op.cit.*, 210–11.
46 PRO: FO 800/728 or CAB 21/3314. 'Memorandum on Relations Between the United Kingdom, the United States and France in the Months Following Egyptian Nationalisation of the Suez Canal Company in 1956', written August, printed 21 October, 1957. Those historians who believe that Macmillan's financial fears were the principle reason for the Cabinet's decision to agree to a ceasefire are: Horne, *op.cit.*, 440; Butler, *op.cit.*, 195; Lucas (1991), *op.cit.*, 292; Kunz (1991), *op.cit.*, 132–3; Rhodes James, *op.cit.*, 574; Nutting, *op.cit.*, 145–6. Other non-committal discussions include: Thomas, *op.cit.*, 161–4; Kyle, *op.cit.*, 464–6; Fullick and Powell, *op.cit.*, 158–60; Dutton, *op.cit.*, 440–2.
47 Interview with Lord Head, conducted by Alistair Horne, cited in Horne, *op.cit.*, 441–2.
48 Kunz, *op.cit.*, 138. It has been argued that Macmillan exaggerated the financial threat to lead Cabinet: Kyle, *op.cit.*, 464; Kunz (1991), *op.cit.*, 132; Dutton, *op.cit.*, 442.
49 Horne, *op.cit.*, 440; Macmillan (1971), *op.cit.*, 164–5.
50 PRO. T236/4189. 'Note of a Meeting at 11 Downing Street on 7 November, 1956'. Kyle, *op.cit.*, 464. Kunz, *op.cit.*, 132, cites the figure as £30.4m.
51 Macmillan (1971), *op.cit.*, 163.
52 Cited in Thomas, *op.cit.*, 163.
53 Papers of Lord Beaverbrook (hereafter referred to as BeP). BBK C58, Bracken to Beaverbrook, 22 November, 1956.
54 SOHP: Interview with Sir Guy Millard.
55 Interview with Lord Sherfield and Lord Home, conducted by Peter Hennessy, cited in 'A Canal Too Far', 18. The American action had the secondary effect of reducing confidence in sterling.
56 Evidence of a Minister, cited in Thomas, *op.cit.*, 164. See also 164n.

57 Carlton, *op.cit.*, 453; Rhodes James, *op.cit.*, 574. For Stuart's feeling see Lloyd, *op.cit.*, 209.
58 Interview with Lord Home, conducted by Peter Hennessy, cited in 'A Canal Too Far', 19.
59 Carlton, *op.cit.*, 453. Rhodes James, *op.cit.*, 574, suggests that Lloyd remained loyal to Eden, but see Lloyd, *op.cit.*, 209.
60 Kyle, *op.cit.*, 467–8; Rhodes James, *op.cit.*, 574.
61 Rhodes James, *op.cit.*, 574; Thomas, *op.cit.*, 162; Eden (1960), *op.cit.*, 549.
62 Lamb (1987), *op.cit.*, 267; Shuckburgh, *op.cit.*, 14; AP 20/1/32. Diary entry for 7 September, 1956; AP 23/5/10B. Eden to Aldrich, 3 May, 1967.
63 Cloake, *op.cit.*, 355.
64 PRO: CAB 128/30. CM(56) 80, 6 November, 1956.
65 Eden (1960), *op.cit.*, 557.
66 Quoted in Carlton, *op.cit.*, 453.
67 AP 33/7ii. Note made of conversation after a visit by Lord Normanbrook, 9 September, 1969. Note made of a conversation after a visit by Lord Head, dictated 23 June, 1975. Templer was another who believed that the Cabinet had shown disloyalty to Eden: Cloake, *op.cit.*, 355.
68 Thomas, *op.cit.*, 165–6; Lucas (1991), *op.cit.*, 295; Kennett Love, *Suez: The Twice Fought War* (London, 1970), 626; Jacques Baeyens, *Un Coup d'Epee dans l'Eau du Canal* (Paris, 1976), 109; Jacques Massu, *Verité sur Suez* (Paris, 1978), 215.
69 Horne, *op.cit.*, 440; Lloyd, *op.cit.*, 211; Kyle, *op.cit.*, 469, see fn. 70.
70 Piers Dixon, *Double Diploma* (London, 1968), 274. Lloyd, *op.cit.*, 209. Kyle, *op.cit.*, 468 and 492. PRO: FO 800/728. Lloyd to Brook, 8 August, 1959. AP 20/2/20. Diary entry for 24 March, 1975.
71 Carlton, *op.cit.*, 454–5.
72 PRO: CAB 128/30. CM(56) 80, 6 November, 1956.
73 Thomas, *op.cit.*, 167; Carlton, *op.cit.*, 455.
74 Evidence of a Junior Minister, cited in Thomas, *op.cit.*, 165.
75 Interview with General Sir Kenneth Darling by Peter Hennessy, cited in 'A Canal Too Far', 19; Thomas, *op.cit.*, 161; Lucas (1991), *op.cit.*, 295–6. However, as Kyle, *op.cit.*, 469, has shown: the Allied Commander-in-Chief, Keightley, had been informed at 11:03 a.m. (British time) that he should be ready for a ceasefire (PRO: AIR 20/9890. COS to Keightley, COSKEY 42, 061103z) and at 1:30 p.m. (British time) he was informed that he should be prepared to ceasefire at 5:00 p.m. when he received the codeword STOP (PRO: AIR 20/9890. COS to Keightley, COSKEY 43, 061330z *FLASH*).
76 SOHP: Interview with Sir Frank Cooper.
77 Interview with General Sir Kenneth Darling and Sir Dermot Boyle by Peter Hennessy, cited in 'A Canal Too Far', 19. An estimate of casualties actually reveals that they were relatively few: British: 22 killed, 97 wounded: French: 10 killed, 33 wounded, cited in Jackson, *op.cit.*, 132.
78 Evidence of a British Commander, cited in Thomas, *op.cit.*, 178.
79 Stockwell Papers. 8/4/1. Templer to Stockwell, 14 November, 1956, cited in Lucas (1991), *op.cit.*, 294.
80 DDE. Ann Whitman Series, Ann Whitman Diary, Box 8, November 1956 Diary (2), Eden to Eisenhower and Eisenhower to Eden, 7 November, 1956, cited in Lucas (1991), *op.cit.*, 299.
81 *Ibid.*
82 DDE. Ann Whitman Series, DDE Diaries, Box 19, November 1956 Diary, Staff Memoranda, Goodpaster memorandum, 7 November, 1956 and DDE, Ann

Whitman Series, Ann Whitman Diary, Box 8, November 1956 Diary (2), Eisenhower to Eden, 7 November, 1956, cited in Lucas (1991), *op. cit.*, 299–300; Nutting, *op. cit.*, 150; Rhodes James, *op. cit.*, 577.

83 Sherman Adams, *First Hand Report: The Inside Story of the Eisenhower Administration* (London, 1962), 209. See also 209–10.
84 See PRO: PREM 11/1177. FO 800/726 and AP 20/27. This 'freeze' was extended to diplomats and Service Missions in Washington and the UN delegation in New York: Kyle. *op. cit.*, 492–3.
85 PRO: PREM 11/1106. PMPT T576/56, No. 1282. Lloyd (New York) to Eden, 18 November, received 19 November, 1956. Lloyd, *op. cit.*, 221.
86 Rhodes James, *op. cit.*, 582; Kyle, *op. cit.*, 503–4: Kyle believes that Evans instructed rest on the evening of 18 November, and that this decision was announced on the 19th; Dutton, *op. cit.*, 447.
87 Nutting, *op. cit.*, 153. It is interesting to note that despite Nutting's earlier conviction of Eden's determination to use force, he saw collusion as 'so completely out of character.'
88 Butler, *op. cit.*, 195.
89 PRO: PREM 11/1548. PMPT T580/56, No. 2010. Eden to Lloyd (New York), 19 November, 1956. Eden's doctors did not know whether the Prime Minister was seriously ill or suffering from exhaustion: Rhodes James, *op. cit.*, 582.
90 BeP. BBK C58, Bracken to Beaverbrook, 22 November, 1956: Viscount Brendan Bracken recognised that the illness was 'not diplomatic'. Bracken was a Trustee of the National Gallery, having been an MP, Parliamentary Private Secretary to the Prime Minister (1940–1941), Minister of Information (1941–1945) and First Lord of the Admiralty (1945).
91 Moran, *op. cit.*, 743. Diary entry for 26 November, 1956.
92 Rhodes James, *op. cit.*, 582–3; Dutton, *op. cit.*, 447. Eden stayed at Goldeneye, the home of Ian Fleming, which was set out many miles, on poor roads, from the Governor's residence, from where any communications would have to be transported.
93 Kyle, *op. cit.*, 504.
94 For an overview, see W. Scott Lucas, 'Suez, the Americans, and the Overthrow of Anthony Eden', *LSE Quarterly*, September, 1987; Lucas (1991), *op. cit.*, 309–23.
95 *FRUS XVI*, Doc. 588, 1150–1152, 19 November, 1956.
96 NAW. RG 59, CDF, 974.7301/11–1956. London to State Department, Cable 2814, 19 November, 1956, cited in Lucas (1991), *op. cit.*, 310.
97 DDE. Ann Whitman Series, DDE Diaries, Box 19, November 1956 Telephone Calls, Aldrich to Eisenhower, 19 November, 1956, cited in Lucas (1991), *op. cit.*, 310.
98 DDE. Ann Whitman Series, DDE Diaries, Box 19, November 1956 Telephone Calls, Eisenhower to Aldrich, 20 November, 1956 and November 1956 Diary, Staff Memoranda, Goodpaster memorandum, 21 November, 1956.
99 PRO: CAB 128/30. CM(56) 85, 20 November, 1956.
100 Lucas (1991), *op. cit.*, 313–16.
101 PRO: CAB 128/30. CM(56) 90, 28 November, 1956.
102 PRO: CAB 128/30. CM(56) 91, 29 November, 1956.
103 PRO: T 236/4190. Rowan to Makins and Makins to Rowan, 30 November, 1956.
104 PRO: CAB 128/30. CM(56) 91, 29 November, 1956. For a fuller description of the economic pressures, see Kunz, *op. cit.*, 138–9. For details of Britain's Sterling Assets, see Kunz, *op. cit.*, 204–6, appendix E.

230 Notes

105 Kunz, *op. cit.*, 132–3; A. J. Davies, *We, The Nation: The Conservative Party and the Pursuit of Power* (London, 1995), 358.
106 Cf. Chapter 7, 158–60.
107 Rhodes James, *op. cit.*, 587.
108 AP 20/25/181. PMPT T592/56. Brook to Eden, 30 November, 1956.
109 PRO: PREM 11/1826. PMPT T593/56, No. 102. Eden to Bishop, 1 December, 1956.
110 Lucas (1991), *op. cit.*, 317; Lamb (1987), *op. cit.*, 296–8; PRO: PREM 11/1107. PMPT T600/56, No. 70. Butler to Eden, 2 December, 1956.
111 PRO: PREM 11/1107. PMPT T609/56, No. 72. Butler to Eden, 3 December, 1956.
112 PRO: PREM 11/1548. PMPT T613/56, No. 117. Eden to Bobby Allan (a private secretary), 4 December, 1956.
113 BeP. BBK C58, Bracken to Beaverbrook, 7 December, 1956.
114 DDE. John Foster Dulles Papers, General Correspondence and Memoranda, Box 1, L-M(2), Macmillan–Foster Dulles meeting, 12 December, 1956, cited in Lucas (1991), *op. cit.*, 320.
115 SOHP: Interview with Sir Guy Millard.
116 Horne, *op. cit.*, 453–6. Macmillan once remarked to Alistair Horne: '[M]y belief is, when you get a chance take it. It was always my philosophy. Chance played such a role in my life – Winston, the war, Algiers, housing ... which made me Prime Minister': 454.
117 Lucas (1991), *op. cit.*, 319–20; Horne, *op. cit.*, 455.
118 SOHP: Interview with Julian Amery.
119 Philip Goodhart, *The 1922: The Story of the 1922 Committee* (London, 1973), 175, cited in Horne, *op. cit.*, 455–6.
120 SOHP: Interview with Julian Amery. An example of this was Alex(ander) Spearman, the Conservative backbencher.
121 'Returned to find everyone looking at us with thoughtful eyes': Clarissa Eden's diary, cited in Rhodes James, *op. cit.*, 591. See also Parliament's reaction on 592.
122 BeP. BBK C 59, Bracken to Beaverbrook, 23 January, 1957.
123 Lucas (1991), *op. cit.*, 322. Hansard, 20 December, 1956.
124 AP 33/7ii. Note made 30 June, 1960: Eden had been informed of the memorandum by Toby Law.
125 MP.MS.Macmillan.dep.c.14. Diary entry for 17 July, 1952.
126 PRO: PREM 11/1548.
127 AP 20/30/1. Prime Minister's Engagement Diary. Diary entries for 2, 3, 4, and 7 January, 1957; AP 33/8. Brook to Eden, 8 January, 1957; Kilmuir, *op. cit.*, 283.
128 The announcement was made at first privately to Macmillan, and then to the Cabinet: Macmillan(1971), *op. cit.*, 180; Eden (1960), *op. cit.*, 583: Butler was also present at this earlier, private meeting. PRO: CAB 128/30. CM(57) 4, 9 January, 1957.

Conclusion

1 SOHP: Interview with Sir Patrick Dean.
2 For example, see Lucas (1991), *op. cit.*, 143, 188, 267, and Kyle, *op. cit.*, 201, 215, 235 and 438–9. Kyle does recognise Mountbatten's fallible memory and desire to promote himself (136) but still uses him as a source.
3 Kyle, *op. cit.*, 137.

4 Butler interviewed by Anthony Howard, 20 June, 1978, cited in Anthony Howard, *RAB: The Life of R.A.Butler* (London, 1987), 235.
5 PRO: FO 800/716. Foreign Secretary's Engagement Diary for October. Lloyd, *op. cit.*, 188.
6 AP 23/11/38. Eden to Lord Boyd, 19 July, 1966.
7 WCP.MS.William Clark.160. Diary entry for 4–5 November, 1956.
8 AP 23/44/77. Lloyd to Eden, 12 August, 1966. Macmillan (1971), *op. cit.*, 106–7.
9 Alistair Horne, 'Yes Suez Did Help Mac.', *The Spectator*, vol. 277, no. 8781, 2 November, 1996.
10 WCP.MS.William Clark.160. Diary entry for 4–5 November, 1956; Shuckburgh, *op. cit.*, 366.
11 For example: SOHP: Interviews with Sir Frederick Bishop, Sir Douglas Dodds-Parker, Sir Evelyn Shuckburgh. Sir Denis Wright, *op. cit.*, 303; Notes made in lieu of a diary, for Sunday 4 November, 1956; Iverach McDonald in conversation with the author, 24 February, 1998.
12 Lord Hailsham, *A Sparrow's Flight: Memoirs* (London, 1991), 289–90.
13 AP 23/56/10. Brook to Eden, 8 November, 1956.
14 Nutting's resignation was not announced until 5 November. AP 20/49: in particular, see AP 20/49/36A and AP 20/49/39. Macmillan 'implored Nutting not to publish what would make people "spit at me, an old man in the street"': AP 23/43/76. Lord Lambton to Eden, 21 July, 1966. For details of the inaccuracies which Eden believed existed in Nutting's account, see: AP 20/49/28B.
15 They were: (1) 'because what Great Britain intended to do contravened the agreement that he had signed with Nasser in 1954'; (2) 'because Britain was acting contrary to the spirit of the Tripartite Declaration'; (3) 'because Britain was breaking the United Nations Charter': SELO 236(3).
16 AP 33/7iii. Note re: Selwyn Lloyd's visit the previous week, dated 30 September, 1971. See also Rhodes James, *op. cit.*, 571.
17 Lucas, *op. cit.*, 221; Kyle, *op. cit.*, 87: *Punch* portrayed Nutting as a glove puppet, labelled 'Eden's Eden'; Dutton, *op. cit.*, 459; Rhodes James, *op. cit.*, 344 and 571.
18 Clark, *op. cit.*, 146–8; WCP.MS.William Clark.160. Diary entry for 4–5 November, 1956.
19 WCP.MS.William Clark.160. Diary entry for 30 October, 1956.
20 Harold Watkinson, *Turning Points: A Record of Our Times* (Salisbury, 1986), 64; Reginald Maudling, *Memoirs* (London, 1978), 63.
21 Lord Home, *The Way the Wind Blows: An Autobiography* (London, 1977), 287–95 and 138. See also 'A Canal Too Far'.
22 Kilmuir, *op. cit.*, 274.
23 SOHP: Interview with Sir Guy Millard; Interview with Sir Guy Millard conducted by the author, 25 February, 1998.
24 See the variety of letters sent to Eden post-Suez: AP 14/4, 5 and 6; AP 15/5; AP 17/1; AP 18/1 and 2; AP 20/36/1–5; AP 23–27.
25 For a discussion of the sense of duty felt by the Civil Service and Ministers, see Hennessy (1990) *op. cit.*, 164–8.
26 For example, see the use of Sir Richard Powell and Sir Donald Logan by Kyle and Lucas.
27 Lucas (1991), *op. cit.*, 166.
28 AP 23/56/15A. Brook to Eden, 14 May, 1958.
29 For press reaction, cf. Introduction, 7–8. For French reaction, cf. Chapter 2, 44–8 and Chapter 4, 94.

30 For example, see: Colin Seymour-Ure, '"War Cabinets", in Limited Wars: Korea, Suez and the Falklands', *Public Administration*, vol. 62, no. 2, Summer, 1984, or Peter Hennessy, 'A Question of Control: UK "War Cabinets" and Limited Conflicts Since 1945', at the Annual Ceser Guest Lecture, University of the West of England, Bristol, May, 1996.
31 Lucas (1991), *op. cit.*, 220; Kyle, *op. cit.*, 277–8, remains undecided.
32 SOHP: Interview with Sir Evelyn Shuckburgh.
33 Butler, *op. cit.*, 195.
34 For Eden's deterioration, see Carlton, *op. cit.*, 466–9 and Rhodes James, *op. cit.*, 602–20. See also the myriad letters between Eden and old colleagues post-Suez.
35 Kyle, *op. cit.*, 144 and Thomas, *op. cit.*, chapter 2, 38–52.
36 Some historians have argued that had Macmillan remained at the Foreign Office, Anglo-American communication could have continued at a high and uncompromised level. However, Macmillan's overriding goal throughout the crisis was to use force, which the Eisenhower Administration were against. Macmillan always believed that he could influence the Americans but they could not condone his bellicosity.
37 For details of the American efforts to derive a solution, 'BETA', see Lucas (1991), *op. cit.*, 87–9; Kyle, *op. cit.*, 96–9.
38 PRO: FO 800/747. A. W. Snelling (at the Commonwealth Relations Office) to Lloyd, 1 August, 1956.
39 Dodds-Parker, *op. cit.*, 101.
40 SOHP: Interview with Sir William Hayter.
41 See WCP.MS.William Clark.160. Diary entries for October, 1956; SOHP: Interview with Sir Frederick Bishop; Shuckburgh, *op. cit.*, 35.
42 It had been hoped that an American would lead the delegation to see Nasser. Cf. Chapter 2, 51–2.
43 Interview with Anthony Nutting conducted by Peter Hennessy, cited in 'A Canal Too Far', 2. SELO 129 (1); Dodds-Parker, *op. cit.*, 102.
44 WP. Reilly to Wright, 1 August, 1986. (Date believed to be 1986 but partially obscured.)
45 Clark cited in 'Suez 1956: Neither War Nor Peace At 10 Downing Street'. Lloyd argued similarly: Lloyd, *op. cit.*, 84.
46 PRO: T236/4834. Meetings of Treasury Officials to co-ordinate policy over Suez Canal Crisis 24.8.56 to 8.10.56.
47 Nicolson (ed.) (1971), *op. cit.*, 282. Diary entry for 2 August, 1956.
48 Clark cited in 'Suez 1956: Neither War Nor Peace At 10 Downing Street'.
49 *Ibid.*
50 SOHP: Interview with Sir Frederick Bishop.
51 PRO: PREM 11/1100. No. 2010. Trevelyan to F.O., 9 September, 1956. Nasser's reply to Menzies.
52 PRO: PREM 11/1177. No. 4061. Eden to Eisenhower, 6 September, 1956; PREM 11/1099. Eden note written 12 August, 1956.
53 PRO: CAB 134/1216. EC(56) 26, 10 September, 1956. Although they were never 100 per cent certain that the American proposal for SCUA would develop.
54 Cf. Chapter 5, 209.

Bibliography

NB: The American Private and Public Papers listed here were consulted via correspondence. Any other US source referred to in the text was cited from a secondary source and has been footnoted as such.

Private Papers

United Kingdom
Alan Lennox-Boyd Papers, Bodleian Library, Oxford.
Avon Papers, Heslop Room, University of Birmingham.
Beaverbrook Papers, House of Lords Record Office, London.
Brendan Bracken Papers, Churchill College, Cambridge.
Butler Papers, Trinity College, Cambridge.
Cilcennin Papers, Carmarthenshire County Archives, Carmarthen, Wales.
Sir William Dickson Papers, Churchill College, Cambridge.
Duncan-Sandys Papers, Churchill College, Cambridge.
Gilbert Murray Papers, Bodleian Library, Oxford.
Gore-Booth Papers, Bodleian Library, Oxford.
Hayter Papers, in the private possession of Lady Hayter.
Kilmuir Papers, Churchill College, Cambridge.
Macmillan Papers, Bodleian Library, Oxford.
Norman Brook Papers, Bodleian Library, Oxford.
Selwyn Lloyd Papers, Churchill College, Cambridge.
Walter Monckton Papers, Bodleian Library, Oxford.
William Clark Papers, Bodleian Library, Oxford.
William Haley Papers, Churchill College, Cambridge.
Wright Papers, in the private possession of Sir Denis Wright.

United States
Bruce Lockhart Papers, Lilly Library, Indiana University, Bloomington, Indiana.
John Foster Dulles Oral History, Seeley G. Mudd Manuscript Library, Princeton.

Public and Institutional Records

United Kingdom

PRO	Public Record Office, Kew, London:
CAB 128	Cabinet Meetings
CAB 129	Cabinet Memoranda
CAB 131	Defence Committee
CAB 134/1216	Egypt Committee Meetings
CAB 134/1217	Egypt Committee Memoranda
DEFE 4	Chiefs of Staff Committee Meetings
DEFE 5	Chiefs of Staff Memoranda

DEFE 32	Chiefs of Staff, Secretary's Standard File
FO 371	General Foreign Office Files
FO 800	Foreign Secretary's Private Files
PREM 11	Prime Minister's Files
T	Treasury Files
WO32	War Office Files on Suez Crisis

United States

NAW	National Archives, Washington
NACP	National Archives, College Park
RG218	Records of the Joint Chiefs of Staff
RG263	Records of the Central Intelligence Agency

Other Records

Cartoon Centre, University of Kent, Canterbury.
Liddell Hart Archive (Suez Oral History Project), Liddell Hart Centre For Military Archives, King's College, University of London.
The Times News Library Archive, News International, London.

Published Official Documents and Records

United Kingdom
Hansard, House of Commons Debates, 1955–57.
HMSO, *Agreement between the Government of Great Britain and Northern Ireland and the Egyptian Government regarding the Suez Canal Base* (October 1954).
HMSO, *The Suez Canal Conference [Selected Documents]* (September 1956).
HMSO, *Exchange of Correspondence between the Suez Committee and the President of the Republic of Egypt regarding the future operation of the Suez Canal, Cairo, 3–9 September, 1956* (September 1956).
HMSO, *The Amphetamines and Lysergic Acid Diethylamide Report* (1970).

United States
FRUS: *Foreign Relations of the United States* (Washington, DC, 1979–90):
  1955–7, Volume XIV: The Arab-Israeli Dispute, 1955.
  1955–7, Volume XV: The Arab-Israeli Dispute, 1 January–26 July, 1956.
  1955–7, Volume XVI: The Suez Crisis, 26 July–31 December, 1956.

France
DDF: *Documents Diplomatiques Français 1956 Tome II: 1 Juillet–23 Octobre* (Paris, 1989).
  Documents Diplomatiques Français 1956 Tome III: 24 Octobre–31 Decembre (Paris, 1990).

Contemporary Press and Periodical Literature

The following have been consulted for 1955–56:

Daily Express, Daily Telegraph, Morning Post, Daily Worker, Le Monde, Manchester Guardian, New York Times, The Economist, The Listener, The New Statesman and Nation, The Observer, The Spectator, The Sunday Times, The Times.

Books and Articles

ADAMS, Sherman, *First Hand Report* (London, 1962).
ADAMTHWAITE, Anthony, 'Overstretched and Overstrung: Eden, the Foreign Office and the Making of Policy, 1951–55', *International Affairs*, vol. 64, no. 2, Spring, 1988.
ADAMTHWAITE, Anthony, 'Suez Revisited', *International Affairs*, vol. 64, no. 3, Summer, 1988.
ALDRICH, Richard J., 'Intelligence, Anglo-American Relations and the Suez Crisis, 1956', *Intelligence and National Security*, vol. 9, no. 3, July, 1994.
ALDRICH, Winthrop, 'The Suez Crisis: A Footnote to History', *Foreign Affairs*, April, 1967.
ALLEN, W. Gore, *The Reluctant Politician: Derick Heathcoat Amory* (London, 1958).
AMBROSE, Stephen E., *Eisenhower, The President 1952–1969* (London, 1984).
ARONSON, Geoffrey, *From Side Show to Center Stage: U.S. Policy Towards Egypt* (Boulder, 1986).
ARONSON, Geoffrey, *Settlement and the Israel–Palestinian Negotiation: An Overview* (Washington, 1996).
ASTER, Sidney, *Anthony Eden* (London, 1976).
AYERST, David, *Guardian: Biography of a Newspaper* (London, 1971).
AZEAU, Henri, *Le Piège de Suez* (Paris, 1964).
BAEYENS, Jacques, *Un Coup d'Épée Dans L'Eau Du Canal: La Seconde Campaigne D'Egypte* (Paris, 1976).
BARDENS, Denis, *Portrait of a Statesman: The Personal Life Story of Sir Anthony Eden* (London, 1955).
BARJOT, Admiral Pierre, 'Reflexions surs les opérations de Suez, 1956', *Revue du Defense Nationale*, 22, 1966.
BARKER, A. J., *Suez: The Seven-Day War* (London, 1964).
BAR-ON, Mordechai, 'David Ben-Gurion and the Sèvres Collusion', in William Roger Louis and Roger Owen (eds), *Suez 1956: The Crisis and Its Consequences* (Oxford, 1989).
BAR-ON, Mordechai, *The Gates of Gaza: Israel's Road to Suez and Back, 1955–57* (Basingstoke, 1994).
BAR-ZOHAR, Michel, *Suez: Ultra-Secret* (Paris, 1965).
BEAUFRE, General André, *L'Expedition de Suez* (Paris, 1967).
BEAUFRE, General André (R. H. Barry trans.) *The Suez Expedition 1956* (London, 1969).
BEVAN, Aneurin, 'Suez: The Excuses are Demolished', *The Tribune*, 7 December 1956.
BIRKENHEAD, Lord, *Walter Monckton: The Life of Viscount Monckton of Brenchley* (London, 1969).
BLACK, Ian and MORRIS, Benny, *Israel's Secret Wars: The Untold History of Israel Intelligence* (London, 1991).
BLAKE Roger and LOUIS, William Roger (eds), *Churchill* (Oxford, 1994).
BOHLEN, Charles, *Witness to History* (New York, 1973).
BOOTHBY, Lord, *My Yesterday, Your Tomorrow* (London, 1962).

BOWIE, Robert R., *Suez 1956: International Crisis and the Role of Law* (London, 1974).
BOWIE, Robert R., 'Eisenhower, Dulles, and the Suez Crisis', in William Roger Louis and Roger Owen (eds), *Suez 1956: The Crisis and Its Consequences* (Oxford, 1989).
BOYLE, Peter G. (ed.), *The Churchill–Eisenhower Correspondence 1953–1955* (Chapel Hill, 1990).
BRADDON, Russell, *Suez: Splitting of a Nation* (London, 1973).
BRADY, C., 'Sir Donald Logan', British Officials and the Suez Crisis Conference, University of Westminster, 10 December 1996.
BRADY, C., 'The Cabinet System and Management of the Suez Crisis', *Contemporary British History*, vol. 11, no. 2, Summer, 1997.
BROAD, Lewis, *Anthony Eden: The Chronicles of a Career* (London, 1955).
BROMBERGER, Merry and BROMBERGER, Serge, *Secrets of Suez* (London, 1957).
BUTLER, R. A., *The Art of the Possible: The Memoirs of Lord Butler* (Harmondsworth, 1973).
CAMPBELL, John, *Edward Heath: A Biography* (London, 1993).
CAMPBELL-JOHNSON, Alan, *Sir Anthony Eden* (London, 1955).
CARLTON, David, *Anthony Eden* (London, 1986).
CARLTON, David, *Britain and the Suez Crisis* (London, 1988).
CATO, *Guilty Men* (London, 1940).
CHALLE, Maurice, *Notre Révolte* (Paris, 1968).
CHARLTON, Michael and CLARK, William, 'Suez: An Unofficial Chronicle', *The Listener*, 22 November 1979.
CHARMLEY, John, *Duff Cooper* (London, 1987).
CHAUVEL, Jean, *Commentaire Volume III: 1952–1962* (Paris, 1973).
CHILDERS, Erskine B., *The Road to Suez: A Study of Western–Arab Relations* (London, 1962).
CHURCHILL, Sir Randolph, *The Rise and Fall of Sir Anthony Eden* (London, 1959).
CLARK, William, 'Turmoil in the Middle East', *The Listener*, 11 November 1956.
CLARK, William, 'Suez', *The Observer*, 3 October 1976.
CLARK, William, *From Three Worlds: Memoirs* (London, 1986).
CLOAKE, John, *Templer, Tiger of Malaya: The Life of Field Marshall Sir Gerald Templer* (London, 1985).
COCKERELL, Michael, *Live from Number 10: The Inside Story of Prime Ministers and Television* (London, 1988).
COCKERELL, Michael, HENNESSY, Peter and WALKER, David, *Sources Close to the Prime Minister: Inside the Hidden World of the News Manipulators* (London, 1984).
COCKETT, Richard, 'The Observer and the Suez Crisis', *Contemporary Record*, vol. 5, no. 1, Summer, 1991.
COLVILLE, John, *Footprints in Time* (London, 1976).
COLVILLE, John, *The New Elizabethans 1962–1977* (London, 1977).
COLVILLE, John, *The Churchillians* (London, 1981).
COLVILLE, John, *The Fringes of Power, 10 Downing Street Diaries 1939–1955* (London, 1986).
CONNELL, John, *The Most Important Country: The True Story of the Suez Crisis and the Early Events Leading to It* (London, 1957).
CONNELL, P. H., *Amphetamine Psychosis* (Oxford, 1958).
COOK, Blanche, *The Declassified Eisenhower* (New York, 1981).
COOPER, Chester L., *The Lion's Last Roar: Suez, 1956* (New York, 1978).
COOPER, Duff, *Old Men Forget* (London, 1957).
COOTE, Sir Colin, *Editorial: The Memoirs of Colin R. Coote* (London, 1965).

COPELAND, Miles, *The Game of Nations: The Amorality of Power Politics* (London, 1970).
COUNCIL ON FOREIGN RELATIONS, *Documents of American Foreign Relations* (New York, 1956–57): 1955 and 1956.
COX, Geoffrey, *See It Happen: The Making of ITN* (London, 1983).
CROSBIE, Sylvia K., *A Tacit Alliance: France and Israel from Suez to the Six Day War* (Princeton, 1974).
CUDLIPP, Hugh, *Walking On The Water* (London, 1976).
DAVENPORT-HINES, R. P. T., *The Macmillans* (London, 1992).
DAVIES, Andrew J., *We, The Nation: The Conservative Party and the Pursuit of Power* (London, 1995).
DAYAN, Moshe, *Diary of The Sinai Campaign* (London, 1967).
DAYAN, Moshe, *The Story of My Life* (London, 1976).
DEEDES, William, 'The Forgotten Side of Suez', *The Spectator*, 25 October 1986.
DICKIE, J., *The Uncommon Commoner: A Study of Sir Alec Douglas-Home* (London, 1964).
DIVINE, Robert, *Eisenhower and the Cold War* (Oxford, 1981).
DIXON, Piers, *Double Diploma: The Life of Sir Pierson Dixon, Don and Diplomat* (London, 1968).
DIXON, Piers, 'Eden after Suez', *Contemporary Record*, Summer, 1992.
DODDS-PARKER, Douglas, *Political Eunuch* (Ascot, 1986).
DONOVAN, Robert, *Tumultuous Years* (New York, 1982).
DOOLEY, Howard J., 'Great Britain's "Last Battle" in the Middle East: Notes on Cabinet Planning During the Suez Crisis of 1956', *International History Review*, August, 1989.
DOUGLAS-HOME, Alec (see also Home, Lord), *Our European Destiny* (London, 1971).
DRUMMOND, Roscoe and COBLENZ, Gaston, *Duel at the Brink: John Foster Dulles' Command of American Power* (London, 1961).
DULLES, John Foster, 'Policy for Security and Peace', *Foreign Affairs*, April, 1954.
DUTTON, David, 'Living with Collusion: Anthony Eden and the Later History of the Suez Affair', *Contemporary Record*, vol. 5, no. 2, Autumn, 1991.
DUTTON, David, *Anthony Eden: A Life and Reputation* (London, 1997).
EAYERS, J., *The Commonwealth and Suez* (Oxford, 1964).
EBAN, Abba, *An Autobiography* (London, 1979).
ECCLES, David, *Life and Politics: A Moral Diagnosis* (London, 1967).
EDEN, Anthony, *Places in the Sun* (London, 1926).
EDEN, Anthony, *England. A Speech by the Right Honourable Anthony Eden* (London, 1933).
EDEN, Anthony, *British Foreign Policy: being a speech by Anthony Eden to the East and West Fulham Conservative and Unionist Association* (London, 1935).
EDEN, Anthony, *England: A speech at the festival banquet of the Royal Society of St. George on April 26th, 1938* (London, 1938).
EDEN, Anthony, *Foreign Affairs* (London, 1939).
EDEN, Anthony, *Anthony Eden talks with you about U.N.O.* (London, 1946).
EDEN, Anthony, *Freedom and Order: Selected Speeches, 1939–1946* (London, 1947).
EDEN, Anthony, *Days for Decision* (London, 1949).
EDEN, Anthony, 'Britain in World Strategy', *Foreign Affairs*, vol. 29, 1950–51.
EDEN, Anthony, 'Britain's Place in the World', *The Listener*, 3 April 1952.
EDEN, Anthony, 'Britain's Foreign Policy', *The Listener*, 10 August 1952.
EDEN, Anthony, 'The Aims of Britain's Foreign Policy', *The Listener*, 8 April 1953.
EDEN, Sir Anthony, 'General Election Broadcast', *The Listener*, 12 May 1955.

EDEN, Sir Anthony, 'The United Nations. Hopes and Achievement', *The Listener*, 30 June 1955.
EDEN, Sir Anthony, 'Impressions of the Geneva Conference', *The Listener*, 4 August 1955.
EDEN, Sir Anthony, 'Impressions of the Anglo-Soviet Talks', *The Listener*, 3 May 1956.
EDEN, Sir Anthony, 'A Very Grave Situation', *The Listener*, 16 August 1956. Originally broadcast on 8 August 1956.
EDEN, Sir Anthony, 'Government Policy in the Middle East', *The Listener*, 8 November 1956. Originally broadcast on 3 November 1956.
EDEN, Sir Anthony, *Memoirs: Full Circle* (London, 1960).
EDEN, Sir Anthony, 'The Slender Margin of Safety', *Foreign Affairs*, January, 1961.
EDEN, Sir Anthony, 'Forty Years On', *Foreign Affairs*, October, 1962.
EDEN, Anthony (as the Earl of Avon), *Memoirs: Facing the Dictators* (London, 1962).
EDEN, Anthony (as the Earl of Avon), *Memoirs: The Reckoning* (London, 1965).
EDEN, Sir Anthony, 'The Burden of Leadership', *Foreign Affairs*, January, 1966.
EDEN, Sir Anthony, *Towards Peace in Indochina* (London, 1966).
EDEN, Sir Anthony, *Another World 1897–1917* (New York, 1977).
EDEN, Anthony, with MACKLEISH, Archibald, *Total War and the People's Peace: Four Addresses by American Leaders* (London, 1942).
EDEN, Anthony, with WALLACE, Henry A., *America Looks to the Future: Four Speeches by American Statesmen* (London, 1942).
EDEN, Sir Timothy, *Tribulations of a Baronet* (London, 1933).
EISENHOWER, Dwight D., *The White House Years: Mandate for Change, 1953–56* (London, 1963).
EISENHOWER, Dwight D., *The White House Years: Waging Peace, 1956–61* (London, 1966).
ÉLY, Paul, *Mémoires: II: Suez... Le 13 Mai* (Paris, 1969).
EPSTEIN, Leon D., *British Politics in the Suez Crisis* (London, 1964).
EVANS, Harold, *Downing Street Diary: The Macmillan Years 1957–63* (London, 1981).
EVELAND, Wilbur, *Ropes of Sand: America's Failure in the Middle East* (London, 1980).
FARNIE, D. A., *East and West of Suez: The Suez Canal in History* (Oxford, 1969).
FAWZI, Mahmoud, *Suez 1956: An Egyptian Experience* (London, 1987).
FEIS, Herbert, 'Anthony Eden and the Cacophony of Nations', *Foreign Affairs*, October, 1965.
FERRELL, Robert H. (ed.), *The Eisenhower Diaries* (New York, 1981).
FERRO, Marc, *Suez: naissance d'un tiers monde* (Brussels, 1982).
FINER, Herman, *Dulles Over Suez: The Theory and Practice of His Diplomacy* (Chicago, 1964).
FISHER, Nigel, *Iain Macleod* (London, 1973).
FISHER, Nigel, *Harold Macmillan* (London, 1982).
FOOT, M. and JONES, M., *Guilty Men* (London, 1957).
FOREIGN POLICY ASSOCIATION, *Nationalisation of the Suez Canal Company* (1970).
FREIBERGER, Steven Z., *Dawn Over Suez: The Rise of American Power in the Middle East, 1953–1957* (Chicago, 1992).
FRY, Michael Graham, 'Decline, Sanctions and the Suez Crisis, 1956–57', *Diplomatic History*, vol. 17, Spring, 1993.
FULLICK, Roy and POWELL, Geoffrey, *Suez: The Double War* (London, 1990).
GAITSKELL, Hugh, 'The Case Against the Government', *The Listener*, 8 November 1956. Originally broadcast on 4 November 1956.

GAUJAC, Paul, *Suez 1956* (Paris, 1986).
GAZIT, Mordechai, 'American and British Diplomacy and the Bernadotte Mission', *The Historical Journal*, September, 1986.
GEORGES-PICOT, Jacques, *The Real Suez Crisis: The End of A Great Nineteenth Century Work* (New York, 1978).
GILBERT, Martin, *Never Despair, Winston Churchill 1945–1965* (London, 1990).
GLADWYN, Lord, *Memoirs* (London, 1972).
GLUBB, J. B., *A Soldier with the Arabs* (London, 1957).
GOLDSMITH, Chris, 'Sir Gladwyn Jebb', British Officials and the Suez Crisis Conference, University of Westminster, 10 December 1996.
GOODHEART, Philip, *The 1922: The Story of the 1922 Committee* (London, 1973).
GOOLD-ADAMS, Richard, *The Time of Power: A Reappraisal of John Foster Dulles* (London, 1962).
GORE-BOOTH, Paul, *With Great Truth and Respect* (London, 1974).
GORST, Anthony, 'Suez 1956: A Consumer's Guide to the Papers at the Public Record Office', *Contemporary Record*, vol. 1, Spring, 1987.
GORST, Anthony and JOHNMAN, Lewis, *The Suez Crisis* (London, 1997).
GORST, Anthony, JOHNMAN, Lewis and LUCAS, W. Scott (eds), *Post-War Britain, 1945–64: Themes and Perspectives* (London, 1989).
GORST, Anthony and LUCAS, W. Scott, 'The Other Collusion: Operation *Straggle* and Anglo-American Intervention in Syria, 1955–56', *Intelligence and National Security*, July, 1988.
GORST, Anthony and LUCAS, W. Scott, 'Suez 1956: Strategy and the Diplomatic Process', *Journal of Strategic Studies*, December, 1988.
GREEN, Stephen, *Taking Sides: America's Secret Relations with a Militant Israel, 1948–67* (London, 1984).
GREENSTEIN, Fred I., *The Hidden Hand Presidency: Eisenhower as Leader* (New York, 1982).
GROMYKO, Andrei (Harold Shukman trans.) *Memories: From Stalin to Gorbachev* (London, 1989).
HAILSHAM, Lord, *The Door Wherein I Went* (Glasgow, 1978).
HAILSHAM, Lord, *A Sparrow's Flight: The Memoirs of Lord Hailsham of St Marylebone* (London, 1991).
HARPER, Paul, *The Suez Crisis* (Hove, 1986).
HARRIES, Owen, 'Anthony Eden and the Decline of Britain', *Commentary*, vol. 83, June, 1987.
HAYTER, Sir William, *The Kremlin and the Embassy* (London, 1966).
HAYTER, Sir William, *A Double Life* (London, 1974).
HEATH, Edward, *The Course of My Life: My Autobiography* (London, 1998).
HEIKAL, Mohammed H., *Nasser – The Cairo Documents: The Private Papers of Nasser* (London, 1973).
HEIKAL, Mohammed H., *Cutting the Lion's Tail: Suez Through Egyptian Eyes* (London, 1986).
HEIKAL, Mohammed H., *Secret Channels: The Inside Story of the Arab-Israeli Peace Negotiations* (London, 1996).
HENDERSON, John T. and AMNON, Til, 'Leadership, Personality and War: The Cases of Richard Nixon and Anthony Eden', *Political Science Quarterly*, vol. 28, December, 1976.
HENNESSY, Peter, *Cabinet* (Oxford, 1986).
HENNESSY, Peter, 'Suez 30 Years On: The Secrets Which Will Stay Secret For Ever', *The Listener*, 11 September 1986.

HENNESSY, Peter, 'Through Egyptian Eyes', *The New Statesman*, 14 November 1986.
HENNESSY, Peter, 'No End of an Argument, *Contemporary Record*, Spring, 1987.
HENNESSY, Peter, 'The Scars of Suez: Reopening the Wounds of Empire', *The Listener*, 5 February 1987.
HENNESSY, Peter, 'Permanent Government: Suez and the Ponting Factors', *New Statesman*, 6 February 1987.
HENNESSY, Peter, *Moneybags and Brains: The Anglo-American Relationship Since 1945* (Glasgow, 1990).
HENNESSY, Peter, *Whitehall* (London, 1990).
HENNESSY, Peter, 'What the Queen Knew', *The Independent*, 21 December 1994.
HENNESSY, Peter, *Muddling Through: Power, Politics and the Quality of Government in Post-War Britain* (London, 1996).
HENNESSY, Peter, 'A Question of Control: UK "War Cabinets" and Limited Conflicts Since 1945', at the Annual Ceser Guest Lecture, University of the West of England, Bristol, May 1996.
HENNESSY, Peter, *The Prime Minister: The Office and its Holders Since 1945* (London, 2000).
HENNESSY, Peter and LAITY, Mark, 'Suez – What the Papers Say', *Contemporary Record*, vol. 1, no. 1, Spring, 1987.
HENNESSY, Peter and SELDON, Anthony (eds), *Ruling Performance: British Governments from Attlee to Thatcher* (Oxford, 1987).
HENRIQUES, Robert, *One Hundred Hours to Suez: An Account of Israel's Campaign in the Sinai Peninsula* (London, 1957).
HENRIQUES, Robert, 'The Ultimatum: A Dissenting View', *The Spectator*, 6 November 1959.
HENRIQUES, Robert, 'The Ultimatum', *The Spectator*, 4 December 1959.
HETHERINGTON, Alastair, *Guardian: Biography of a Newspaper* (London, 1971).
HEUSTON, R. F. V., *Lives of the Lord Chancellors 1885–1940* (Oxford, 1964).
HOME, Lord (see also Douglas-Home, Sir Alec), *The Way the Wind Blows: An Autobiography* (London, 1977).
HOOPES, Townsend, *The Devil and John Foster Dulles: The Diplomacy of the Eisenhower Era* (Boston, 1973).
HORNE, Alistair, *Macmillan, Volume I, 1894–1956* (London, 1988).
HORNE, Alistair, *Macmillan, Volume II, 1957–69* (London, 1989).
HORNE, Alistair, 'Yes Suez Did Help Mac.', *The Spectator*, vol. 277, no. 8781, 2 November, 1996.
HOWARD, Anthony, *RAB: The Life of R. A. Butler* (London, 1987).
HOWARD, Anthony, 'The Real Demon King of Suez', *The Times Literary Supplement*, 24 May 1991.
HOWARD, Anthony and WEST, Richard, *The Making of the Prime Minister* (London, 1965).
HUDSON, W. J., *Blind Loyalty: Australia and the Suez Crisis, 1956* (Melbourne University Press, 1989).
HUGHES, Emmet, *The Ordeal of Power: The Inside Story of the Eisenhower Administration* (London, 1963).
HUGHES, Emrys, *Macmillan: Portrait of a Politician* (London, 1962).
HUTCHINSON, George, *The Last Edwardian At No. 10: An Impression of Harold Macmillan* (London, 1980).
HYDE, H. Montgomery, *Walter Monckton* (London, 1991).

JAY, Douglas, *Change and Fortune: A Political Record* (London, 1980).
JENNINGS, Sir Ivor, *Cabinet Government* (Cambridge, 1965).
JOHNMAN, Lewis, 'Defending the Pound: The Economics of Suez Crisis, 1956', in Anthony Gorst, Lewis Johnman and W. Scott Lucas (eds), *Post-War Britain, 1945–64: Themes and Perspectives* (London, 1989).
JOHNMAN, Lewis, 'Sir Gerald Fitzmaurice', British Officials and the Suez Crisis Conference, University of Westminster, 10 December 1996.
JOHNSON, Edward, 'Sir Pierson Dixon', British Officials and the Suez Crisis Conference University of Westminster, 10 December 1996.
JOHNSON, Paul, *The Suez War* (London, 1957).
KEIGHTLEY, General Sir Charles, 'Operations in Egypt, November to December, 1956', *Supplement to the London Gazette*, 10 September 1957.
KELLY, Saul, 'Sir Roger Makins', British Officials and the Suez Crisis Conference, University of Westminster, 10 December 1996.
KHRUSHCHEV, Nikita (Strobe Talbot trans.) *Khrushchev Remembers* (London, 1971).
KILMUIR, Lord, *Political Adventure* (London, 1964).
KINGSEED, Cole C., *Eisenhower and the Suez Crisis of 1956* (Baton Rouge, 1995).
KIRKPATRICK, Ivone, *The Inner Circle* (London, 1959).
KIRKPATRICK, Ivone, *Mussolini: Study of a Demagogue* (London, 1964).
KUNZ, Diane, 'Did Macmillan Lie Over Suez?', *The Spectator*, 3 November 1990.
KUNZ, Diane, *The Economic Diplomacy of the Suez Crisis* (Chapel Hill, 1991).
KYLE, Keith, 'Morality and Conscience in Politics', *The Listener*, 18 May 1967.
KYLE, Keith, 'Death of a Plan', *The Listener*, 13 January 1972.
KYLE, Keith, 'Suez: What Really Happened?', *The Listener*, 11 November 1976.
KYLE, Keith, 'Footnotes to Suez', *The Listener*, 16 December 1976.
KYLE, Keith, 'Interpretations of Suez', *The Listener*, 22 June 1978.
KYLE, Keith, 'Israel Holds The Key to the Last Secret of Suez', *The Listener*, 20 November 1986.
KYLE, Keith, *Suez* (London, 1991).
KYLE, Keith, 'Suez and the Waldegrave Initiative', *Contemporary Record*, vol. 9, no. 2, Autumn, 1995.
KYLE, Keith, 'Sir Norman Brook', British Officials and the Suez Crisis Conference, University of Westminster, 10 December 1996.
L'ETANG, Hugh, *The Pathology of Leadership* (London, 1969).
LAMB, Richard, *The Failure of the Eden Government* (London, 1987).
LAMB, Richard, 'Was Eden's Premiership a Failure?', *Contemporary Record*, vol. 1, no. 4, Winter, 1988.
LAMB, Richard, *The Macmillan Years 1957–1963: The Emerging Truth* (London, 1995).
LANE, Ann, 'Sir Ivone Kirkpatrick', British Officials and the Suez Crisis Conference, University of Westminster, 10 December 1996.
LAPPING, Brian, *End of an Empire* (London, 1986).
LAQUEUR, Walter Z, *Communism and Nationalism in the Middle East* (New York, 1956).
LAQUEUR, Walter Z, *The Israel–Arab Reader: A Documentary History of the Middle East Conflict* (London, 1969).
LAWRENCE, Alan and DODDS, Peter (eds), *Anthony Eden, 1897–1977: A Bibliography* (London, 1995).
LENNOX-BOYD, Alan, 'The Suez Question and the Colonies', *The Listener*, 27 September 1956. Party Political Broadcast originally on 22 September 1956.
LITTLE, Douglas, 'Strategies R Us: America's Road to Suez'?, *Diplomatic History*, vol. 17, Summer, 1993.

LLOYD, Selwyn, 'The London Conference and the Suez Canal', *The Listener*, 16 August 1956.
LLOYD, Selwyn, 'The Government's Middle East Policy', *The Listener*, 15 November 1956. Party Political Broadcast on 7 November 1956.
LLOYD, Selwyn, *Suez 1956, A Personal Account* (London, 1978).
LLOYD, Selwyn and HARRIS, Ken, 'A Foreign Secretary Remembers', *The Listener*, 4 November 1976.
LOCKHART, Sir Robert Bruce, *Friends, Foes and Foreigners* (London, 1957).
LOGAN, Sir Donald, 'Suez: Meetings at Sèvres, 22–25 October, 1956' (24 October 1986, unpublished).
LOGAN, Sir Donald, 'Collusion at Suez', *The Financial Times*, 8 November 1986.
LOUIS, William Roger and BULL, Hedley (eds), *The Special Relationship: Anglo-American Relations since 1945* (Oxford, 1986).
LOUIS, William Roger and OWEN, Roger (eds), *Suez 1956: The Crisis and Its Consequences* (Oxford, 1989).
LOVE, Kennett, *Suez: The Twice Fought War* (London, 1970).
LOW, Anthony and LAPPING, Brian, 'Did Suez Hasten the End of Empire?', *Contemporary Record*, vol. 1, no. 2, Summer, 1987.
LUCAS, W. Scott, 'Suez, the Americans and the Overthrow of Anthony Eden', *LSE Quarterly*, September, 1987.
LUCAS, W. Scott, 'Neustadt Revisited: The Suez Crisis and the Anglo-American Alliance', in Anthony Gorst, Lewis Johnman and W. Scott Lucas (eds), *Post-War Britain, 1945–64: Themes and Perspectives* (London, 1989).
LUCAS, W. Scott, 'Redefining the Suez "Collusion": A Regional Approach', *Middle Eastern Studies*, vol. 26, January, 1990.
LUCAS, W. Scott, 'Biography as History: Eden, Macmillan and Suez', *Contemporary Record*, vol. 2, Spring, 1989.
LUCAS, W. Scott, 'Path to Suez: Britain and the Struggle for the Middle East, 1953–1956', in Anne Deighton (ed.), *Britain and the First Cold War* (London, 1990).
LUCAS, W. Scott, 'NATO, Alliance, and the Suez Crisis', in Beatrice Heuser (ed.), *NATO and the Cold War* (London, 1991).
LUCAS, W. Scott, *Divided We Stand: Britain, the US and the Suez Crisis* (London, 1991).
LUCAS, W. Scott, 'A Most Peculiar War: Britain and the Suez Crisis', *Modern History Review*, vol. 7(2), November, 1995.
LUCAS, W. Scott, *Britain and the Suez Crisis: The Lion's Last Roar* (Manchester University Press, 1996).
LUCAS, W. Scott, *Divided We Stand: Britain, the US and the Suez Crisis* (London, 1996). Revised introduction.
LUCAS, W. Scott, 'Escaping Suez: New Interpretations of Western Policy in the Middle East 1936–1961', *Intelligence and National Security*, vol. 12(2), April, 1997.
LUETHY, Herbert and RODMICH, David, *French Motivations in the Suez Crisis* (Princeton, 1956).
MACKINTOSH, J. P., *The Government and Politics of Britain* (London, 1970).
MACMILLAN, Harold, *Tides of Fortune 1945–1955* (London, 1969).
MACMILLAN, Harold, *Riding The Storm 1956–1959* (London, 1971).
MACMILLAN, Harold, *The Past Masters; Politics and Politicians 1906–39* (London, 1975).
MAKINS, Sir Roger (see also Sherfield, Lord) 'The World Since the War: The Third Phase', *Foreign Affairs*, October, 1954.
MANSFIELD, Peter, *Nasser's Egypt* (Harmondsworth, 1957).

MANSFIELD, Peter, *Nasser* (London, 1970).
MARGACH, James, *The Abuse of Power: The War Between Downing Street and the Media from Lloyd George to Callaghan* (London, 1978).
MASU, Jacques, *Verité sur Suez 1956* (Paris, 1978).
MAUDLING, Reginald, *Memoirs* (London, 1978).
MAY, Annabelle and ROWAN, K. (eds), *Inside Information: British Government and the Media* (London, 1982).
McDERMOTT, Geoffrey, *The Eden Legacy and the Decline of British Diplomacy* (London, 1969).
McDONALD, Iverach, *A Man of The Times: Talks and Travels in a Disrupted World* (London, 1976).
McDONALD, Iverach, *The History of the Times, Volume V: Struggles in War and Peace 1939-1966* (London, 1984).
McGHEE, George C., 'Turkey Joins the West', *Foreign Affairs*, July, 1954.
McGHEE, George C., *Envoy to the Middle World* (New York, 1983).
MEIR, Golda, *My Life* (New York, 1975).
MENZIES, Sir Robert G., *Speech Is Of Time* (London, 1958).
MENZIES, Sir Robert G., *Afternoon Light* (London, 1970).
MONCRIEFF, Anthony (ed.), *Suez: Ten Years After: Broadcasts from the BBC Third Programme* (London, 1967).
MONROE, Elizabeth, *Britain's Moment in the Middle East* (London, 1963 and 1981).
MORAN, Lord, *Churchill: The Struggle for Survival* (London, 1968).
MORGAN, Janet, *The Backbench Diaries of Richard Crossman* (London, 1981).
MORRIS, Benny, *Israel's Border Wars 1949-56: An Arab Infiltration, Israeli Retaliation and the Countdown to the Suez War* (Oxford, 1993).
MOSLEY, Leonard, *Dulles: A Biography of Eleanor, Allen and John Foster Dulles and Their Family Network* (New York, 1978).
MURPHY, Robert, *Diplomat Among Warriors* (London, 1984).
NASSER, Gamal Abdul, *Egypt's Liberation: The Philosophy of the Revolution* (Washington, 1955).
NASSER, Gamal Abdul, 'The Egyptian Revolution', *Foreign Affairs*, January, 1955.
NASSER, Gamal Abdul, 'My Side of Suez', *The Sunday Times*, 24 June 1962.
NEFF, Donald, *Warriors at Suez: Eisenhower Takes America into the Middle East* (New York, 1981).
NEGRINE, Ralph, 'The Press and the Suez Crisis: A Myth Re-examined', *The Historical Journal*, vol. 25, 1982.
NEWMAN, Sarah, 'The Commonwealth and the Suez Crisis of 1956', *Contemporary Review*, vol. 259, October, 1991.
NICOLSON, Nigel (ed.), *Harold Nicolson: Diaries and Letters 1930-39* (London, 1970).
NICOLSON, Nigel (ed.), *Harold Nicolson: Diaries and Letters 1939-45* (London, 1970).
NICOLSON, Nigel (ed.), *Harold Nicolson: Diaries and Letters 1945-62* (London, 1971).
NICOLSON, Nigel, *Long Life: Memoirs* (London, 1997).
NUTTING, Anthony, *I Saw for Myself: The Aftermath of Suez* (London, 1958).
NUTTING, Anthony, *Disarmament, an Outline of the Negotiations* (London, 1959).
NUTTING, Anthony, *No End of a Lesson: The Story of Suez* (London, 1967).
NUTTING, Anthony, *Nasser* (London, 1972).
NUTTING, Anthony, 'Sir Anthony Eden', in Herbert Van Thal (ed.), *The Prime Ministers* (Vol. II. London, 1975).
NUTTING, Anthony, 'Another Eden', *The Spectator*, 1 May 1976.
NUTTING, Anthony, 'Collusions and Delusions', *The Spectator*, 8 July 1978.

NUTTING, Anthony, *No End of a Lesson: The Story of Suez* (London, 1996), with a revised introduction.
OREN, Michael B, 'Secret Egyptian–Israeli Peace Initiatives Prior to the Suez Campaign', *Middle East Journal*, vol. 26, July, 1990.
PACH, Chester and RICHARDSON, Elmo, *The Presidency of Dwight D. Eisenhower* (Lawrence, Kansas, 1991).
PARMENTIER, Guillaume, *The British Press in the Suez Intervention* (Paris, 1978).
PARMENTIER, Guillaume, 'The British Press in the Suez Crisis', *The Historical Journal*, vol. 23, no. 2, 1990.
PEARSON, Lester, *Memoirs, Volume II, 1948–57: The International Years* (London, 1974).
PELLING, Henry, *Winston Churchill* (London, 1974).
PELLING, Henry, *Churchill's Peacetime Ministry, 1951–55* (London, 1997).
PERES, Shimon, *David's Sling* (London, 1970).
PERES, Shimon, *Battling For Peace: Memoirs* (London, 1995).
PETERS, A. R., *Anthony Eden at the Foreign Office 1931–1938* (New York, 1986).
PFEIFFER, Rolf, 'New Zealand and the Suez Crisis of 1956', *Journal of Imperial and Commonwealth History*, vol. 21(1), January, 1993.
PHILBY, Kim, *My Silent War* (New York, 1968).
PICKERING, Jeffrey, *Britain's Withdrawal from East of Suez* (London, 1998).
PICKLES, Dorothy, *The Uneasy Entente: French Foreign Policy and Franco-British Misunderstanding* (OUP, 1996).
PINEAU, Christian, *1956: Suez* (Paris, 1976).
RAMSDEN, James, 'Rab did Miss Tricks which Macmillan Managed to Take', *The Listener*, 19 March 1987.
RAMSDEN, James, *The Age of Churchill and Eden* (London, 1995).
RANELAGH, John, *The Agency: The Rise and Fall of the CIA* (London, 1987).
RATHMELL, Andrew, *Secret War in the Middle East: The Covert Struggle for Syria 1949–1961* (London, 1995).
RAWNSLEY, Gary David, 'Cold War Radio in Crisis: The BBC Overseas Services, the Suez Crisis and the 1956 Hungarian Uprising', *Historical Journal of Film, Radio and Television*, vol. 16(2), June, 1996.
RAWNSLEY, Gary David, 'Overt and Covert: The Voice of Britain and Black Radio Broadcasting in the Suez Crisis, 1956', *Intelligence and National Security*, vol. 11(3), June, 1996.
REES-MOGG, William, *Sir Anthony Eden* (London, 1956).
REYNOLDS, David, 'Eden the Diplomatist, 1931–56: Suezide of a Statesman', *History*, February, 1989.
RHODES JAMES, Robert, 'Hugh Gaitskell and Suez', *The Listener*, 13 December 1979.
RHODES JAMES, Robert, 'Eden at Suez: The Diplomat Who Went Uncertainly to War', *The Times*, 27 October 1986.
RHODES JAMES, Robert, 'Anthony Eden and the Suez Crisis', *History Today*, vol. 36, November, 1986.
RHODES JAMES, Robert, *Anthony Eden* (London, 1987).
RICHARDSON, Louise, 'Avoiding and Incurring Losses: Decision-Making during the Suez Crisis', *International Journal*, vol. 47, no. 2, Spring, 1992.
RICHARDSON, Louise, *When Allies Differ: Anglo-American Relations During the Suez and Falklands Crises* (Basingstoke, 1996).
ROBERTS, Andrew, *Eminent Churchillians* (London, 1995).
ROBERTSON, Terrance, *Crisis: The Inside Story of the Suez Conspiracy* (London, 1965).

ROOSEVELT, Archie, *For the Lust of Knowing: Memoirs of an Intelligence Officer* (London, 1988).
ROSKILL, Stephen, *Hankey, Man of Secrets. Volume III 1931–1963* (London, 1974).
ROTHWELL, Victor, *Anthony Eden: A Political Biography 1931–57* (Manchester, 1992).
ROYAL INSTITUTE OF INTERNATIONAL RELATIONS, *Documents on International Affairs* 1951–1957 (London, 1954–60).
RUANE, Kevin, 'Eden, the Foreign Office and the War in Indo-China: October 1951 to July 1954', Ph.D., University of Kent, 1991.
RUANE, Kevin, 'Anthony Eden, British Diplomacy and the Origins of the Geneva Conference of 1954', *The Historical Review*, vol. 37, March, 1994.
SAINSBURY, Keith, *The Turning Point* (Oxford, 1986).
SAMPSON, Anthony, *Macmillan, a Study in Ambiguity* (London, 1968).
SELDON, Anthony, *Churchill's Indian Summer: The Conservative Government, 1951–55* (London, 1981).
SELDON, Anthony, 'Prime Ministers and Near Prime Ministers: Lord Hailsham interviewed by Anthony Seldon', *Contemporary Record*, vol. 1, no. 3, Autumn, 1987.
SEYMOUR-URE, Colin, '"War Cabinets", in limited wars: Korea, Suez and the Falklands', *Public Administration*, vol. 62, no. 2, Summer, 1984.
SHAW, Tony, 'Government Manipulation of the Press during the Suez Crisis', *Contemporary Record*, vol. 8, no. 2, 1994.
SHAW, Tony, *Eden, Suez and the Mass Media: Propaganda and Persuasion During the Suez Crisis* (London, 1996).
SHAW, Tony, 'Sir Alexander Cadogan', British Officials and the Suez Crisis Conference, University of Westminster, 10 December 1996.
SHEPHERD, Robert, *Iain Macleod: A Biography* (London, 1994).
SHERFIELD, Lord (see also Makins, Sir Roger), 'The Suez Crisis: The Makins Experience' (unpublished).
SHINWELL, Emanuel, *I've Lived Through It All* (London, 1973).
SHUCKBURGH, Evelyn, *Descent to Suez: Diaries 1951–1956* (London, 1986).
SLADE-BAKER, J. B., 'Can the Anglo-American Gulf be Bridged?', *The Listener*, 18 March 1954.
SPIEGEL, Steven L., *The Other Arab-Israeli Conflict: Making America's Middle East Policy from Truman to Reagan* (Chicago, 1985).
STEVENSON, Sir Ralph, 'Colonel Nasser and the Future of Egypt', *The Listener*, 14 June 1956.
STOCKWELL, General Sir Hugh, 'Suez From the Inside', *The Sunday Telegraph*, 30 October and 6 November 1966.
STOCKWELL, General Sir Hugh, 'A General Remembers: Suez 1956', *The Listener*, 29 November 1979.
STOOKEY, Robert, *America and the Arab States* (New York, 1975).
STRANG, Lord, *The Foreign Office* (London, 1957).
STRANG, Lord, *The Diplomatic Career* (London, 1962).
SUMMERSKILL, W. H., DAVIDSON, Esther, SHERLOCK, Sheila and STEINER, R. E., 'The Neuropsychiatric Syndrome Associated With Hepatic Cirrhosis And An Extensive Portal Collateral Circulation', *Quarterly Journal of Medicine*, New Series, vol. xxv, no. 98, April, 1956.
SWINTON, Earl of, *Sixty Years of Power: Some Memories of the Men Who Wielded It* (London, 1966).
TEMPLETON, Malcolm, *Ties of Blood and Empire: New Zealand's Involvement in Middle East Defence and the Suez Crisis, 1947–57* (Auckland University Press, 1994).

THOMAS, Abel, *Comment Israel Fut Sauve: Les secrets de l'expedition de Suez* (Paris, 1978).
THOMAS, Hugh, *The Establishment: A Symposium* (London, 1959).
THOMAS, Hugh (ed.), *Crisis in the Civil Service* (London, 1968).
THOMAS, Hugh, *The Suez Affair* (Harmondsworth, 1970; 1st edn 1967).
THOMAS, Hugh, 'The Demigod that Failed', *The New Statesman*, 21 January 1977.
THOMAS, Hugh, 'Chronicling the Crisis', *The Times Literary Supplement*, 30 November 1979.
THOMAS, Hugh, *The Beginnings of the Cold War* (London, 1986).
THORNHILL, Michael T., 'Sir Humphrey Trevelyan', British Officials and the Suez Crisis Conference, University of Westminster, 10 December 1996.
THORPE, D. R., *Selwyn Lloyd* (London, 1989).
THORPE, D. R., *Alec Douglas-Home* (London, 1996).
TOURNOUX, J. R., *Secrets d'état: Dien Bien Phu, les Paras l'Algerie, l'affaire Ben Bella, Suez, la cagoule, le 13 mai, de Gaulle au pouvoir* (Paris, 1960).
TREVELYAN, Humphrey, *The Middle East in Revolution* (London, 1970).
TREVELYAN, Humphrey, *Diplomatic Channels* (London, 1974).
TROEN, S. I. and SHEMESH, M. (eds), *The Suez–Sinai Crisis 1956: Retrospective and Reappraisal* (London, 1990).
TRUKHANOVSKII, V. G. (Ruth English trans.), *Anthony Eden* (Moscow, 1984).
TURNER, John, *Macmillan* (London, 1994).
URQUHART, Brian, *Hammarskjöld* (London, 1972).
VERRIER, Anthony, *Through the Looking Glass: British Foreign Policy in an Age of Illusions* (London, 1982).
VERRIER, Anthony, 'Harsh Truth at the Heart of Suez', *The Financial Times*, 22 June 1991.
VERRIER, Anthony, 'Why America Wanted Nasser Down But Not Out', *The Financial Times*, 12 October 1991.
WARNER, Geoffrey, 'Collusion and the Suez Crisis', *International Affairs*, April 1979.
WARNER, Geoffrey, 'The United States and the Suez Crisis', *International Affairs*, vol. 67, April, 1991.
WATKINSON, Harold, *Turning Points: A Record of Our Times* (Salisbury, 1986).
WATT, Donald Cameron, *Documents on the Suez Crisis* (London, 1957).
WEST, Nigel, *The Friends: Britain's Post-War Secret Intelligence Operations* (London, 1990).
WILLIAMS, Philip, *Hugh Gaitskell* (London, 1979).
WILLIAMS, Philip (ed.), *The Diary of Hugh Gaitskell 1945–1956* (London, 1983).
WILSON, Harold, *A Prime Minister on Prime Ministers* (London, 1977).
WINT, Guy and CALVOCORESSI, Peter, *Middle East Crisis* (Harmondsworth, 1957).
WRIGHT, Sir Denis, 'The Memoirs of Sir Denis Wright 1911–1971' (Vol. II, unpublished).
YOUNG, John W., *Cold War Europe 1945–1989: A Political History* (London, 1992).
YOUNG, John W., 'The Geneva Conference of Foreign Ministers, October – November 1955' (Diplomatic Studies Programme No. 9, University of Leicester, Department of Politics, September, 1995).
YOUNG, Kenneth, *Sir Alec Douglas Home* (London, 1970).
ZACHER, Mark W., *Dag Hammarskjöld's United Nations* (New York, 1970).
ZIEGLER, Philip, *Mountbatten: The Official Biography* (London, 1985).
ZIEGLER, Philip (ed.), *From Shore to Shore: The Final Years: The Diaries of Earl Mountbatten of Burma 1953–1979* (London, 1989).

ZIEGLER, Philip, 'When Britain Went to War over Suez', *The Sunday Express*, 13 October 1993.

Radio and television documentaries

'Anthony Eden – a Historian's Assessment', Martin Gilbert in conversation with Douglas Stuart for BBC Radio 4, *The World Tonight*, partial transcript in *The Listener*, 20 January 1977.

'Grim Times When the Cupboard Was Bare', interview with Kenneth Harris for BBC1, *The Reckoning*, partial transcript in *The Listener*, 13 January 1977.

Suez 1956: Neither War Nor Peace At 10 Downing Street: William Clark in Conversation with Michael Carlton, BBC Radio 3, recorded 10 October, transmission 22 November 1979.

A Canal Too Far, BBC Radio 3, presented 31 January 1986.

Secrets of Suez, BBC 2, presented 12 November 1986.

Living with Anthony, BBC Radio 4, presented 1990.

The Suez Crisis, BBC TV, presented 1996.

Index

Acheson, Dean, 14, 18
Aldrich, Winthrop, 21, 120, 163, 166
Alexander, Harold, 32
ALPHA, 14, 16, 18, 20, 264
Amery, Julian, 7, 45, 140, 141, 159, 168
Amory, Derick Heathcoat, 159
Amory, Robert, 160
Ardalan, Ali Qoli, 59
Asquith, Herbert, 49
Attlee, Clement, 8, 68

Baghdad Pact, 10, 12, 21, 40, 175
Barjot, Pierre, 44
Bar-On, Mordechai, 151
Beeley, Harold, 54
Bedell-Smith, Walter, 165
Ben-Gurion, David, 94, 121, 149, 151, 152
Berry, Pamela, 7
Biggs-Davidson, 140
Bishop, Frederick, 14, 16, 21, 28, 33, 74, 75, 110, 125, 140, 142, 167
Bohlen, Charles ('Chip'), 57
Bourgès-Manoury, Maurice, 164
Boyle, Dermot, 24, 169
Bracken, Brendan, 167
Brook, Norman, 3, 4, 33, 115, 118, 126, 142, 147, 164, 167, 170, 172, 173
Buchan-Hepburn, Patrick, 159
Bulganin, Nikolai, 16, 57, 112, 161
Butler, R.A. ('Rab'), 17, 28, 56, 105, 106, 109, 111, 121, 127, 142, 143, 149, 159, 163, 164, 166, 167, 168, 169

Caccia, Harold, 21, 31, 32
Canadian reaction to crisis, 28
Canal Users' Association, 4, 26, 47, 64–7, 69, 71–9, 81–94, 98–103, 105, 108, 109, 111, 115–18, 122, 126–31, 133, 135, 136, 138, 143, 147, 149, 169, 179, 180
CASU, *see* Canal Users' Association

Challe, Maurice, 131, 137, 138, 141, 143, 145, 146, 147, 149, 150, 154, 173, 180
Chamberlain, Austin, 10, 177
Chamberlain, Neville, 9
Chapman-Andrews, Edward, 111, 112
Chauvel, Jean, 21, 44, 45, 47, 130, 131, 143
Chiefs of Staff, 22, 23, 24, 25, 38, 46, 47, 68, 69, 139, 161, 165
Churchill, Randolph, 140
Churchill, Winston, 7, 8, 9, 14, 17, 25, 28, 46, 47, 92, 94, 95, 96, 97, 106, 107, 118, 140, 141, 159, 166, 177, 180
CIA, 13, 14, 64, 111
Cilcennin, Lord, 42
Clark, William, 22, 55, 75, 88, 89, 97, 98, 105, 109, 111, 116, 125, 158, 160, 163, 169, 170, 171, 172, 178
collusion, 2, 3, 4, 5, 22, 24, 55, 117, 138, 144, 145, 148, 153, 154, 155, 156, 168, 169, 170, 172
Constantinople Convention, 37, 51, 52, 58, 59, 63, 64, 72, 73, 81, 84, 85, 87, 93, 100, 102, 119, 123, 126, 127, 128, 130, 131, 134, 135
Cooper, Chester, 14, 111, 160, 161
Cooper, Frank, 23, 24, 114, 165
Coote, Colin, 140
Crosthwaite, Moore, 60

Daily Express, 42, 68, 103, 140
Daily Herald, 29
Daily Mail, 29, 42
Daily Mirror, 81
Daily Telegraph, 7, 28, 29, 97, 103, 104, 118, 122, 135, 140, 180
Daily Worker, 81
Davis, William, 55
Dayan, Moshe, 4, 93, 94, 113, 121, 150, 153
D-Day, 55, 59, 62, 68, 72, 139, 178
de Zulueta, Philip, 14

Dean, Patrick, 106, 154, 155, 169
Dickson, William, 24
Dictators, 6, 9, 80, 112, 115, 172, 174
Dillon, Douglas, 75
disgorge, 3, 37, 41, 44, 49, 51, 53, 57, 99, 108
Dixon, Pierson, 84, 99, 113, 158, 160, 161
Douglas, Lewis, 103
Douglas-Home, Alec, 21, 28, 106, 125, 163, 171
dual-track policy, 1, 2, 20, 26, 27, 35, 42, 62, 66, 125
dues, Canal, 30, 48, 51, 65, 67, 76, 78, 83, 84, 86, 88, 89, 90, 98, 101, 104, 109, 110, 117, 128, 129, 131, 132, 134, 135, 136, 147, 149, 179, 180
Dulles, Alles, 64
Dulles, John Foster, 3, 10, 11, 12, 13, 14, 18, 23, 30, 31, 32, 33, 34, 36, 37, 38, 39, 40, 41, 44, 48, 51, 52, 53, 54, 55, 57, 58, 59, 60, 61, 63, 64, 65, 66, 67, 69, 70, 71, 72, 75, 76, 77, 78, 79, 80, 81, 82, 83, 84, 85, 86, 87, 88, 89, 90, 91, 92, 93, 98, 99, 103, 106, 108, 109, 110, 115, 116, 118, 120, 121, 122, 123, 124, 126, 127, 128, 129, 130, 135, 136, 143, 146, 147, 153, 160, 161, 165, 169, 174, 175, 177, 179, 180

Eban, Abba, 128
Eden, Anthony, illness, 2, 9, 11, 15, 17, 97, 111, 120, 125, 126, 138, 143, 156, 165, 166, 171, 173, 180; memoirs, 3, 172; influence of Churchill, 8–9, 46–7, 94–7; policy of 'peace through strength', 10, 34, 37–8, 111; attitude towards Soviets, 11, 56–7; relationship with Eisenhower, 14; relationship with Dulles, 14–15; character, 15–16, 176; nationalisation of the Canal, 21–2; policy to reinternationalise Canal, 25–6; relationship with Iverach McDonald, 27; meeting with newspaper editors, 43; fear of possible Israeli involvement, 45; withholding of transit dues, 48; fear of public support for force, 48–9; reaction to Menzies Mission, 59, 61–3, 177, 179; belief in a canal users' association, 63, 66, 67, 73, 88, 179–80; fears of military plan, 67–9; move to UN, 69–75, 82, 98–100, 179; hospitalised, 125; rejection of Menon proposals, 127; belief in Security Council, 134; October 14 meeting, 138; influence of Suez Group, 140–1; decision to use force, 145–8; leaves country, 165–6; resignation, 168; effect of dictators on, 174; importance of collective responsibility of government, 178
Eden, Clarissa, 16, 125
Eden Must Go Campaign, 7
Egypt Committee, 23, 27, 37, 38, 40, 42, 46, 48, 50, 52, 54, 55, 59, 60, 62, 68, 69, 71, 72, 79, 82, 84, 102, 103, 106, 111, 113, 114, 122, 125, 127, 129, 136, 143, 145, 149, 152, 156, 157, 160, 169, 171, 172, 173, 177, 178, 179
1888 Convention, *see* Constantinople Convention
Eighteen Power Resolution, 60
Eisenhower, Dwight D., 6, 10, 11, 14, 18, 23, 26, 27, 29, 30, 31, 32, 33, 35, 36, 44, 48, 51, 58, 60, 61, 62, 63, 64, 65, 70, 77, 78, 80, 85, 93, 95, 106, 107, 108, 112, 118, 123, 124, 125, 134, 135, 136, 139, 141, 147, 160, 161, 164, 165, 166, 167, 174, 175
Evans, Horace, 17, 125, 166, 168, 174

Farouk, King of Egypt, 13
Fawzi, Mahmoud, 122–4, 127, 128, 130–3, 135, 138, 146, 149, 150
Feisal, King of Iraq, 20
First Sea Lord, 2, 24, 50
Fitzmaurice, Gerald, 114
Foster, Andrew, 21, 23, 31, 32, 54, 55, 61, 63

Gaitskell, Hugh, 21, 29, 81
Gazier, Albert, 137, 141, 143, 145, 173, 180
Glubb, John Bagot, 1, 15, 176
Goodhart, Philip, 168
Gulf, 8, 49, 50, 131

Hailsham, Lord, 24, 156, 159
Haley, Sir William, 27, 44, 46, 47
Hammerskjøld, Dag, 122–4, 130, 131, 133, 135, 146, 149, 150, 164
Hankey, Lord,
Hapte-wold, Ato Aklilou, 59
Harkavi, Yehoshafat, 131
Harcourt, Lord, 30
Hayter, Iris, 57
Hayter, William, 16, 56, 57, 94, 161
Head, Antony, 4, 162, 163, 164
Heath, Edward, 167
Henderson, Loy, 59, 62
Hitler, Adolf, 29, 57, 63, 112
Holland, Sidney, 28, 42, 50
Hoover, Herbert Jr, 23, 30, 31, 32, 34, 80, 160, 165
House of Commons, 2, 9, 22, 25, 29, 78, 79, 81, 84, 95, 168, 178
Hussein, King of Jordan, 15, 176

IMF (International Monetary Fund), 161, 167

Jebb, Gladwyn, 4, 47, 55, 69, 109
JIC (Joint Intelligence Committee), 160, 161, 169

Keightley, Charles, 68, 69, 161
Khedive, 20
Khrushchev, Nikita, 16, 57
Kilmuir, Lord, 21, 144, 159, 167, 171, 173
Kirkbride, Alexander, 15
Kirkpatrick, Ivone, 53, 62, 63, 114, 115, 118, 142, 146, 173

League of Nations, 10, 118, 123, 177
Lennox-Boyd, Alan, 25, 129, 163
Llandudno Conservative Party Conference, 7, 140, 141, 144
Lloyd, Selwyn, 3–6, 11, 14, 20, 21, 23, 30–2, 34, 38, 39, 44, 45, 47, 49, 51, 54, 56, 57, 61, 64, 70, 73, 76, 78–80, 84, 87, 89, 90, 93, 98–100, 103, 108–10, 114, 122–39, 141, 143, 146–53, 155, 157, 159–66, 169, 170
Lloyd George, David, 49
Lloyd George, Gwilym, 71

Lodge, Herbert Cabot, 99, 165
Logan, Donald, 127–30, 142, 151–5
London Conference, First, 37–40, 42, 44, 47, 48, 49, 51–3, 56–60, 93, 98, 106, 127, 177
London Conference, Second, 83, 86–91, 101, 104, 109, 110, 116, 179
'Lucky Break', 13

Maclachlan, Donald, 7
Macleod, Ian, 16
Macmillan, Harold, 2, 7, 8, 11, 12, 16, 28, 29, 31–4, 37, 45–7, 52–6, 65–7, 72–5, 81–3, 86, 88, 89, 96–8, 102, 103, 106–9, 111–13, 117, 118, 140, 143, 146, 147, 154, 155, 159–64, 166–70, 173, 174, 177
Makins, Roger, 30, 31, 34, 60, 64, 70, 71, 76, 78, 80, 85, 99, 107, 108, 115, 116, 120, 121, 123, 146, 163
Manchester Guardian, 81, 139
Massingham, Hugh, 164
Maudling, Reginald, 171
McDonald, Iverach, 3, 16, 17, 27, 28, 35, 36, 38–40, 43, 55, 88, 92, 97, 98, 100, 112, 116, 117, 149
Menon, Krishna, 114, 127, 128
Menzies, Robert, 28, 42, 59, 60, 62–4, 66, 67, 69, 72, 73, 76, 87, 89, 92, 93, 101, 109, 134, 173, 177, 179
Menzies Mission, 59, 62
MI6, 13, 84, 117, 175
Millard, Guy, 3, 16, 21, 33, 35, 102, 125, 126, 138–40, 148, 158, 163, 167, 170, 171
Mollet, Guy, 29, 41, 45, 69, 110, 117, 133, 136, 137, 145, 148, 149, 164
Monckton, Walter, 28, 43, 68, 74, 102, 103, 125, 142, 147, 156, 159
Montague-Browne, Anthony, 96
Moran, Lord, 95, 140, 166
Morrison, Herbert, 29
Mountbatten, Lord, 21, 23, 24, 42, 156, 169, 172
Murphy, Robert, 30–4, 36, 65, 67, 90, 106, 112, 177
Musketeer, Operation, 68, 72, 115
Musketeer Revise, Operation, 67, 69, 105, 139, 157
Mussolini, Benito, 29, 44, 57, 112, 161

Nasser, Gamal Abdul, 1, 3, 4, 7, 9–13, 15–18, 20–49, 51–4, 56–70, 72–90, 92–115, 117, 118, 120, 122, 124–7, 129, 132–6, 138, 139, 143, 146–8, 150, 151, 153–5, 157, 160, 161, 164, 165, 170, 172–80
nationalisation, of the canal, 1, 15, 19–23, 31, 35, 37, 44, 45, 51, 52, 68, 83, 132, 140, 157, 172, 173, 175–7
NATO, 10, 20, 34, 37, 56, 60
Neguib, Mohammed, 84
New Zealand, 28, 34, 42, 50, 87
News Chronicle, 42, 68, 81
Nicolson, Harold, 178
Nicolson, Nigel, 74
Nomy, Henry Michel, 44
northern tier, 12
Nuri es-Said, 13, 20, 45, 49, 54, 100, 101, 141, 172
Nutting, Anthony, 4, 12, 13, 98, 112, 116, 127, 136, 141, 142, 146, 147, 152, 156, 163, 165, 170, 171

oil, 6, 8, 9, 18, 25, 26, 28, 30, 37, 53, 54, 56, 83, 85, 89, 101, 107, 122, 126, 138, 153, 160, 167, 170, 176, 179
OMEGA, 13, 36, 93, 108, 109, 160, 175, 176

Panama Canal, 36, 37, 98, 104
Pan-Arabism, 9, 10, 13, 35, 40, 49, 161, 175
peace through strength, policy of, 10, 20, 177
Phleger, Herman, 99, 160
Pinay, Antoine, 12
Pineau, Christian, 3, 25, 29–31, 69, 70, 75, 86, 93, 94, 99, 100, 104, 109, 110, 113, 119, 123, 124, 130–7, 143, 146, 148, 151, 153, 154, 164
Pitblado, David, 106, 141
Powell, Richard, 24, 94, 102, 103, 142, 156, 158, 171
precautionary measures, 42, 49, 61, 62, 156

Reading, Lord, 84
Reilly, Patrick, 64, 93, 178
reinternationalisation of the Canal, policy of, 21, 25–7, 36, 40, 42, 46, 48, 49, 62, 84, 89, 114, 123, 129, 134, 138, 147, 177, 180
Ricketts, Dennis, 56
Roberts, Chalmers M., 121
Robertson, Norman, 92
Roosevelt, Kermit, 9
Ross, Archibald, 146
Rountree, William, 77, 160
Rowan, Leslie, 56
Royalist, New Zealand Frigate, 50, 87
Rusk, Dean, 121

Salisbury, Lord, 21, 28, 55, 56, 86, 141, 142, 159, 163, 164, 166–8, 173
sanctions, 13, 20, 30, 35, 36, 48, 53, 55, 56, 65–7, 87–9, 104, 106, 143, 149, 160, 173, 180
SCUA, *see* Canal Users' Association
scuttle, 6, 7, 97
SEATO, 12
Second World War, 5, 6, 25, 29, 31, 44, 123, 174
Security Council, role of, 4, 21, 42, 56, 57, 60, 63, 64, 68, 69, 71–3, 76, 77, 81, 82, 84–6, 89, 90, 92, 98–100, 104, 105, 108–10, 113, 117, 118, 120, 122–4, 126–37, 143, 146, 150, 156, 180
Sèvres Meeting, 2, 4, 151, 152, 154, 155, 158, 169
Shepilov, 52, 57, 123, 124
Shuckburgh, Evelyn, 8, 10, 13–16, 18, 46, 47, 96, 97, 141, 142, 170, 176
Soames, Christopher, 96
SOE (Special Operations Executive), 34
Soviet, 3, 7, 11, 12, 18, 21, 31, 37–9, 43, 52, 53, 56, 57, 60, 63, 81, 90, 97, 103, 117, 123, 133, 134, 137, 158, 161, 175, 177
Spaak, Paul-Henri, 56, 100, 133
Spectator, The, 3
St Laurent, Louis, 28
Sub-Committee of the Official Middle East Committee, 50
Suez Canal Company, 1, 27, 30, 34, 40, 45, 52

Suez Canal Users' Association, *see* Canal Users' Association
Suez Group, 7, 140, 141, 143
Sunday Times, 4, 126

Templer, Gerald, 24, 69, 163, 165
Thorneycroft, Peter, 163
Times, The London, 16, 27, 29, 44, 51, 81, 88, 116, 123, 125
Trevelyan, Humphrey, 60, 62, 80, 87, 88, 101, 102, 126, 150
Trieste, 6
Turco–Iraqi Pact, 13

UN (United Nations), 1, 3, 14, 20, 21, 43, 45, 52, 56, 58, 60, 64, 66–70, 81, 84, 90, 92–4, 98–107, 110–15, 118–20, 122–4, 126–8, 130–5, 138, 139, 158, 160, 161, 179
Unden, Osten, 59
users, 26, 37, 39, 47, 48, 51, 64, 69, 71–3, 75, 80, 82, 83, 85, 88–91, 93, 98, 99, 103, 104, 112, 118, 132, 147

Washington Post, 121
Waterhouse, Charles, 140
Watkinson, Harold, 171
White, Dick, 175
Wilson, Harold, 2, 160
Winter Plan, 139, 157
Wright, Denis, 142, 146
Wright, Michael, 21, 100–2, 118

Young, George, 175